France in the Era of Fascism

France in the Era of Fascism

Essays on the French Authoritarian Right

Edited by
Brian Jenkins

Berghahn Books
New York • Oxford

First published in 2005 by
Berghahn Books
www.berghahnbooks.com

© 2005 Brian Jenkins

Library of Congress Cataloging-in-Publication Data

Jenkins, Brian, 1944-
France in the era of fascism : essays on the French authoritarian right / Brian
Jenkins.
    p. cm.
Includes bibliographical references.
ISBN 1-57181-537-6
    1. Fascism--France--History--20th century. 2. Right-wing extremists--France-
-History--20th century. 3. France--Politics and government--1914–1940. I. Title.

DC369.J46 2005
320.53'3'094409041--dc22

2004053832

British Library Cataloguing in Publication Data

A catalogue record for this book is available
from the British Library.

Printed in Canada on acid-free paper.

ISBN 1-57181-537-6 hardback

Contents

Preface

The idea for this book grew out of the preparations for a conference. The editor was one of the organisers of the annual conference of the Association for the Study of Modern & Contemporary France (ASMCF) held at the University of Portsmouth in September 2001. The theme was '*La France exceptionnelle?* Comparisons and Intercultural Perspectives', and in this context it was decided to organise a panel on the issue of France's supposed immunity to fascism between the wars. Although not all of the contributors to this volume were able to attend the conference, it was the problematic notion of French 'exceptionalism' that provided the intellectual impetus for this book. My thanks are therefore due to the ASMCF for its initial financial and organisational support, and to my conference coorganisers, Dr Tony Chafer and Dr Emmanuel Godin, for helping to give shape to the original idea.

I must also thank all my contributors. Though some of the material in this volume has been translated or revised from earlier published versions, the construction of this collection of essays has been a genuinely collaborative enterprise. The editor received valuable advice from all the authors throughout the process. It was intended from the outset that everyone involved would see the entire manuscript, and would be given the chance to take account of what others had written and to revise their own text accordingly. Several colleagues availed themselves of this opportunity; indeed, as editor, I would like to acknowledge the many helpful suggestions I myself received from the contributors concerning my introduction, conclusion, and the biographical notes that preface each chapter. I am also indebted to the reader commissioned by Berghahn Books, whose insights led to some significant revisions in the final stages.

I am grateful to the following publishers for their permission to reproduce material in this volume: Editions Complexe for my abridged translation of Professor Sternhell's new preface to the 3rd edition of his *Ni droite ni gauche*; University of Chicago Press for Professor Paxton's amended version of an article which first appeared in the *Journal of Modern History*, no 70 (1998).

Finally I would like to thank the staff at Berghahn Books, and in particular Marion Berghahn and Mark Stanton, for their patience and professionalism.

Brian Jenkins
Leeds, 2004

List of Abbreviations

AD	Alliance Démocratique
AF	Action Française
CF	Croix de Feu
EVP	*Equipes volantes de propagande*
FR	Fédération Républicaine
JP	Jeunesses Patriotes
OVRA	Organisation for Vigilance and Repression of Antifascism [Italy]
PCF	Parti Communiste Français
PDP	Parti Démocratique Populaire
PNF	Partito Nazionale Fasciste [Italy]
PPF	Parti Populaire Français
PSF	Parti Social Français
RPF	Rassemblement du Peuple Français
SA	*Sturm-Abteilung*
SF	Solidarité Française
SFIO	Section Française de l'Internationale Ouvrière
UNC	Union Nationale des Combattants
UPR	Union Populaire Républicaine

1

Introduction: Contextualising the Immunity Thesis

Brian Jenkins

Brian Jenkins is the editor of this collection of essays. His interest in the interwar French extreme Right dates back to the 1970s when he prepared his doctoral thesis on the Paris riots of 6 February 1934. Since then he has worked mainly on the history and theory of nationalism, both in the context of France and within a wider contemporary European framework. He has written extensively on these questions, and in particular he is the author of *Nationalism in France: Class and Nation since 1789* (1990) and co-editor of *Nation and Identity in Contemporary Europe* (1996). His approach emphasises the plurality of nationalism(s), their political and ideological malleability, their dependence on the specific political dynamics of each historical context, the dangers of taking their self-proclaimed lineage and rationale at face value.

In some respects, he brings a similar methodological perspective to bear on the debate about France and fascism between the wars: one which is suspicious of typologies based on fixed *essences*, sensitive to the nuances of historical context and political conjuncture, sceptical about the way political movements define themselves. His articles in this field include a critical evaluation of Robert Soucy's work (in *Modern and Contemporary France*, vol. 4, no. 2, 1996) and a recent essay on Action Française (in M. Dobry, ed., *Le mythe de l'allergie française au fascisme*, 2003).

Brian Jenkins is Research Professor in French Studies at the University of Leeds.

In an edited collection like this one it seems necessary to prepare the ground for the reader. Experts in a specialised field have little time in the restricted space of an essay to introduce their subject; they must move quickly to a sophisticated level and assume the reader can follow them. Thus it falls to the editor to make the terrain more accessible by providing some helpful signposts and reference points. In this particular case, for example, it seems necessary to fill in some historical background and to offer a synoptic overview of the political crisis of the 1930s in France. But before we begin to address the substance of our subject, we should first draw attention to the fact that this is a deeply sensitive field of study, and one which has become increasingly controversial over the last thirty years. While it would be inappropriate in an introductory essay to start exploring the key elements of that debate, it seems important to recognise from the outset that we are dealing with an area where passions run high and where more is at stake than purely academic pride.

The immunity thesis

The nature of France's response to the rise of European fascism during the 1930s, and subsequently to the Nazi occupation of 1940–44, has been a difficult subject for the nation's historians. In the three decades that followed the Liberation, what might be described as an 'optimistic' version of events (already embedded in political discourse and in popular consciousness) was given the *imprimatur* of academic respectability, rationalised and institutionalised into an historical orthodoxy. According to this, France's democratic culture and its well-established indigenous ideological traditions had rendered the country largely immune to the appeal of fascism between the wars. Those movements that displayed fascist characteristics were for the most part superficial imitations of something essentially 'foreign', and their political significance was anyway marginal. As for La Rocque's Croix de Feu, a real mass movement which has to be taken more seriously, this was authoritarian conservative rather than genuinely fascist, a prefiguration of postwar Gaullism, respectful of *'la légalité républicaine'*. And anyway, by 1938 the Republic had largely 'seen off' the extremes of Right and Left, and had found stability under Daladier's two-year centrist coalition when external events intervened. Vichy was an artificial by-product of military defeat and occupation, a regime that would never have come about in the normal run of things and whose excesses were perpetrated under pressure from the occupying power. By the same token Vichy's popular roots were shallow, collaboration was a limited phenomenon effectively dealt with by the *épuration*, the majority of French people had been sympathetic to the Resistance, and the Liberation allowed France to revert to democratic norms after what was essentially an historical parenthesis or aberration.

This picture has gradually been subverted, not least by the work of non-French historians. It was the American Robert Paxton who in the early 1970s first assembled and presented exhaustive evidence of the extent of collaboration, and above all of Vichy's direct and willing implication in the persecution of Jews and their transportation to the death camps.[1] In this field of study at least, some of the taboos that inhibited historical enquiry have gradually been lifted and a more balanced picture has begun to emerge. There is certainly greater willingness to acknowledge and explore the Vichy regime's true record and the extent of its responsibilities. This does not of course resolve the persistent question of whether or not it was fascist, which still remains contentious. Nor does it necessarily help us evaluate the nature of Vichy's popular support - was it largely circumstantial or was it more deep-rooted? But the growing body of research certainly favours the view that the regime had a considerable historical hinterland, both intellectual and political, arguably stretching back to the closing years of the nineteenth century.

This perspective inevitably exposes the interwar period to greater scrutiny, but here the proposition that France was largely immune to fascism in the 1930s, first developed by René Rémond and subsequently refined by another generation of French historians,[2] has remained obstinately intact. It has been challenged from various angles, again largely by foreign scholars like the Israeli Zeev Sternhell and the American Robert Soucy,[3] but although quite significant theoretical adjustments have sometimes been made in order to accommodate new research data, the proponents of what Michel Dobry has called the *thèse immunitaire* (immunity thesis) have refused to abandon its central tenets.[4] Unlike the Vichy case, where the sheer weight of empirical evidence eventually shifted the terms of debate, the bone of contention over the *entre-deux-guerres* seems to be interpretive rather than factual. As Dobry himself notes below, when they are writing more discursively about the politics of the period, these selfsame historians are often quite happy to concede that France experienced a profound political crisis in the 1930s.[5] It is only when they have their 'immunity thesis' hats on that the emphasis suddenly switches from the Republic's vulnerability to its proven resilience.

What is at stake is a set of interrelated questions. Did fascism have roots in France, or was it a foreign import? Did fascism have a significant following in interwar France? Were conditions in France conducive to the development of fascism? Bearing in mind, of course, that all of these formulations invite another vital question – namely how to define 'fascism', and indeed whether it should be seen primarily as cultural phenomenon, political ideology, political movement, developmental process or regime – the 'immunity thesis' is fairly unequivocal in its conclusions. While it is willing to acknowledge that some of the ideological antecedents of fascism are to be found in France (so the phenomenon is not entirely 'alien'), and that some of the extraparliamentary movements active in interwar France displayed fascist characteristics (so the phenomenon is not entirely 'marginal'), it nonetheless maintains that French society was strongly resistant to the contagion.

In support of this argument, mainstream French historiography insists on the differences of ideology and temperament that distinguish authentic 'fascism' from indigenous French right-wing political traditions, claiming for example that the French extraparliamentary Right lacked certain *essential* or *typical* features of fascism such as social radicalism, incipient totalitarianism, or aggressive expansionism. The case is powerfully supplemented by references to those historical conditions which allegedly made France particularly unreceptive to fascism: its deeply-entrenched democratic political culture, the lack of ideological 'space' for new movements, the absence of French territorial ambitions after 1918, the relatively low levels of recorded unemployment in France during the Great Depression, and so on. As we shall see, there are weaknesses, contradictions and inconsistencies in all these arguments, but this intricate web of defences with its numerous fallback positions is nonetheless an impressive construction. Equally remarkable is the united front maintained by so many leading French historians in their commitment to this cause.

The immunity syndrome

These are, of course, profoundly sensitive issues for a country that has prided itself on being in the vanguard of democratic progress and enlightenment, and where intellectuals (and historians not least)[6] enjoy unusual status and public visibility. Coming to terms with these difficult areas in the nation's past has been a long and painful process, which has underlined the profoundly political and ideological nature of historical interpretation and enquiry. A whole generation of postwar political leaders was legitimated by the Resistance 'myth' and therefore had a stake in the 'optimistic' version of events referred to above. The much-publicised trials for crimes against humanity of Klaus Barbie, Paul Touvier and Maurice Papon, as well as the increasing salience of race issues with the rise of the Front national, have ensured the contemporary resonance of historical debates. Only in this context is it possible to understand how intellectual disagreement has sometimes bred deep personal animosity between academics working in this field, as exemplified by the so-called 'Sternhell controversy' of the early 1980s.[7] The 'immunity thesis' (or what Robert Soucy, following William Irvine, has called 'the consensus school of French historiography')[8] is very much the 'ghost at the feast' in the present collection of essays. Though not all our contributors have explicitly and deliberately set out to refute the 'consensus' position, their work has certainly helped to weaken its credibility. As we shall see, their individual approaches are very different, indeed they are often directly critical of one another. At this introductory stage, it would be premature to explore these differences, or to suggest how they might be reconciled. Nor shall we attempt to investigate any further the key characteristics of the 'immunity thesis' itself, for these emerge in some detail in the chapters that follow, and especially in the essays by Sternhell, Soucy and Dobry. It does seem appropriate in this introduction, however, to consider another question. Why have French historians generally been so resistant to the idea that their country produced a serious fascist movement between the wars, or that the Vichy regime had significant fascist characteristics? It is perhaps not surprising that, with the exception of Michel Dobry, our contributors all come from outside the hexagon and bring to bear the sceptical eye of the outsider.

It is not our intention here to question the professionalism of the many distinguished historians who have aligned themselves with the so-called 'immunity thesis', nor indeed to suggest that they have consciously geared their historical interpretation to a particular political agenda. However, none of us can escape the prejudices and perceptions of the time and place in which we live, and it would be naïve indeed to imagine that the 'immunity thesis' emerged in a social and political vacuum. Henry Rousso has shown in his classic *Le syndrome de Vichy* how memories of the Occupation and representations of the Vichy regime have been constantly reappropriated and refashioned since the war in line with changing political strategies and historical circumstances.[9] Similarly, the study of the French extreme Right between the wars (and its relationship to fascism) has also been conditioned by subsequent contextual factors. The two subjects are of course linked, and the authors of the 'immunity thesis' have often been subject to the same intellectual pressures that influenced historians of Vichy. However, because their terms of reference are different, they work in rather different registers. The official history of Vichy (pre-Paxton) rested on the assumption that it was the product of exceptional circumstances, somehow in historical parentheses, disconnected from what preceded and what followed. The political turmoils of the 1930s, however, required a more sophisticated theoretical explanation.

René Rémond's study of *La Droite en France* first appeared in 1954, was periodically updated, and since 1982 has been repeatedly reprinted as *Les Droites en France*. As Sternhell notes below, this book became virtually a 'bible' for successive generations of students[10] and, through its coverage of the 1930s and Vichy, it made the 'immunity thesis' an established orthodoxy. But the original text dates, it should be remembered, from the early 1950s when a very distinctive and constraining political climate prevailed.

First of all, the atmosphere in postwar France was scarcely conducive to a spirit of open historical enquiry into the painful and divisive events of the 1934–44 period. Most people, irrespective of their individual experiences and allegiances, had little desire to probe too thoroughly into what had happened. And this public mood chimed perfectly with the great reforming agenda of immediate postwar governments, where the accent was on economic and social regeneration, on looking forward rather than back. The restoration of national pride and self-respect also required that, after the initial (emblematic) purges, the extent of wartime collaboration be played down and the issue be treated as resolved. All those political parties which could claim resistance credentials (and especially the Gaullists and the Communists) quickly recognised, not only that this was a vital source of legitimacy, but that it was in their own interests for as many people as possible to feel able to identify with this patriotic resistance legacy (and therefore with *them*). The aspiration to build broad-based popular movements therefore meant defining collaboration as narrowly as possible and not discouraging those with a bad conscience. To delve too deeply into the past would anyway focus attention on events that the parties which now wore the Resistance mantle would rather forget – the eighty-eight Socialist deputies who had voted full powers to Pétain in July 1940, or the ambivalence of the PCF in the twenty-two months from the Nazi-Soviet pact until Hitler's invasion of the USSR.

Those who had much more to hide were happy to collude in this collective amnesia. Thus, for example, many conservative voters who had been receptive to Vichy's Révolution nationale now transferred their allegiance to formations with a resistance pedigree, first to the Catholic Mouvement Républicain Populaire,[11] and then to De Gaulle's Rassemblement du Peuple Français (RPF). Anyway, at a more pragmatic level the postwar shortfall in administrative and political personnel with experience and expertise made it difficult to envisage a total renewal of elites, and a blind eye was inevitably turned to the *curriculum vitae* of those who had made themselves indispensable. In short, however tempting it was for the parties identified with Resistance to mobilise memories of Vichy and collaboration against their political enemies, in the new realities of the postwar era there were powerful countervailing factors which discouraged this from being done systematically.

By the early 1950s the hopeful mood of postwar reconstruction had very much given way to the new international realities of the Cold War, but this also contributed to the intellectual climate in which the 'immunity thesis' began to take shape. The concept of 'totalitarianism', launched by American political science at this time,[12] can now be seen more clearly in its ideological context. It was designed to cement the 'free world' against the communist bloc by focusing on features that the existing Soviet state supposedly shared with the defeated and universally reviled Nazi and Fascist regimes.[13] However, to make the charge stick, fascism itself had to be defined in a way that emphasised its parallels with communism. Whence the tendency to insist on the radical or even revolutionary nature of fascist ideology and fascist movements; on their capacity to mobilise antibourgeois sentiments, to attract personnel from the Left, to appeal to the 'working class'. Whence also the insistence on the 'totalitarian' nature of fascist regimes, thereby distinguishing them from (less invasive) 'authoritarian' conservatism. As we shall see in later chapters, this view of fascism as radical is one that proponents of the 'immunity thesis' tend to share, though, ironically enough, so do some of their critics.[14] The 'totalitarian' dimensions of fascism also allowed certain other regimes to be excluded from the definition, not least right-wing dictatorships (within the American sphere of influence) like Franco's Spain and Salazar's Portugal, but also – by retrospective association – Vichy and the prewar French extreme Right.

Rémond's initial framing of the 'immunity thesis' thus took place against this twin background: the multifaceted French reluctance to address the historical realities of the period, and the retrospective redefinition of fascism in line with Cold War imperatives. As Bruno Goyet has also noted, however, the updated editions of *La Droite en France* from the 1960s onwards had to take account of the arrival of the Fifth Republic and the need to interpret the significance of Gaullism.[15] Many on the Left regarded De Gaulle's return to power in 1958 essentially as a *coup d'état*, and his new regime as an elective dictatorship. The communists, indeed, who had depicted De Gaulle's earlier RPF movement (1947–53) as fascist, saw the Fifth Republic as a new form of concentrated political power typical of the era of 'State Monopoly Capitalism'. By contrast, Rémond's rival interpretation can be seen as a form of legitimation. His famous model of 'les trois droites', whereby the whole history of the French Right since the mid-nineteenth century could be understood in terms of three enduring political traditions (Legitimism, Orleanism and Bonapartism)[16], proved quite capable of dealing with these new developments. Gaullism is thus defined as a mature and modernised form of Bonapartism, where nationalism has finally been reconciled with the requirements of democracy, and where the more liberal impulses of the Orleanist tradition are effectively accommodated in practice. No need to look outside French history for explanations, no need to import extraneous concepts (whether fascism or anything else), the Gaullist Republic has its own distinctive and respectable national pedigree: one which incidentally includes La Rocque's prewar Parti Social Français, here presented as a pale precursor of Gaullism rather than as a fascist mass movement (see further below).[17]

It seems inevitable that this complex political environment weighed heavily on the initial articulation and elaboration of the 'immunity thesis'. What is harder to explain is how the interpretation was able to maintain its academic hold throughout the 1960s and 1970s,[18] and was then endorsed, updated and systematised by a new cohort of historians in the early 1980s.[19] Why this closing of ranks in response to the work of Zeev Sternhell? After all, the previous ten years or so had seen the subject of Vichy and collaboration opened up for discussion, not least by the dissemination of Robert Paxton's research and the intense media coverage of Marcel Ophuls's banned film Le Chagrin et la Pitié.[20] In the aftermath of 1968, the 1970s may indeed now be seen as a transitional period during which what George Ross has called 'Resistance-Liberation Left discourse'[21] retreated before the more libertarian New Left values of a generation less afraid of digging into the sensitive past. So why did French historians react so violently to Sternhell's argument that fascist ideas were widespread in France before the war? And why do so many scholars, including those who have since become the leading authorities in the field, continue to build their arguments around the central tenets of the Rémondian model, when these tenets have been progressively undermined by subsequent research (including their own!)?

We will avoid speculation here about the ties of patronage, loyalty or collective solidarity that may or may not operate in this or any other section of the French academic community.[22] We will merely note that the Rémondian framework for analysing the French Right has held sway for a very long time, that it is seductively neat and comprehensive, that the immunity thesis is an integral part of it, and that it would take nerve to bring such a venerable edifice crashing down. More importantly, however, the notion that France was immune to fascism is also a vital component in a powerful historical narrative about French exceptionalism and the distinctive character of *la République*. It is perhaps this above all which explains why the immunity thesis has won support among academics of differing political persuasions, including some who almost certainly do not share the rather conservative perspectives of René Rémond himself. For what makes France exceptional, what makes *la République* exemplary for the rest of humanity, is not presented in identical fashion in rival political discourses.

For some, *la République* is a consensual term designed to unify the nation around widely accepted constitutional principles, and certain shared values like civil liberties and the rule of law. But for others it may denote the more radical and dynamic notion of the unfulfilled *République sociale*, those transcendent egalitarian ideals derived from the French Revolution and momentarily reincarnated in the period of the antifascist struggle and the Resistance. The story of that struggle has a powerful mythic quality. It is a key chapter in an unfolding historical metanarrative (democratic and socialist) about human progress towards a better society. Challenges to the immunity thesis may (superficially at least) appear to be debunking that story, to be casting doubt on the significance of the resistance legacy, and thereby undermining not only French faith in the Social Republic, but also the faith of all those who have seen France and its revolutionary heritage as a beacon for humanity at large.

Those who have challenged the immunity thesis would, of course, protest that they are not in any way setting out to devalue the antifascist movement and its ideals. Indeed, they might argue that the more we know about the extent of fascism in 1930s France, or the true character of the Vichy regime, the greater should be our admiration for those who opposed them. But, of course, books that set out to expose these unpalatable facts do not dwell long on the more positive features. As both Robert Paxton and Zeev Sternhell discovered to their cost,[23] this is dangerous territory, especially for foreign scholars who were also too young to have 'lived' the events they study. They are easily presented as unwelcome intruders into a domestic dispute, as irresponsible iconoclasts who do not respect the terrible dilemmas of those caught up in exceptional circumstances. Nonetheless, it is thirty years since Paxton's work was first published in France, twenty years since the 'Sternhell controversy'. Those who directly experienced the events are now thin on the ground, and it might be assumed that national sensibilities are now less easily offended. Certainly most of the historians who still defend the immunity thesis are not of the wartime generation, and yet there is no doubt that this remains a sensitive issue within the academic community.

In *Le syndrome de Vichy*, Henry Rousso makes the telling point that, in the aftermath of the Liberation, the resistance legacy of *minorités agissantes* (as celebrated in particular ideological groups like the Gaullists and the Communists) was progressively assimilated to the whole nation (*résistancialisme*).[24] There is an analogy here with the *thèse immunitaire*, which rather than focusing on the historical detail of the prewar political crisis and the antifascist struggle, imbues the whole of French society with inbuilt defence mechanisms which spontaneously reject fascism (as if vaccinated by its 'democratic political culture'). This is undoubtedly a difficult position to retreat from, because it is strategically linked to totalising concepts of French exceptionalism and national identity, notions which are themselves under siege in the contemporary world. In the era of globalisation, when France is sometimes regarded as the only source in the developed world of ideological opposition to *la pensée unique*, it is perhaps unfortunate that the best-known critics of the immunity thesis come from the United States and Israel! But to attach any significance to that fact is to fall precisely into the trap we are endeavouring to warn against.

Contesting the immunity thesis

This volume brings together five authors whose work has played a key role in opening up this area of debate. While all of them would reject the notion of French society being somehow exempt from or especially protected against fascism, they approach the subject from very different directions and bring very different resources to bear. Indeed, they are often directly critical of each other, as we shall see. However, there is some common ground, and even evidence of a degree of convergence between several of our contributors, as they take stock of their own researches and the wider interpretative environment. To help the reader appreciate such revisions or shifts of emphasis, each essay is preceded by a brief editorial preamble which summarises that author's previous interventions.

It has not been easy to decide in which order to present the essays that follow, but for many reasons it seems natural to start with the contribution by Zeev Sternhell. It was, after all, his intervention that first made this such a controversial subject some twenty-five years ago, and his corpus of work is still regarded by French historians as the most significant challenge to their position. His insistence that the ideological origins of fascism are to be found in France between 1885 and 1914 gives his approach a broader historical sweep than that of other contributors, as well as a more radical cutting edge. In this particular essay, Sternhell develops the most comprehensive refutation of the immunity thesis to date, claiming that in 1930s France anti-democratic values and attitudes were widespread, and that this counterculture not only produced some of the most sophisticated intellectual elaborations of pure fascist ideology, but also a genuine fascist mass movement (the Croix de Feu) and, in Vichy, an authentic fascist regime.

Robert Soucy's essay focuses more sharply on the 1930s, and in particular on La Rocque's Croix de Feu/Parti Social Français. This movement, with at least a million members in 1938, is of course pivotal to this whole area of discussion. The argument that it was not fascist is absolutely crucial to the immunity thesis. Soucy sets out systematically to dismantle the case that has been developed by mainstream French historiography, making ample use of comparative data in order to show that the supposed differences between the CF/PSF and 'authentic' fascist movements in Italy and Germany are more apparent than real. His chapter also provides an interesting contrast with Sternhell's approach: a greater concern with the programmatic expression of ideology rather than with its intellectual underpinnings, a more sceptical view of the antibourgeois and anticapitalist components in fascist discourse, and deep reservations about the argument that 'authentic' fascism was a revision of Marxism.

Our remaining authors all seek, in different ways, to distance themselves from the definitional questions that have dogged the debate, and from the impulse to measure French examples against a single concept of fascism based on fixed essences. Robert Paxton thus argues that fascism is not driven by ideology or doctrine like other '–isms', but that it should be perceived more in terms of the functions it fulfils. It is thus shaped by the political space and historical context in which it operates, and is best understood as a 'process' or indeed as a 'cycle' typically running through a number of stages, each of which requires different modes of analysis. Michel Dobry goes a step further, denying the utility of the whole notion of generic fascism, and seeking to break entirely with the *logique classificatoire*. His critique of the 'immunity thesis' focuses above all on its methodological flaws, and he advocates a *perspective relationnelle* whereby movements will be properly set in context, namely within a complex web of political relationships, rather than rigidly categorised according to ideological parentage.

Finally, Kevin Passmore's essay may, in many ways, be seen as seeking to move beyond the whole debate about the impact of fascism in France. His investigation of the concept of the 'stalemate society' and of the tensions between conservatism and modernisation within French social and political elites between the wars, admittedly sheds tangential light on the question. The notion that the Third Republic was based on a conservative compromise between peasantry and middle classes, which was highly resistant to social and economic change (and therefore, for some historians, to fascism), has certainly underpinned the 'immunity thesis', and Passmore's conclusion that there was no such consensus behind the regime's institutions therefore has serious implications. However, his chapter also proves that there are other ways of conceptualising the political crisis in 1930s France than through the grid of the fascism debate, and that to ask new questions of historical events may be the best way to enrich our understanding of them.

The extreme Right in France and the political crisis of the 1930s

The task of setting the historical scene for this volume is a tricky one. How are we to provide an adequate introduction to our subject without getting bogged down in detail or intruding too much on the patience of the informed reader? A comprehensive chronological narrative has therefore to be ruled out: it would anyway raise difficult questions about where to begin and how far afield to look geographically. A more selective thematic approach seems the best option, though here the risk is that the process of selection already involves a degree of interpretation. Where the subject is so contentious, all pretence to editorial neutrality evaporates. To see one particular event as more significant than another, to regard this set of explanatory factors as more relevant than that, is to intervene in the debate you purport to be introducing. Nevertheless, for all its pitfalls that is the approach we have chosen.

The main historical focus of the essays in this volume is the political crisis of the Third French Republic in the 1930s, as exemplified above all by the emergence of extraparliamentary movements of the extreme Right, whether in the shape of the 'leagues' or, after the 1936 ban on paramilitary formations, in the guise of full-blown political parties like La Rocque's Parti Social Français (PSF) or Doriot's Parti Populaire Français (PPF). However much historians have been divided in their interpretation of such organisations, there is nonetheless a measure of agreement that France in the 1930s did indeed experience something akin to a political 'crisis'. This, of course, is not a reference to the recurrent *crise ministérielle*, an unexceptional event which punctuated the life of the Republic at a frenetic rate throughout the decade (twenty-nine governments between February 1930 and June 1940) – though this in itself was symptomatic of more deep-seated problems. We refer, rather, to the remarkable effervescence of ideological innovation and experimentation, to the intensity of class antagonisms and pent-up social grievances, to the violent polarisation of party politics, to the radical dealignment of partisan allegiances especially on the Right of the political spectrum, and finally to the process which saw support for the liberal-democratic Republic dwindle (in enthusiasm as much as in extent) in favour of an increasing willingness to endorse more authoritarian solutions.

The 'longue durée'

There are several different 'time frames' that may be invoked to help with the intepretation of these developments. First of all, there is a *longue durée* stretching back at least as far as the establishment of the Third Republic in 1870, but also taking account of the whole legacy of the Enlightenment and the Revolution. On the one hand, this perspective can be used to remind us that the ideals associated with liberal democracy have a long history in France, and that in the interwar period the French people already had fifty years' continuous experience of adult male suffrage,[25] elective and accountable government at both local and national level, open access to public office, freedom of the press and association – in contrast with neighbouring Italy and Germany, where such practices were arguably far less developed. Hence the proposition that France had a well-established 'democratic' political culture which was highly resistant to fascism. This same timescale was also a reminder, of course, that the embryonic Republic had struggled to survive the clerical-monarchist challenge in the 1870s, and that it had warded off further attacks from Boulangism in the late 1880s and from the anti-Dreyfusard coalition at the turn of the century. Recognition that the Republic had enemies, especially on the Right, might be seen as a corrective to an over-complacent view about the solidity of French democracy. However, this notion of an ongoing '*guerre franco-française*' dating back to the Revolution also favours an interpretation of the interwar right-wing leagues exclusively in terms of French historical traditions (like Rémond's '*trois droites*'), as the recurrent flourishes of *la Réaction* – troublesome but ultimately not dangerous, and therefore a further reason to be dismissive about the influence of fascism in France.

The 'age of mass politics'

Where Rémond's *trois droites* (Legitimism, Orleanism, Bonapartism) imply a pedigree extending back to 1815, some of his successors, like Serge Berstein and Michel Winock, are more willing to acknowledge that the last quarter of the nineteenth century was an historical watershed in France as in other European countries. Against a background of rapid economic modernisation and social change, these years saw the consolidation of the modern nation-state and the entry of the masses onto the political stage, and consequently the emergence of movements and ideologies (socialism, syndicalism, nationalism) designed to attract, organise and mobilise these masses. In this context, for example, French historians have recognised that the new racist and populist nationalism that developed in the years between the Boulanger and Dreyfus Affairs cannot be adequately understood just as a derivative of Bonapartism, and have invented terms like 'national-populism' to encompass it[26] (and, once again, to avoid equating it with fascism). By contrast, Zeev Sternhell has seen the intellectual encounters between 'integral nationalism' and branches of revolutionary syndicalism in France in the early years of the twentieth century as the very birthplace of pure fascist ideology, which was thus initially a French product before it was first used effectively as an instrument of political mobilisation in Italy.[27]

The 'Great War and Russian Revolution' perspective

From another angle, the Great War and the Russian Revolution were an equally decisive watershed, and are the primary historical reference points in any discussion of the rise of fascism, or indeed of the French extraparliamentary Right in the 1930s. Sternhell has been criticised for adopting a history-of-ideas approach that neglects the importance of such vital contextual factors, though the classic Rémondian model[28] seems no less guilty in this respect. The human costs of the 1914–18 conflict, both physical and psychological; the economic and demographic repercussions; the social dislocation and bitter political animosities; the deep resentments, anxieties and unresolved tensions bequeathed by the Versailles settlement; the unprecedented bourgeois fear of social revolution that followed the establishment of the Soviet Union as the first workers' state; the deep divisions that the same event created on the European Left: the effect of all these developments was to destabilise societies internally, and to destabilise the international order. On the one hand, this perspective warns against parochialism, and reminds us that France was locked into a much wider European experience in these years. On the other hand, arguments have been deployed to suggest that France was crucially different from Italy or Germany in at least one important respect – victorious rather than humiliated in 1919, a net beneficiary of the Versailles Treaty with no frustrated territorial ambitions, deeply impregnated with a politically diffuse pacifism between the wars, the country was supposedly unpropitious terrain for the aggressive expansionism that some see as an essential element in fascism.[29]

The 'société bloquée'

To return briefly to the longer timespan, the durability of the Third Republic has often been attributed to a 'psycho-social compromise' between the middle classes and the peasantry.[30] The regime consolidated its mass base above all by safeguarding the interests and values of these key property-owning constituencies. However, the cultivation of this social consensus (for example via low taxes, protectionism etc.) antagonised not only industrial workers eager for social welfare and labour reform, but also the more dynamic sectors of big business. It appeared that in order to preserve the social and political stability supposedly afforded by widespread property-ownership, policies were designed to suppress the natural forces of urbanisation and economic modernisation – France was, in Stanley Hoffmann's phrase, a 'société bloquée'.[31] In this context, the question arises of how far this model of society had been disrupted by the Great War and its revolutionary aftermath, how far the balance and nature of social class relations in France were transformed, and how far the political system was undermined by any shift in its social foundations. On the one hand, it certainly seems that the Republic faced unprecedented social and economic problems between the wars, and that the traditional model of economic liberalism was under challenge in France as much as elsewhere. It was no doubt this widely perceived need for greater state intervention, and thus for stable government and continuity of policy, that made the endemic problem of ministerial instability suddenly appear so much more serious in the interwar period. On the other hand, commentators traditionally point out that the world economic Depression of the early 1930s, which was such a vital backdrop to Hitler's accession to power in Germany, had a much less spectacular impact in France; that although the effects of the Depression were prolonged and debilitating, the diversified structure of France's less developed economy did in fact cushion the country against the social upheavals on which fascism supposedly feeds.[32]

The conjunctural perspective

Another approach would give much greater weight to the changing political conjuncture of the interwar years. From this perspective, no matter how important the various contextual factors mentioned above in shaping attitudes, it was the response of political organisations to the specific issues of the day that determined their likelihood of success. The themes exploited by extraparliamentary movements of the extreme Right between the wars were carefully chosen. In the 1920s the main preoccupation was the campaign against the scaling down of German war reparations ('L'Allemagne paiera'), which of course tapped into the longstanding Germanophobia of right-wing nationalism ever since the Boulanger episode, but which also fed on the financial uncertainties caused by inflation and the collapse of the franc. In the early 1930s the switch to the theme of political scandal, culminating in the Stavisky Affair and the riots of 6 February 1934, also drew on a well-established extreme-Right tradition of targeting Republican corruption, though again public receptiveness was sharpened by the first inroads of the world Depression into France. In the mid-to late 1930s the threatening international situation increasingly affected how other issues were perceived, and in this context there was ample scope for linking together the widespread fear of war with anti-Bolshevism and contempt for parliamentary democracy.

However, the intensity of extreme-Right activity correlates most closely with another political variable, namely the presence of a left-of-centre coalition in government. In three of the five general elections between the wars, the centrist Radical Party formed an electoral alliance with the socialist Section Française de l'Internationale Ouvrière (SFIO) and won a parliamentary majority as a result. Although in both 1924 and 1932 the SFIO refused to allow its deputies to become ministers in Radical-led cabinets, the mere fact that governments were Socialist-supported was enough to alarm conservative bourgeois opinion. The Popular Front election victory of 1936 was, of course, an even more threatening prospect – the government was now led by a Socialist, the electoral alliance had been extended leftwards to include the Communists, and the elections had triggered off a massive wave of strikes and factory occupations. The social and economic reforms introduced by the June 1936 Matignon Agreements were regarded by many employers as the first salvos of the social revolution, creating a climate of class warfare which lasted until the definitive collapse of the Popular Front coalition in October 1938. It is this calendar more than any other which reveals a developmental pattern in the growth and fortunes of the extraparliamentary extreme Right.

The period of the so-called Cartel des Gauches parliamentary majority saw the fall of seven Radical governments between June 1924 and July 1926, as big business interests withdrew their confidence. The nationalist extreme Right were quick to link the financial crisis to the Republic's failure to secure German reparations, and against the background of street demonstrations largely orchestrated by the Action Française, two new right-wing leagues emerged – Pierre Taittinger's Jeunesses Patriotes and Georges Valois's Faisceau. This first upsurge ran out of steam when the conservative Raymond Poincaré formed a government of National Union in July 1926, which stabilised the economy and tied the Radicals into a Centre-Right coalition where they remained for the 1928 elections. Four years later, however, the Radicals renewed their winning electoral alliance with the Socialists, and this once again created propitious circumstances for the extreme Right. As Radical cabinets again tumbled, this time against the backdrop of the world recession and Hitler's accession to power, two new organisations were born in 1933 – Jean Renaud's Solidarité Française and Marcel Bucard's Francisme, while a little-known war veteran's association called the Croix de Feu was being transformed into a right-wing political movement under a new leader, Colonel François de La Rocque.[33]

The events of February 1934 were a decisive turning-point in many respects.[34] The Stavisky scandal, which implicated several Radical Party politicians, provided a new focus for extreme-Right street mobilisations, culminating in the resignation of the Chautemps government at the end of January. The incoming Prime Minister Daladier, as part of an administrative reshuffle, sacked the conservative Paris Prefect of Police, Jean Chiappe, in what was perceived as an inept ploy to win Socialist parliamentary support. This triggered off the Paris riots of 6 February[35], orchestrated by the right-wing leagues, which claimed nineteen lives[36] and forced Daladier's resignation the following day. The immediate consequence was the setting up of a National Union government under former President of the Republic Gaston Doumergue, a repeat of the Poincaré formula of 1926, which detached the Radicals from the Socialists in favour of a Centre-Right parliamentary majority. This time, however, any hopes that this would stabilise the situation were soon dashed because a new dynamic had been set in motion, a process of popular mobilisation and political polarisation which would overshadow parliamentary politics for the next two years. The Left had quickly identified the riots as an attempted fascist coup, and this produced a massive counter-demonstration on 12 February where, for the first time, Socialists and Communists marched together. The new theme of antifascism launched the vast social movement of the Popular Front, which would bring with it organisational cooperation between the Socialist and Communist parties, and the eventual incorporation of the Radical Party into an electoral alliance that would win the April-May 1936 elections and pave the way for France's first Socialist-led government under Léon Blum. But in parallel to the rise of the Popular Front, La Rocque's Croix de Feu grew at a spectacular rate from an estimated 35,000 on the eve of the 6 February 1934 riots to 500,000 in early 1936, entirely eclipsing its rivals on the extraparliamentary Right and indeed giving it the largest membership of any party in France at that time.

As René Rémond himself recognised,[37] the Croix de Feu is the crux of the debate about whether or not there was a mass fascist movement in France, and the subject preoccupies nearly all of the contributors to this volume. A major question is how far the movement changed when it was transformed into the Parti Social Français in 1936, following the Popular Front government's dissolution of the right-wing leagues. For some historians, its continuing dramatic growth to around one million members at the end of 1937, more than the combined membership of the Socialist and Communist parties, can only be explained by a supposed moderation of its image, making it more attractive to mainstream conservative voters. In this version, the PSF is often contrasted with Doriot's supposedly more combative Parti Populaire Français, which attracted many of the remnants of the other leagues and is often given the label 'fascist' by supporters of the immunity thesis. Others, however, would argue that La Rocque's movement grew consistently and dramatically from February 1934 onwards on a rising curve of anxiety about the prospect of a Popular Front government, and when this became a reality in May 1936, far from these fears abating they grew more intense. In other words, the PSF's continuing upward growth, against a background of domestic class conflict and heightened international tension, reflected not the movement's moderation but the radicalisation of conservative opinion.[38]

Daladier's April 1938 govermment may have defused these tensions by reviving the Radicals' alliance with the parliamentary Right in October, revoking the Popular Front social reforms a month later and breaking the subsequent attempted general strike. Indeed, Daladier's two-year tenure until March 1940 recalled the longevity of Poincaré's term of office, and some have identified this as a stabilisation of the Republic, which would have survived but for external events. Others have argued, however, that the catastrophe of June 1940 was not just a military defeat, that France had been weakened and demoralised from within, and that the Republic had proved itself incapable of resolving the deep-seated social and economic problems that so divided the country in the 1930s.[39] Such speculation is of course fruitless, but it does at least reveal how tendentious it is to conclude unequivocally that 'the Republic survived', and to use this teleologically to minimise the extent of the challenge to liberal democracy in France between the wars.

The 'relational' perspective

There is one last 'perspective' on the political crisis of the 1930s which needs briefly to be identified, and to which we shall return in our conclusion. Dubbed *'perspective relationnelle'* by Michel Dobry, and made methodologically explicit in his essay below, this approach involves recognising that political movements operate in a dynamic competitive environment. Their ideology, programmes, discourse, behaviour are not manifestations of some fixed and bounded identity or essence, shaped definitively by historical tradition. They are also the product of constant interaction with other movements, of manoeuvres seeking to gain competitive advantage over rivals and allies, of attempts to reposition or even redefine the organisation in response to new strategic or tactical opportunities. Clearly such a perspective might involve taking account of the entire political spectrum, including the parties of the Left: for example, in the early 1930s the inability of Radicals, Socialists and Communists to work together caused acrimonious splits inside all three parties, raising the possibility of partisan realignment which might benefit the extreme Right. In the event it did lead some well-known politicians of the Left to succumb to what Philippe Burrin calls *La dérive fasciste*,[40] but in fact this had little organisational or electoral impact on the parties they abandoned. Indeed, the subsequent development of the Popular Front temporarily produced a popular groundswell of Left unity which tended to stabilise working-class political allegiances in the mid-1930s. Admittedly, the process of political polarisation between 1934 and 1938 had taken its toll on the centrist Radical Party, which lost a sixth of its vote at the 1936 elections, but this seems above all to have benefited the parties to its left, thus helping to sustain an old argument – that fascism could only progress in France at the expense of the Radicals, and that their survival proves it never took root.[41]

However, many others would argue that the *sine qua non* of a significant fascist movement is that the main political formations regarded as the guardians of the existing social and economic order, namely the mainstream liberal and conservative Right, should begin to lose public confidence and support. There can be little doubt that this occurred in France. It is, of course, true that right-wing politics under the Third Republic had a history of fragmentation, weak discipline and volatility, but nonetheless what occurred in the 1930s, under the destabilising influence of economic depresssion and intense social division, has been described by Michel Dobry as 'nothing less than a political earthquake across the entire political spectrum of the Right'.[42] If by 1934 the credibility of the parliamentary Right (collectively '*les modérés*') had already been undermined (the combined membership of the extraparliamentary leagues was probably around 300,000 by this time), the rise of the left-wing Popular Front movement triggered a process of polarisation whose effect on the Right at the 1936 elections was to weaken the more moderate elements (liberal Alliance Démocratique and Christian-democrat Parti Démocrate Populaire) in favour of the more conservative Fédération Républicaine. As we have seen, an even more dramatic effect was the exponential growth of La Rocque's Croix de Feu which, as the Parti Social Français after 1936, had a membership whose size threatened to eclipse the electoral prospects of the Fédération Républicaine at the parliamentary polls due in May 1940.

Robert Soucy has, of course, long explored the interface between 'conservatives' and 'fascists' in France, insisting on the permeability of the boundaries between them.[43] The picture that emerges is one, not of rigidly demarcated ideological spheres, but of a common pool of similar ideas, sentiments and programmes; of regular interchanges and movements of personnel across the divide between parliamentary and extraparliamentary, mainstream and 'extreme'; of multiple allegiances and constantly shifting loyalties among both activists and voters. And this proximity in itself bred intense rivalry. Kevin Passmore's study of the *Right in a French Province 1928–1939* reveals a process of conflict and fragmentation on the Right, arguing that the spectacular growth of the Croix de Feu, both in the Rhône region and nationally, 'represented a mobilisation of conservative rank-and-file in response to the divisions of the established Right'.[44]

The competitive nature of this environment is nowhere better illustrated than in the affair of the so-called Front de la Liberté in the spring of 1937. This loose anti-communist alliance was devised by PPF leader Jacques Doriot, with the connivance not only of the remnants of the other leagues but also of Louis Marin's parliamentary Fédération Républicaine. All of these organisations shared a desire to neutralise the burgeoning PSF, and by inviting La Rocque to join the alliance, Doriot seems to have been setting a trap for him. If La Rocque accepted, Doriot hoped to outmanoeuvre and discredit him in the eyes of his followers, using the alliance to 'pluck the PSF chicken' (plumer la volaille PSF).[45] And if La Rocque refused, he risked being isolated and marginalised, possibly with the same effect.

The episode is instructive for a number of reasons. It certainly confirms how alarmed other right-wing organisations were at La Rocque's growing ascendancy. But it also reveals that the real political dynamics of the time are too complex to be understood in terms of sharply defined ideological traditions. Why would the conservative nationalists of the parliamentary Fédération Républicaine form an alliance with the extraparliamentary PPF (supposedly the nearest thing to a mass fascist formation in France) against the (Bonapartist? authoritarian populist? national-caesarist? authoritarian republican? Christian-nationalist?) PSF?[46] To dismiss it as pure opportunism or as *une alliance contre-nature* whilst still insisting on the primacy and validity of these ideological distinctions is hardly convincing. The *perspective relationnelle* surely suggests that in a climate of destabilisation and radicalisation on the French Right, the behaviour of the various formations is not best explained by the traditional analysis of the ideological nuances that separated them, but rather by the intense competition and tactical calculations of organisations that were in fact drawing very much on the common stock of ideas referred to by Dobry below – antiparliamentarism, hatred of democracy, the seductive appeal of authoritarian regimes in neighbouring states, anti-Marxism etc.[47] And arguably, from this perspective the attempt to measure this or that individual French movement against generic definitions of fascism begins to look like a rather sterile exercise.

Notes

1. R.O. Paxton, *Vichy France: Old Guard and New Order, 1940–44*, New York, 1972; M. Marrus and R.O. Paxton, *Vichy France and the Jews*, New York, 1981.

2. R. Rémond, *La droite en France de 1815 à nos jours*, Paris, 1954 and subsequent editions, notably *Les droites en France*, Paris, 1982. See also S. Berstein, 'La France des années 30 allergique au fascisme: à propos d'un livre de Zeev Sternhell', *XXe siècle*, no. 2, April 1984; P. Burrin, 'La France dans le champ magnétique des fascismes', *Le Débat*, no. 32, November 1984; J. Julliard, 'Sur un fascisme imaginaire: à propos d'un livre de Zeev Sternhell', *Annales ESC*, 39 no. 4, July–August 1984, M. Winock, 'Fascisme à la française ou fascisme introuvable?', *Le Débat*, no. 25, May 1983; P. Milza, *Fascisme français*, Paris, 1987; P. Burrin, *La Dérive fasciste*, Paris, 1986; P. Burrin, 'Le fascisme', in *Histoire des droites en France* vol. 1, Politique, ed. J.-F. Sirinelli, Paris, 1992.

3. Notably Z. Sternhell, *La droite révolutionnaire: les origines françaises du fascisme*, Paris, 1978; *Ni droite ni gauche. L'idéologie fasciste en France*, Paris, 1983. R. Soucy, *French Fascism: The First Wave, 1924–1933*, New Haven, 1986; *French Fascism: The Second Wave, 1933–1939*, New Haven, 1995.

4. See Dobry, chapter 5 below, p. 132.

5. Ibid., section on 'Political cultures, values and calculations', pp. 145–47.

6. For example, the summoning of historians as expert witnesses during the 1998 trial of Maurice Papon (for his role in the deportation of Jews when general secretary of the Gironde préfecture 1942–43), and the very public divisions among leading historians during the so-called Aubrac affair (following the publication in 1997 of a book by the journalist Gérard Chauvy, which questioned the wartime role of Resistance heroes Lucie and Raymond Aubrac, and the veracity of their testimony). See G. Chauvy, *Aubrac: Lyon 1943*, Paris, 1997. Annie Collovald has given a telling evocation of this new social role of the historian: 'If they find themselves virtually summoned to assume a "civic" role (as witnesses and judges in their specialist fields of political history) when there is in fact no agreement between them, they also find themselves required collectively to defend their historical interpretation of the Vichy regime, and their version of this past which has returned to haunt the present'. A. Collovald, 'Le "national-populisme" ou le fascisme disparu. Les historiens du "Temps Présent" et la question du déloyalisme politique contemporain' in *Le mythe de l'allergie française au fascisme*, ed. M. Dobry, Paris, 2003, p. 286. [Editor's translation].

7. See Sternhell, chapter 2 below, p. 23.

8. *The Second Wave*, p. 6; W. Irvine, 'Fascism in France and the strange case of the Croix de Feu', *Journal of Modern History*, vol. 63, June 1991, p.294.

9. H. Rousso, *Le syndrome de Vichy (1944–198...)*, Paris, 1987.

10. See Sternhell, chapter 2 below, 'France immune to fascism?', pp 27–35.

11. Summed up by the Communist jibe that MRP stood for *Machine à Ramasser les Pétainistes*.

12. For example, H. Arendt, *The Origins of Totalitarianism*, New York, 1951; J. Talmon, *The Origins of Totalitarian Democracy*, London, 1952; C. Friedrich, ed., *Totalitarianism*, proceedings of a conference held at the American Academy of Arts and Sciences in March 1953, Cambridge, MA, 1954; C. Friedrich and Z. Brzezinski, *Totalitarian Dictatorship and Autocracy*, Cambridge, MA, 1956.

13. See B. Goyet, *Charles Maurras*, Paris, 2000, pp.118–19.

14. Notably Sternhell goes much further in identifying some of the ideological roots of fascism as not just radical but distinctly left-wing (see in particular his *La droite révolutionnaire*). Earlier Ernst Nolte had identified fascism as a reaction to and imitation of communism ('Fascism is anti-Marxism which seeks to destroy the enemy by the evolvement of a radically opposed yet related ideology, and by the use of almost identical, but typically modified methods, always however within the unyielding framework of national self-assertion and autonomy', E. Nolte, *Three Faces of Fascism*, London, 1965, pp. 20–21.)

15. Goyet, *Charles Maurras*, p. 125.

16. For more detailed discussion of Rémond's model, see Sternhell, chapter 2 below.

17. For Rémond's discussion of La Rocque's movement, see *Les droites en France*, pp. 211–16. Rémond does nonetheless recognise that the question of whether or not the Croix de Feu was fascist is 'le pivot du débat' (p.211). That is why the analysis of the Croix de Feu/PSF is central to all the chapters in the present volume.

18. For example, the largely 'Rémondian' line taken in E. Weber, *Action Française: Royalism and Reaction in 20th Century France*, Stanford, 1962; J. Plumyène and R. Lasierra, *Les fascismes français, 1923–63*, Paris, 1963; S. Berstein, *Le 6 février 1934*, Paris, 1975, and reproduced in most general histories of the Third Republic or of the interwar years published in the 1960s and 1970s.

19. See note 2 above.

20. Paxton, *Old Guard and New Order*; Marcel Ophuls's film *Le Chagrin et la Pitié* was composed in 1967–68, and first screened in a small venue in the Latin Quarter in 1971, but it was not finally shown on French television until 1981. See Rousso, *Le syndrome de Vichy*, pp. 114–31.

21. G. Ross, 'Adieu vieilles idées: the Middle Strata and the Decline of Resistance-Liberation Left Discourse in France', in *Contemporary France: A Review of Interdisciplinary Studies*, Vol. 1, ed. J. Howorth and G. Ross, London, 1987, pp. 57–83.

22. Jean-François Sirinelli has referred to the Sciences-Po historians around René Rémond as the 'corporation' (see Sternhell, chapter 2 below, note 56).

23. For an account of the reception in France of Paxton's *La France de Vichy* (French translation of *Old Guard and New Order*) in 1972, see Rousso, *Le syndrome de Vichy*, pp. 267–71.

24. Rousso, *Le syndrome de Vichy*, p. 20.

25. Adult male suffrage was introduced by the Second Republic in 1848, and maintained under the Second Empire (1851–70) for elections to the Legislative Body. The powers of that assembly were, however, very seriously circumscribed. It was only under the Third Republic, therefore, that adult male suffrage was combined with parliamentary sovereignty and acquired real political weight.

26. For a critical discussion of the uses recently made by French historians of the term 'national populism', see Collovald, 'Le "national-populisme" ou le fascisme disparu'.

27. See Sternhell, *La Droite révolutionnaire*, and Z. Sternhell (with M. Sznajder and M. Asheri), *Naissance de l'idéologie fasciste*, Paris, 2000.

28. This applies in particular to Rémond himself, and to a lesser extent to Milza, Berstein and Burrin, none of whom (in this author's view) adequately convey how the Great War and the Russian Revolution transformed social and political attitudes in France. Michel Winock and Jacques Julliard both criticise Sternhell for failing to do just this, but they omit to point out that Rémond's model of 'les trois droites' is equally insensitive to such contextual factors. (Julliard, 'Sur un fascisme imaginaire'; Winock, 'Fascisme à la française ou fascisme introuvable?').

29. Burrin, 'Le fascisme', pp. 643–44.

30. See K. Passmore, *From Liberalism to Fascism: The Right in a French Province, 1928–1939*, Cambridge, 1997, pp. 6–7.

31. S. Hoffmann, *In Search of France: Renovation and Economic Management in the Twentieth Century*, New York, 1963.

32. Kevin Passmore does, however, point out that the economic depression in France did have a major impact on social groups that were vulnerable to fascism. See his discussion in *From Liberalism to Fascism*, pp. 163–85.

33. The Croix de Feu had been founded by Maurice d'Hartoy in 1927, as an elite war veterans' association with no political vocation. La Rocque joined in 1929 and by 1931 had become its president. He quickly transformed it into a political movement with a mass membership.

34. Serge Berstein's study (*Le 6 février 1934*, Paris, 1975) confirmed the standard interpretation of the events developed in the 1960s, and was long regarded as the definitive work, remaining virtually unchallenged until Michel Dobry's 1989 article. See Dobry, chapter 5 below.

35. See Berstein, *Le 6 février1934*; M. Le Clère, *Le 6 février*, Paris, 1967; M. Chavardès, *Une campagne de presse: la droite française et le 6 février 1934*, Paris, 1970; B. Jenkins, 'The Paris riots of February 6th 1934: the crisis of the Third French Republic', (unpublished Ph.D. thesis, University of London, 1979); P. Pellissier, *6 février 1934*, Paris, 2000.

36. Pellissier, *6 février 1934*, p.320, records that 15 were killed by gunfire that evening, two more died shortly afterwards from their wounds, and a further four deaths can be attributed to wounds sustained on this occasion.

37. Rémond, *Les droites en France*, p. 211.

38. For an interesting recent discussion of these conflicting interpretations, see D. Leschi, 'L'étrange cas La Rocque', in Dobry, ed., *Le mythe de l'allergie française au fascisme*. Leschi argues that between 1934 and 1940, La Rocque increasingly places his movement outside and against the parliamentary system, while Doriot (so often presented as La Rocque's more radical counterpart) plays the card of bourgeois respectability by doing a deal with the parliamentary Right via the 'Front de la Liberté'.

39. Julian Jackson finds evidence of an upturn in France's political mood in the last twelve months before war was declared, and confirms how difficult it is to reach a balanced judgement: 'It is too often alleged, in the light of defeat, that the French Republic in the 1930s was in a state of terminal decline. On the other hand, one should not go too far in the opposite direction. The divisions of the 1930s had not been forgotten. Hatreds bubbled close beneath the surface, and Daladier's public image of earthy solidity was a façade.' J. Jackson, *The Fall of France: the Nazi invasion of 1940*, Oxford, 2003, p.119.

40. P. Burrin, *La Dérive fasciste: Doriot, Déat, Bergery, 1933–1945*, Paris 1986.

41. As Michel Dobry has pointed out, many 'immunity thesis' historians seem to contradict their own case when they write about other topics. Thus, when Serge Berstein writes about the subject on which he is the leading expert (the French Radical Party), he has no hesitation in acknowledging that the party was 'in crisis' during the 1930s (S. Berstein, *Histoire du Parti radical*, vol. 2 'Crise du radicalisme', Paris, 1982). When arguing that France was largely immune to fascism, however, he again presents the resilience of the Radical Party as one of the foundations of France's 'democratic culture' (Berstein, 'La France des années trente allergique au fascisme'). M. Dobry, 'La thèse immunitaire face aux fascismes' in Dobry, ed., *Le mythe de l'allergie française au fascisme*, p. 26.

42. See Dobry, chapter 5 below, 'The autonomisation of the non-parliamentary Right'.

43. Soucy, *The Second Wave*.

44. Passmore, *From Liberalism to Fascism*, p. 8.

45. Jacques Nobécourt reminds us that, as an ex-communist, Doriot was very familiar with the PCF tactic of establishing 'front' organisations, nominally nonpartisan alliances open to all comers, but really a device for drawing in and then poaching the membership of close rivals – usually the SFIO ('plumer la volaille *social-democrate*'). As leader of the PPF, Doriot was simply using the same tactic, this time against La Rocque ('plumer la volaille PSF'). J. Nobécourt, *Le Colonel de La Rocque 1885–1946 ou les pièges du nationalisme chrétien*, Paris, 1996, p. 572.

46. These various terms have been applied to the PSF by Rémond (Bonapartist), Passmore (authoritarian populist), Burrin (national-caesarist), Berstein (authoritarian republican), Winock and Nobécourt (Christian-nationalist).

47. See Dobry, chapter 5 below, 'On imprecision and the boundaries of ideologies', pp. 138–40.

2

Morphology of Fascism in France*

Zeev Sternhell

In the year 2000 Fayard published new editions of Zeev Sternhell's trilogy of books on French fascism (*Maurice Barrès et le nationalisme français, La droite révolutionnaire, Ni droite ni gauche*), while Gallimard did the same for his coauthored *Naissance de l'idéologie fasciste*. In each of them the author has written a substantial new preface. While this would anyway appear entirely appropriate, given the interest they have provoked in France and the length of time that has elapsed since they first appeared (more than thirty years in the case of the book on Barrès), such a focused enterprise strongly suggests a taking-stock or reappraisal. The essay that follows is an abridged translation of the new preface to the most controversial of these volumes, *Ni droite ni gauche*. The reader will judge to what extent this marks a restatement, a refinement, or an adjustment of the author's previous line of argument as briefly summarised below.

Of all the contributors to this volume, Zeev Sternhell is the one who has attracted the most hostility from the supporters of the so-called 'immunity thesis'. Through his work in the early 1970s on Boulangism and Paul Déroulède, and then on Maurice Barrès, he developed the key ideas that were later elaborated in his trail-blazing study *La droite révolutionnaire, 1885–1914: les origines françaises du fascisme* (1978), namely that fascist ideology had its origins in a heresy of the Left before being transformed into a doctrine of the revolutionary Right, and that turn-of-the-century France was its key intellectual laboratory, above all in *milieux* that might be described as

* This essay is a considerably abridged translated version of the author's extensive new preface to the revised third edition of *Ni droite ni gauche* (Fayard, 2000, pp. 11–112). In its original version *Ni droite ni gauche* is available in English: *Neither Right nor Left: Fascist Ideology in France* (Princeton University Press, 1995).

'national-syndicalist'. Controversial though it was to see France as the intellectual seedbed of European fascism, this book was not perceived as immediately threatening by proponents of the 'immunity thesis'. It was only when Sternhell turned his attention to the interwar period that the alarm bells began to ring.

In his *Ni droite ni gauche: L'idéologie fasciste en France* (1983) Sternhell continued to underline the synthetic nature of fascist ideology, the radical Right constantly replenished by dissident intellectual deserters from the Left. Thus when he brings this perspective to bear on the 1920s and 1930s in France, it is not the 'usual suspects' (Doriot, Bucard, Drieu la Rochelle, Brasillach) who attract his attention, but the antimaterialist revisionists of Marxism from Georges Sorel to Henri de Man and Marcel Déat, along with the *personnalistes* like Emmanuel Mounier and the 'spiritual' nationalists around Thierry Maulnier. To have singled out these intellectually intriguing but numerically insignificant coteries might seem rather innocuous, but Sternhell drew two much more startling conclusions: first, that the doctrines developed in these *milieux* represented fascism in its purest ideological form, uncontaminated by the inevitable compromises of political action or the exercise of power; and second, that these tips of the ideological iceberg reflected the deep impregnation of French intelligentsia and French society between the wars with fascist attitudes. In both respects, Sternhell presented France, far from being 'immune' to fascism, as being its ideological progenitor and intellectual repository. But where Sternhell's analysis really hurt was in his perception of fascism as the hard core of a much more widespread phenomenon: the revolt against liberal democracy. *Ni Droite ni gauche* showed the centrality of that revolt to French political culture.

The indignant reactions provoked by this interpretation are discussed at the start of the essay that follows. Elsewhere, Zeev Sternhell has referred to it as 'truly a very rough affair', and one of his more measured and perceptive critics, Philippe Burrin, has since acknowledged that 'it is regrettable that the polemic unleashed by *Ni droite ni gauche* has not allowed [… Sternhell's analysis] to be discussed in its entirety'. One wonders if the reason Sternhell stirred up such a hornets' nest was that he was confronting his opponents on their own territory – namely the history of ideas. As we shall see, many supporters of the 'immunity thesis' (following their mentor René Rémond) base their conclusions largely on the supposed *ideological* distinctions between 'genuine' fascism and its French analogues. Sternhell was ploughing the same ground, but turning up different material and reaching opposite conclusions. The fury of the response seems to indicate both indignation at Sternhell's intrusion, and relish at the prospect of fighting on familiar terrain.

In the essay below Professor Sternhell takes a reflective look at the controversy, sheds some fascinating light on the whole intellectual tradition which produced the historical method associated with René Rémond and his successors, and addresses some of the recent refinements of the immunity thesis, notably in the work of Philippe Burrin. However, there were some other critics of *Ni droite ni gauche*, notably Jacques Julliard, who criticised Sternhell precisely for being too preoccupied with the history of ideas at the expense of what he called *le vécu* or 'lived history'. In some respects, the essay which follows may be seen as a sustained response to this particular critique. It dwells at some length on the political and social history of the Vichy regime, drawing significant comparisons with Mussolini's rise to power and the political realities of the Italian fascist dictatorship. It then goes on to look at two substantial French extraparliamentary movements in which Sternhell has not previously shown sustained interest – La Rocque's Croix de Feu and Dorgères's Greenshirts. In concluding that France produced not only a fully-fledged and widely disseminated fascist ideology, but also (in the Croix de Feu-PSF) a genuine fascist mass movement, and eventually an authentic fascist regime, Sternhell continues to present the most comprehensive and radical challenge to the 'immunity thesis'.

In order to meet editorial requirements, the translated essay that follows has been substantially abridged to around half the length of the original French version. Inevitably, in the process the weight and force of some arguments has been significantly reduced. The title of the original preface was *Morphologie et historiographie du fascime en France*: the removal of the reference to historiography in the amended title below gives some clue to the nature of the cuts that have been made.

Zeev Sternhell is currently Léon Blum Professor of Political Science at the Hebrew University of Jerusalem, Israel.

The contours of the debate

'Few books on European history in recent memory have caused such controversy and commotion' wrote Robert Wohl in an important historiographical article on the American edition of *Ni droite ni gauche*.[1] The numerous other major essays which greeted the book's appearance indicate the scale of the debate it aroused.[2]

Despite the lapse of time it still seems astonishing that it provoked such extreme reactions. There were many different reasons for the ferocity of the debate, but they can be reduced to a few essential points. First of all, there is the notion of French exceptionalism, and more specifically the assumption that France was somehow immune to the phenomenon of fascism. France was, so the reasoning goes, protected by its republican tradition and was therefore by definition incapable of producing anything resembling a national brand of fascism. The implications of this assumption are clear enough. It would mean that the long tradition of historicism, the rejection of the Enlightenment, the radical critique of democracy which erupted at the turn of the twentieth century and assumed a particularly violent form between the two world wars, the moral and intellectual revolt against the liberal Republic – should all be regarded as minor phenomena. Since their existence cannot be denied, their importance has been minimised. The nationalism of *La Terre et les Morts*, the veneration of Barrès, the legacy of Drumont still celebrated by Bernanos in the 1930s, the magisterial influence of the Action Française over a significant fraction of the cultured classes, the persistance of the anti-Dreyfusard tradition – these are treated as relatively innocent manifestations, disconnected from society at large. The long tradition of Catholic antiliberalism (which implicates not only the Church, the religious orders and men like Claudel but also the likes of Maritain and Mounier), the importance of the antidemocratic press, the attractive power and numerical strength of the leagues and first and foremost the Croix de Feu, the continuous street agitation – in the eyes of apologist historiography all of this is superficial distraction bordering on folklore. If there were a few traces of such sentiment, they were soon swept away by the epic tide of the Resistance. So it inevitably follows that Vichy can have been no more than a mishap, a passing sickness, a momentary bout of fever. Indeed, in the historiography of the apologists it is almost as if the Vichy episode barely merits a mention at all except as a period of transition, and that it could quite easily be wiped from the nation's memory without doing any damage to History.

The second dimension of the debate concerns the proper place that should be assigned within historical analysis to the history of ideas. This discipline (which explores the structure of systems of thought, their logic and their influence in a long timeframe) was from the very outset bound to be suspect. For it revealed how the collapse of democracy in France, as in Germany and Italy, emanated from a long tradition which contested the philosophical principles and moral bases of democracy. Thereby it surely touched a raw nerve. What other discipline can bring out so clearly the continuities of a tradition, the lineage of ideas, their trajectory, often adventurous and strange but always fascinating? What other discipline is better able to grasp the significance of intellectual constructs, the forces that shake the values of a civilisation, the translation into politics of processes of change?

Furthermore, did not the history of ideas reveal that intellectual constructs had a power of their own, and that what happened in the world of ideas quickly assumed social and political significance? And this raised questions about the nature of the intimate links between philosophical reflection, historical research, literary production and politics. Whereas in France intellectual history was the poor relation, in Italy, Germany and England, and in the United States under the influence of the great wave of German immigrants, there was a veritable intellectual renewal from the 1930s and throughout the postwar period, involving a process of self-examination. This reflection on the European catastrophe often involved asking some hard questions about 'historicism', in other words asking what risks might be involved for a whole civilisation when it rejects the notion of universal values. The history of ideas thus assumed a new status pretty well everywhere, except in France.

This weakness owed as much to the prestige enjoyed by the Annales school as to the fact that the history of ideas in France had no one of the stature of Cassirer,

Meinecke, Croce, Arendt, Lovejoy, or in more recent times Isaiah Berlin, H. Stuart Hughes, George Mosse or Fritz Stern. And this remained true when the Annales school was well past its peak and, alongside a few magisterial works, was beginning to produce (under the cover of social history) something more like factual or even anecdotal history. Raymond Aron, who wrote a fine book on the history of ideas in 1967, did not dare adopt the appropriate title for this exemplary series of essays on Montesquieu, Tocqueville, Marx and Weber. To achieve respectability they had to be collected under the rubric *Les Etapes de la pensée sociologique*.[3]

In these conditions, it was possible in the France of the 1970s and 1980s [during the long debate provoked by Sternhell's work: *Editor's note*] to use the campaign against the history of ideas, and in particular the argument that ideas do not represent reality, as a cover under which to dispute the historical importance of the persistent antidemocratic tradition. It was possible to deny that there were any causal links between the turn-of-the-century intellectual crisis, the revolt of the 1930s, and the establishment of the nationalist dictatorship of 1940. Thus by giving immediate political circumstances primacy over the longer timeframe, it was possible to present the whole attack on the intellectual principles and philosophical infrastructure of democracy (an attack which was implicit in the whole idea of crisis which dominated the first half of the twentieth century), as an innocent exercise, scarcely more than intellectual recreation. But it would never have occurred to anyone to dispute the contribution made by intellectuals to the rise of German nationalism in its most extreme and barbaric forms. Of course, this is not to say that philosophers, historians, jurists and writers, from Herder and Fichte to Spengler, from Moser and Adam Muller to Langbehn, Lagarde, Moeller Van den Bruck and Junger, from Savigny to Carl Schmitt, from Ranke to Treitschke, actually created German nationalism, but they shaped it and gave it a certain character.

Similarly in France it wasn't the likes of Taine, Renan, Barrès, Drumont, Maurras or Thierry Maulnier, of Céline, Brasillach or Drieu La Rochelle and their many fellow travellers who produced all on their own the nationalism of *La Terre et les Morts* and its corollary anti-Semitism. But by conceptualising a deep seated social, emotional and intellectual need, they had as much impact on history as their German analogues and thus carry the same responsibility. Similarly, Vichy was not created by the intellectual rebels of the 1930s, but could the government of the National Revolution have carried out its destruction of democracy, largely with the support of the elites, if the soil had not already been prepared and the seed sown? Is it possible to imagine Vichy without the prior work of moral and intellectual destruction undertaken by Maurrassians of every persuasion, as they eulogised Mussolini's Italy, its regime and its leader, and loudly demanded the establishment of a dictatorship in France?[4] It is impossible to insist enough on the process which saw the intellectual Right, from its Maurrassian core outwards, increasingly seduced by fascism; or indeed on the role of these intellectuals in creating a climate which allowed fascism to hold sway.[5]

At the eye of the storm provoked by my book, however, was this notion of French exceptionalism. Whereas it was normal enough to ask the question why, throughout Europe, fascism exercised such a powerful influence over so many worthy people, to pose the same question in France in the early 1980s was to commit the crime of *lèse-majesté*. What was normal and natural for the London of Ezra Pound, Wyndham Lewis and T.S. Eliot, the Bucharest of Mircea Eliade and Emil Cioran, the Lisbon of Fernando Pessoa or the Brussels of Hendrik de Man (with Germany and Italy, of course, at the centre of our problematic), ceased to be acceptable as soon as one stepped onto French soil. To ask why fascism held such attractive power for such diverse social classes, how it was able to be both a mass movement and an elitist intellectual construct capable of seducing some of the most sophisticated avant-garde thinkers of the day, was normal as long as the thesis of French immunity was not challenged. To try to understand why fascism was able to seduce both the ill-educated and some of the great names of the century's intellectual life was acceptable as long as France was excluded from the field of research.

So when *Neither Right nor Left* appeared at the start of 1983, the very idea that French political culture might not be an exception, and that forms of revolt against democracy and liberalism, including fascism, might have exercised considerable appeal across broad swathes of society, provoked outrage in certain quarters. The idea that celebrated figures in postwar France, with Resistance credentials, including prominent intellectuals, had loyally served the Vichy regime before changing horses in midstream, was hard to stomach. And to have to face the question of why these dignitaries of the new France had enthusiastically supported the National Revolution despite Vichy's anti-Jewish laws, the round-ups and the deportation of children, was simply intolerable.

There is nothing particularly surprising about this reaction. When it comes to anything to do with nationalism, anti-Semitism, Vichy, and more generally the whole nature and importance of the revolutionary Right between the wars, one thing must be remembered. By the time the book appeared, not only those men and women who for various reasons felt themselves directly implicated, but also the whole French historical and political science establishment, had spent thirty years sanitising and dedramatising the narrative. The received wisdom was that neither fascism (mischievously copied from abroad), nor Vichy (a reactionary and anachronistic regime totally dominated by the occupier) were really part of the nation's history.

France immune to fascism?

The idea of French exceptionalism, based on the notion of the permanence of political traditions since the Revolution, took shape immediately after the Liberation. Our concern here is not with the 'refoundation myth' bequeathed to France by Gaullism (and which is discussed in the new edition of *La Droite révolutionnaire*),[6] but with official French historiography. The tone was set by the 'most eminent representative' of French political science, André Siegfried.[7] In the years that followed the Liberation, the author of *Tableau politique de la France de l'Ouest sous la Troisième République*, professor at the Collège de France since 1933, member of the Institut, and later president of the board of directors of Sciences-Po, enjoyed unparalleled academic authority. Furthermore, it should be emphasised that Siegfried's influence was not limited to university circles. Elected to the Académie Française in 1944, columnist on Le Figaro, he was a pillar of the 1940s and 1950s cultural establishment.

Siegfried genuinely founded a school. We are not concerned here with his contribution to electoral sociology, or rather electoral geography, but with his global interpretation of the relationship between political forces. The fundamental principle, which shapes the whole of his interpretation, is a form of ethnic and psychological determinism, which he defines in terms of 'temperament'. Just as there are individual temperaments, so 'there are regional and national temperaments', there is 'a temperament derived from one's milieu': thus 'beneath those elements that change quickly (social classes, political parties)' lies 'a social structure which changes slowly'. But the essential point is that 'deep down we finally discover, in population groups, these collective political temperaments, geographically localised, which over nearly half-a-century have remained virtually unchanged.'[8]

The principles laid down in *Tableau politique de la France de l'Ouest*, and which had already appeared a few years earlier in *Le Canada, les deux races* (1906), provided the explanatory framework within which Siegfried operated throughout his career. Thus Siegfried established a strict correlation between human behaviour and ethnic origin, which is of course the classic feature of racism. He applies his ideas entirely without discrimination, and in this respect remains true to his profession. Whether his ideas might have had dangerous implications in certain critical circumstances was a different matter altogether. For if there is indeed a Breton race and a Breton soul, a Breton temperament and character supposedly unchanged since the day the first soldiers of the great Celtic chieftain Nomenoé alighted on the shores of the land that would become Brittany, then why should there not also be a Jewish race, with the same mental habits and behaviour patterns as the one which left the desert for Europe after the Roman conquest of Judea? If, in order to explain the electoral behaviour of Western France, it is necessary to invoke wars and migratory movements dating back fourteen centuries, is it not also logical when endeavouring to understand the Jewish character and temperament to return to the first century of the Christian era?

Siegfried answers such questions unceremoniously in a book which appeared in 1950, *L'Ame des peuples*. 'In the collective psychology of peoples there is always an element of permanence. We are still, in many of our features, similar to our Gallic ancestors, and the characteristics that Tacitus observed in the barbarians or in the Jews of his time are still recognisably present in the Germans or Israelis of today.'[9] Here Siegfried borrows from the racist anthropology of Vacher de

Lapouge: 'the physical features of the Germanic peoples have not changed since Roman times, if we trust the description supplied by Tacitus: they are dolichocephalic, tall and strongly built, blond or red-haired, fair-skinned and blue-eyed.' But there is also 'a second type of German who is not of true Germanic stock ... brachycephalic, of medium build and increasingly small as we move south-east ... they are Alpine people, sometimes referred to as Celts'.[10] The same criterion is used to describe 'the races which combined to form the Mediterranean type. The oldest and most representative of these are the Iberians: white, dolichocephalic, slightly-built, small with a dark complexion. They are both geographically and physically distinct from the Negroes, who are dolichocephalic but black, and from the Scandinavian or Nordic races, who also are dolichocephalic but blond and fair-skinned.'[11]

Siegfried is so convinced of the validity and utility of these methods that he is still using the cephalic index during the Second World War. (The 'cephalic index', devised by Vacher de Lapouge, was obtained by dividing the width of the skull by its length, and multiplying the result by 100.) In what claims to be an anthropological study, *Vue générale de la Méditerranée*, published in 1943, he seeks to establish a classification of races, not just for the purposes of the Mediterranean region, but in order to 'evoke the destiny of the West as a whole'.[12] Indeed, this work is devoted not just to the supposedly 'scientific' analysis of the ethnic character of the Mediterranean peoples, but also to the defence of the West. It is the 'European section' of the white race which, 'straddling Asia and Europe, has created Western civilisation: in their opposition to the Persians, the Greeks of Antiquity were already authentic Westerners; for us Marathon should be a place of pilgrimage!'[13] There follows an analysis of 'ethnic zones' where we learn that 'the Mediterranean race has distinctive physical characteristics ... the dolichocephalic skull, verging on the mesocephalic – usually an index of less than 75 – is generally the rule'.[14]

Five years after the war, Siegfried returned to the conclusions he drew in 1943: 'if Western civilisation is partly the product of an environment, it is also the achievement of a race'.[15] He then pursues his reflections on the problems of race, and this leads him, apparently without any discomfort, to tackle the Jewish question. While the author of *L'Âme des peuples* pays homage to Abraham as the founder of monotheism,[16] he regards Jews with the same eye as his mentor Barrès. What troubles him is that oriental influence of which Jews are the medium: that is why 'we must still talk about the Jews, even after Hitler's massive persecution of them'.[17] To understand the causes of anti-Semitism, the celebrated political scholar, who took a great interest in the Jews throughout his career, turned not only to his own country but also towards Germany and the United States.

Indeed, according to Siegfried the end of the First World War saw a new type of immigrant arrive in Berlin, 'rather similar to those who came with the Jewish invasion of New York. Interestingly enough, the activity of these new arrivals, who achieved considerable influence under the Weimar Republic, was not limited to finance as had previously been the case: they were to be found, so to speak, at the intersection of the business and the intellectual worlds. The press, the theatre, the cinema, the art trade, medicine, the law increasingly belonged to them'.[18] Siegfried concludes that 'their role under Weimar was decisive, and Hitler's anti-Semitism was the reaction'.[19] Here, Siegfried adds another explanation which, like the myth of Jewish power under Weimar, had already done the rounds in Nazi propaganda and which resurfaced in Germany in the 1980s during the 'historians' debate' (*Historikerstreit*): the Jewish invasion carries with it the danger of communism. 'Through this intrusive influence, which extended from avant-garde art to financial advertising and communist propaganda, a subtle soviet presence was somehow projected into the German capital city, displaying traits that were in some curious way nonwestern, surreptitiously Russian.'[20] That is why Berlin, 'so aggressively western in outward appearance, harboured within it, largely thanks to the Jews, insidious germs of the East. These circumstances provoked the persecution we all know about'.[21]

Clearly these learned perambulations indicate that Nazism was a defensive double-reflex, natural and perfectly justified, to a foreign invasion which was both ethnic and ideological: to sum up the position of the celebrated scholar, the Jews alone are responsible for anti-Semitism. Apparently this is equally true of the United States: there too anti-Semitism is in response to a Jewish takeover. Whether he comes from the aristocracy of London or Frankfurt, or from the ghettos of Poland or the Ukraine, whether he changes his name from de Schönberg to Belmont, or from Jonas to Jones, the Jew always provokes the same reaction. It is not just that he offers stiff competition in the contest for attractive positions, whether in the world of business or academia; it is because, bound together as they are by 'racial ties', the Jews cannot be assimilated. Naturally therefore, they have led 'the Protestant American to adopt a hostile attitude which has then developed into an anti-Semitic movement'.[22]

The case of France is no different. Anti-Semitism is explained in the same terms: in the last analysis it is the innate character of the Jew that triggers the defensive reflex. Like Barrès, André Siegfried sees Jews through the eyes of the militant *anti-Dreyfusard*.[23] In the notes for his 1957 lecture course, he quotes Barrès to describe the Jewish temperament, their 'nomadic instincts': 'the Jewish intellect manipulates ideas with the dexterity of a banker counting money'. For them, ideas are no more than 'coins being sorted on a cold marble counter'. In the end, he concludes that the Jew is 'the irreducible residue in the melting-pot': and thus anti-Semitism is 'not economic in nature, but a doctrinal reaction against the Jewish approach to problems'. To be sure, the Jews do bring – and here he uses one of his favourite quotes, borrowed from Bismarck – 'a certain sparkle, but it is dangerous to exceed the stated dose':[24] ideas like these were aired quite freely, without even provoking a raised eyebrow, in Siegfried's lectures at the Paris Institut d'études politiques between 1947 and 1957.

The conceptual framework devised by Siegfried underpins all those analyses which prioritise notions of temperament (which avoids saying 'character'), of continuity, of permanence in general, and of the plurality of temperaments, especially on the Right. Clearly the infrastructure is based on determinism. The disciples of Siegfried reject his scarcely concealed racism, his mild anti-Semitism, an anti-Semitism which is the logical by-product of his methodology, but they nonetheless adopt the analytical principles that derive from it, namely that 'in politics, differences of temperament sometimes run deeper than differences of programme'.[25]

It is in this notion of the permanence of attitudes and temperaments from the Restoration until today that we find the bedrock for the principle whereby the existence of fascism in France is a virtual impossibility. This idea is at the heart of the most famous book by René Rémond, *La Droite en France*, which has provided a rallying-point for the Sciences-po chapel. First published in 1954, and regularly reprinted since 1982 as *Les Droites en France*, this book (in the words of Jean-François Sirinelli) 'was destined to leave a profound and lasting imprint on the historiography of the subject'.[26] In fact this judgement seems too modest: Pierre Birnbaum is nearer the mark when he tells us that the book was virtually a bible for several generations of students.[27] Indeed, with very few exceptions, it was not until the 1990s that French academics raised any doubts about the semi-official status of the general interpretation developed by the Siegfried-Rémond school.

For René Rémond 'the whole problem of the Right hinges on this alternative: *unity or plurality through time*'.[28] His choice is to align himself firmly with what he calls 'the tendency of contemporary historians' to emphasise the continuity, permanence and stability of public opinion through successive regimes, and in support he invokes the sledgehammer argument: the authority of Siegfried and Goguel. 'One of the most valuable contributions of the work launched 40 years ago by André Siegfried's *Tableau politique de la France de l'Ouest* (1913) is to have restored the threads of history that seemed on the surface to have been severed, and to have revealed the existence in France of large blocs of opinion, of practice, of religious behaviour, whose territorial homogeneity is less striking than their persistence down the ages.'[29] As for Goguel, 'by demonstrating so forcefully the existence of two stable and well-defined political temperaments [Order and Movement: Editor's note], his interpretation of the history of parties has revealed with unprecedented clarity the fundamental determinants of Right and Left'.[30]

Moving further down this path, Rémond discovers 'three varieties of the Right, each equipped with all the attributes of an authentic political tradition, with its own system of thought, temperament, clientele. They appeared at successive moments in France's political evolution. The first borrows its doctrine from the *ultras* of the Restoration, that of counter-revolution. The second, conservative and liberal, inherits its essentials from Orleanism. The third brings together several heterogeneous elements under the banner of nationalism, with Bonapartism as a precursor.'[31]

The conclusion soon follows: 'there was no French fascism because it would have been difficult for anything of the sort to establish itself in France. Despite appearances, public opinion in that country is peculiarly resistant to the appeal of fascism'.[32] The three right-wing traditions, which have always occupied and will always occupy the terrain, ensure that 'there is no future for fascism in France if the past is anything to go by: all attempts to embark on the road to fascism have been diverted down the path of classical reaction.'[33] Thus France was immunised, once and for all, by its three right-wing traditions, or in other words by its history.

To avoid any comparison with fascism, Vichy's racial laws are not even mentioned in Rémond's work, and indeed the place awarded to Vichy suggests it was some minor episode in the nation's history, squeezed between the Third and Fourth Republics. From the first edition of *La Droite en France* mentioned above to the last edition in 1982, the one which is still regularly reprinted and used as a textbook in all higher education establishments throughout France, the cover design has changed and so has the division of chapters, but the content remains (but for a few details) set in stone: chapter XI, entitled '1940–44: Vichy, the National Revolution and the Right', still totals a little less than eight pages.

Thus the main contours for the explanation of the Vichy phenomenon were fixed for a generation. The conceptual framework imagined by Siegfried and developed by Rémond is in fact virtually immobile: fixedness itself is a transhistorical feature, and short of the whole edifice crashing down, the system of the three right-wing traditions, based as it is on the continuity, stability and permanence of political temperaments, brooks neither modification nor exception. Neither the opening of archives, nor the accumulated evidence of numerous, often remarkable works conducted on this subject over recent years, have been able to change the basic position: Vichy can be assimilated either to the Legitimist-reactionary tradition, to the Orleanist-liberal tradition, or to the Bonapartist-plebiscitary tradition. There are no other choices on offer. The conclusion is that, since fascism does not belong to any of these three families, it can never have got a foothold in France, it can never have been more than a vague imitation, marginal and without real roots. In short, fascism cannot by definition be part of the nation's history. René Rémond himself put his finger on the key point: if it was established that a French fascism did exist, 'it could not easily be confused with the tradition founded by Bonapartism'.[34]

If René Rémond's model takes account of nineteenth-century realities up until the opening years of the Third Republic, it no longer works after Boulangism. With Boulangism we enter the era of mass politics. The modernisation of the European continent, the technological revolution, the democratisation of political life created a new social and ideological reality. It was these conditions, born out of industrialisation and the growth of large urban centres, which produced the new Right, a revolutionary Right, a popular Right, proletarian even, but violently anti-Marxist and secreting an organic, tribal nationalism, a nationalism of *La Terre et les Morts*, of *Blut und Boden*. This new Right reflected the problems of modern society where Bonapartism expressed the realities of preindustrial society. The revolutionary Right, the prefascist Right and later the fascist Right responded to needs that Bonapartism could not even envisage.

To be sure, the revolutionary Right which produced fascism borrowed elements from different systems of thought, ideological traditions and intellectual families, but it was able to forge them into a new, powerful and attractive synthesis. This Right was also a tributary of Bonapartism, but a whole world separated this new ideology, which had integrated the great intellectual revolution of the turn of the century, from the simple authoritarianism of earlier times. The revolutionary Right was derived from the revolt against the French Enlightenment and its heritage, against ideological modernity, against both liberal and marxist 'materialism'. Can this global rejection of a whole model of society, which often draws on social Darwinism and racism, be assimilated to Bonapartism? Does Bonapartism contain this living image of the biological unity of the nation expressed in the 'cult of the dead and the land where they lived', the song intoned by Soury and Barrès in the wake of Taine?[35]

The revolutionary Right is rooted, rather, in the social psychology of Le Bon, in the physiological determinism of the Barresian antinomy of self and anti-self which erupted at the time of the Dreyfus Affair and which anticipated Carl Schmitt's famous antinomy of friend/enemy.[36] As in the case of the latter,[37] who was the real thinker behind German fascism, so for the men of the French revolutionary Right, whether disciples of Maurras or Barrès, the concept of politics presupposes the concept of an enemy: that is why anti-Semitism has a central place in their system. Finally, does not Barrès, the theoretician of the French version of blood-and-soil nationalism, also embrace the Nietzschean revolt against the Enlightenment, even though the great German thinker abhorred both nationalism and anti-Semitism?

On the political level, whereas Bonapartism thought in terms of a *coup d'état* supported by the mass of peasants longing for stability, and for whom the referendum was a means of protecting public order and private property, the revolutionary Right seeks to fashion a new morality, a new kind of society, and new rules of political behaviour. Cultural integration, mass national consciousness, rising levels of literacy, daily access to the press – all of this politicised society to an unprecedented degree. Thus began the struggle to influence public opinion, a struggle for or against the prevailing system, for or against the preservation of the existing order.

It was at this time that within the Right two blocs took shape, which remained opposed to one another from Boulangism until the defeat of 1940: on the one hand, liberals and conservatives who accepted the rules of the game under liberal democracy, and, on the other hand, the revolutionaries who wished to smash the political structures and sweep away the value system of this self-same liberal democracy. These revolutionaries had little in common with Bonapartism which, despite its populist and authoritarian character, belonged to a society where political participation was very limited, and which lacked – how could it be otherwise at the time – these two essential ingredients: anti-Marxist radicalism and an organic nationalism, biological in character. That is why Bonapartism lacked that degree of intellectual autonomy which was a distinctive feature of the revolutionary Right. It had no ideology that was uniquely its own, and which had been elaborated by some of the leading intellectuals of their time, and it was not able to exploit that 'intellectual power' which gave the revolutionary Right such influence throughout the half-century that preceded the disaster of 1940.

In fact, the rise of the revolutionary Right at the turn of the century, that Right which between the wars and then at the time of Vichy would take the form of fascism, was the product of a general European phenomenon: France was not immunised by the Revolution of 1789, nor by the revolutions of the nineteenth century, nor by the foundation of the Third Republic (in other words by its 'republican tradition'). The rejection of the Enlightenment was a constant and powerful theme in nineteenth-century France, and by the turn of the century it was clear that the land of the Rights of Man had ended up producing not one (single and unique) but two political traditions: on the one hand, a universalist and individualist tradition, rooted in the French Revolution, rationalist, democratic (be it Jacobin or liberal), a tradition which was dominant from the foundation of the Third Republic until the summer of 1940; and on the other hand, a particularist and organicist tradition, taking shape as a local variety of biological and racial nationalism, very close to the *volkisch* tradition in Germany.[38]

What is beginning to emerge here might seem paradoxical at first. Despite their very different political histories, French nationalism and German nationalism had at the turn of the last century reached virtually the same point. In terms of intellectual content, they were closely related. There was the same introspection, the same rejection of universal values, the same hatred of the Enlightenment, both in the country which a century earlier had just completed the most important liberal revolution in history, and in the lands of a German Empire where the tradition of law of nature and natural rights had never really penetrated. Furthermore there were similar controversies in the two countries about the criteria for defining the national collectivity: on the one hand in France, the first nation-state of continental Europe, forged by a long political process extending over seven centuries, the product of a unique form of juridical and administrative centralisation; and on the other hand in Germany, which until shortly before the arrival of Napoleon had still been divided into several hundred more or less independent statelets and where the process of national unity had only been completed in the second half of the nineteenth century.

While it is understandable that national identity should have been a problematic concept in Germany, why should the same type of questions have been posed in France? Why during the 1890s should the political and juridical foundations of the idea of nation, conceived as an aggregate of free individuals with equal rights, have come under attack? Why redefine the nation instead as a great family, as a tribe clustered around its churches and cemeteries, communing in ancestor-worship? Why, when defining the criteria for membership of the nation, replace the concept of freely exercised individual choice by objective, historical, ethnic, racial, religious criteria? Why, at the turn of the century, pose the question to which Vichy's race laws gave the concrete answer: is it the same thing to be a French citizen, and to be a member of the French nation? Is every French citizen by definition French? Is French identity defined in political and juridical terms or, on the contrary, is it a product of ethnic, biological, racial factors? Can human beings who are not linked by ties of kindred enjoy the same rights?

All the principles that underpinned the Vichy legislation are inscribed in the nationalist programme of the 1890s. This other tradition, contrary to a widespread and comfortable fallacy, was far from being a marginal ideology in twentieth-century France. On the contrary, it had considerable influence on the development of social attitudes and it permeated society to a far greater extent than anyone would care to acknowledge. From the rebels of Boulangism and the anti-Dreyfus campaign to the militants of the National Revolution, these two traditions coexist, sometimes even within the same mental construct. In fact, it would not be difficult to depict the intellectual history of France since the Revolution as a constant confrontation between these two rival conceptions of what is politically desirable, these two opposing philosophies of history. The great crisis which in many respects marks the opening of the French twentieth century, the Dreyfus Affair, is a striking example of this, and it exemplifies the continuity of these two traditions.

Thus Vichy was not the product of pure expediency or opportunism. The new regime did not emerge from an ideological vacuum: the death of liberal democracy had been the stated intention of the revolutionary, nationalist and nonconformist Right ever since the last decade of the nineteenth century. For those defeated in the Dreyfus Affair and their intellectual heirs, the defeat of 1940 provided the opportunity to enact the principles they had defended forty years earlier: at Vichy the historicist, organicist and particularist tradition momentarily gained the ascendancy. The rebels of the turn of the century, like those of the 1930s, felt that ideas counted, that they had a power of their own, and that what happened in the world of ideas had immediate social and political significance. The men who came to power in the summer of 1940 were morally and intellectually prepared to go to work, just as much as the Nazis in 1933 and perhaps more than the Italian fascists in 1922.

The National Revolution and fascism

When *Ni droite ni gauche* first appeared, Jacques Julliard raised a fundamental objection by questioning the role of ideas in history. He cast doubt not only on the coherence of fascist thought in France, but on the very existence of fascism.[39] As Vincent Duclert explains, Julliard pointed to what he regarded as an essential contradiction between the 'ideal type' of French fascism, as produced notably by the turn-of-the-century prefascists, and the fact that this 'idea' never materialised historically.[40] He took me to task for basing *Neither Right nor Left* on the assumption that (as he put it) 'the application of an ideology implies "compromises" with reality which change its original significance'. 'This', he went on, 'leads us back to a rather traditional form of philosophical and historical idealism which takes little account of the achievements of social history. After all, for the social historian, that is to say for any historian, pure ideas have no reality; historical incarnation is the only real test of their truth. Or, to put it like Hegel, *Die Weltgeschichte ist das Weltgericht*; for social ideas as for human societies, it is history, that is to say lived experience, which offers the final judgement'.[41]

It is not my intention here to embark on a debate about whether social history is the only worthwhile history; I think that to reduce history to social history would not be very productive. Similarly, I do not think that to recognise the intrinsic importance of the history of ideas necessarily involves reverting to traditional idealism. But since it is required of us that we produce evidence of 'lived experience', let us start with Vichy. Let us look at this everyday reality, this great tribunal of history which opens before us.

Can the regime of the National Revolution be understood other than as the logical culmination of the intellectual revolt against the universalist, individualist, hedonist and secular heritage of the French Enlightenment? Was the nationalism of *La Terre et les Morts* not the very core of the National Revolution? Was it not precisely the aim of all Vichy legislation to reverse, in a great burst of revolutionary fervour, all the achievements of the century-and-a-half struggle to democratise, liberalise and secularise French society? Did military defeat necessarily imply the setting-up of a brutal anti-Semitic dictatorship, the basis of a 'new order' which would purge the nation of its impurities? In what way was the ideology of Vichy, the first Vichy, the 'good' Vichy,[42] Pétain's Vichy, the Vichy that transformed both public and private life in the six months betweeen June and December 1940, in what way was that Vichy, let alone the Vichy of the Milice, different from the fascist ideology analysed in *Neither Right nor Left*? And what exactly distinguished this regime in its essentials from the Mussolini regime? How did its blue-print for society, its power structures, differ from those of fascist Italy? Where was police repression most severe, and where between 1940 and 1942 were there more concentration camps for foreigners, political refugees and other undesirables: in Italy or in the French unoccupied zone? Did a Jew feel safer in Italian-occupied Nice or in Marseilles, in Libya – the Italian colony governed by Italo Balbo, one of the most famous founders of the regime – or in North Africa under Darlan, Pétain's heir apparent? Dispatched far from Rome because his presence in the capital was regarded as dangerous for the Duce, renowned throughout the world for his exploits as an aviator until his accidental death in 1940, Balbo had practically blocked the enactment of the race laws. As for the cult of traditional values – the land, family, religion – and all that arsenal of weapons forged to fight individualism, liberalism, 'materialism' whether Marxist or bourgeois, this was just as powerful at Vichy as it was in Italy or Nazi Germany, not to mention the Romanian Iron Guard which had also come to power in 1940. And the same goes for the cult of leadership and the support of the elites.

The process whereby the Italian Fascists took power was no more violent than the one which allowed Pétain to become head of the 'French State': indeed, it was the political and administrative elites led by the former Prime Ministers Giolitti and Salandra, one a liberal, the other more conservative, which allowed Mussolini (when invited by the King to form a government on 29 October 1922) to assume power. There was never any coup d'état in Italy, and the March on Rome did not involve the seizure of power. As was the case later in Germany, it was the crisis of liberal democracy, the weakness of its structures combined with an extraordinary atmosphere of moral and psychological distress, which allowed fascism to take hold. It was this feeling that a world was coming to an end which provoked the abdication of liberal and conservative elites and led them to regard the dictators as national saviours. And it was thanks to a comparable crisis (triggered by military defeat, but in long preparation since the beginning of the century, just as in Italy and Germany) that the French elites handed power to Marshall Pétain and pledged themselves to his service. The cult of the dictator and the willingness of the elites to serve, along with the extraordinary efforts made to mould youth and to create a 'new man' – none of these features differ in any significant degree from what was practised in neighbouring countries.

So here is the 'lived experience'. Dictatorship, the cult of the leader, war on anything remotely connected with the principles of '89, Enlightenment, the Rights of Man, all of these found concrete expression at Vichy. Anti-Semitism, from Barrès and Drumont to Maurras and Brasillach, along with the whole phalanx of anti-Dreyfusards and their descendants, the hatred preached by the popular press since the 1890s, all found their 'lived experience' in the racial laws, the round-ups and deportations. Neither Franco, nor Salazar, nor Mussolini went so far. Furthermore, large sections of opinion between the wars had participated in this war against democracy, against its principles as well as its institutions, and thus a climate was created of progressive delegitimisation of the Republic. When disaster struck, the democratic system in France had barely more support than it had had in neighbouring countries.

As in Italy, the revolt against the Enlightenment or, in concrete political terms, against liberalism, democracy and socialism, was the point of intersection for all the dissidents who subscribed to the National Revolution, from the hard-line fascists who found the new regime too moderate, to those who were horrified at the totalitarian aspects of Pétainism but, at the same time, could not resist the attraction of the spiritualistic and idealistic dimension of this long-awaited revolution.

True enough, Vichy never had the *parti unique*, and never was a single-party regime. But in Germany, as in Italy, the party was never more than an instrument in the struggle for power within the democratic system. The National Fascist Party (PNF), like the Nazi party, had been founded with this end in view: in both cases their arrival in power was the product of a political process which had culminated in a crisis of the regime. In October 1922, Mussolini, as everyone knows, did not march on Rome: he waited quietly in Milan for a telephone call which informed him that the political old guard had failed in its attempt to construct a coalition from which the Fascists would be excluded. He knew that the acting Prime Minister, Luigi Facta, who had taken office in February 1922 at the head of a centre-right coalition, was himself in favour of the Fascists entering government. He also knew that former Prime Minister Antonio Salandra, a right-wing liberal, had declared himself an 'honorary Fascist'. Fascism enjoyed warm support within the royal family as well as in the Army. Benedetto Croce had just proclaimed that, all things considered, fascism was compatible with liberalism.[43] Once in power, in order to govern without tearing society apart Mussolini was obliged to make the same sort of compromises that socialists have always found it so hard to avoid. He drew his collaborators not from the ranks of the party but from the existing elites: from the civil service, the law, the police and the Army. He gave the command of the security forces not to one of the party faithful but to a senior civil servant. He did everything he could to neutralise the provincial Fascist leaders, the *ras*, and to this end he eventually used the state bureaucracy and the traditional elites – industrialists, the *haute bourgeoisie*, the Church – against them.

Thus Mussolini came to power at the head of a parliamentary coalition government made up of liberals of both tendencies, Catholics, a nationalist, a social democrat, an independent close to the Fascists (Giovanni Gentile, Minister of Education), two generals (the War and Navy ministries) and only three Fascists out of thirteen ministers. At thirty-nine, Mussolini was the youngest Prime Minister Italy had ever had, but apart from that, this was an entirely normal government and the regime may be described as semi-constitutional.[44] Between 1922 and 1925 the only exceptional measures were those taken against the Communists, and these were not very different from the measures introduced by the Daladier government in France in 1939. Parliament, where the opposition was free to express itself, willingly granted the new Prime Minister the power to govern by decree for one year; this was a perfectly constitutional provision, written into Italian law. In the meantime the new head of government had to deal with a deep identity crisis within the Fascist party, divided into half-a-dozen antagonistic tendencies. Even after the April 1924 elections, sprinkled with acts of violence and intimidation, and where the Fascist list, which included moderates and conservatives, fraudulently claimed 66 per cent of the vote, it was still not clear which direction Mussolini would take. And this was not the case with Pétain.

The move to dictatorship was a gradual process which accelerated in 1926 against the background of four attempts on Mussolini's life. It was only after the last of these that all political parties were banned and special measures against subversion were introduced. At Vichy the break with the democratic past was more brutal than in Italy and the transition was enacted more speedily and with greater determination.

As was later the case at Vichy, the Rome revolution was carried out at the top. Such is the nature of fascist revolution: it is a political, intellectual and moral upheaval, but it leaves the social and economic structures intact. Mussolini, who took the title 'head of government' (*capo del Governo*) – the King remaining head of state – exercised his dictatorial power though the normal state machinery. The administrative levers of command responded smoothly, which meant there was virtually no need to change the administrative personnel. The provinces were administered by the prefects rather than by the Fascist *ras*, the purge of the bureaucracy was minimal, and there was little interference in the running of the judicial system. The Fascist violence in the first half of 1921,[45] the *squadrismo*, the terror in the countryside, all belong to the period before the accession to power. Throughout the whole Fascist period, five thousand people were imprisoned for political reasons and a further ten thousand were sentenced to internal exile (*confino*). Up until 1940, nine capital sentences were pronounced and carried out, mainly on Slovenian terrorists. A further seventeen executions occurred in the war years, between 1940 and 1943.[46]

Of course, the regime was also responsible for political assassinations abroad, as in the case of the Rosselli brothers, but all in all Italian fascism may have been oppressive and brutal, but it was not sanguinary. It probably caused less suffering than the National Revolution. Even after it fell under the tutelage of Germany, even after the introduction of the 1938 race laws, the comparison with Vichy is not particularly favourable to the French regime, which had no hesitation in handing over anti-Nazi refugees and four thousand Jewish children, even though the Germans did not want them. There is no comparison between the outrages committed by the Vichy *Milice* and the conduct of the Italian security forces, notably the political police, the *OVRA*.

It goes without saying that the brutality of a regime is not the sole determinant of its fascist character. It is nonetheless interesting to note that the Nazification of the Italian state was opposed by a significant fraction of the Fascist party under the leadership of the regime's founders – Grandi, Balbo, Bottai, De Stefani, Federzoni. It was Dino Grandi who presented to the Fascist Grand Council of 24–25 July 1943 the motion to remove the head of government from office. The end of fascism in Italy was brought about by an internal revolt, and this was not the case at Vichy, another interesting point of comparison.

To return to the *parti unique*, the absence of such a structure at Vichy has been seized on as the decisive argument by all supporters of the 'immunity thesis'.[47] But if, in the words of that shrewd and penetrating historian of ideas Alain-Gérard Slama (who borrows the formula from Stanley Hoffmann), Vichy was a 'pluralist dictatorship',[48] Mussolini's Italy was no different. The classic function of the single party is to mobilise popular support in favour of a regime and an ideology, and, after gaining power, to govern the State. If Italy is our reference point, the party never governed there. Not only was it never able to impose its hegemony, but its leader did everything he could to prevent it from doing so. In November 1926, with the abolition of all civil liberties and human rights guarantees, Italy became a police state, but the dictatorship of a monolithic party never materialised.[49]

Thus, just like Vichy, Italy had a pluralist or semi-pluralist dictatorship, where all the important sectors of social, economic and cultural life enjoyed considerable autonomy. This is true of the Army, and the world of business, banking and industry. As we have seen, the central bureaucracy was not purged, and the traditional separation of political and administrative functions was preserved. The judiciary was also relatively unscathed and able to maintain its autonomy. In this pluralist system the Fascist militia retained some independence, but were nonetheless placed under the control of the Army and police. The number of political detainees can be counted in hundreds, and certainly never exceeded a few thousand.[50] Overall it is hard to see any major difference between the regime of the National Revolution and that of fascist Italy.

The great task of the Italian Fascist Party was the mobilisation of opinion. The Duce required it to impregnate the state apparatus with a fascist spirit, and no more than that. Mussolini and Gentile proclaimed the totalitarian character of the regime: the objective of fascism was to forge a new national consciousness, a new way of life, a new kind of Italian. To this end the regime invoked anti-individualist, antimaterialist, martial values, the cult of youth and strength, memories of the Great War: it was no different at Vichy. And if territorial expansionism and the glorification of war are meant to be a special feature of fascism, then these were as much in evidence in interwar France as they were in Italy, at Vichy as much as across the Alps. In autumn 1935 a thousand writers hostile to sanctions against Italy signed Henri Massis's famous manifesto for the 'Défense de l'Occident'.[51] This declaration of aggressive, expansionist and racist nationalism shows that the Italians did not have the monopoly on hard-line fascist invective. The weakness of this particular argument of the 'immunity' school, provided by Philippe Burrin in his first book, and which Azéma still accepts, is plain to see.[52]

The worship of force and violence was peculiar to turn-of-the-century nationalism, from gang-leaders like Morès to Barrès, Drumont and Maurras and their numerous disciples. Sorel added the extra dimension of violence as a cult, similar to that of the futurists. In the wake of the 1918 victory, the glory of French arms and of her victorious warriors was constantly celebrated. The whole nationalist press and all the leagues, including the most important of them, the Croix de Feu, founded by nationalist and Catholic war veterans, extolled military virtues, discipline, obedience, sacrifice. The 'great war leaders' were constantly venerated, the processions of ex-servicemen and torchlight tattoos were endless. The length and breadth of the Hexagon rang with hymns to the 'colonials', to the Empire, and such was the reputation of Marshall Lyautey that he toyed with the idea of a coup d'état. Here again, Italian fascism was hard put to outstrip the French fascist and semi-fascist movements of the 1930s.

Clearly the regime of the National Revolution could not harbour expansionist ambitions, but Michel Bergès has shown how Vichy compensated for its occupied status. For four years, the Empire and France's greatness oversees provided a sort of sublimated glory. This kind of discourse quickly restored to the army and navy their lost prestige.[53] Furthermore, Vichy's warlike rhetoric took up the classic theme of all organic nationalisms, and of all fascisms (which, it must be remembered, are first and foremost nationalisms): ancestor worhip and the celebration of a mythical past were the pillars of youth education and mass moblisation. In this process war veterans played a vital role, but they were not the only transmission belt for an ideology which extolled youth, the body, physical strength, tribal solidarity against the 'other', the foreigner, the outcast, the traditional 'anti-self' of Barrès. As Bergès again observes, an unambiguous paramilitary ideology permeated all official institutions, vaunting the merits of priestly rule, reviving heroes from history, celebrating the exploits of departed warriors. The lust for war found refuge in the compensatory violence of language, even that of the intellectual review *Idées*.[54] This ideological journal of the National Revolution, launched by former editors of the *Revue Universelle*, read like any of the theoretical reviews that spoke for Italian fascism.

Undoubtedly the great beneficiary of fascist rule in Italy, as under the regime of the National Revolution, was the Church. From 1922 the Vatican gave its blessing to the fascist movement and to the Mussolini government. The 1929 agreements sealed the collaboration of the Church with the fascist state: not only did the Pope regain his liberty, but religion was restored to its place in social life, notably in the schools, and the Church launched into a campaign to rechristianise the country. These well-known facts need repeating because, according to Jean-Pierre Azéma, the French state's recognition of the 'legitimacy of privileged bodies like the Church' is decisive proof of the regime's nonfascist purity.[55] If the regime established in Italy between 1922 and 1929 was fascist, it is difficult to see in what way the Vichy system was more open, less totalitarian than the Italian regime.

It is not the existence of a fascist party with monopoly status that made the regime dictatorial, but the suppression, in the name of the Motherland and the State, of all civil liberties, the ambition to create a new man and a society purified of all the germs of destruction: individualism, humanism, universalism, 'materialism', or in other words, utilitarianism. Fascism is the commitment of all authority, of all state power concentrated in the hands of the leader, to the service of new values. Fascism is a revolt against Enlightenment principles, or, in concrete terms, against democracy, Marxian socialism and liberalism. Vichy was no different.

The rise of Pétain to power was easier than that of Mussolini or Hitler. He reached the summit without having to compete with other political forces. Once in power he found himself in control of all the levers of command, almost without exception and without rivals. To establish himself in power, Hitler had to liquidate the populist and genuinely anticapitalist elements in his party; Mussolini had to deal with his earliest associates, the revolutionary syndicalists, with Marinetti's futurists, with D'Annunzio and his Fiume fighters. Even in Germany the party was far from having a free hand: the army was virtually closed to its influence, the senior administration including the law continued to operate almost normally, implementing the new legislation and the new codes of practice. Thus Fascist Italy and Nazi Germany were far from being monolithic dictatorships, a fact worth remembering when the relative heterogeneity of Vichy and its internal struggles are used as proof that it was different, more conservative, even downright reactionary and anachronistic.

Marshall Pétain bestowed on France 'the gift of his person'. He was hailed as a saviour without ever having to fight for power, and was greeted as a hero in Paris right up until the last weeks before the Liberation. Pétain enjoyed a freedom of movement and a popularity that Mussolini would certainly have envied, disavowed as he was in the end by his peers on the fascist Grand Council, imprisoned on the king's orders and liberated by the Germans. Pétain had total freedom of manoeuvre and thus didn't need a party: far from it, any new organisation would simply have impeded the smooth operation of the state apparatus. Furthermore a party, albeit a single party, would inevitably have become a hornet's nest of internal squabbles, rivalries and endless scheming. The hero of Verdun, both head of state and head of government, had a status closer to that of Hitler than of Mussolini.

When Déat and Bergery presented their famous plan for a single party, they were brushed aside, but this had not the slightest effect on the dictatorial and totalitarian nature of the regime. At the same time the law of 29 August 1940 created the French Legion of Veterans. Xavier Vallat, a disabled veteran of the Great War, was placed at its head at the same time as he took office as secretary of state for ex-servicemen. The Legion was to assume the mobilising role of a single party. This was very much Pétain's style. His priority was to eliminate all traces of the 'old order', indeed all traces of political life itself. Democracy was destroyed in the space of a few weeks, so what better proof could there be that the regime was revolutionary? For the task was not just to demolish the institutions of democracy – Parliament, parties, all elective offices – but to extinguish the democratic spirit.

Let us return briefly to the nature and role of the 'immunity thesis' produced by some of the members of the Sciences-Po group. For these historians, who willingly describe themselves as a 'corporation'[56] or as a shadowy '*nébuleuse*', French fascism has always been a 'marginal' phenomenon and 'the Vichy regime does not belong to the same category as what took shape between the wars in Italy and Germany'.[57] This view, initiated by René Rémond, has been taken up in more or less extreme form by several of his disciples, in the wake of the debate opened by the publication of *Ni droite ni gauche*.[58]

Michel Dobry, writing about the crisis of 6 February 1934, has developed a devastating critique of the immunity thesis, its historical errors and contradictions, its fundamental historicism. As Michel Bergès, who shares Dobry's conclusions, has pointed out, Dobry warns against the epistemological presuppositions of this approach.[59] He attacks the whole intellectual stance of the immunity school, which consists of intepreting historical processes according to their 'outcomes'. This false orientation lies behind the notion that French society was 'allergic' to fascism. It shapes the questions that these historians direct at their subject, it defines their problematic, it leads them to identify 'authentic' fascism with the 'finished product' of the fascist regimes.[60] Such an approach, which makes comparative study very difficult, necessarily distorts our understanding of the true nature of a crisis like that of the 6 February 1934 riots, a movement like La Rocque's, or a regime like that of the National Revolution.

For if society really had been 'immunised', there would have been far fewer people between the wars who despaired of democracy and looked abroad to solutions of the fascist type. Social elites would not have thrown themselves into the National Revolution with quite the same enthusiasm. There would perhaps have been fewer books, like Jouvenel's *Après la défaite,* articles and pamphlets, written by some of the great names of intellectual life, which attributed Germany's victory to the moral superiority of the Nazi system. The Resistance movement might have been a little less isolated before 1943, and might have had less difficulty overcoming the blank incomprehension of public opinion. There were, of course, men and women from all walks of life who very early on took a stand against the new order being imposed on their country by the National Revolution. Ordinary French men and women are not our concern here, any more than middle-ranking officers can be held responsible for the battle of France: it is the elites who must be called to account.

Pierre Laborie's rhetorical question is entirely justified: where indeed, in those last terrible weeks of spring 1940, could a devastated and exhausted France have possibly found the resources to change the outcome?[61] But, once again, what about the nation's elites? Why this 'general abdication' of which De Gaulle has spoken, and which he evokes in such striking terms by reminding us that these were men whose role it was, especially in times of crisis, to lead society?[62] Laborie, as he seeks to fathom the state of mind, that is to say the behaviour, of the French people, draws a picture in muted tones.[63] However, while the mood of the majority of the French people can be described pretty safely as one of 'wait-and-see', as full of ambiguity, it is difficult to accept the verdict that 'popular support for the new regime' was 'short-lived' and that collaboration met with 'almost immediate rejection'[64]: all the work of recent years, which analyses the behaviour of specific sectors of opinion and spheres of activity – the civil service, academia, the law – points in the opposite direction.

As it was, the 'wait-and-see' attitude itself worked in favour of the regime, and indeed of collaboration. For *attentisme* also reflected the desire to return to normal life as soon as possible, and this meant not obstructing the wheels of bureaucracy: neither the government of the French state nor the occupying power could have asked for anything more. But in fact the picture presented by Laborie has already been corrected by Anne Grynberg, whose recent work reveals public opinion to have been quite sympathetic to the government, thus actually facilitating the work of the authorities.[65]

How is it that a regime dedicated to building a new France on the ruins of democracy was able to generate both popular enthusiasm and elite connivance? The explanation lies in the realm of ideas. The war on democracy is a constitutive element of fascism, and the regime of the National Revolution went to work with drums beating. The elites harnessed themselves to this revolutionary enterprise with alacrity. Here is another aspect of 'lived experience' that gives little satisfaction to the immunity thesis. If practice is the only acceptable criterion for judging historical phenomena, as the afficionados of *'l'histoire politique'* insist, then the balance-sheet of the work conducted in recent years is alarming indeed. The same picture emerges in virtually every domain: in the civil service, in education from primary school level to the *Collège de France*, at the bar, in the world of publishing, the arts and letters.[66]

The relations between society and its elites are dialectical ones. If the French elites for the most part lined up with the new regime, or adopted a position of benevolent neutrality, it was not just out of conformity, but because they identified in various degree with the rejection of democracy, and with the recasting of institutions and society, which had been undertaken with such extraordinary vigour ever since the first days of the National Revolution. It is also because they felt that, by embarking on this road, they were responding to the deep aspirations of society at large. The long process of fascist impregnation had finally given shape to a mode of behaviour, a type of politics.

After (or, to be exact, *before*) the administration, the law and *l'Université*, the French Catholic Church lent its precious support to the executioners of French democracy. There were exceptions, of course, from simple parish priests to Monseigneur Saliège to the Jesuit father Gaston Fessard, author of the Manifesto 'France prends garde de perdre ton âme'. But as a whole the Church preferred to back the dictatorship in its campaign against the Enlightenment, against secular education, against Rousseau (who had denied Original Sin), against Voltaire and the men of '89, against the Separation law.[67]

A remarkable study by Philippe Burrin has produced a balance-sheet which is indeed damning. Under the cover of cautious language and phrases designed not to offend national sensitivities – 'accommodation' sounds better than 'collaboration' – the author of *la France à l'heure allemande* paints the harshest but also the most realistic overall picture that has been produced so far of these four years that many would have liked to have seen wiped from the nation's history.[68]

In France, a large majority of the population not only believed in the legitimacy and legality of the Vichy government,[69] but also regarded the National Revolution (as long as it was not accompanied by measures like the compulsory labour draft) as necessary to public safety. The end of democracy, the destruction of political parties and representative institutions, the coming to power of the 'strong man' many of them had summoned in their prayers for fifty years, the opportunity to undo the separation of Church and State, to banish secularism and restore religion to its place in society, all of these were largely acceptable initiatives. Similarly, the *statut des juifs* was not regarded as a reason to change one's attitude towards the new regime. Taken *en bloc*, all these measures do not seem to have offended the deeper sensibilities of men who, after all, could have suspended their public activities without seriously prejudicing their livelihoods: publishers, writers, academics, artists, even many civil servants.

The National Leadership School at Uriage, vividly depicted by Bernard Comte and John Hellman[70] each from their own perspective, was a venture which exemplified the appeal of the *Révolution nationale* in its early stages. These authoritarian Catholics and militants of the *Révolution nationale* rallied to the Resistance out of patriotism, the refusal to become vassals of Germany, rather than from any instinctive revulsion against the destruction of democracy or the introduction of the race laws. As long as the new regime was building a new France, authoritarian and Catholic, exclusionary and even fascist, the 'knights' of Uriage found it entirely acceptable. Men who, after the Liberation, would become pillars of the new France threw themselves into the Révolution nationale with the fervour of crusaders: having flaunted their contempt for the liberal Republic in the 1930s, they joined the great antisecular revolution and seized the chance in 1940 to build a France that conformed to their own desires. Three years later their anti-German patriotism led them into the Resistance.

This would also be the path of La Rocque, who joined the Resistance in 1943, was deported and met his death as a result. His exemplary conduct in the face of the enemy does not alter one iota the poltical stance he adopted in the 1930s. Even Dorgères, who was loyal to the National Revolution until the very end, disliked Hitler, and some have drawn the conclusion that his nationalism somehow exonerates him from the charge of fascism. Nothing could be further from the truth. One could be a fascist and anti-German just as one could be a fascist and a collaborator. One could despise democracy, the Enlightenment and the secular Republic, but still fight the occupier, precisely because he was the occupier and not because he too was an enemy of democracy.

Here is one of the fundamental reasons for the desire to wipe the Vichy slate clean, which persisted until the very last decade of the twentieth century. Judgement on Vichy was usually based on a single criterion, or rather a single dichotomy: collaboration with the enemy versus anti-German patriotism. But the essential reason for the whole effort, launched immediately after the Liberation, to consign the Vichy period to oblivion, was that support for Vichy was so routine and commonplace. It would hardly have been realistic to call to account all those with professional qualifications and positions of responsibility. To have despised the Enlightenment, democracy, political parties, Freemasons, Communists and Jews could not be made a crime. Many people considered that in the context of this exceptional period it was simply not possible to judge men or events by the usual moral criteria or political norms. Even those who understood that this was the fruit of fifty years of war against the institutions, principles and philosophy of democracy, knew that it was impossible to demand a genuine purge without running the risk of a civil war comparable to the Terror or the Commune.

The test of reality: ideologies and movements

The passionate controversies provoked by *Ni droite ni gauche* were never limited only to the academic community. On the continent of Europe, in contrast to Britain and the United States, fascism is a lived history, a concrete experience which, as Jean-Pierre Rioux has written, deeply affects national sensibilities.[71] Jacques Julliard attributes the tensions around the subject to the fact that the epithet 'fascist' is so loaded politically and ethically that genuine scientific discussion becomes difficult.[72] The fear of the word 'fascism' is such that Vichy is happily described as a dictatorship, as totalitarian, as a 'totalitarian but not fascist' system, in the words of that great Vichy specialist Alain-Gérard Slama,[73] as a regime 'controlled by the extreme right', according to Jean-Pierre Azéma:[74] any definition goes, any euphemism is acceptable, as long as the fateful word is not uttered.

In this context it is worth dwelling briefly on Philippe Burrin's article in *Histoire des droites en France*.[75] Let me say straight away, Burrin does not make the error of dismissing the importance of the history of ideas. He has examined my analysis of fascism with a fine-toothed comb to alight on two central areas of disagreement: my conception of fascist ideology, and the role played by men who came from the Left.

On the first of these points, I have explained in *Naissance de l'idéologie fasciste*[76] why Nazism is not included in my definition of fascism: the biological determinism which is at the heart of Nazism is not a constitutive element of fascism. On a point of methodology, I thus see Nazism as a phenomenon that *resembles* fascism because of their shared revolt against the Enlightenment and their organic concept of the nation, but racial determinism is not in itself a *necessary condition* of fascism. Far from limiting the concept, if anything this definition actually widens it, because it throws serious doubt on the convenient but for the most part artificial distinction drawn between fascism and authoritarianism, authoritarianism and totalitarianism. Not that such distinctions do not exist or are not useful, but they are far less clear cut, and their boundaries are much more fluid, than is often imagined.

On the second point, I have no doubt either about the essential contribution made to fascism by the antimaterialist revision of Marxism. Linked to organic nationalism and the rejection of the Enlightenment, and to the war against the whole humanist and rationalist culture, this revision fired the fascist synthesis. This synthesis was born in France, reproduced in Italy, and permeated French cultural and political life from the turn of the century. It was this process of impregnation – fascist, or tending to fascism, antiliberal, authoritarian, 'antimaterialist' – which explained the abdication of elites under Vichy, and indeed which allowed the formation of mass movements in the 1930s.

This mood of rejection was both deep and widespread. As it now appears, French society in the twentieth century was not only not immunised against fascism by its republican tradition (which always had to contend with the rival tradition of *La Terre et les Morts*), but neither was it protected by virtue of being a so-called '*société bloquée*'.[77] True, the forces of social conservatism were powerful in France, but no more than in Germany or Italy. As in neighbouring countries, the desire to safeguard the gains of capitalism and its social structures had never been incompatible with cultural and political revolt. On the contrary, to destroy the intellectual and moral bases of liberalism and bourgeois society whilst preserving the market economy and the social structures derived from it, such were indeed the objectives of fascism, and it was this combination which constituted fascism's novelty and originality.

At this point, I must admit to having adjusted my view about both the function and the importance of fascism in France as a political force and mass movement. That is to say, this powerful ideology, whose elite appeal was as vigorous as that of communism and which came into its own after the defeat of 1940, nourished not only the regime of the National Revolution, but also the mass movements of the 1930s which paved the way for Vichy. The results of research over the last decade are quite conclusive: France did indeed produce, both in urban settings and in the countryside, authentic fascist movements.

Of course, if to qualify as truly 'fascist' it is not enough that a paramilitary movement should despise the very principles of democracy and all its manifestations, that it should maintain a constant presence in the street and show utter contempt for all the norms of universal suffrage; if the only way to merit the title is to be a carbon copy of the most hard-line tendency in the Italian Fascist Party – why then, of course, fascism has never existed anywhere in Western Europe. On these criteria, even Mussolini's movement taken overall, and the regime established in Italy in 1925, cannot claim to have been entirely fascist. Anyway, this kind of argument fails to recognise that the PNF was very different not only from the German national-socialist party, but also from the Romanian Iron Guard or the British Union of Fascists. Comparable ideas, identical or at least similar principles, when put into practice inevitably depend on context. In the French context, once proper account is taken of the resistance offered by the Republic, then the Croix de Feu and the Greenshirts were fascist movements.

That is why a distinction must be made between the conditions which favour the birth of fascism, and those which permit it to come to power. The conditions which made the rise of fascism possible were already present before 1914 (as I have shown in *La droite révolutionnaire*) and they existed in equal measure in France between the wars. In France, however, as in Italy and Germany, the conditions for the seizure of power only materialised in the wake of national disaster, and in France this did not happen until the defeat of 1940. The National Revolution was thus the product of conditions created in the aftermath of the battle of France, but its ideological content and its structures were welcomed favourably because they were already deeply engrained in cultural life and responded to the aspirations of a vast mass movement in the 1930s.

I was always sceptical of the view that the Croix de Feu involved nothing more sinister than 'the adult fantasy of reliving one's childhood by indulging in a great boy-scout adventure'.[78] But nonetheless, for a long time I too made the mistake of underestimating the fascist character of the largest of the leagues. Although I was sceptical about the sudden conversion of the Croix de Feu units into a Parti social français supposedly devoted to democracy, it took several years for me to be convinced that France had produced not only a well-structured fascist ideology but also a genuine mass movement, and finally a regime.

Unlike René Rémond, who sees La Rocque's conversion as genuine, I do not believe the colonel renounced his principles at all, he simply became more prudent. The dissolution of the leagues announced on 18 June 1936 by the Blum government convinced the leader of the Croix de Feu that any attempt at insurrection would be crushed without hesitation. The fact that La Rocque and his entourage had been persuaded by experience that the tactics of the leagues were doomed to failure does not in any way prove, as Rémond seems to think, that the former league had suddenly converted to democracy when it became a party.[79] There is nothing in the Croix-de-Feu press, nor in La Rocque's writings, nor in the political behaviour of his lieutenants to support this conclusion. It is hard to find any difference of tone or content in material published before and after June 1936. If La Rocque thought it wise not to chance his arm, this was no doubt because of the resolute attitude of the authorities, and indeed because he had every prospect of seeing a hundred PSF deputies enter the Palais Bourbon at the legislative elections of 1940. It was certainly no proof that the 'Croix de Feu were not really a fascist league' and that 'the temptation of fascism had far less hold on public opinion than the desire for harmony and the respect for legality'.[80]

Furthermore, the fact that La Rocque could only count on the support of eight or ten deputies elected in May 1936 tells us nothing about the potential of the movement. In 1928 Hitler had obtained less than 3 per cent of the vote, and Mussolini came to power at the head of a parliamentary group of thirty-five members. Mussolini had been invited to lead the government in order to put an end to a crisis which the political elite had been unable to resolve. This was not the case in France where the Left, anxious to avoid the disasters that had befallen their neighbours, closed ranks and established an eventually victorious Popular Front. Hitler, who had misread the significance of the 'March on Rome', attempted his Munich *putsch* in 1923: crushed by the army, sent to prison, he never tried it again. He too decided to put his faith in the ballot box. La Rocque had also learned this lesson and he understood perfectly well the process by which democracies fall, as indeed did Dorgères.

Jacques Nobécourt's biographical study *Le Colonel de la Rocque*,[81] which is intended to confirm the image of La Rocque as the champion of democracy, and thus add grist to the mill of the 'immunity thesis',[82] ironically achieves precisely the opposite result. The author offers the reader a mass of primary material which in fact demonstrates that La Rocque's movement was essentially 'available' for any venture. To free his hero from any suspicion of 'fascism', Nobécourt defines fascism as a 'nationalism based on biological racism, and thereby justifying the principle that anyone foreign to the community should be excluded'[83]: this is a reasonable definition, if rather partial and limited, of Nazism rather than of Italian fascism, at least until the 1938 racial laws. But what supporters of the immunity thesis forget is that this definition can certainly be applied to the policies of Vichy, which in this respect was closer to Nazism than to the Mussolini regime. Furthermore, the book's one thousand pages clearly contradict the author's conclusion about the ultimate objective of the movement and its leader: supposedly to serve 'a Prince known as the Republican State'.[84]

The Croix de Feu was just one of the many leagues of the interwar years, but it was the only one that became a mass movement. The exact figures are not known, but specialists agree that after a rapid period of growth in the wake of 6 February 1934, it had reached between 400,000 and 500,000 members on the eve of dissolution. According to Philippe Machefer, the Croix de Feu-PSF movement had grown to 600,000 members by November 1936, more than the Communist Party (284,000) and Socialist Party (200,000) combined, and claimed 4,000 mayors and municipal councillors.[85] Towards the end of the 1930s, the PSF had around 700,000 members, according to Passmore, Irvine and Soucy,[86] or between 700,000 and 1.2 million according to Machefer, who at the beginning of the 1970s was the research pioneer in this field.[87] By way of comparison it is worth noting that the total number of blackshirts on the eve of the takeover in Italy did not exceed 200,000 for the whole peninsula. These figures show why it has become so important to decide what exactly the Croix de Feu was: the author of *Les Droites en France*, like all those who follow him on this point, knows very well that the Croix de Feu is the nub of the whole debate.[88] And make no mistake, these people were not engaged in 'political boy-scouting for adults',[89] they were there to fight for their ideas and for their brand of politics.

The strength of fascist ideology having been confirmed beyond doubt, the extent of its impact on broad sectors of public opinion amply demonstrated, the only open question was what significance should be bestowed on the most important of the leagues. Today, it seems, there is no longer room for doubt on that either:[90] this huge army of activists was committed to an ideology whose core was a 'Christian nationalism', antiliberal, authoritarian, calling for the destruction of the existing order: such was the spirit of the *réforme de l'Etat* invoked by La Rocque. His main work, *Service Public*, sits comfortably in the classical canon of fascist thought:

> We have shown all those willing to listen that it is possible to be concerned about social issues without renouncing one's obligations to the nation, and to be a nationalist without abandoning one's commitment to social progress. Resurrection will come when the passionate ranks of the Left unite spontaneously with the revived forces of the Right, shaking off their false leaders.[91]

In August 1932 *Le Flambeau* demanded 'a more honest and meaningful convergence than the short-lived coalitions devised by our politicians … [L]ogic requires it, the force of events will produce it. Men of the Left, men of the Right, new men, real *men*, will unite in a sort of Committee of Public Safety'.[92] This was no different from what Doriot, Brasillach, Drieu La Rochelle or Jouvenel would say. In the 1930s the synthesis of the '*national*' and the '*social*', constructed around the '*profession organisée*' or corporation, which would replace political parties and traditional trade unions, was the code-name for this third way between liberalism and Marxism which opened the door to fascism. In *Service Public* La Rocque goes to war against the class struggle, against trade unions unwilling to accept a strictly professional role; but in practically every issue of *Le Flambeau* he launches a ringing appeal to the unemployed, to the 'little people': 'most of our supporters are from the popular classes',[93] he claimed. He campaigned for 'the spiritual fusion of social classes', for the corporation, but without seeking his example abroad.[94]

For La Rocque the fear of being accused of imitating Mussolini, or of being in thrall to a foreign power, was a constant preoccupation. He knew that his authoritarian solutions would be equated with fascism, an absurd accusation according to him, for 'the only true fascism is that of the Duce'.[95] The word bothered him much more than the content, however, and despite his proclamations of independence and his efforts to distance himself from the Italian dictator, the leader of the Croix de Feu could not help paying homage to the 'genius of the Duce'. 'That Mussolini deserves our admiration is indisputable',[96] he writes, and if 'we must have some reservations about his accomplishments' it is for reasons of foreign policy and the 'need to look after our external interests'.[97] Similarly in the case of Germany, the hatred of the former and eternal enemy has no limits, but this aversion is not directed, he claims, against 'the personality, still it seems to me rather difficult to grasp, of Adolf Hitler'.[98]

Fascism does not, of course, automatically imply racism. In the 1930s La Rocque denied being in any way anti-Semitic: 'France is by nature assimilationist and racism is contrary to our culture', he wrote in an important article. But at the same time he required Jews to prove their loyalty: to be free of suspicion they should 'reveal their aversion for Marxism, all its dealings and all those who support it'. No, of course La Rocque was not anti-Semitic, despite the misdeeds of 'the Jewish ministerial clique appointed by M. Blum to undertake their work of destruction'.[99] He would not raise the race issue, only the problem of foreigners, but he would delicately remind us that 'Hitler's racism ... forces us to take on board without any guarantees a teeming and virulent horde of *outlaws*'.[100] Under the National Revolution the tone becomes harsher still. 'We want a France for the French', he proclaimed.[101] La Rocque cursed the dechristianisation of the country, demanded that 'the Jewish question be resolved' and 'the masonic lodges be smashed forever'.

Behind this more orderly and less vulgar brand of fascism, this fascism which dared not declare itself because the term denoted something foreign, La Rocque placed the weight of his enormous organisation, and people were afraid of it. The fact that the movement gained the endorsement of Lyautey, whose attitude to the Republic was well known, and then of Weygand, could only exacerbate fears of a possible *coup d'état*.[102] Allusions to the so-called H-hour of the uprising did little to calm nerves, but the leader of the Croix de Feu was a prudent and experienced military officer who had no intention of throwing his troops into a vain assault on an impregnable stronghold. In an important editorial of August 1930 La Rocque replied to all those who reproached him for his inaction, and set out his line of conduct

> As for our plan of action! Let the hotheads calm down and the *agents provocateurs* shut up! We will choose our own forms of intervention according to the circumstances. We will choose our time, and when that time comes we will be there ... Action requires long preparation. It should not be unleashed prematurely. [103]

The leader of the largest of the leagues returned to this same theme, the need to avoid adventurism, on the first anniversary of the 6 February riots, and replied vigorously to the harsh criticisms directed against him for his refusal to seize the initiative that day when, according to some, everything was possible. 'A movement like ours is not at anyone's beck and call. It's not there to be used in support of just any old cause at the slightest opportunity ... We will know how to seize our moment because we will have had the patience to wait for it.'[104]

La Rocque was convinced of the strength of the movement that bore him, and he refused to waste its potential. Because he found himself at the head of an organisation that held the key to the situation, and because he was aware of the dangers of an insurrection when the regime had not yet been destabilised by a major crisis, La Rocque decided to play for time. 'To have gone looking for a fight would simply have reinforced the Popular Front', he wrote in December 1936.[105] It was not out of respect for democracy and its institutions that he chose not to launch an attack, it was simply a matter of opportunity and common sense. In the meantime he paraded his men, and even Nobécourt admits that he seemed willing to risk a trial of strength and civil disorder. Nobécourt gives his subject credit for being haunted by the communist menace and the deficiencies of national security:[106] Was there ever a fascist movement which did not claim to be the guardian of public order, and to be no more than a *response* to the communist threat? La Rocque never stopped expressing his '"disgust" at the games of parliamentary politics':[107] was this any different from other fascist leaders before they took power? What fascist leader did not claim to be reacting to the danger posed to national defence and national pride by communists, socialists and their liberal-centrist allies the Radicals, who would soon collaborate in the Popular Front? What fascist leader did not deploy the rhetoric of the trenches and call for unity and fraternity? Which of them did not regard the electoral process, and indeed democracy itself, as a form of decadence? Which did not declare war on 'materialism'?

The movement's paramilitary style, the '*dispos*' with their motorcycle cavalcades and their constant states of alert, the grandiose rallies and imposing processions, the flag-raising ceremonies, the use of civil aircraft, the meetings where section leaders from all over the country gathered around La Rocque to discuss urgent and secret orders, the constant warnings that the situation was critical – all of this helped create a permanently feverish climate. If the Croix de Feu did not attempt an armed seizure of power, it was not out of respect for legality but because the regime had shown it was determined to resist. After the dissolution of the leagues, La Rocque made no pretence of changing his behaviour: the PSF was 'extending the work of the Croix de Feu', he told the Popular Front government in August 1936.[108] The Croix de Feu made not the slightest adjustment to their programme, their activities, the tone and spirit of their propaganda. They continued to wait for the propicious moment, but H-hour never struck.[109]

Indeed, to judge by *Le Flambeau* in 1936–37, if there was any change at all it involved taking a tougher line. On 2 March 1935 the weekly adopted a new format and henceforth carried a slogan which would one day become famous – '*Travail, Famille, Patrie*'. Under banner headlines calling for a war against domestic traitors, the tone becomes more violent, the style more demagogic, the attacks on the Left, Blum and the Popular Front more crude. If the movement experienced spectacular growth after the dissolution of the leagues, it was not, as historical apologists suggest, because this mass of new recruits were joining a movement newly won over to the virtues of democracy, but on the contrary because more and more people felt disgusted with the existing order. To take out a PSF card, after the dissolution of the Croix de Feu, was a gesture of defiance, a cry of revolt, a desire to translate ideas into action. The new arrivals were demonstrating their commitment to the forces fighting liberal democracy. They were taking their place alongside the most powerful of the disbanded leagues to proclaim that the time had come to do away with the disgraced regime.

If rural fascism could not compete in terms of organisation and numerical strength with its urban counterpart, its potential was no less impressive. That is the conclusion to be drawn from the latest book by Robert Paxton. Interestingly enough, while the book's title, *French Peasant Fascism*,[110] is quite categorical, in chapter 5, which offers an overall evaluation of the Dorgères phenomenon, the author adds a crucial question mark. The subsection 'A village fascism?' poses a question which the author eventually answers in the affirmative, but only after much beating about the bush and without ever committing himself explicitly. It is almost as if he had resigned himself to the conclusion, defeated by his own material.[111] But no professional historian devotes more than fifteen years to a project and scours the archives from one end of the country to the other unless he has good reason to believe that the subject merits all the effort.

Dorgères' movement[112] never published exact membership figures, and these were anyway very volatile. At the beginning of 1935, the peasant defence committees must have had around 35,000 members. By the autumn the leader claimed this figure had quadrupled. In 1943 Dorgères would claim that his movement had reached 420,000 on the eve of the war.[113] But anyway, its strength was not organisational solidity or stable membership, but its capacity to mobilise massive peasant audiences around particular grievances.

The Greenshirt movement, founded in the summer of 1935, grew rapidly: 10,000 people attended the first annual rally held in December of the same year.[114] Their motto – *Believe, Serve, Obey* – was what you would expect, as was their style and their storm-trooper rituals, their uniforms and emblems, their slogans and anthems.[115] The same was true of their programme: anyone who reads Dorgères' 1935 book-manifesto,[116] or *l'Almanach des chemises vertes*[117] would get the same clear impression: what Dorgères led was a mass fascist movement.

In fact, without always being conscious of it, Paxton (like Nobécourt with La Rocque) himself supplies all the material necessary to prove the fundamentally fascist character of Dorgères' movement. His description of it leaves no doubt: 'Despite his tactical denials, Dorgères' language and rhetoric make him appear tempted by fascism. He was passionately antiparliamentary. He had only scorn for democratic institutions. The world had gone wrong, he thought, with the individualism of the French Revolution and the collectivism of the industrial revolution. He rejected the liberal market system in economic matters, preferring a planned and managed economy run by the organised professions – that is, corporatism. He was frequently and crudely antisemitic and occasionally anti-Islamic.' The next section reveals the very essence of fascist thought – 'he said he wanted revolution, but it was public authority and morals he wanted to change, not the social and economic hierarchy. He placed little value on due process and legal remedies, preferring to intimidate his enemies by force'.[118]

However, in Paxton's view, Dorgères' ardent defence of the family and the profession or trade as the foundations of the future social order place him closer to traditional authoritarianism than to fascism. Why? Because the supporters of authoritarianism envisaged an organic society ruled by natural elites, whereas fascists wanted to replace traditional social authorities with 'a new "mechanical solidarity", leveling and egalitarian and embodied in the party'.[119]

Let us say it right away: the idea that the notion of organic society belongs to authoritarianism and not to fascism is absurd: no other ideology has such a corporeal vision of the nation, seen as a great tribe bound together almost physically. Furthermore, the cult of the biological family was at the heart of Fascist policy in Italy and Nazi policy in Germany. No regime has so passionately promoted the model of the large family and of woman as the guardian of hearth and home. Dorgères said nothing different. Of course, fascism did want to replace traditional social authorities by a new elite, one raised in the trenches or forged in its own organisations. It was this elite, based on merit rather than birth, which alone could bring about the organic, physical, near-tribal unity of the nation. But neither the Fascists nor the Nazis had the time or the means to accomplish such a huge task, and traditional elites prospered in Italy and Germany, businessmen as well as military leaders and civil servants, industrialists as well as intellectuals, on condition that they did not openly oppose the regime. In fact, not wishing to tear society apart, neither Mussolini nor Hitler really tried to replace traditional elites in posts of responsibility, except at the very summit of the state.

In reality the only important element which separated Dorgères from the ideal type of fascism was his defence of the countryside against the town. This political divide prevented him from transcending class interests and appealing to the whole nation. So finally Paxton is obliged to acknowledge the truth: 'Despite an imperfect fit with fascism, Dorgères remains the French farmers' leader who came closest to occupying the niche of French rural fascism at the moment of maximum fascist successes in Europe'.[120]

But what does this notion of 'an imperfect fit' with fascism mean once we accept that no fascism ever existed, whether as movement or regime, which corresponded to the ideal type of fascism?[121] At the end of the 1960s we find an American specialist writing: 'Italy under fascism was not a fascist state'.[122] Thirty years later Paxton makes the great discovery that 'no regime in 1930s Europe was 100% fascist, although many authoritarian leaders had taken a few steps in that direction'.[123] What sense is there in the question – 'are we so sure that fascism is best defined by its programs and by its stage settings?' – and the reply given a few lines later: 'the most useful definition of fascism may be a functional one, based more on how it works than on what it says.'[124] If this is a methodology, then it is not valid unless it can be applied to all political movements, right, left and centre. But is it possible to separate ideology from behaviour, the myth from its application, a movement's self-image from its power to attract? Should we forget that no political movement has ever been able to implement all its principles? Such an approach has never been adopted in any reputable study of conservatism, liberalism, socialism or Nazism, or at least not when the investigators are people capable of incorporating a broader vision of cultural issues into historical analysis: so why should the study of fascism be seen as a special case?

So if in Italy we find 'the incomplete fascism of Mussolini, who shared power with Italian conservatives', and if in Germany 'even Hitler shared power with conservatives',[125] what exactly should we make of the 'test of power', or in other words, what is the historical reality of fascism? Surely this *test* demonstrates precisely that, in France as elsewhere – and just like communism, socialism, liberalism – fascism was at the same time a concept, an intellectual construction, and an historical reality whether expressed as a movement or as a regime. Furthermore a reply should once again be given to the question raised earlier by Michel Dobry and which Pascal Ory had also posed even longer ago: 'To qualify as a fascist is it necessary to have been successful?'[126] Is the failure of a movement, for example the Greenshirts or the Croix de Feu, to overthrow democracy proof of its non-fascism? Some think so, it seems: Jacques Julliard, for example, who, after reading *Ni droite ni gauche*, once again advanced the argument we have already encountered above: 'What exactly is this French fascism which never manages to materialise?'[127] The great mass movements which in the 1930s unfolded across the towns and villages of France, and which culminated in the experiment of the National Revolution, surely give that question an unequivocal response.

I have shown in *Neither Right nor Left* and in *The Birth of Fascist Ideology* the crucial function of ideology, conceived as a body of ideas designed to promote, explain and justify the objectives of any form of organised social action. That is the *raison d'être* not only of political ideology but also of political philosophy. Fascism is no exception: to understand fascism you must examine its philosophy of history, its vision of society and of the relationship between the individual and society. You must look at its intellectual content and at its style. Fascism was a product of a crisis of the liberal democratic culture, and fascist movements and regimes were instruments for the building of a new man and a new social order.

'*Idee und Gestalt*', according to Eric Michaud in a magisterial study of the Nazi myth, was a generic expression used in the title or sub-title of countless brochures and books published by the Nazi ideologues. National Socialism sought to emulate a process it saw at work both in Art and in Christianity, namely the capacity to translate the idea into substance.[128] Ideas, style and behaviour are intimately linked, always and everywhere: all the twentieth-century fascist or semi-fascist dictators believed, as Paul Valéry so fittingly put it in his preface to a book on Salazar in 1934, that 'all politics tends to treat human beings as things'. And later 'inside the dictator there is an artist, and within his schemes there is an aesthetic. Thus he must fashion and work his human material, mould it to his designs.'[129]

This explains why dictators hold such fascination for so many intellectuals. Hubert Beuve-Méry[130] had visited Portugal, admired the Salazar regime and gave its youth movement a very favourable presentation in the publications of the Uriage School.[131] At the same time, a young student, François Mitterrand, was loitering on the fringes of Thierry Maulnier's pro-fascist review *Combat*.[132] One of Mitterrand's friends from this period, François Dalle, has captured perfectly the intellectual climate of the 1930s: 'At that time we talked a lot about fascism. The Mussolini and Salazar versions were attractive. We did not think Mussolini would follow Hitler. We were students, bourgeois, catholic, blithely unconcerned about money. We were influenced by *Gringoire* and *Je suis partout*, and though we were not anti-semitic ourselves, it could be said we were guilty by association.'[133] Just before his death Mitterrand, who had still been pro-Vichy in the spring of 1943 and had received the regime's decoration, the *francisque*,[134] registered this plea in his own defence: 'It is unfair to judge people for mistakes which are explained by the particular atmosphere of the time.'[135]

In one sense, François Mitterrand was right. A young student who despised liberal democracy, a soldier returning from captivity to serve the Révolution nationale, then joining the Resistance at a time when the outcome of the war was no longer in doubt, there is nothing particularly unusual about this kind of political trajectory. It is no more unusual than the case of those *personnalistes*[136] and social Catholics who, after conducting a remorseless campaign against 'materialism', ended up after the war on the extreme Left, or those socialists and communists who by sliding towards fascism in the 1930s had already followed the same path, but in the opposite direction.

It was only with the national catastrophe of 1940 that this accumulated potential was finally released. This triggered a crisis which French democracy was unable to resist, despite having a history that differed in every respect from that of Italy or Germany. To be sure, France had three major advantages which delayed the collapse of democracy. First, she had two political traditions locked in fierce combat, not just one single historicist, authoritarian and bureaucratic tradition as in Germany. Second, she had a strong state, unlike Italy. Third, she had escaped the economic and psychological disasters that had beset both her neighbours. But these differences were not sufficient for French society to claim immunity. These two antagonistic political traditions were engaged in relentless struggle throughout the Third Republic's life and – this is the vital point – they both impregnated society with their values. But the precarious balance was broken the day that the country was overwhelmed by military catastrophe: this finally created the conditions for the anti-Enlightenment tradition to achieve power. For many, defeat proved the fundamental inferiority of democracy: in the summer of 1940 democracy, liberty, and the Rights of Man collapsed like a house of cards. And this shows us that no society, whatever its history (and whatever its contribution to history conceived as the history of liberty, as Benedetto Croce would have put it), is immunised against those forces of destruction that are an integral part of our civilisation, today just as much as yesterday.

In fact, the intellectual and moral conditions were already in place that would allow fascist ideology to take shape in the closing years of the nineteenth century, and fascist movements to become a reality in the political and cultural life of the interwar period. Fascism was a product of civilised society, and France did not escape it. Indeed, it was not just a matter of her being *implicated* in this crisis of civilisation, this crisis of modernity – France was in fact its test-bed. The conviction that the whole rationalist and individualist civilisation of the Enlightenment had culminated in this colossal failure called democracy was already part of the repertoire of some of the leading figures in France at the end of the nineteenth century: the most advanced liberal society in Europe also produced the intellectual engine of this machine for the annihilation of democracy known as fascism. As time passes, this view seems increasingly difficult to refute.

The French case is enormously significant, and is a stark reminder of how fragile are those principles and traditions which we fondly believe to be part of the natural order of things. For even if it took a military disaster to set the Révolution nationale in motion, the defeat did not in itself make the establishment of a fascist dictatorship inevitable. The same was true of Italy and Germany: the defeat of 1918, unemployment and inflation, the Soviet Revolution are not sufficient to explain the rise of fascism and Nazism. The catastrophe became possible because economic and social crisis aggravated an existing state of moral and intellectual distress. Too many people across Europe had been convinced too long and too deeply that the Enlightenment tradition – rationalist, universalist and humanist – was morally and intellectually inferior to its rival, the tribal culture of a nationalism rooted in Blood and Soil.

(Translated from the French original by Brian Jenkins)

Notes

1. R.Wohl, 'French Fascism both Right and Left: Reflections on the Sternhell Controversy', *The Journal of Modern History*, vol. 63, March 1991, pp. 91–98.
2. The most significant are: A. Costa-Pinto, 'Fascist Ideology Revisited: Zeev Sternhell and His Critics', *European History Quarterly*, vol. 4, no. 16, 1986, pp. 465–80; R. Eatwell, 'On Defining the Fascist "Minimum": the Centrality of Ideology', *Journal of Political Ideologies*, vol. 1, October 1996, pp. 303–19; F. Germinario, 'Fascisme et idéologie fasciste. Problèmes historiographiques et méthodologiques dans le modèle de Zeev Sternhell', *Revue française des idées politiques*, vol. 1, no. 1, 1995, pp. 39–79; S. Romano, 'Sternhell lu d'Italie', *Vingtième Siècle. Revue d'histoire*, no. 6, April-June 1985, pp. 75–81. See also the remarkable Masters dissertation presented by Magali Balent at the Université Pierre Mendès France, Grenoble in June 1997 on 'La réception des thèses de Zeev Sternhell par les historiens français'. I confess that I had forgotten some of the material published at the time. Thanks to the work of Magali Balent, I have now been able to rediscover some important elements of this debate.

3. R. Aron, *Les Etapes de la pensée sociologique*, Paris, 1967.
4. On this point it is worth consulting the excellent work by C. Foureau, *La Revue universelle (1920–1940)*, a doctoral thesis prepared at Princeton University under the direction of Thomas Pavel, May 1999.
5. To avoid any misunderstanding, I will underline the point further. If the historian of ideas is to give more than a simple narrative, whether chronological or thematic, if he really wishes to understand social and cultural phenomena, it is difficult for him to avoid having recourse to the methodological device of the ideal-type. This method, as we know, is above all associated with the work of Max Weber, but in fact it can be traced back to Tocqueville and Montesquieu, and thus to the founders of historical sociology and political science. For Weber the ideal-type is an intellectual construct which the historian will never find reproduced anywhere in its conceptually pure form. It is difficult to exaggerate the role of Weber in contemporary research, and the history of ideas is no exception: the author of *The Protestant Ethic and the Spirit of Capitalism* was also a great historian of ideas, after all. In this respect, Ernst Cassirer and Raymond Aron are two exemplary cases: the philosopher Cassirer and the sociologist Aron were equally historians of ideas working in the wake of Max Weber. Their work lives on because, like Tocqueville (who always sought the '*idée-mère*', a principle that Taine adopted in identical terms) and indeed like Weber himself, they knew how to find what was essential, how to bring out the key characteristics of a phenomenon, though fully aware that in so doing they were not able to evoke every feature, every last detail of any given historical situation.

    In the thought of Max Weber, based as it is on the interdependence of history and sociology, the ideal-type is a conceptual tool for understanding causality, and its function is to organise and make intelligible an extremely diverse and fragmented reality. The ideal-type should help us understand an historical reality, but it does not encompass it in every detail. The construction of ideal-types is an attempt to make material intelligible by revealing its internal rationality, in the event even by construing this rationality from material that is only half-formed. It is worth reminding ourselves again that an historical concept seeks to capture what is typical, essential. It is not some average derived from quantitative data, it is an accentuation of qualitative features. In my work on fascism, and here on French fascism, I am trying to reconstruct a phenomenon on the basis of what is typical and original about it. The purpose is not to convey a cultural, ideological or political reality in all its details, but to show what is essential about this phenomenon. To put it in terms Raymond Aron might have used, it involves the stylised, rationalised reconstruction of an intellectual and political reality.
6. See the new introductory essay, 'La droite révolutionnaire entre les anti-Lumières et le fascisme', which opens the latest edition of Z. Sternhell, *La Droite révolutionnaire 1885–1914: les origines françaises du fascisme*, Paris, 2000.
7. F. Goguel, 'En mémoire d'André Siegfried', *Revue française de science politique*, vol. IX, no. 2, June 1959, p. 333.
8. '... il y a des tempéraments régionaux et des tempéraments nationaux ... le tempérament d'un milieu ... sous ce qui change vite (classes sociales, partis politiques) [...] une structure sociale qui change lentement ... plus profondément nous trouvons enfin, dans les populations, des tempéraments politiques collectifs, géographiquement localisés, qui, à un demi-siècle près, sont pratiquement immobiles.' A. Siegfried, *Tableau politique de la France de l'Ouest*, presentation by Pierre Milza, Paris, 1995, pp. 365–69.
9. 'Il y a dans la psychologie des peuples un fond de permanence qui se retrouve toujours. Nous sommes encore, par combien de traits, semblable aux Gaulois nos ancêtres, et les caractéristiques que Tacite notait chez les Barbares ou les juifs de son

temps sont encore reconnaissables dans les Allemands, les Israéliens d'aujourd'hui.' A. Siegfried, *L'Ame des peuples*, Paris, 1950, p. 5.

10. 'Les traits des Germains n'ont pas changé depuis les Romains, si nous en croyons la description de Tacite: ils sont dolichocéphales, grands et forts, blonds ou roux, avec des yeux bleus, une complexion claire ... une seconde série d'Allemands, qui ne sont pas des Germains ... brachycéphales, de taille moyenne et d'autant plus petit qu'on avance vers le sud-est ... ce sont des Alpins, qualifiés parfois de Celtes.' Ibid., pp. 116–17.

11. '... les races qui ont contribué à former le type humain méditerranéen. La plus ancienne, la plus représentative aussi, est celle des Ibères: blanche, dolichocéphale, d'une structure osseuse légère, petite et de teint brun. Elle s'oppose, en se distinguant d'eux géographiquement, soit aux Nègres, qui sont dolichocéphales mais noirs, soit aux Scandinaves ou aux Nordiques, qui sont eux aussi dolichocéphales, mais blonds et de teint clair.' Ibid., pp. 28–29.

12. '... évoque la destinée de l'Occident tout entier.' A. Siegfried, *Vue générale de la Méditerranée*, Paris, 1943, p.14.

13. '... à cheval sur l'Asie et l'Europe ... a crée la civilisation occidentale: par opposition aux Perses, les Grecs de l'Antiquité étaient déjà, authentiquement, des Occidentaux: Marathon devrait être, pour nous, un lieu de pèlerinage.' Ibid., p. 14.

14. 'La race méditerranéenne possède des caractères physiques qui lui sont propres ... La dolichocéphalie, tirant sur mésocéphalie, indice d'ordinaire inférieur à 75 – est générale.' Ibid., pp. 69–72.

15. 'La civilisation occidentale, si elle est le résultat d'un milieu, est aussi l'oeuvre d'une race.' Siegfried, *L'Ame des peuples*, p. 201.

16. Ibid., p. 207.

17. 'Il nous faut encore parler des juifs, même après la massive persécution hitlérienne.' Ibid., p. 118.

18. '... assez sembalable à celui de l'invasion juive new-yorkaise. Chose intéressante, l'action de ces nouveaux venus, fort influents sous le régime de Weimar, ne se limitait plus comme précédemment à la finance: on les trouvait en quelque sorte à l'intersection des affaires et de l'intelligence. Les journaux, les théâtres, le cinéma, les antiquités, la médecine, le Palais tendaient de plus en plus à leur appartenir.' Ibid., p. 119.

19. 'Leur rôle est décisif sous Weimar dont l'antisémitisme d'Hitler est la réaction.' Quoted in P. Birnbaum, 'La France aux Français', *Histoire des haines nationalistes*, Paris, 1993, p. 154.

20. 'Du fait de cette intervention insinuante, qui allait de la thèse artistique d'avant-garde à la publicité financière et à la propagande communiste, une présence soviétique subtile se trouvait en quelque sorte projetée dans la capitale allemande, dont certains traits non occidentaux, subrepticement russes, se manifestaient curieusement.' Siegfried, *L'Ame des peuples*, p. 119.

21. '... agressivement occidentale dans son cadre extérieur, recelait en soi, largement à cause des juifs, d'insidieux germes de l'Orient. Ces circonstances ont attiré la persécution que l'on sait.' Ibid., p.120.

22. '... l'Américain protestant à adopter une attitude hostile qui s'est développée en un mouvement antisémite.' A. Siegfried, *America Comes of Age. A French Analysis,* New York, 1927, pp. 25–27.

23. I have examined the anti-Semitism of Barrès in Z. Sternhell, *Maurice Barrès et le nationalisme français*, Paris, 1972 (new edition: Paris, 2000).

24. 'Ces intelligences juives ... manient les idées du même pouce qu'un banquier les valeurs ... des jetons qu'ils trient sur un marbre froid ... un résidu non fusible dans le creuset ... n'est pas de nature économique [mais] une réaction doctrinale contre

l'approche juive des problèmes … un certain mousseux … mais à dose excessive, danger (quota).' Quoted in Birnbaum, 'La France aux Français', pp. 149–50.

25. 'En politique, les différences de tempérament vont parfois plus profond que les différences de programmes.' Siegfried, *Tableau politique de la France de l'Ouest*, p. 104.

26. '… allait marquer profondément et durablement l'historiographie de la question'. J.-F. Sirinelli, ed., 'Introduction générale', in *Histoire des droites en France*, vol. 1, *Politique*, Paris, 1992, p. xxiii.

27. P. Birnbaum, 'Sur un lapsus présidentiel', *Le Monde*, 21 October 1994.

28. 'Tout le problème de la droite tient dans cette alternative: *unicité ou pluralité dans le temps.*' R. Rémond, *La Droite en France de la première Restauration à la Ve République* (2nd edition), Paris, 1963, p. 17 (italics in the original text).

29. 'C'est un des apports les plus précieux du mouvement amorcé, il y a quarante ans, par le *Tableau polique de la France de l'Ouest* d'André Siegfried (1913), que d'avoir renoué le trame en apparence interrompue par les déchirures superficielles, et révélé l'existence en France de larges blocs d'opinion, de pratique, de comportement religieux, dont l'homogénéité territoriale nous touche moins vivement que la constance à travers les époques.' Ibid., p. 18.

30. 'En mettant très fortement en évidence l'existence de deux tempéraments politiques stables et définis, … [son] interprétation de l'histoire des partis a éclairé avec une netteté sans précédent les déterminations profondes de la droite et de la gauche.' Ibid., p. 38. In the 1982 edition, the version which has been constantly reprinted under the title of *Les Droites en France* (Aubier-Montaigne), René Rémond insists on his autonomy in relation to Siegfried: 'No doubt I should have given a more detailed explanation of what I mean by this notion of the continuity of a tradition of thought. It is quite different from the persistence of territorially-defined cultures, which André Siegfried has brought out so effectively … What I have in mind is the permanence of families of thought, the existence of stable traditions'.

31. '… trois droites, dotées chacune de tous les attributs d'une authentique tradition politique, ayant en propre système de pensée, tempérament, clientèle. Elles sont apparues è des moments successifs de l'évolution politique de la France. La première emprunte aux *ultras* de la Restauration sa doctrine, la contre-révolution: elle est la tradition faite système et érigée en politique. La seconde, conservatrice et libérale, hérite son fond de l'*orléanisme*. La troisième a opéré un amalgame d'éléments sous le signe du *nationalisme*, don't le bonapartisme est un précurseur.' Rémond, *La Droite en France,* p. 22.

32. 'Il n'y a pas eu de fascisme français parce qu'il pouvait difficilement s'en établir en France. L'opinion y est, en dépit des apparences, particulièrement réfractaire aux prestiges du fascisme.' Ibid., p. 224.

33. 'Il n'y a pas d'avenir en France pour le fascisme, si l'on en juge par le passé: les tentatives qui semblaient amorcer un départ vers une expérience fasciste se sont bientôt fourvoyées dans le chemin de la réaction classique.' R. Rémond, 'Y a-t-il un fascisme français?', *Terre Humaine*, 2e année, no. 19–20, July–August, 1952, p. 45. In this article Rémond lays down the explanatory principles which will be developed in *La Droite en France*.

34. '[l'existence du fascisme] … ne pourrait que difficilement être confondue avec la tradition fondée par le bonapartisme.' Rémond, *Les Droites en France*, 1982 edn, p. 40.

35. J. Soury, *Campagne nationaliste 1894–1901*, Paris, 1902, p. 65.

36. See the new preface written for my *Maurice Barrès et le nationalisme français*, Paris, 2000.

37. See C. Schmitt, *La Notion de politique*, Preface by Julien Freund, Paris, 1972, p. 65 etc. It is also worth consulting the fascinating study by H. Meier, *The Lesson of Carl*

Schmitt: Four Chapters on the Distinction between Political Theology and Political Philosophy, Chicago, 1998, p. 26.

38. I would refer the reader here to my essays 'La droite révolutionnaire entre les anti-Lumières et le fascisme', in *La Droite révolutionnaire* and 'The Political Culture of Nationalism' in *Nationhood and Nationalism in France from Boulangism to the Great War, 1889–1918*, ed. R. Tombs, London and New York, 1991, pp. 22–37.

39. J. Julliard, 'Sur un fascisme imaginaire: à propos d'un livre de Zeev Sternhell', *Annales ESC*, 39e année, no. 4, July–August 1984, pp. 849–59. On this subject, see the excellent clarification of the key issues in this debate by V.Duclert, 'Histoire, historiographie et historiens de l'affaire Dreyfus (1894–1997)', in *La Postérité de l'affaire Dreyfus*, ed. M. Leymarie, Lille, 1998, pp. 174–76.

40. V. Duclert, 'L'affaire Dreyfus', p. 175.

41. 'La réalisation d'une idéologie implique des 'compromissions' avec le réel qui en altèrent la portée: nous voilà ramenés à un idéalisme philosophique et historique assez traditionnel, et qui ne tient guère compte des acquis de l'histoire sociale. Car enfin, pour l'historien social, c'est-à-dire pour l'historien tout court, il n'y a pas de réalisme des idées pures; leur incarnation historique est pour elles la véritable épreuve de vérité. Ou encore, pour parler comme Hegel, *Die Weltgeschichte ist das Weltgericht*; pour les idées sociales comme pour les sociétés humaines, c'est l'histoire, c'est-à-dire le vécu, qui est le véritable jugement dernier.' J. Julliard, 'Sur un fascisme imaginaire', pp. 850–51.

42. André Siegfried was the author of the theory of the 'two Vichys', contrasting the Vichy of Pétain (Révolution nationale) with the Vichy of Laval (collaboration). A. Siegfried, *De la IIIe à la IVe République*, Paris, 1956 (see in particular chapter VI, entitled 'Le Vichy de Pétain, le Vichy de Laval'.

43. S.G. Payne, *A History of Fascism 1914–1945*, Madison, 1995, p. 107.

44. Ibid., p. 110.

45. A list of these characteristic cases of violence can be found in a new reference work: A. De Bernardi and S. Guarracino, *Il fascismo. Dizionario di storia, personaggi, cultura, economia, fonti e dibattito storiografico*, Milan, 1998, p. 22 etc. See also the opening chapter of R. De Felice's unrivalled *Mussolini il fascista. I. La conquista del potere 1921–1925*, Turin, 1966.

46. Payne, *A History of Fascism 1914–1945*, pp. 112–17.

47. The term 'thèse immunitaire' was used by Michel Dobry in an important article: 'Février 1934 et la découverte de l'allergie de la société française à la "Révolution fasciste"', *Revue française de sociologie*, vol. XXX, no. 3/4, July–December 1989, pp. 511–33. (See chapter 5 below.)

48. A.-G. Slama, 'Vichy était-il fasciste?', *Vingtième Siècle. Revue d'histoire*, special issue, July–September 1986, p. 42.

49. A. Lyttelton, *The Seizure of Power: Fascism in Italy, 1919–1929* (2nd edition), London, 1987, p. 297.

50. Payne, *A History of Fascism 1914–1945*, pp. 119–22.

51. Foureau, *La Revue universelle (1920–1940)*, p. 126.

52. J.-P. Azéma, 'Le régime de Vichy', in *La France des années noires. I.: De la Défaite à Vichy*, ed. J.-P. Azéma and F. Bédarida, Paris, 1993, p. 179

53. M. Bergès, *Vichy contre Mounier. Les non-conformistes face aux années quarante* (preface by J.-L. Loubet del Bayle), Paris, 1997, p. 361.

54. Ibid.

55. Azéma, 'Le régime de Vichy', p. 179.

56. J.-F. Sirinelli, 'Les intellectuels', in *Pour une histoire politique*, ed. R. Rémond, Paris, 1988, p. 206. Sirinelli goes on to say 'The corporation's serene and tempered response to Zeev Sternhell's arguments on French fascism tells us one thing about this school of

historians: that they have together studied the inter-war period for long enough to feel confident and united in their determination to preserve what they have scientifically established, and that this transcends the rivalries that are endemic to any small community.' In other words, and to quote Magali Balent, this reflects the corporation's desire to 'preserve its legitimacy' ('La réception des thèses de Zeev Sternhell par les historiens français', p. 130)

57.   P. Milza, *Fascisme français. Passé et présent*, Paris, 1987, p. 8. On the composition of the group and the links which bind its members together, see the unsigned introduction to the collective work *Pour une histoire politique* (see note 56 above). For Milza, 'this "*nébuleuse*", essentially grouped around René Rémond, and which includes most notably the contemporary historians at the university of Nanterre-Paris X and the Institut d'Etudes Politiques', has boldly assumed the right to speak on behalf of 'French academic history': I do not recall, for example, that someone like Maurice Agulhon, emeritus professor at the Collège de France and author of a superb *Histoire de France* ('Pluriel') covering the period from 1880 to the present day, ever gave the historians of Sciences-Po the right to speak in his name.

58.   See the telling critique of the immunity thesis developed by Michel Dobry, 'Février 1934', p. 511. 'The debate around the works of Zeev Sternhell on fascist ideology and its origins has given a group of French historians the opportunity to update and systematise a curious historical interpretation: that French society in the 1930s was "allergic" to fascism (the immunity thesis).'

59.   Bergès, *Vichy contre Mounier*, pp. 354–55.
60.   Dobry, 'Février 1934', pp. 513–14.
61.   P. Laborie, *L'Opinion française sous Vichy*, Paris, 1990, p. 330.
62.   Ch. De Gaulle, *Mémoires de guerre: L'Appel, 1940–1942*, Paris, 1954, pp. 94, 104.
63.   Laborie, *L'Opinion française sous Vichy*, p. 332.
64.   '[l'] adhésion effective au nouveau régime ... [un] échec précoce ... [un] refus quasi immédiat.' Ibid., p. 331.
65.   A. Grynberg, *Les Camps de la haine: les internes juifs des camps français, 1939–1944*, Paris, 1999, pp. 164–71.
66.   See, for example: C. Singer, *Vichy, l'Université et les juifs. Les silences et la mémoire*, Paris, 1992; Hachette, <Pluriel>, 1996; R. Badinter, *Un antisémitisme ordinaire. Vichy et les avocats juifs (1940–1944)*, Paris, 1997; R. Poznanski, *Etre juif en France pendant la Seconde Guerre mondiale*, Paris, 1994; M.O. Baruch, *Servir l'Etat français. L'Administration en France de 1940 à 1944*, preface by J.-P. Azéma, Paris, 1997; P. Hébey, *La "Nouvelle Revue Française" des années sombres, 1940–1941: des intellectuels à la dérive*, Paris, 1992; P. Assouline, *Gaston Gallimard: un demi-siècle d'édition française*, Paris, 1984.
67.   See P. Burrin, *La France à l'heure allemande, 1940–1944*, Paris, 1995; A. Fleury, 'La Croix devant la marée brune', *Vingtième Siècle. Revue d'histoire*, no. 9, January-March 1986.
68.   Burrin, *La France à l'heure allemande*, p. 250.
69.   P. Novick, *L'Epuration française, 1944–1949*, Paris, 1985, p. 231.
70.   B. Comte, *Une utopie combattante. L'Ecole des cadres d'Uriage, 1940–1942*, Paris, 1991; J. Hellman, *The Knight-Monks of Vichy France: Uriage 1940–1945*, Montreal, 1993. Although Comte presents these men who offered their service to Vichy as beyond reproach, as fearless and unblemished knights, in the end the image that emerges is not so very different from the one depicted by his Canadian counterpart.
71.   See Rioux's foreword to the article by Serge Berstein, 'La France des années trente allergique au fascisme. A propos d'un livre de Zeev Sternhell', *Vingtième Siècle. Revue d'histoire*, no. 2, April 1984. In his view, *Ni droite ni gauche* 'is damaging to national identity' and, he adds, 'Zeev Sternhell disturbs too many illusions not to be regarded with suspicion' (p. 83). Magali Balent has devoted some ten pages to this question ('La réception des thèses de Zeev Sternhell', p. 132.)

72. Julliard, 'Sur un fascisme imaginaire', p. 850.
73. Slama, 'Vichy était-il fasciste?', p. 43.
74. Quoted by Foureau, *La Revue Universelle*, p. 241.
75. Ph. Burrin, 'Le fascisme', in *Histoire des droites en France*, vol. I, *Politique*, pp. 603–47.
76. Z. Sternhell, M. Sznajder and M. Asheri, *The Birth of Fascist Ideology*, Princeton, 1994.
77. The expression belongs to S. Hoffmann, 'Paradoxes de la communauté politique française', in *A la recherche de la France*, ed. S. Hoffmann et al., Paris, Seuil, 1963, p. 26.
78. '... sentiment exaltant pour des adultes de revivre leur enfance en participant à une sorte de grand jeu scout.' Rémond, *Les Droites en France*, p. 214.
79. Ibid.
80. 'Les Croix de Feu n'étaient pas réellement une ligue fasciste ... la tentation du fascisme était infiniment moins forte sur l'esprit public que l'aspiration à la concorde et le respect de la légalité.' Ibid., p. 215.
81. J. Nobécourt, *Le Colonel de La Rocque, 1885–1946, ou les pièges du nationalisme chrétien*, Paris, 1996.
82. Before the arrival of Nobécourt's study, the (uncompleted) thesis of one of Rémond's associates, Janine Bourdin, was used by the Institut d'Etudes Politiques as 'oral testimony': this is the source used by Pierre Milza in his treatment of La Rocque's movement (Milza, *Fascisme français*, p.136 etc.)
83. '... nationalisme fondé sur le racisme biologique, justifiant le principe de l'exclusion de tout étranger à la communauté.' Nobécourt, *Le Colonel de La Rocque*, p. 177.
84. 'Un Prince qui est l'Etat républicain.' Ibid., pp. 16, 963.
85. See R. Soucy, 'French fascism and the Croix de Feu: A Dissenting Interpretation', *Journal of Contemporary History*, vol. 26, 1991, p.160.
86. K. Passmore, *From Liberalism to Fascism. The Right in a French Province, 1928–1939*, Cambridge, 1997, p. 17. W.D. Irvine, 'Fascism in France and the Strange Case of the Croix de Feu', *The Journal of Modern History*, vol. 63, no. 2, 1991, p. 272. R. Soucy, *Le Fascisme français*, Paris, 1989, p. 8.
87. Ph. Machefer, 'Le Parti social français en 1936–1937', *L'Information historique*, March-April 1972, p. 74, and 'L'Union des droites: le PSF et le Front de la Liberté, 1936–1937', *Revue d'histoire moderne et contemporaine*, XVII (1970), p. 113.
88. See Rémond, *Les Droites en France*, p. 211; Milza, *Fascisme français*, pp.138–39; Ph. Burrin, *La Dérive fasciste. Doriot, Déat, Bergery, 1933–1945*, Paris, 1986, p. 25.The most recent example is in the review *L'Histoire*, no. 219, March 1998, p. 7, where La Rocque is praised for his 'legalism'.
89. Rémond, *Les Droites en France*, p. 214.
90. The three authors cited earlier, Soucy, Irvine and Passmore, agree unequivocally on the fascist character of the movement.
91. 'Nous avons fait comprendre aux hommes de bonne volonté qu'on peut être social sans cesser d'être national et qu'on peut être national sans abandonner sa recherche du progrès social. Le signe de la résurrection est la conjoncture spontanée des forces ardentes de la gauche avec les forces ranimées de la droite, les unes et les autres débarrassées de leur faux chefs.' Lt-Colonel de La Rocque, *Service public*, Paris, 1934, p. 226. In the Bibliothèque nationale in Paris (BNF) this book is only available on microfiche.
92. '... un regroupement plus pur et plus solide ques les 'concentrations' politiciennes ... La logique l'annonce; la force des choses l'engendrera. Des hommes de gauche, des hommes de droite, des hommes nouveaux, des hommes 'tout court' s'uniront en une sorte de Comité de Salut public.' La Rocque, 'Bab Allah', *Le Flambeau*, no. 36, August 1932, p. 1.

93. 'La majorité de nos amis est populaire.' La Rocque, 'Fait nouveau', *Le Flambeau*, 3e serie, no. 89, 9 January 1937.

94. '… la fusion spirituelle des classes.' La Rocque, *Service public*, pp. 125–51.

95. 'Il n'est véritablement de fascisme que celui du Duce.' Ibid., p. 256.

96. 'L'admiration méritée par Mussolini ne se discute pas.' Ibid., p. 177.

97. '[une] juste réserve quant à la pérennité de son oeuvre s'impose … la surveillance de nos intérêts étrangers.' Ibid., pp. 177–78.

98. '… la personnalité, encore assez confuse à mes yeux, d'Adolphe Hitler'. Ibid., p. 178.

99. 'La France est par nature assimilatrice et le racisme est contre à son génie … manifester leur aversion pour le marxisme, ses hommes et ses procédés … l'équipe juive installée par M. Blum aux postes de destruction.' La Rocque, 'Repères', no. 71, *Le Flambeau*, 22 August, 1936.

100. 'Le racisme hitlérien … nous condamne à héberger une foule grouillante, virulente d'*outlaws* que rien ne garantit.' La Rocque, *Service public*, p. 159.

101. 'Nous voulons la France française … régler la question juive … briser à jamais les Loges.' La Rocque, *Disciplines d'action*, Clermont-Ferrand, 1941, p. 99.

102. See for example the editions of *Le Flambeau* in January (no. 15) and May (no. 19) 1931.

103. 'Notre volonté d'action! Que les impatients se calment, que les agents provocateurs se taisent! Nous choisirons notre mode d'intervention, au mieux des circonstances. Nous choisirons notre heure: l'heure venue, nous serons là … L'action ne se prépare pas sans un long travail. Elle ne doit pas être déclenchée sans être mûre.' Lt-Colonel de La Rocque, 'Le repos avant l'action', *Le Flambeau*, no. 10, August 1930, p. 1. Pierre Milza (*Fascisme français*, p. 135) regards the invocation of 'H hour' as a myth. In fact it was indeed a myth, but a mobilising myth in the Sorelian sense of the term, a working tool to be brandished repeatedly, a revolutionary weapon constantly sharpened in readiness for the day of opportunity when it would be put into effective use.

104. 'On n'annexe pas un mouvement comme le nôtre. On ne l'utilise pas pour ouvrir n'importe quelle voie devant n'importe quelle improvisation … Il saura saisir son heure parce quil aura su l'attendre.' La Rocque, 'Gloses', *Le Flambeau*, no. 67, 1 February 1935.

105. 'Rechercher la bagarre, c'eût été cimenter le Front populaire.' La Rocque, 'Réalisme', *Le Flambeau*, no 34, 5 December 1936.

106. Nobécourt, *Le Colonel de La Rocque*, p. 231.

107. '[sa] 'nausée' devant les jeux du parlementarisme'. Ibid., p. 233.

108. Lt-Colonel de La Rocque, 'Dérèglement', *Le Flambeau*, no. 69, 1 August 1936.

109. Kevin Passmore's study, *From Liberalism to Fascism*, op.cit., analyses the battle engaged by the Croix de Feu in the Rhône department against both the conservative Right and the Left. At the end of his meticulous investigation, the author reaches an unequivocal conclusion: this was indeed a fascist movement in action. [Editor's note: It should be noted that in Passmore's view the movement ceased to be fascist when it became the PSF.]

110. R.O. Paxton, *Le Temps des chemises vertes. Révolte paysanne et fascisme rural, 1929–1939*, Paris, 1996. [Editor's note: all page references below are to the English edition of this book: R.O. Paxton, *French Peasant Fascism: Henri Dorgères' Greenshirts and the Crises of French Agriculture, 1929–1939*, Oxford, 1997.]

111. Paxton, *French Peasant Fascism*, p. 154.

112. Dorgères was the pen-name of Henri-Auguste d'Halluin.

113. Paxton, *French Peasant Fascism*, p. 211, note 36.

114. Ibid., p. 65.

115. Ibid.

116. H. Dorgères, *Haut les fourches*, Paris, 1935.
117. *Almanach des chemises vertes* de 1936, no publisher's name, no date. This large brochure can be consulted at the BNF under the catalogue number 8-S-20385.
118. Paxton, , *French Peasant Fascism*, pp. 156–57.
119. Ibid., p.158.
120. Ibid., p.159.
121. See Z. Sternhell, 'Fascist Ideology', in *Fascism. A Reader's Guide: Analyses, Interpretations, Bibliography*, ed. W. Laqueur, Berkeley, 1976, pp. 315–76.
122. N. Kogan, 'Fascism as a Political System', in *The Nature of Fascism*, ed. S.J. Woolf, London, 1968, p. 16.
123. Paxton, , *French Peasant Fascism*, p.158.
124. Ibid., p. 157.
125. Ibid., p.158.
126. 'Pour être fasciste faudrait-il avoir réussi?' P. Ory, 'Le dorgérisme: Institution et discours d'une colère paysanne (1929–1939)', *Revue d'histoire moderne et contemporaine*, t. XXII, April-June 1975, p.186.
127. 'Qu'est-ce donc que ce fascisme à la française qui ne se réalise jamais?' Julliard, 'Sur un fascisme imaginaire', p. 859.
128. E. Michaud, *Un art de l'éternité. L'image et le temps du national-socialisme*, Paris, 1996.
129. 'Toute politique tend à traiter les hommes comme des choses ... il y a de l'artiste dans le dictateur, et de l'esthétique dans ses conceptions. Il faut donc qu'il façonne et travaille son matériel humain, et le rende disponible pour ses desseins.' P. Valéry, 'L'ideé de dictature', quoted in Michaud, *Un art de l'éternité*, p. 16.
130. [Editor's note: Hubert Beuve-Méry, who was much influenced by the ideas of Emmanuel Mounier, became Director of Studies at the Vichy regime's Uriage leadership training school and initially placed some hope in the National Revolution. He joined the Resistance forces in 1942, and in 1944 was the founder-editor of the *Le Monde* newspaper, a position which gave him considerable influence in French intellectual circles for the following twenty-five years.]
131. J. Hellman, 'Wounding Memories': Mitterrand, Moulin, Touvier and the Divine Half-Lie of Resistance', *French Historical Studies*, vol. 19, no. 2 (Autumn 1995), p. 469.
132. P. Péan, *Une jeunesse française. François Mitterrand, 1934–1947*, Paris, 1994, pp. 77–78.
133. 'A cette époque on s'interrogeait beaucoup sur le fascisme. Ceux de Mussolini et de Salazar étaient attirants. On croyait que Mussolini n'allait pas suivre Hitler. Nous étions des étudiants bourgeois, catholiques, éloignés de l'argent ... On était influencé par *Gringoire* et *Je suis partout* et, sans être antisémite, on pouvait parler à notre sujet d'ostracisme par contamination.' Ibid., p. 99.
134. Ibid., pp. 220–21, pp. 288–89, p. 310, p. 475.
135. 'C'est injuste de juger des gens sur des erreurs qui s'expliquent dans l'atmosphère de l'époque.' Ibid., p.18.
136. [Editor's note: *Personnalisme* was a doctrine associated above all with Emmanuel Mounier and his social-Catholic collaborators on the review *Esprit*, but its main tenets chimed with many of the anti-materialist themes of dissident intellectuals in 1930s France. The abstract and atomised '*individu*' of economic and political liberalism, defined in terms of opinions and interests, would be replaced by the concrete '*personne*' complete with all the affective ties of family, trade and community that constitute real social life: the human spirit would be rescued from the dehumanising effects of both the rationalist and the industrial revolutions.]

3

Fascism in France: Problematising the Immunity Thesis

Robert Soucy

The essay that follows is a considerably revised and much extended version of a paper with the same title presented at the Annual Conference of the Association for the Study of Modern and Contemporary France at the University of Portsmouth on 6–8 September 2001. The theme of the conference was 'La France exceptionnelle? Comparisons and Intercultural Perspectives', and it was in this broad context that Professor Soucy contributed to a panel on the debate on French fascism between the wars.

Like Zeev Sternhell, Robert Soucy's early work in this field was on Maurice Barrès, his book *Fascism in France: The Case of Maurice Barrès* (1972) being published in the same year as Sternhell's own study. However, Soucy's attention subsequently shifted to the interwar period: in 1979 he published *Drieu La Rochelle: Fascist Intellectual*, and in a journal article in 1981 he attracted attention by applying the term 'centrist fascism' to the rather underresearched extraparliamentary right-wing movement, the Jeunesses Patriotes. His first decisive intervention, however, was his book *French Fascism: The First Wave, 1924–1933*, published in 1986. This was an exhaustive archival study of the extreme-Right leagues of the 1920s, focusing principally on Pierre Taittinger's Jeunesses Patriotes and Georges Valois' Faisceau. It made sufficient impact for Philippe Burrin, in a landmark essay in 1992, to cite Robert Soucy, alongside Ernst Nolte, Zeev Sternhell and Klaus-Jürgen Müller, as one of the principal foreign critics of the Rémondian orthodoxy. Soucy's long-awaited sequel, *Fascism in France: The Second Wave, 1933–1939* appeared in 1995, and looked primarily at Jean Renaud's Solidarité Française, Jacques Doriot's *Parti Populaire Français*, and most crucially and controversially at François de La Rocque's Croix de Feu/Parti Social Français. Soucy and the Canadian historian William Irvine had already, in separate articles in 1991, challenged the orthodox view that La Rocque's movement was merely authoritarian conservative, and in *The Second Wave* Soucy mobilised extensive archival evidence behind the uncompromising claim that it was indeed a fascist organisation.

Although Robert Soucy's intervention provoked some critical reviews and references, and in particular a letter to *Le Monde* from La Rocque's son Gilles vigorously denying that his father had supported Vichy's anti-Semitic laws or the idea of 'continental collaboration' with Nazi Germany, overall the response was rather muted in comparison with the controversy aroused by the work of Sternhell or indeed Robert Paxton. This on the face of it seems rather surprising, for the interpretation of the Croix de Feu/Parti Social Français is absolutely central to the whole debate, as several of the essays in this volume amply testify. If Soucy is right about the nature of this organisation, then its huge membership certainly makes it that mass fascist movement which supporters of the immunity thesis have always denied ever existed in France.

Professor Soucy's starting point is a very different understanding of 'fascism' from the one shared by most proponents of the immunity thesis. Unlike them (and, incidentally, unlike Sternhell too) he regards fascism as differing only in degree and in tactics from conservatism. They share similar social and economic interests, notably their deep hostility to Marxism, and in critical circumstances the boundaries between the two become increasingly permeable, allowing for a growing convergence around other themes like antiparliamentarism, antiliberalism, anti-'decadence', paramilitarism, etc. Thus Soucy is deeply sceptical about the supposed anticapitalist 'radicalism' of the Italian Fascist or German Nazi parties, and their capacity to win significant working-class support. Beneath the superficial trappings of antibourgeois rhetoric fascist movements are 'deeply counter-revolutionary', and on this basis he has no difficulty classifying the full range of extraparliamentary right-wing leagues in interwar France as fascist.

Given their fundamentally different visions of what constitutes 'fascism', there is little basis for productive intellectual exchange between the Soucy position and the immunity thesis. Indeed, the problem is exacerbated by the methodological gulf between them. While the disciples of René Rémond feel most comfortable on the terrain of ideas (and are thus quite happy doing battle with Sternhell), Soucy approaches the subject as an unashamed empiricist. Philippe Burrin, who draws a sharp distinction between 'authoritarian conservatives' and 'fascists', complains that Soucy 'does not make explicit the foundations of his definition of fascism', offering instead what Burrin calls 'a very broad conception of what constitutes French fascism'. The main weight of the argument in *The Second Wave* is that once direct comparisons are made at the level of membership, discourse, programme and political practice, the differences between the allegedly nonfascist 'conservative' Croix de Feu/PSF and movements that are more widely recognised as authentically 'fascist' (whether *Solidarité Française* or Doriot's PPF, or more importantly the Italian Fascist or German Nazi parties) are far less significant than is commonly claimed. Although, in a review of *The Second Wave* in Le Monde, Nicolas Weill wrote that Soucy's dossier of evidence was sufficiently weighty 'for historians of our country to re-open the debate on French fascism without any concession', the plea seems to have fallen on deaf ears in France. There has not been any attempt by supporters of the immunity thesis systematically to repel this particular line of attack, and Soucy's *The Second Wave* has had to wait eight years before finding a French publisher. In the essay that follows, the author updates his thesis in the light of recent publications in the field.

Robert Soucy is Emeritus Professor of History at Oberlin College, Ohio.

In 1989 Michel Dobry took issue with scholars who claimed that France was highly resistant to fascism during the interwar period. He called their view '*la thèse immunitaire*' (the immunity thesis) and was particularly critical of those who denied that Colonel de La Rocque's mass movement, the Parti Social Français (PSF), successor to the Croix de Feu (CF), was fascist.[1]

The PSF, because of its size, is central to the debate over the extent of French fascism in the 1930s. By 1938, as part of the right-wing backlash to the Popular Front's coming to power in 1936, it had become the largest political movement on the French right, with nearly a million members, comparable in size to the Nazi Party in Germany in 1932 and much larger than the Fascist Party in Italy in 1922.[2] It had more party members than the French Socialist and Communist parties combined. If the PSF was indeed fascist, the immunity thesis becomes problematic – and even more so if one adds to its membership figures the approximately 100,000 members of Jacques Doriot's French fascist movement in 1938, the Parti Populaire Français (PPF).[3]

But was the PSF 'fascist'? A number of scholars have said no.[4] Indeed, since 1952, when René Rémond wrote his article 'Y-a-t-il un fascisme français?', it seems that every ten years or so some historian or political scientist adds a new argument to the growing corpus of arguments as to why the PSF was not fascist, in some cases scrapping older arguments for newer ones. Although these scholars have disagreed with one another on various points, they have all agreed that the PSF was not fascist. William Irvine, one of the first scholars to challenge this conclusion, has called this the 'consensus' view of French fascism. Dissenters have been few.[5] The following is a critique of some of the major arguments and suppositions found in consensus historiography, starting with the assumption that one of the reasons La Rocque was not a fascist was because he was not pro-German in the 1930s.

Nationalism, anti-Semitism, Christianity

Fascism, it has been suggested, came to France as a 'foreign' ideology, and La Rocque was too nationalistic to be classified as a fascist.[6] Yet by this standard,

Mussolini was not a fascist prior to 1936 when he opposed Hitler's designs on neighbouring Austria and helped finance the Austrian Heimwehr movement, which was also fascist and also opposed to a German takeover. In 1939 many Polish fascists fell resisting the German invasion of their homeland, while others were later condemned to Nazi concentration camps. A number of anti-German Hungarian fascists were imprisoned or executed under the German occupation.[7] Before 1940, there is not one French fascist that I know of who desired a German invasion of France, and some French fascists even joined the Resistance. Non-German fascists could be just as nationalistic towards their countries as German fascists were towards theirs. In the 1930s, La Rocque went out of his way on numerous occasions to deny that he was a 'fascist', partly no doubt to avoid being seen by the French public as a lackey of Germany or Italy, that is, as less nationalistic than others on the French Right.[8]

Some consensus historians have suggested that La Rocque was not fascist because in the 1930s he criticised Nazi racial theory, welcomed Jews into his movement, and attended services for Jewish war dead at Rabbi Kaplan's synagogue in Paris – the assumption apparently being that all fascists are racist and anti-Semitic.[9] Again, it is an assumption that would eliminate Mussolini from being classified a fascist, at least between 1922 and 1933 when his regime repeatedly denounced anti-Semitism in Germany and accepted Jews into the Italian Fascist Party. According to Susan Zuccotti, by 1933 approximately 10 per cent of Jewish-Italians had joined the party, 'about the same percentage as Italians as a whole'.[10] In Austria, prior to the Anschluss, the clerico-fascist governments of Engelbert Dollfuss and Kurt von Schuschnigg also rejected anti-Semitism, which helps explain why some Austrian Jews, including Sigmund Freud, regarded them as a bulwark against Nazism.[11] In France in 1926, Pierre Taittinger, chief of the fascist-saluting Blue Shirts of the Jeunesses Patriotes (JP), declared that his position towards other religious creeds was one of absolute tolerance and that the JP would defend all the religions of France, whether they were those of 'Catholics, Protestants, or Israelites'.[12] In 1927 Georges Valois, the leader of the Faisceau, and in 1936, Doriot, the leader of the PPF, both considered fascist by most consensus historians, accepted assimilated, right-wing Jews into their movements.[13] Only after 1936 did Doriot turn sharply and extensively in an anti-Semitic direction.

Not until October 1940 did La Rocque begin speaking of Jewish 'purulence' abetted by Freemason 'conspiracies'. In *Disciplines d'Action* (1941) he accused Jews 'chased out of Central and Eastern Europe' of having undermined French 'morality' and 'health' and, along with the Freemasons, of having sought the 'de-Christianization' and 'despiritualization' of France.[14] This was not a completely new position for La Rocque, since in *Service public* (1935) he had pandered to cultural and political anti-Semitism by distinguishing between unassimilated and left-wing Jewish immigrants and those assimilated French Jews who were 'patriotic'.[15] In the 1930s, members of the CF and PSF in some of the provincial and North African sections of his movement were blatantly anti-Semitic, and in 1938, under pressure from the PSF in Algeria, La Rocque insisted that 'our friends in Constantine abstain from all relations, commercial or political, with members of [the Jewish] community'.[16]

Several consensus scholars have suggested that one of the characteristics of La Rocque's movement that distinguished it from fascism was its Christianity, particularly its allegiance to Social Catholicism.[17] Stanley Payne has defined fascism as essentially a pagan, secular, anti-Christian ideology, and therefore fundamentally different from La Rocque's. For Payne, one reason La Rocque was not a fascist was because he 'was strongly Catholic and preached the "cult of tradition"', whereas fascism 'presupposed a post-Christian, postreligious, secular, and immanent frame of reference'.[18] Pierre Milza finds that the Croix de Feu's attachment to 'the Christian tradition, to the primacy of the spiritual and to traditional moral values' makes one think more of 'a social patriotic Christianity' than of nihilistic fascism.[19] Philippe Burrin writes that 'La Rocque referred to Christianity and declared that he found his inspiration in Social Catholicism, while, for all of Hitler's and Mussolini's exploitation of religion, their ideology's contradiction with Christianity was evident to anyone who paid attention to their remarks'.[20]

However, as Payne acknowledges, there existed throughout Europe and the world in the 1930s 'specific examples' of 'religious and would-be "Christian fascists"'. And indeed the examples are many. José Antonio Primo de Rivera's Falange in Spain portrayed itself as a defender of the Catholic Church against atheistic Marxists and anticlerical liberals, as did fascist movements in Poland, Portugal, Austria, Hungary, Croatia, Bolivia, Argentina, Chile, and Brazil.[21] In Brazil, as Payne points out, Catholic priests were active in the mid-level leadership of the Integralist Action Party, and several Catholic bishops praised this fascist party in the 1930s.[22] In the 1930s fascists in Austria and Hungary expressed their devotion to the 'Christian National' principle, and Polish fascists tried to surpass the religious conservatism of the Pilsudski regime by defending ultramontane Catholicism. In Romania, the head of the fascist Iron Guard, Corneliu Codreanu, said he wanted to model his life after the crucified Christ revealed by the Orthodox Church. During the Second World War, the Croatian fascist movement, the Utasha, formed a government allied with Germany that combined aggressive Catholicism with racism. In Fascist Italy, where there were competing versions of fascism, large numbers of fascist conservatives were practising Catholics. After the signing of the Lateran Accords in 1929, there was an influx of Catholics into Mussolini's party which, as the historian Alexander De Grand notes, 'created a clerical fascism which vied with other ideologies for the "true fascist mantle." ... Thus, rather than retreating into a private sphere, Catholics were able to fill a vacuum in the public arena with their own version of fascism.'[23]

Before he came to power in Germany, Hitler often posed as a friend of Christianity, and even after he came to power, he was careful not to go too far in antagonising German Catholics and Protestants, whose support – or, at the very least, whose passivity – he needed in order to carry out his policies. Although it now seems clear that Hitler ultimately wished to abolish all brands of Christianity and replace them with a racist form of warrior paganism, this was much less clear to many Germans in the 1930s. In 1933 and 1934 a number of Protestant periodicals in Prussia described Hitler as a protector of the Christian family against cultural modernism and praised him for cracking down on prostitution and abortion.[24] According to Ronald Rychlak, in a meeting with German church officials in 1933, Hitler 'essentially justified his policies by citing Catholic traditions'.[25] John Cornwell in *Hitler's Pope* claims that as late as 1939 a quarter of Himmler's SS were Catholics.[26]

Under the Third Reich, thousands of pro-Nazi Protestant Christians found a home in the enormously successful 'German Christian' movement, which taught that Jesus had been a blond-haired, blue-eyed Aryan, and that the males in its movement were 'SS men for Christ'. In July 1933 its representatives won two-thirds of the votes cast in Protestant church elections across Germany. That same year a number of mass church weddings occurred between SS-men and their brides. According to Doris Bergen, 'most Christians in Germany did not share [Dietrich] Bonhoeffer's conviction about the fundamental opposition between [National Socialist ideology and Christianity]'. German Christians preached that Nazi ideology and Christianity were 'not only reconciliable but mutually reinforcing. ... [They] gave voice to the yearning of many Germans for the comfort of familiar religious ritual and custom without the demands of ethical standards'.[27]

Not any brand of Christianity, of course, would do for such a fusion – not, for example, the Christianity of Dr Erich Klausner, president of the German Catholic Action movement, who was assassinated by Hitler's Brownshirts in 1934, or that of Heinrich Brüning, head of the Catholic Centre Party in Germany, who pleaded with members of his own party not to sign the Enabling Act and who urged Pius XI not to sign concordats with Hitler. Nor was the form of Christianity practised by Nazi Christians the same as that of the courageously outspoken Catholic editor of *Der Gerade Weg*, who in 1933 was nearly beaten to death in the magazine's office by Brownshirts and then sent to a concentration camp where he was murdered a year later.[28] On the other hand, the Catholic Centre Party in Portugal was much less attached to political democracy in 1926 when the Portuguese Republic was overthrown and a military dictatorship established. The historian António Costa Pinto recounts how 'the Catholic Church blessed the 1926 coup and immediately offered up its secular members for possible ministerial positions'.[29] Obviously, there are different kinds of Christianity, including different kinds of Catholic Christianity.

To be compatible with fascism, at least with Italian Fascism and the Dollfuss brand of Austrian fascism, the Christianity espoused need not be racist. But it does have to permit an antidemocratic, super-nationalistic, ascetic, 'manly', martial and punitive approach to politics – punitive especially where its 'decadent' or 'degenerate' opponents are concerned. The Catholicism of Colonel de La Rocque displayed all these characteristics, as did the Catholicism of several other French fascist movements during the interwar period, including Georges

Valois's Faisceau, Pierre Taittinger's Jeunesses Patriotes, Marcel Bucard's Francistes and Jean Renaud's Solidarité Française.[30] Even Doriot, a former Communist, praised 'the spirit of the cathedrals of France' after he lost much of his working-class support and became a fascist. The writer Pierre Drieu La Rochelle, a supporter of Doriot and a self-proclaimed fascist, extolled the 'virile male Catholicism' of the Middle Ages and the 'warrior Christianity' of the crusades; and Robert Brasillach, editor of the fascist journal *Je suis partout*, described the Spanish Civil War in 1936 as a conflict between Catholic fascism and atheistic Marxism.[31]

That most members of La Rocque's movement were Catholics is not in itself proof that they were not fascists. To be sure, the Christianity of La Rocque's movement was not identical to that of the German Christians – it was not German, nor racist, nor Protestant – but neither was the Christianity of many Catholic fascists in Austria and France, nor that of the conservative wing of Mussolini's party.[32]

As for La Rocque's Social Catholicism, Kevin Passmore has pointed out that the Social Catholic movement in Lyon in the 1930s stretched 'from the pro-socialist Jeune république to the anti-democratic far right'.[33] La Rocque's brand of Social Catholicism was far more conservative than progressive, insisting, for example, that only workers 'faithful' to their employers should be given additional benefits and that these benefits be dispensed by employers rather than by the government. One PSF pamphlet condemned the sitdown strikes of 1936 as a form of terror, called the strikers unpatriotic, and chastised moderate conservatives for their 'pusillanimity' in responding to them.[34]

Political moderation and Republican legality

Another consensus argument is that La Rocque was too much of a political moderate to be a fascist, that is, too committed to political democracy and republican legality, especially after June 1936 when the PSF succeeded the antiparliamentary and paramilitary CF.[35] Indeed, some scholars see the PSF as having acted as a force *against* fascism for this reason, attracting potential supporters of fascism to the cause of moderation.[36] And it is true that in the 1930s La Rocque maintained that fascism was 'contrary to the French temperament', that he was 'ferociously opposed to any copy of dictatorial regimes', and that he was 'firmly attached to republican liberties'.[37]

There are problems, however, with taking La Rocque's conversion to moderation in 1936 at face value. The most obvious is how it was contradicted by many of the public statements he made before 1936 and by many of the actions his followers engaged in prior to the founding of the PSF. On 5 February 1934, for example, La Rocque called for the replacement of the Daladier government by a team 'rid of politicians of any sort'. In *Service public* (1935) he made no secret of his contempt for political democracy, claiming that politicians were inevitably corrupted by 'electoralism' and calling the coming national elections an exercise in 'collective decadence'. He spoke of the 'genius' of Mussolini, said that 'the admiration which Mussolini merits is beyond dispute', and called for 'continental solidarity' with Fascist Italy. He also asserted in 1935 that France needed 'healthy' institutions and an 'orderly' people in order to compete effectively with Germany.[38]

Pierre Milza's claim in 1987 that 'La Rocque did not mix his movement with the enterprises of the other [extreme Right nationalist] leagues' does not apply to the CF. Sean Kennedy, who has produced what is currently the best researched and best written study of La Rocque's movement, points out that in the months that followed the 6 February 1934 riots, CF activists on more than one occasion held joint meetings or demonstrations with members of the the Action Française (AF), Jeunesses Patriotes (JP) and Solidarité Française (SF) – and eventually absorbed many of their members into the CF.[39]

Prior to 1936, La Rocque and other CF spokesmen repeatedly expressed their disgust for French moderates. As Kevin Passmore has pointed out, in 1935 La Rocque condemned moderates for paving the way to communism and threatened that on the final day of reckoning these 'custodians who were unworthy of their responsibilities' would be placed at the head of the list of guilty men.[40] In March 1935, in a front-page editorial in *Le Flambeau*, the party newspaper, La Rocque condemned *les modérés* for falling prey to 'compromise and hesitation' and called upon the French people to 'stand up against revolution and its sordid ally moderation'.[41]

In the winter of 1935–36, however, La Rocque changed his tune, explaining to his followers why they needed to master their antidemocratic feelings, at least for the time being, and engage in the very electoral process they had so often condemned. Although he told them that 'even the idea of soliciting a vote nauseates me', he maintained that reversing the movement's public opposition to political democracy had become a necessity.[42] His reasoning was more fascist than liberal: 'To scorn universal suffrage ... does not withstand examination. Neither Mussolini nor Hitler ... committed that mistake. Hitlerism, in particular, raised itself to total power through elections ... Hitlerism became a preponderant political force only on the day when, in [1930] it achieved 107 seats of its own in the Reichstag.'[43] Six months later La Rocque founded the allegedly democratic PSF.

As Roger Griffin has observed, such opportunism is not uncommon among fascist movements:

> Though they oppose parliamentary democracy and their policies would in practice inevitably lead to its destruction, they may well choose to operate tactically as democratic electoral parties. Indeed, they may go to considerable lengths to camouflage the extent of their hostility to liberalism through euphemism and dishonesty, reserving their rhetoric of destruction of the system and of revolution for the initiated.[44]

Kennedy says of the founding of the PSF in 1936:

The Croix de feu had embarked upon a constitutional path and its leader had resisted calls for the use of force; these facts are often cited as proof of the latter's moderate intentions. On this point, there can be no doubt that by late 1935 he had concluded that direct participation in the political process was the most effective path to power. ... Such actions only prove that La Rocque was a realist; they do not demonstrate that he had become a democrat. ... He realized that the Republican state was a strong one, and that visible displays of strength, while creating enthusiasm, were unlikely by themselves to lead the movement to power. The relative caution of the Croix de feu on 6 February – and on subsequent occasions – can be explained in such terms.[45]

Nor was the PSF's engagement in electoral politics unique in the history of French fascism, since in the 1920s members of both Taittinger's JP and Charles Maurras's Action Française (AF) had done the same. In 1935, Henry Dorgères, leader of the Greenshirts, ran for the Chamber of Deputies. The fact that Taittinger, Maurras and Dorgères had all condemned 'parliamentarianism' on many occasions did not deter them from utilising the electoral 'weapon' when it served their purposes.[46] La Rocque was not unlike earlier French fascists in this regard. So too were Jacques Doriot and Simon Sabiani when they conducted electoral campaigns for the PPF.

But what about La Rocque's followers? Were they more moderate than La Rocque himself? Did the thousands of members of the CF who continued into the PSF, people who had previously shared La Rocque's contempt for political democracy, really believe that La Rocque had become a genuine democrat in 1936? Only a small minority, led by Pozzo di Borgo, abandoned La Rocque at that point; the overwhelming majority stayed with him. Julian Jackson and others have attributed the rising popularity of the PSF after 1936 to its rejection of extremism rather than the reverse. 'Even if there was a degree of political opportunism in [La Rocque's] rallying to the Republic', Jackson writes, 'the significant point is that de la Rocque achieved his greatest influence when he appeared at his most moderate.'[47] But did the new recruits, the 'moderates' who flocked to the PSF after June 1936 really believe that La Rocque had seriously changed his stripes? Were they, too, victims of mass amnesia? And if they themselves were moderates looking for a like-minded political party to support, why did they not remain with or go over to the well-established moderate parties already in existence, socially conservative but political democratic parties like the Fédération Républicaine (FR), the Alliance Démocratique (AD), the Parti Démocrate Populaire (PDP) or, in Alsace, the Union Populaire Républicaine (UPR)?[48]

Did the PSF between 1936 and 1940 woo thousands of newcomers *from* fascism or *to* fascism? Given La Rocque's previous antiparliamentarianism, given the pressures of the social and economic crisis brought on by the Depression, given the fear, anger and humiliation felt in conservative circles as a result of the election of the Popular Front in 1936 and the sitdown strikes that followed, and given the failure of French moderates to prevent the Popular Front from coming to power in the first place, it seems unlikely that a desire for more moderation was behind the phenomenal growth of the PSF between 1936 and 1939. As Zeev Sternhell has said of this growth, it was not because the new members had 'suddenly been won over to the virtues of democracy, but, on the contrary, because more and more people felt disgusted with the existing order'.[49] Kennedy offers a similar explanation as to why thousands of former moderates flocked to the PSF after June 1936:

> Was it because the party provided material aid and sociability? Because it was stronger on the 'social question' than the traditional right? There were certainly those who emphasized that it was above all the message of unity and sense of mystique which attracted them to the PSF. ... But the timing of the PSF's most impressive period of growth – 1936–37, the period of the Popular Front government -suggests that the reaction to the latter is of integral importance in explaining why moderate conservatives and previously apolitical individuals signed up. ... Given the sociopolitical upheavals of 1936–37, ... many moderates were radicalized and politicized and saw the PSF as the best vehicle of opposition to the Popular Front, even if they had previously considered the Croix de feu distasteful.[50]

La Rocque was not the first leader on the French far right during the interwar period to cultivate discontented moderates. In 1926, according to a lengthy report compiled by the French Minister of the Interior, Georges Valois sought his clientele 'exclusively from the conservative and moderate parties', that is, from those who had been disturbed by the electoral victory of the Cartel des Gauches in 1924.[51]

Some consensus scholars have suggested that even the 'moderates' who had earlier joined the PSF's predecessor, the CF, were opposed to authoritarianism, a view which Kennedy disputes:

> There can be no doubt that the Croix de feu did attract large numbers of people who were moderate in outlook and eminently respectable in the eyes of their fellow citizens. ... It is important to keep in mind, however, that these moderates found the Croix de feu appealing in a time of sharp political conflict. ... The rhetoric of local speakers was not only intended to convert people to a programme; it no doubt echoed the sentiments of their audiences as well. In the Aisne, prospective members were told of 'the intense life of the Group', but also that its aim was 'to reconstruct the French state by installing an authoritarian republic'. In Nantes a speaker called for 'a true France, armed, militarized, disciplined'.[52]

Not all consensus scholars would disagree with Kennedy on this point, since Julian Jackson and others have described the CF as more authoritarian than the PSF, emphasising how Pozzo di Borgo and his followers abandoned La Rocque in 1936 when he opted for the electoral path to power. Kevin Passmore, for example, has categorised the CF, but not the PSF, as fascist.[53] Kennedy finds, however, that 'if there were militants who in 1935 opposed the transformation into [an electoral] party, there were also those who believed that the Croix de Feu should play such a role'. He notes, for example, that even though the Algerian sections of the CF were quite anti-Semitic, they 'were eager to engage in electoral politics from an early stage' thus demonstrating that adopting a '"constitutional" path did not necessarily lead to moderation in political opinions'.[54]

Kennedy recounts how, following the creation of the PSF in 1936, a host of moderates whom he describes as 'no longer feeling quite so moderate' joined the party, but so too did a number of 'extremists'. Not only did most members of the CF remain loyal to La Rocque (in the Nord, for example, 'police estimated that the overwhelming majority of CF members continued into the PSF'), but also many former members of the AF, JP and SF joined the PSF as well, 'people who were generally considered bitter opponents of the Third Republic'. Kennedy writes: 'That in 1935–36 La Rocque rejected the demands of "militants" for more drastic action does not mean that he was a moderate conservative. The willingness of members of the other leagues to join the PSF in 1936–37, and the latter's competition for members with the PPF, suggests that extremists not only remained welcomed but were actively sought out'.[55]

In some local PSF sections, former members of the Faisceau, the JP and the SF held leadership positions. A PSF slogan linking the openly antidemocratic CF to the allegedly democratic PSF ('The French Social Party equals the Croix de feu plus electoral politics') may have eased their passage.

This is not to deny, as Kennedy points out, that 'the diverse nature of the PSF membership meant that La Rocque was subjected to conflicting pressures' or that some of the new recruits who joined La Rocque's movement after 1936 were moderates 'who may have wanted the Popular Front out of power but in some cases little beyond that'. But moderates of the latter sort never dominated the PSF. On the contrary, a PSF effort in 1937–38 to win over members of the Radical Party to its own 'centrist/conservative consensus' was based on offering Radicals not more centrism, but less. Kennedy concludes that, while most of the rhetoric and tactics of the PSF were more democratic than those of the CF, its ethos was consistently hierarchical: 'the Croix de feu and the PSF were fundamentally the same'.[56]

Michel Dobry cautions against judging whether the PSF was fascist or not by the way Mussolini or Hitler behaved *after* they came to power.[57] By this standard, Hitler was not a Nazi between 1928 and 1933 when he engaged in electoral politics, nor Mussolini a Fascist in 1923 when, still in the process of consolidating his power, he claimed that he wanted to save Italian parliamentary democracy, not destroy it. Similarly, when Robert Zaretsky takes the view (following the distinction which Juan Linz makes between fascism and conservative authoritarianism) that the PSF was not fascist because fascism required a 'single mass party, the mobilization of the population, and the elimination of all intermediate institutions between the state and the individual', he is comparing a movement which never came to power to those that did (as well as ignoring the PSF's considerable success at mass mobilisation in 1936–38).[58] Such ahistorical litmus tests ignore the differences between 'fascism in motion' and 'fascism in practice'. It is easier for a fascist to be more openly absolutist when he is in power than when he is not, and these two stages of fascism should not be confused.[59]

Some consensus historians have argued that the fact that La Rocque never attempted a coup d'état is proof of his respect for republican legality.[60] However,

La Rocque himself had another explanation as to why he had not 'acted' after the Popular Front came to power in 1936 and outlawed the CF. Speaking to a PSF audience in February 1937, he declared: 'Do you understand today that if in the month of June I had ordered you to descend into the streets, you would have been crushed ?'[61] In 1941 he explained further: 'We would have had to overcome the double shock of masses of people drunk with [Popular Front] demagoguery and of public authorities obedient to the orders of the government : the victory of the 'reds' would have been certain.'[62] These were not the words of a man committed to republican legality. As Robert Paxton has written:

> We need to recall that fascism has never so far taken power by a coup d'état, deploying the weight of its militants in the street. Fascist power by coup is hardly conceivable in a modern state. Fascism cannot appeal to the street without risking confrontation with future allies – the army and police ... Resorting to direct mass action also risks conceding advantages to fascism's principal enemy, the Left, which was still powerful in the street and workplace of interwar Europe.[63]

Paxton also does well to remind us that fascism in both Italy and Germany came to power legally.

La Rocque knew that it was foolish to attempt a coup d'état when the chances of success were slim, a view which in 1936 was shared by a large majority of CF members.[64] It was also the same position which three leaders on the French fascist right – Valois, Taittinger and the leader of the Solidarité Française, Jean Renaud – had previously taken on the same issue. They too had argued that a failed coup was all the government needed to ban their organisations and that it was a 'trap' to be avoided.[65] Nor should it be forgotten that Hitler, having proclaimed his adherence to republican legality in 1930, took measures in 1931 to curb the Sturm-Abteilung (SA) when some of its members ignored his directives and began talking of overthrowing the government by force. Like La Rocque in 1936, Hitler in 1931 feared that such 'noise' might bring down a second government ban on his party, the first having occurred after the Munich putsch of 1923. Hitler responded by appealing to the loyalty of SA members, by defending the 'constitutional' path to power, and by purging some five hundred of the guilty from the ranks of the SA.[66] In La Rocque's case, the passionate right-wing backlash to the Popular Front and to the sitdown strikes in 1936 provided him with an opportunity that had been largely missing before, that of coming to power through electoral means. It was both a more promising and less risky option that resorting to armed rebellion.

The professed moderation of the PSF between 1936 and 1940 did not prevent vestiges of the movement's previous authoritarianism from cropping up. Indeed, Zeev Sternhell finds that following the founding of the PSF, *Le Flambeau* grew less rather than more moderate. Sternhell writes: 'Underneath the enormous headlines calling for war against domestic treason, the tone became more violent, the style more demagogic, the attacks against the Left, Blum, and the Popular Front more vulgar.'[67] After the Croix de Feu was banned in 1936, its *dispos* (paramilitary units 'available' to act on short notice) were renamed EVP, *équipes volantes de propaganda* (flying propaganda squads), only now their mobilisation exercises were fewer and more discreet. A PSF pamphlet in 1936 declared that it was up to the state to 'forbid' all teaching likely to harm the 'health' of the nation; otherwise, it said, the state would be behaving in a 'criminal' fashion.[68] In July 1937, the PSF's new mass circulation daily, *Le Petit Journal*, defended the AF's Charles Maurras, whose venom against liberalism and democracy was well known. It also congratulated General Francisco Franco, who in 1937 was in the process of crushing the democratically-elected government of Spain, for being '*autant chef d'État que militaire* [as much a head of State as a military leader]' In 1938 La Rocque declared that France would never be secure until it was as 'politically strong' as Germany. In 1939 he called for an entente between France and Germany and asserted that hostility between Rome and Paris was 'contrary to the nature of things'.[69]

Violence and repression

Philippe Burrin has contended that one reason La Rocque was not a fascist was because his speeches contained no 'eulogy to force' or 'incitement to violence'.[70] It is true that in the late 1930s La Rocque repeatedly called for class reconciliation 'without violence' and 'without civil war'.[71] And yet, a major reason for the original paramilitary organisation of his movement was to create a force that could help defeat Communist violence with anti-Communist violence, revolution with counterrevolution. In condemning Nazi violence in 1935, he pointedly added that this did not mean that he feared using violence if it were necessary to defeat the 'criminal' designs of the Popular Front.[72]

On a number of occasions, when it was still relatively safe for his movement to do so, La Rocque either instigated or praised acts of political violence committed by his followers. Between 1931 and 1933, CF militants, with La Rocque's approval, disrupted several pacifist meetings. On 27 November 1931, in one of his first public acts as the new head of the CF, La Rocque himself led over a thousand of his followers in breaking up a pacifist conference at the Trocadero in Paris, creating such an uproar that the police had to be called in and the auditorium evacuated. Kennedy notes that in November 1933, following a 29 October attack by CF members on a meeting of conscientious objectors in Laon, 'La Rocque remarked how this action, along with "numerous" others in the history of the association, showed how a prepared and disciplined use of force, whether "preventative" or "curative" in nature could, with the advantage of surprise, overwhelm a numerically superior enemy'.[73] And, of course, the columns of CF troops who marched towards the rear of the Chamber of Deputies on 6 February 1934, while indeed more disciplined than the AF, JP, SF, and Franciste rowdies in the Place de la Concorde, clearly sought to intimidate the Daladier government with a show of paramilitary force. The next day, La Rocque boasted that the CF 'had surrounded the Chamber and forced the deputies to flee'.[74] In the weeks that followed, a host of new recruits poured into his movement.

In the summer and fall of 1935, with the Popular Front on the rise, La Rocque repeatedly called upon his dispos to prepare for H hour, which he implied was near. This rhetoric was hardly meant to discourage CF militants from being violent when the time came. La Rocque's urging his troops to remain 'ready' but 'calm' in the meantime was not an argument against violence itself. Pierre Milza has dismissed La Rocque's talk of direct action and H-hour as never being more than 'a project and a myth'.[75] If La Rocque's better judgement finally reduced his references to H hour to that, it was nevertheless a project and a myth that helped attract thousands of new militants to the CF in 1935.

Even after the PSF was founded and faced with the threat of dissolution, there were militants within the movement who ignored La Rocque's pleas for caution. Some of them took matters in their own hands in response to the wave of strikes and factory occupations that followed the electoral victory of the Popular Front in 1936.[76] Kennedy writes that 'La Rocque himself soon felt the need for a show of force'. When the Communists proposed to hold a rally in Paris at the Parc des Princes, La Rocque responded with a counter-demonstration. On 4 October, 1936, between 15,000 and 20,000 PSF activists (the party claimed 40,000) turned up to contest the rally, only to be turned back after clashing with some 20,000 police and *garde mobiles*. Stones were thrown at buses carrying leftists to the stadium, and thirty police and an unspecified number of PSF rioters were injured. A month later, La Rocque described the event as a great success for the PSF, as 'a spontaneous *levée en masse* of 40,000 Parisians' which had stopped 'the rise toward power of a Communist plot'.[77] Presumably, praising a violent '*levée en masse*' qualifies as incitement.

Following the clash at the Parc des Princes, the Blum government threatened to ban the PSF on the grounds that it had reconstituted the CF. Police raided the Parisian headquarters of the PSF and searched La Rocque's residence and those of several party leaders: a total of fifty searches. The government's legal offensive failed to stop PSF violence completely, as some PSF sections in the provinces launched other 'direct actions' in 1936 and 1937.[78] In 1938 there was more PSF violence, this time against members of Doriot's PPF and Taittinger's JP, rivals of the PSF on the French far right.[79]

Had La Rocque cracked down on the perpetrators in 1936–38 as firmly as Hitler had on the SA in 1931, he might have alienated PSF 'extremists' whose continuing support he wished to keep. Indeed, in 1940 the PSF had hoped to run Philippe Barrès, one of the former leaders of the Faisceau, against Taittinger in Paris. La Rocque was torn between pleasing tactically cautious 'moderates' within his movement and hungry-for-action firebrands, which was much like the problem Valois, Taittinger and Renaud had previously faced with their own followers – and which they also had tried to manage, some with more success than others.[80] It was also similar to the problem Hitler had faced with the SA in 1931.

There are a number of reasons why CF and PSF activists did not engage in more political violence, none of which required an allegiance to republican legality. After the 6 February 1934 riots, it was clear that much of the French

Right was against threats to public order, whether these threats came from the Left or the Right. La Rocque's dispos had gained prestige on 6 February by acting in a disciplined manner, while members of the AF, JP and SF had been part of an uncontrolled mob. Following the riots, several right-wing newspapers praised La Rocque's troops for their discipline and urged those who had rioted to desist from further such actions. The fear of public disorder was even manifested in the reaction of these same newspapers six months later to Hitler's 'Night of the Long Knives' in Germany. Several of these journals ran headlines with variations of 'Hitler Restores Order in the Reich!'[81] Reading them, one can almost hear a collective sigh of relief. This does not mean that some of these same conservatives, including François de Wendel, head of the *comité des forges* (steel trust) and a major financial supporter of the CF/PSF, would have opposed defensive violence by the PSF had the Communists attempted a revolution. But short of such an eventuality, they preferred to discourage violence.[82] Fear of public disorder was particularly strong on the French Right after the outbreak of civil war in Spain in 1936, the kind of conflict which few conservatives wanted to see occur in France, especially since there was no guarantee that the Right would win out. La Rocque's insistence that the PSF was opposed to 'civil war' and 'class conflict' was meant both to allay this fear and to blame the Left for causing it.

The banning of the CF in 1936 also restricted PSF violence. The government's threat to dissolve the PSF as well, if it behaved too provocatively, hung over La Rocque's movement like Damocles' sword – especially after the Parc des Princes and 'Clichy Massacre' affairs.[83] Moreover, even if this threat lessened, as it no doubt did after the parliamentary defeats of Popular Front governments in 1937 and 1938, there was another reason to avoid confrontations. When street clashes did occur between militants in La Rocque's movement and their Communist and Socialist opponents, the former regularly lost and sometimes had to be escorted to safety by the police. This was especially the case when La Rocque's followers attempted to hold political meetings in 'red' neighbourhoods. Such setbacks were not unique to La Rocque's movement. As Bernd Weisbrod has pointed out, even Hitler's Brownshirts, before they came to power, were hesitant to take on German leftists in neighbourhoods where the odds were against them. 'The SA', Weisbrod writes, 'hardly ever ventured into hostile working-class districts without some sort of police protection.'[84]

La Rocque hardly rejected political violence on principle, but, as a former lieutenant-colonel in the French army, he preferred controlled uses of force under the right circumstances to rowdier kinds under the wrong circumstances. 'Defensive' violence against a Communist revolution, which would have had the support of large sections of the population, was one thing; 'offensive' violence against political opponents prior to such a revolution, which would have had much less public support, was another. This was the same position which three French fascist movements in the 1920s, Antoine Rédier's Légion, Taittinger's JP, and Valois's Faisceau had taken.[85] Kennedy writes of the Faisceau:

> In the 1920s the Faisceau had its blueshirted Legionnaires, but they were rarely employed offensively. Georges Valois, the movement's leader, and his lieutenant, Philippe Barrès (son of Maurice) 'considered street brawling to be childish and counterproductive' and feared it would alienate potential members. ... No one has argued that the Faisceau was somehow not fascist because Georges Valois saw brawling as counterproductive.[86]

Indeed, if brawling is the standard by which fascism is defined before it comes to power, the PSF tolerated much more fascism within its ranks between 1936 and 1939 than did the Faisceau between 1924 and 1927. No one has claimed that the Faisceau was not fascist because it engaged in less violence than the PSF.

La Rocque was no less opportunistic than Mussolini or Hitler when it came to choosing the moments when he would – or would not – employ violence. It should not be forgotten that after the Matteotti assassination in 1924, Mussolini, who was sensitive to the public outcry and whose hold on power was still tenuous, reined in the *squadristi* in an attempt to defuse domestic and international criticism. Had Hitler launched the 'Night of the Long Knives' in June 1931 rather than in June 1934, that is, *before* he came to power (an onslaught that included not only the house arrests of the Crown Prince of Germany and Franz von Papen but also the murders of several of von Papen's supporters, of the Catholic leader Erich Klausner and of General and former Chancellor Kurt von Schleicher and his wife), then this would doubtless have alienated many respectable conservatives whom Hitler was still courting in 1931.

There is little reason to believe that La Rocque would have hesitated to repress his political opponents had he had the power to do so (which is not to say that he would have been as bloodthirsty as Hitler). In 1933 La Rocque wrote that no elections should take place without a preliminary 'cleansing' of government committees and the press, adding that 'our initial intervention will consist of reducing to silence the agitators of disorder'.[87] In April 1936 a CF manifesto called for 'severe sanctions against groups, parties, and journals that conducted campaigns against military duty, civic duty, and loyalty to the country's institutions'.[88] (It did not mention La Rocque's own criticism of electoral institutions the year before.)

In June 1936, the very month the PSF was founded, La Rocque called for a 'reconciliation' that would 'eliminate' noxious forces in French political life, 'punish' those who robbed the people of their savings, and 'outlaw' those whose private lives did not conform to their public declarations.[89] A PSF pamphlet in 1936 demanded 'penal sanctions' for French schoolteachers who undermined national loyalty.[90] In 1941, free from republican constraints, La Rocque labelled Léon Blum and Edouard Daladier 'traitors', complained that the Riom trial was taking too long to condemn them, and declared that France had reached the bottom of its 'degeneracy' in the elections of 1936 ('degenerate' being one of La Rocque's favorite pejoratives). He advocated 'pitiless' sanctions against France's internal enemies and the 'integral extirpation of contaminated elements' in French society.[91] He also called upon the Vichy regime to 'make examples' of those guilty of treason and recalled how, as a former colonial officer in Morocco, he had saved the lives of his troops by having firing squads execute any 'native convicted of treason or of passing intelligence to our adversaries'.[92]

This is not to suggest that had La Rocque come to power, he would have been as brutal or as totalitarian as Hitler, but then – as historians Tobias Abse, Joel Blatt and Alexander De Grand have observed – neither was Mussolini. Once again, one need not equate La Rocque with Hitler – or, for that matter, Mussolini with Hitler – to classify La Rocque a fascist. Abse points out that the Italian Fascist regime had no real equivalent of the Gestapo or the SS and that its OVRA (Organisation for Vigilance and Repression of Antifascism) was little more than a slightly better organised version of the political section that had always existed within the traditional police. Abse writes: 'Repression did not reach German levels: if political murders of anti-Fascists occurred in 1920–5 and again in 1943–5, for the bulk of the regime's existence *squadrismo* gave way to very traditional police methods: imprisonment and internal exile, not death, were the standard penalties for political dissidence'.[93] Although Blatt regards OVRA 'as more efficient than the traditional police, as having ambitions for greater control and having fewer countervailing forces with which to contend', he agrees with Abse that its brutality was 'not on the scale of Hitler and Stalin'.[94] Nor, as De Grand has shown, was Mussolini's regime as totalitarian in cultural matters, since it 'rejected the option of a massive purge of the universities and the forcible imposition of its will on the intellectual community'.[95]

Because La Rocque never achieved the power that Mussolini did, we cannot be sure how he would have behaved had he done so – although, if his remarks under the Vichy regime calling for 'pitiless' sanctions and the 'extirpation of contaminated elements' are any indication, it seems unlikely that he would have been inclined to practise what he condemned in 1935 as moderate 'hesitation and compromise'. We do know that in 1941 La Rocque not only returned to denouncing political democracy but also called for 'continental collaboration' with the Germans.[96] In early 1942, he turned against the Germans and created his own Resistance organisation, which led to his deportation to Germany in 1943. Michel Winock has suggested that these last two facts should exonerate La Rocque from all charges of collaborationism.[97] La Rocque's reversal, however, does not erase his prior attacks on France's 'degenerate' and 'treasonous' internal enemies, his call for collaboraton with the Germans, his praise for the 'ardent vitality of fascist and Hitlerian regimes', his declaration that the 'theory of "families of good stock who have their roots in the earth" leads us to conclusions not far from [those of] Walther Darré, Minister of Agriculture for the Reich', and his insistence that the French people follow Marshal Pétain with 'total discipline'. His previously 'firm' attachment to republican liberties was nowhere in sight in 1941 when he wrote that 'no dissidence will be legitimate [or] supportable'.[98]

Social and economic conservatism and Leftist populism

Another consensus argument is that La Rocque was too socially and economically conservative to be a fascist, the assumption being that 'authentic' fascism was a socially radical, passionately antibourgeois phenomenon – even if it had to 'compromise' with traditional conservatives during and after its rise to power.[99] Pierre Milza, for example, has argued that one reason La Rocque was not a fascist was because he 'implicated neither the bourgeois order nor the economic foundations of the system'.[100] But then neither did Italian Fascism nor German Nazism. Milza's view is based more on fascist rhetoric and aspirations in the cultural sphere than on fascist constituencies and policies in the economic sphere. Historians Adrian Lyttelton, Tobias Abse, Robert Paxton and Alexander De Grand have all remarked on how Fascists in Italy, even before 1920, often sounded more socially revolutionary than they actually were.[101]

Moreover, if one focuses, as De Grand does, 'on the nature of Fascism's constituencies, why they adhered to the movement, what they expected, and how they fared', then far more important than the small number of dissident syndicalists and even smaller number of futurist literati who supported early Italian Fascism were the large numbers of social conservatives and cultural traditionalists who poured into the movement after 1920 and transformed it into a party of 'bourgeois resurgence'.[102]

Roger Griffin's assertion that nothing precluded a member of the working class from being susceptible to fascism's myth of palingenetic nationalism is true but misleading, since it was far truer in the exception than in the rule. As Abse has noted, Italian Fascism during its rise to power had little success among working-class constituencies. The great majority of industrial workers in northern and central Italy were fiercely hostile to fascism.[103] Any appeal that palingenetic nationalism might have exerted on them was undermined by the regime's union busting and wage cuts.[104] Mussolini's 'leaky totalitarianism' was applied far more to the subversive Left than to the traditional Right. Blatt points out that Italian Fascism 'compromised with conservative elites – industry, business, large landowners, the army, the police, the King, the Catholic Church – but crushed the Left'.[105] In Germany – as historians Ian Kershaw, Michael Kater, Bernd Weisbrod, and Tilla Siegel have shown – Nazism's inroads into the industrial working class were also marginal, both before and after Hitler's coming to power. Workers were underrepresented in the Nazi Party.[106]

Many of Hitler's supporters in Germany in 1932, like La Rocque's in France in 1936, were middle-and lower middle-class businessmen, tradesmen, large and small landowners, and white-collar workers who feared the Left. According to Weisbrod, this fear was also present among many members of the 'liberal' professions – doctors, lawyers, engineers, technicians, high school teachers, university professors – and was shared by thousands of high school and university students who aspired to these professions. In the midst of the Depression, feeling that their careers or career ambitions were threatened, they turned to the Nazis for protection. In doing so, they proved willing to sacrifice some bourgeois values (certain 'notions of civilised behavior') to other bourgeois values (economic security and social status).[107] Thus, it should come as no surprise that, as Michael Kater has demonstrated, individuals from Germany's most 'educated' classes, the middle and upper middle classes, were overrepresented in the Nazi Party.

As historians George Mosse, Fritz Ringer and John Weiss have amply demonstrated, 'higher' education per se was hardly a prophylactic against Nazism, since many German academics and intellectuals were propagating Volkish ideology long before Hitler came to power.[108] Indeed, De Grand remarks that in both Italy and Germany, 'intellectuals led the fawning crowd' in calling for a strong man to reverse the process of degeneration they attributed to democracy. In France in the mid-1930s, large numbers of students from the nation's *grandes écoles,* especially from the École Polytechnique, belonged to La Rocque's movement. In 1936 half of the members of the CF's 'Students of the National Volunteers' in Paris came from the medical and law schools. In May of that year, some 1,500 students, professors and doctors were present when La Rocque spoke at a meeting of the university branch of the CF.

None of this is to deny that some of the social and economic programmes of European fascist movements during the interwar period displayed left-wing features, as did the writings of the various 'nonconformist' French and Italian intellectuals that Zeev Sternhell has described. So too did the Twenty-Five Points of the Nazi platform in Germany in 1920 and the party programmes of Marcel Déat's Neo-Socialists and Gaston Bergery's Front Commun in France in 1936.[109] The original programme of Italian Fascism in 1919 called for an eight-hour work day, an increase in the minimum wage, worker participation in management, confiscation of excess war profits, confiscation of Church lands, abolition of the existing monarchical constitution, and the vote for women and eighteen-year-olds. Some early fascists in Italy were national syndicalists, that is, dissidents from mainstream internationalist syndicalism, although many of them later abandoned fascism when they thought they were being turned into 'watchdogs' for the big landowners.[110]

When Mussolini's embryonic Fascist Party was badly beaten in the elections of 1919, it dropped the radical planks of its platform and looked to more conservative groups for support. De Grand writes:

What we know as fascism ... was not born on March 23, 1919 in Milan. The membership and outlook of the initial fascio had little chance of finding political space in Italy. The true birth of fascism came in countless towns throughout rural Italy between the autumn of 1920 and the spring of 1921. After the electoral debacle of November 1919, when the Fascists in Milan received fewer than 5,000 votes out of 275,000, much of the original membership (mainly syndicalists, socialists, and futurists) drifted off. From a low point in December 1919, when there were only 31 fasci (local sections) with 870 members, the movement made a spectacular recovery as the party of bourgeois resurgence. By the end of 1920 there were already 88 fasci with over 20,000 members. Two forces coalesced to produce this result: an urban movement led by Mussolini and a few associates from his early days, and a vast movement of agrarian reaction against the Socialist peasant leagues.

> By the time that the movement transformed itself into a political party in 1921, it was already a heterogeneous coalition and would become increasingly so after the March on Rome, when large numbers of conservatives flocked to the winning side. Thus, any effort to seek in the radical Fascist program of 1919 the true essence of the movement runs up against the reality that Mussolini's first leftist and nationalist fascism was a total failure. Once transformed into a mass party of the middle class, the Fascist movement found it impossible to return to the supposed purity of its radical origins.[111]

As a result, as Paxton remarks, 'Mussolini…went from being one of the most popular figures in the Socialist party to a virtual outcast'.[112]

In Germany, the economically radical aspects of Nazism's original Twenty-Five Points were also scrapped on Hitler's road to power, except for those applying to Jews.[113] In May 1933 Hitler destroyed Germany's labour unions and sent many of their leaders to concentration camps. Robert Ley, the Nazi Minister of Labour, announced that the new policy was to 'restore absolute leadership to the natural leader of the factory – that is, to the employer'. Henceforth, the employer was to be 'the master of the house'.[114] In short, social radicalism is hardly a sine qua non for fascism, and therefore La Rocque's social and economic conservatism is no grounds for excluding him from this category.

In recent years, some consensus historians have put a new twist on what might be called the 'fascism as leftism' argument. Once again it is suggested that lower-income and less-educated persons are more likely to support fascism than wealthier and more educated individuals, only this time the alleged motivation for the former is not national 'socialism' but national 'populism'.[115] According to this view, fascists are populists who seek to mobilise the masses and replace traditional elites with their own counter-elite. Traditional elites, by contrast, are said to be antipopulist, distrustful of the masses, and opposed to their mobilisation. This formula ignores the fact, as Gustave Le Bon famously did not, that wealthy conservatives can both distrust the masses and *want* their mobilisation – as long as 'the crowd' can be manipulated for right-wing ends. As La Rocque put it, 'The crowd need not be penned up but judiciously arranged, partitioned, oriented', since left to itself it can become a chaotic 'tidal wave'.[116] In other words, a disciplined and supportive right-wing crowd was acceptable, an undisciplined and threatening left-wing crowd was not. Christopher Hitchens's observation that 'kings and bishops and billionaires often have more say than most in forming the appetites and emotions of the crowd' is also pertinent when discussing populism.[117] Nor should fundamental differences between left-and right-wing populisms be ignored.[118]

Nevertheless, in the debate over the nature of French fascism, it is sometimes assumed that fascist populism is incompatible with upper-class conservatism. Philippe Burrin, for example, has contended that one reason La Rocque was not a fascist was because he was supported by notables and came himself from an aristocratic background.[119] Pierre Milza, calling attention to the underrepresentation of farm and factory workers and the overrepresentation of small business people, white-collar workers, and 'leisured' city dwellers in the CF, concludes that 'Colonel de La Rocque's movement thus presented a less plebeian, more bourgeois character than fascist organizations'.[120] Roger Griffin, who also views La Rocque as non-fascist, has described fascism as a populism that seeks to 'destroy' traditional hierarchies. For Griffin there is a 'sharp distinction' between 'fascist regimes in Italy and Germany bent on creating a revolutionary new social and ethical order on the basis of mass mobilization' and authoritarian right-wing regimes 'whose fundamental aim is the reactionary one of using mechanisms of social engineering and repression to maintain the social status quo'.[121]

In contrast, De Grand describes how Italian fascism after 1921 was overwhelmingly conservative and how after 1924 it received a good deal of support from the nation's traditional elites. 'The Fascist regime', he writes, 'never disturbed social hierarchies and only tampered with private property under the impact of the Depression.'[122] Italy's traditional elites, including its 'intermediate elites', benefited from the Fascist regime more than other sections of the population.[123] John Weiss observes that in both Italy and Germany: 'Property and income distribution and the traditional class structure remained roughly the same under fascist rule. What changes there were favored the old elites or certain segments of the party leadership'.[124]

Authoritarian conservatism and traditional elites

There are some consensus historians, Robert Paxton and Philippe Burrin, for example, who, while acknowledging the 'complicity' of some conservatives with fascists at times, are at pains to distinguish between authoritarian conservatives and fascists. Indeed, as Paxton has remarked, 'nothing provokes a fight – or a lawsuit – faster than being latitudinarian about fascism in France'.[125] For Paxton and Burrin, La Rocque was an authoritarian, not a fascist. For Burrin, it is a distinction which applies to the Vichy regime as well. One reason the Vichy regime was not fascist, he writes, was because of 'the power of conservative elites at the head of state'. These elites were 'solid elements' who 'provided a barrier to the development of fascism'. As long as the traditional right held 'control of the terrain', the Vichy regime remained non-fascist.[126] Even Paxton, who is hardly an apologist for Vichy, insisted in 1995, speaking of European fascism in general, that there were major differences between 'mechanical' (or new) elites who supported fascism and 'organic' (or traditional) elites who did not – although he conceded that the borders between the two were sometimes 'blurred'.[127] For Griffin, the borders were not even blurred, given the 'sharp' distinction between the two.

And yet in Italy in the 1920s and in Germany in the 1930s not only were the borders indeed blurred, but many fully-fledged crossovers to fascism occurred. In Germany, scores of authoritarian conservatives, especially younger ones from socially or educationally elite backgrounds, joined the Nazi Party and, as Michael Kater has shown, were given a disproportionate share of leadership positions: 'While the elite was consistently overrepresented in the rank and file of the party, this situation was more evident in the cadres: the higher the cadre, the greater the degree of overrepresentation. ... The Nazi functionary corps was not a counterelite composed of "marginal" men on the fringe, from largely plebeian origins, as Daniel Lerner and others have stated.'[128]

In Italy after 1919, social and cultural conservatives became a major faction within the *Partito Nazionale Fasciste* (PNF), whose membership jumped from 80,000 to 180,000 between April and May 1921. De Grand notes that the PNF was no monolithic block but rather a 'heterogeneous coalition' composed of six 'hyphenated' fascisms: (1) syndicalist Fascism, (2) modernist intellectual Fascism, (3) rural Fascism, (4) technocratic Fascism, (5) nationalist Fascism, and (6) conservative Fascism.[129] After 1924, the conservative and the nationalist Fascists (who agreed on economic policy) became the two most dominant factions within the PNF. In 1924 an alliance was forged between the Fascist regime and industrial and financial elite groups, with the Italian Association of Joint Stock Companies tapping its members for contributions to the Fascist electoral fund. Conservative Fascists were given prominent positions within the state bureaucracy, from which the *squadristi* leadership was largely excluded.

The *squadristi* were generally lower-middle-class Fascists from small towns who wished to move into the governing class and who resented Mussolini's siding with Italy's traditional elites. These 'new men', however, were hardly leftists, since they despised 'the reds' as much as wealthier Fascists did. In 1920 and 1921, as Blackshirts, they had helped repress Socialist strikes and organisations in the countryside. They believed in upward social mobility not Marxist egalitarianism. They came from the intermediate elites whom Mussolini favoured over factory and farm workers, but who were favoured much less than the country's top elites. These 'populists' lost out to their economic superiors, although not nearly as much as the syndicalist Fascists did.[130] After he came to power, Mussolini made major concessions to the Vatican and to Italy's industrialists, large landowners and army leaders – all bastions of traditional conservatism.[131]

Within the Italian Fascist Party itself, conservatives also held sway. In his study of the social composition of the PNF, Marco Reveilli speaks not only of the 'conspicuous presence' of industrialists, upper-class landowners, and higher civil servants within the party in 1927 but also of their 'hegemony'. Between 1927 and 1933, the PNF expanded its membership but continued to be an organisation 'based on petty and middling bourgeois rank and file membership and *haute bourgeois* hegemony (industrialists and landowners)'.[132] Indeed, Reveilli finds that the party was so firmly under the control of industrial *haute bourgeois* in areas where large-scale capitalist enterprises existed that 'the Fascist Party functioned at times as if it was simply the extension into public life of decisions taken at the company level'. At the same time, in predominantly rural areas, the party was the expression of 'the political demands of landowners'.[133] In 1928, among the ninety-three federal secretaries of the PNF were two marquises, two barons, one count, one duke and seven university lecturers. In 1929, 16.8 per cent of the new Fascist assembly elected by plebiscite were landowners, industrialists, bankers and senior public or private officials; 9.5 per cent were university lecturers. Among the four hundred new members there were twenty-seven nobles.[134] Every governor of Rome during the Fascist era, except one, came from the aristocracy. This was Fascist 'populism'.

Culturally, many conservative Fascists, particularly in rural areas, were highly traditionalist. 'Their influence,' De Grand writes, 'was already evident in the 1921 platform of the party, which abandoned populist, republican, and anticlerical rhetoric in favor of a free enterprise fascism compatible with both the Church and the monarchy.' De Grand states that 'in the end the regime's collaboration with traditional culture enhanced the passive consensus that grew up around fascism during the early thirties, but it also reinforced the status quo against any effort by Fascist extremists to push toward a radical break with the past'.[135]

To argue that Colonel de La Rocque was not fascist because he supported his country's organic elites and many of their members supported him would eliminate many conservative Fascists in Italy from this classification as well. This presents a problem for Burrin because he has written that Italian fascism is the 'obligatory point of departure' for any definition of fascism.[136]

In Germany, too, as mentioned previously, the Nazi Party won the support of many from elite backgrounds. Shelley Baranowski has documented the widespread moral bankruptcy that took place among Germany's Protestant elites, including prominent church leaders, both before and after Hitler came to power.[137] In the Wehrmacht, young Junker aristocrats were among the many lieutenants, captains and majors who favoured Hitler before 1933. The generals were more sceptical, but in 1934 the SA was repressed by Hitler to assuage them (a loyalty oath to his person was the price they paid in return). Baranowski reminds us that the attempt on Hitler's life by Colonel Claus von Stauffenberg on 20 July 1944 only took place after eleven years of Nazi rule and only after military setbacks had weakened the Führer's support in the army. Moreover, the conspirators themselves had once been 'far from immune to the enticements of National Socialism'.[138]

There is another problem with the contrast which Paxton and Burrin draw between fascism and conservative authoritarianism which also bears on the debate over Colonel de La Rocque and French fascism. These scholars object to any view of fascism which ignores its different stages and reduces fascism to a 'fixed essence'. Burrin objects to dwelling on a 'supposed essence' of fascism which ignores its various deviations, and Paxton criticises specialists who 'treat generic fascism in a static manner'. For Paxton, it is better to study fascism 'in motion, paying more attention to processes than to essences'.[139] This is good advice, since fascists were often opportunistic in reacting to changing circumstances and appealing to different clienteles. Yet when it comes to describing traditional conservatives who 'compromised' with fascism, the two historians seem to switch analytical gears, attributing to these conservatives an essence which remained nonfascist despite the support which they gave to fascism.

Although Paxton acknowledges that the frontiers between conservative authoritarianism and fascism may be 'fluid' and that conservatives and fascists may cross them in either direction, he describes upper-class conservatives who supported fascism in Italy and France as 'allies' or 'accomplices' of fascism rather than as fascists themselves, as persons who 'coopted' fascists but were not coopted in return.[140] In this presentation, conservatives who engage in 'reciprocal flexibility' with fascists remain conservatives. Fascism changes as it passes through different stages, but conservatism does not. The selective essentialism of this interpretation spares members of organic elites, but not those beneath them, from being considered fascists.[141] Paxton's interpretation differs strikingly from De Grand's and Reveilli's, which treat conservative Fascists within the PNF as fully-fledged members of a Fascist coalition, indeed as the *most influential* members within that coalition. De Grand and Reveilli regard them as no less Fascist because the constituencies they represented were not plebeian.

Paxton's approach raises a number of questions. In his account of Henry Dorgères's Greenshirts in *French Peasant Fascism*, he describes Adolphe Pointier and Jacques Le Roy Ladurie, who actively supported Dorgères, as 'two of the most influential conservative agrarian leaders in France'. Did their belonging to an organic elite prevent them from becoming fascists? Were they allies or accomplices of fascism but not fascist themselves, not even temporarily? Was their essence unchanged by their acts? Were they any less fascist than the rural thugs Dorgères used to intimidate striking farm workers in the countryside, thugs whose actions served the material interests of these very same notables? At what point do organic conservatives *become* fascists, and at what point do they *cease* to be?[142] If fascism is best understood, as Paxton rightly contends, by the 'function' it serves for its followers – and organising a more muscular opposition to the political Left was certainly a major part of that function in the 1920s and 1930s – then did not Pointier and Le Roy Ladurie *behave* like fascists, if only for a few months? And if it was a matter of some organic conservatives becoming fascists and others not, did the former have to abandon their conservatism for the conversion to occur?

Fascism on a continuum

Paxton's useful notion that there is a point on a 'continuum' where a person or a movement or a regime may be considered more fascist than not is marred by his assumption that fascism is only 'complete' when it is no longer compromised by conservatism :

> The frontiers between authoritarianism and fascism are at best imprecise … . They were never more fluid than in the 1930s, when fascism was ascendant. In that decade a continuum ran from the clerical authoritarianism of Franco, Salazar, or Dollfuss – all colored to some degree by fascist borrowings in their décor and one-party systems – through the incomplete fascism of Mussolini *who shared power with conservatives* [italics mine], to the most integrally fascist regime of all, Nazi Germany. *But even Hitler shared power with conservatives* [italics mine]. No regime in the 1930s was 100 per cent fascist, although many authoritarian leaders had taken a few steps in that direction.[143]

Paxton applies the same standard when he judges Dorgères to be much closer to fascism than Colonel de La Rocque. 'Dorgères belongs somewhere along that continuum of fascist-authoritarian mixtures', Paxton writes. 'He was authoritarian in his organic conception of society, but he leaned toward fascism in his glorification of action, his uniformed young men, and his cult of the "chief".'[144] La Rocque, on the other hand, was further from fascism because he had 'a less confrontational style' and 'was perceived by both supporters and disappointed hotheads after 1936 as reassuringly traditional and orderly'. La Rocque was also no fascist because he 'appealed to a broader constituency than the uniforms, fascist salutes, oaths, and sweaty shirtsleeves of Doriot'.[145] That La Rocque also glorified action (when it was opportune), that the PSF also had a cult of the chief, that it was not opposition to confrontations in principle but fear of losing them in practice that gave the colonel pause, and that Mussolini and Hitler also appealed to broad constituencies beyond their Blackshirts and Brownshirts are missing from Paxton's analysis. As for the reference to fascist uniforms, two years later Paxton agreed with Orwell that the clothing fascists wore was far less important than the functions fascists performed.[146] For all their differences, the primary appeal of La Rocque's, Dorgères's and Doriot's movements was their offer to resist the political left more decisively than democratic rightists had, a function that was far more basic to fascism throughout Europe at the time than Doriot's sweaty shirtsleeves.

Both Paxton and Burrin see La Rocque as more akin to Franco in Spain or Salazar in Portugal than to Mussolini in Italy or Hitler in Germany: like La Rocque, the Iberian leaders are considered too conservative to be fascist, even if they borrowed some of the 'décor' of fascism. They too were authoritarians, not fascists. Once again, the emphasis is on dichotomies rather than syntheses and on differences of *kind* rather than differences of *degree*. In their studies of the Salazar and Franco regimes, António Costa Pinto and Paul Preston take a less essentialist approach. Employing a concept of 'fascistization', Pinto concludes that the Salazar regime never became *preponderantly* fascist but that, in reaction to the electoral victory of a Popular Front coalition in 1936 in neighbouring Spain, it became, for a time, *increasingly* fascist.[147] Similarly, Preston demonstrates how Franco, following the death in 1936 of José Antonio Primo de Rivera, cultivated the support of Spanish fascists (more than once speaking at their rallies in a fascist uniform and on at least one occasion joining the crowd in singing the Falangist anthem *Cara al sol*). Not only did Franco welcome the Falange into his ruling coalition, but in 1941, Preston writes, he 'gave free reign to his proHitlerian rhetoric', declaring that the Allies were on 'the wrong side' of the war and paying homage to 'these moments when the German armies lead the battle [against the Soviet Union] for which Europe and Christianity have for so many years longed'.[148]

This is not to say that there were no differences between fascist and nonfascist authoritarian conservatives in interwar Europe (the most obvious being, where German Nazism was concerned, the rejection of biological racism by many conservatives) but rather that these differences were often more a matter of degree than of irreconcilable essences. Fascists had (1) a *greater* tendency to apply military values to civilian life and to extol its own paramilitary units and youth organisations as safeguards against Marxism (whereas some authoritarian conservatives, when it came to crushing revolutionary threats from the Left, were more inclined to leave it completely up to the army and the police); (2) a *greater* hatred of cultural 'decadence' and 'degeneration'; (3) a *greater* desire to create a mass of nondecadent 'new men', but new men committed to upward social mobility for the few not to more social egalitarianism for the many (again the model was more military than civilian); (4) a *greater* appeal to the young ('virility' was the catchword); and (5) a *more intense* nationalism. Fascists also displayed (6) a *greater* willingness to engage in mass mobilisation, but a mass mobilisation which essentially served socially conservative not socially radical ends and which taught that material differences were unimportant compared to 'spiritual' values and the unity of the Volk (class conflict was to be replaced with an 'integral' nationalism which would allow a poor fascist and a rich fascist to become comrades despite the remaining economic divide between them); (7) a *greater* interest in promoting populism, but a right-wing populism which did not threaten traditional property relationships and which fiercely opposed leftists who did; (8) a *more virulent* demonology, blaming *more harshly* Communists, Socialists, Freemasons, internationalists, and, in many but not all cases, Jews for most of the nation's ills; and (9) a *greater* taste for repression in dealing with these 'unpatriotic' souls, especially when it was safe to gratify that taste. La Rocque's movement displayed all these features.[149]

The more authoritarian conservatives felt threatened by the Left, the greater their susceptibility to fascism. Rather than abandoning their conservatism to join fascism, many believed, with considerable justification, that they were preserving it. There *was* a continuum, and along it were increasing degrees of fascistisation, but at the point where fascism prevailed, no assault on traditional elites or their economic interests was required, at least in peacetime.

There was far more cooperation than conflict between organic and mechanical elites under fascist regimes. This was abetted by a fascist version of 'the American Dream', which taught that superior individuals not born into wealth might move into the highest reaches of government and society where they would share power with, not overthrow, those who *had* been born into wealth. Just as in the American Dream Horatio Alger did not attack J.P. Morgan, in the Fascist Dream the paramilitary youth did not attack the established landowner, industrialist or businessman (indeed, he was their saviour) – except, of course, in cases where fascists judged them incorrigibly wedded to political democracy, cultural liberalism or some other form of 'decadence'. In the mid-1920s, the Faisceau's Georges Valois praised the 'great idea' of careers open to talent, as did Colonel de La Rocque in the mid-1930s. Valois also proclaimed class conciliation, not class warfare, as one of the major goals of fascism, as did other fascists of the era and as did La Rocque.[150] Like careers open to talent, this ideal, too, favoured cooperation, not conflict, between organic and mechanical elites.

Charisma, imperialism and irrationalism

Another consensus argument is that fascism is distinguished from authoritarian conservatism by the charisma of its leaders, and La Rocque, who was a 'cold' public speaker, lacked such charisma. Certainly, his personality was not the same as Hitler's or Mussolini's, but, then, charisma comes in many versions. Like La Rocque, Charles de Gaulle (who was no fascist) had an austere military manner, but this seems to have enhanced rather than diminished his charisma. At the same time, as Ian Kershaw has pointed out, compared to other aspects of fascism, the role of charisma can be greatly overrated.[151]

It has also been suggested that the PSF was not fascist because it failed to adopt the aggressive imperialism of Nazi Germany and Fascist Italy. This view discounts the fact that it had less need to do so, inasmuch as France already had important imperial possessions in North Africa and Indochina. La Rocque was a strong defender of this empire, and the PSF, like previous French fascist movements, enjoyed considerable popularity among the European population of Algeria. A territorially satisfied fascist is still a fascist.

A final consensus argument is that fascism appealed primarily to irrationalism, and La Rocque was opposed to 'contagions of madness'.[152] Stanley Payne has argued that traditional conservatives were more rational and pragmatic than fascists, who glorified vitalism and irreason.[153] Eugen Weber has referred to fascism as more a 'fever' than an ideology.[154] Paxton has written that fascists 'despise thought and reason' and 'subordinate thought and reason not to faith, as did the traditional Right, but to the promptings of the blood and the historic destiny of the group'.[155] Griffin maintains that a myth of palingenetic ultranationalism, a myth meant to arouse strong emotions, was at the 'core' of fascism.[156] There were indeed strong nationalistic emotions involved in fascism, and the PSF, too, did its best to arouse them. 'France for the French' was one of its rallying cries.

But there were also strong rational reasons why certain constituencies supported fascism during the interwar period, that is, reasons that served the particular social, economic, political or cultural interests of these groups. To be sure, there was little that was liberal, democratic or humanitarian about this rationality. The 'rational', after all, need not be fair.[157] As many scholars have emphasised (De Grand, Weisbrod, Abse, Lyttelton, Kershaw, Kater, and Paxton being among the more recent), defending various middle- and upper-class economic and status interests against threats from the Left played a major role in the rise of European fascism – and, *on balance*, it seems to me, played a far greater role than irrationalism. Even increasing antagonism towards Jews in France in the mid-1930s had its coldly rational side, coinciding as it did with the objections of some French citizens to competition from Jewish immigrants in the 'liberal' professions and with concerns that impoverished immigrants might become a burden to French taxpayers.[158] Nor should one underestimate how irrational beliefs, including the most callous, can sometimes rationalise the material desires of their believers, however 'spiritual' the latter may claim to be.

Was 'France' fascist?

Finally, what if one does conclude that La Rocque's movement in the late 1930s was substantially fascist, especially if one compares it to Italian Fascism? What if the various consensus arguments that have been contested here are indeed problematic and that both the CF and the PSF were very much drawn to the magnetic field of fascism? Does this mean that 'France' was fascist in the late 1930s? Obviously not, obviously not the whole of France. Most French Radicals, Socialists and democratic conservatives remained opposed to fascism during the interwar period, and even French Communists who bowed to the Nazi-Soviet pact of 1939 were hardly converts to domestic fascism.[159] At worst, as in Italy and Germany when political democracy still operated, no more than a third, probably no more than a sixth, of France's adult population was tempted by fascism. Just as the great majority of Italians were not Fascists in 1922 and the great majority of Germans were not Nazis in 1932, the great majority of the French were not fascists in 1937.

I only state this truism because it seems to me that one of the favourite ploys of French fascists and of extreme nationalists in general is to equate their countries with themselves when they or their cohorts are criticised. Anyone who finds fault with their political or military behaviour, especially if he or she is a foreigner, is accused of attacking the whole nation. Appealing to nationalism thus becomes a clever way of avoiding criticism and winning sympathy.[160] To equate criticisms of the PSF with criticisms of France entire is similarly fallacious. One part of France is not all of France and, in this case, hardly the best part. France is not indivisible.

By the same token, the fact that La Rocque's movement was not a majority movement does not mean that France was as immune to native fascism during the interwar period as consensus scholars have claimed. Italian Fascism and German Nazism were not majority movements either before they came to power.[161] Indeed, had the timing of events been different, had Hitler's 'Blood Purge' of 1934 not alienated many French conservatives from fascism by murdering certain prominent German conservatives and Catholics, had the Popular Front not helped break the agricultural strikes in France in 1936, and, above all, had the Popular Front itself not been defeated by parliamentary means in 1937 and 1938, France might have been even less immune.[162]

Notes

1. M. Dobry, 'Février 1934 et la découverte de l'allergie de la société française à la "Révolution fasciste"' *Revue française de sociologie*, July–December 1989, p. 511.
2. Serge Berstein estimates that by 1938 the PSF had some 800,000 party members (though Philippe Machefer and Philippe Burrin have put the figure at closer to a million.) The Italian Fascist Party had no more than 200,000 party members on the eve of its coming to power in 1922. The PSF's membership was roughly the same size

as the Nazi Party in Germany in 1932, which had approximately 850,000 members (950,000 if one counts Nazi Youth), and France's population was only two-thirds as large as Germany's.

3. See R. Soucy, *French Fascism: the Second Wave, 1933–1939*, New Haven, London, 1995, pp. 204–79.

4. R. Rémond, 'Y a-t-il un fascisme français', *Terre Humaine*, vol. 7–8, 1952, pp. 37–47; R. Rémond, *Notre Siècle, 1918–1988*, Paris, 1988, pp. 216, 105; P. Machefer, ' Sur quelques aspects de l'activité du Colonel de La Rocque et du "Progrès Social Français" pendant la seconde guerre mondiale', *Revue d'histoire de la deuxième guerre mondiale*, 58, 1963, p. 54; M. Winock, *Nationalism, Anti-Semitism, and Fascism in France*, Stanford, 1988, pp. 177–94; S. Berstein, 'La France des années trente allergique au fascisme : à propos d'un livre de Zeev Sternhell', *XXe siècle*, no. 2, April 1984, pp. 83, 89, 92–94; J. Nobécourt, 'Le Pen a-t-il pris la suite du colonel de La Rocque?', *Le Monde*, 8–9 May, 1988; J. Nobécourt, *Le Colonel de La Rocque*, Paris, 1996, p. 954; P. Milza, *Fascisme français passé et présent*, Paris, 1987, pp. 135–42; P. Burrin, 'Le fascisme', in *Histoire des droites en France*, ed. J.-F. Sirinelli, Paris, 1992, vol. I, pp. 603–52; P. Burrin, *Fascisme, nazisme, autoritarisme*, Paris, 2000, pp. 257–59; J. Jackson, *The Popular Front in France: Defending Democracy, 1934–38*, Cambridge, 1988, pp. 253, 107; R. Eatwell, *Fascism: A History*, New York, 1995, pp. 202–5; R. Griffin, *Fascism*, Oxford, 1995, p. 10; K. Passmore, 'Boy Scoutism for Grown-Ups ? Paramilitarism in the Croix de Feu and the Parti Social Français', *French Historical Studies*, vol. 19, Fall 1995, pp. 527–57; K. Passmore, *From Liberalism to Fascism: The Right in France in a French Province, 1928–1939*, Cambridge, 1997, p. 251; K. Passmore, 'The Croix de Feu and Fascism : A Foreign Thesis Obstinately Maintained', in *The Development of the Radical Right in France*, ed. Edward J. Arnold, New York, 2000, pp. 100–18. (Passmore regards the Croix de Feu as fascist, but not the PSF); E. Weber, *The Hollow Years: France in the 1930s*, New York, London, 1994, p. 120; S. Payne, *A History of Fascism*, Madison, Wisconsin, 1995), pp. 15, 294–95; R. Paxton, 'Review of Robert Soucy, "French Fascism"', *French Politics and Society*, vol. 13, no. 4, Fall 1995, p. 108; S.M. Kennedy, 'Reconciling the Nation Against Decadence : the Croix de Feu, the Parti Social Français and French Politics', *Ph.D thesis*, York University, North York, Ontario, Canada 1998. Kennedy is critical of many consensus arguments but finally concludes, like Paxton and Burrin, that La Rocque was an 'authoritarian conservative', not a fascist.

5. For nonconsensus views see : W. Irvine, 'Fascism in France and the Strange Case of the Croix de Feu', *Journal of Modern History*, vol. 63, June 1991, pp. 271–95; R. Soucy, *French Fascism: the First Wave, 1924–1933*, New Haven and London, 1986; Soucy, *The Second Wave*; Dobry, 'Février 1934', p. 511; and S.H. Goodfellow, *Between the Swastika and the Cross of Lorraine: Fascisms in Interwar Alsace* , DeKalb, IL, 1999, pp. 135–48; Z. Sternhell in *Le Monde*, November 15, 1996; and Z. Sternhell, *Ni droite ni gauche: L'idéologie fasciste en France*, Brussels, 2000, pp. 83–92.

6. R. Rémond, *La Droite en France de 1815 à nos jours*, Paris, 1954, pp. 12, 211–18; S. Berstein, 'La France des années trente allergique au fascisme', pp. 83, 89, 92–94. Nobécourt writes that La Rocque's denials of fascism 'only indicate that nationalism itself forbade La Rocque to think of himself as a fascist'. Nobécourt, *Le Colonel de La Rocque*, pp. 176–77.

7. S.J. Woolf, ed., *European Fascism*, New York, 1968, pp. 183, 142–43.

8. See Soucy, *The Second Wave*, p. 140.

9. Ibid., pp. 152–55. Rémond, *Notre Siècle*, pp. 216, 105; Milza, *Fascisme français*, p. 137; Nobécourt, 'Le Pen a-t-il pris la suite du colonel de La Rocque ?', p. 8. For La Rocque's critique of Nazi racial theory and his acceptance of right-wing Jews into the CF, see La Rocque, *Service public*, pp. 154–61, 199 and Soucy, *The Second Wave*, pp.152–56.

10. S. Zuccotti, *The Italians and the Holocaust*, Lincoln, NB, 1987, p. 27. Michael Ledeen has described Mussolini's opposition to anti-Semitism before 1933 and explained why it was not uncommon at the time for Italian Jews to join the Fascist Party. M. Ledeen, 'Italian Jews and Fascism', *Judaism: A Quarterly of Jewish Life and Thought*, vol. 18, no. 3, Summer 1969, p. 282. Fascist racial laws against Jews in Italy were not passed until 1938, but there were earlier occasions, starting in 1933, when Mussolini unleashed anti-Semitism in the fascist press when it suited his immediate political purposes and leashed it again when it no longer did. In 1936 it was revived in a more sustained way and prepared the way for the Italian racial laws of 1938. See Zuccotti, pp. 28–51. See also J. Blatt, 'The Battle of Turin, 1933–1936', *Journal of Modern Italian Studies*, vol. I, no. 1, 1995, p. 31. Alexander De Grand notes that since Italian Fascism 'had no internal defenses against Nazi racism' and ' there was no moral core to the movement or regime', part of the Fascist coalition could easily be turned in an anti-Semitic direction. Email from De Grand to Soucy, 14 January, 2002. Michael Marrus and Robert Paxton have pointed out the lack of popularity of anti-Semitism with the Italian public under Mussolini's regime and how as late as 1943 Fascist Italy remained a haven for Jews escaping Vichy France. M. Marrus and R.O. Paxton, *Vichy France and the Jews*, New York, 1981, pp. 316–18.

11. Payne, *A History of Fascism 1914–1945*, p. 250.

12. Pierre Taittinger, *Les Cahiers de jeune France*, Paris, 1926, p. 28.

13. Georges Valois, *Le Fascisme*, Paris, 1927, pp. 57–58, 60; Jacques Doriot in *L'Emancipation nationale*, 14 November 1936. In the same article, Doriot made it clear that he welcomed only assimilated Jews into the PPF. The same was true for Valois, who had previously been highly anti-Semitic as a member of the Action Française but who adopted a more tolerant posture as head of the Faisceau. He drew a distinction between 'pious' Jews who contributed to the 'spiritual treasure' of France and 'emancipated' Jews who worshipped the 'golden calf'. It is true, as Samuel Kalman has pointed out, that some Faisceau spokesmen employed a number of anti-Semitic stereotypes in condemning left-wing and 'greedy' Jews and that Valois himself denounced Jews who were part of the 'international financial plutocracy'. Valois also employed a coded anti-Semitism when he focused his denunciations of foreigners in France on individuals with Jewish names. However, his solution to 'the Jewish problem', i.e. to Jews who were greedy, left-wing, or unassimilated, was not their extermination or deportation but their integration into a Christian economy and their eventual conversion to Christianity. S. Kalman, 'Reconsidering Fascist Antisemitism and Xenophobia in 1920s France: The Doctrinal Contribution of George Valois and the Faisceau', *French History*, January 2003. As for those whom Valois considered 'good' Jews (including Jean Mayer and Jacques Marx, who contributed articles to the Faisceau's newspaper, *Nouveau Siècle*, and Victor Mayer and an engineer named Salomon, who helped finance the movement), Valois had only positive things to say. In his book *Fascism*, he wrote that the people of Israel had certain virtues which would contribute significantly to the economic renewal of France: an 'appetite for change' and an 'incontestable creative fever' (p. 60). For more on Valois's attitude towards Jews, see Soucy, *The First Wave*, pp. 134–35, 152–54, 171–72. For possible reasons why Valois felt the need to reject blanket anti-Semitism as head of the Faisceau, see R. Soucy, 'Functional Hating: French Fascist Demonology between the Wars', *Contemporary French Civilization*, vol. XXIII, No. 2, Summer/Fall 1999, pp.158–61. Some of the same considerations may have affected La Rocque's 1930s position on anti-Semitism as well, along with his soldierly respect for Jews who had fought for France in the First World War. The fact that the circulation of the newspaper of the notoriously anti-Semitic Action Française fell from 60,000 to just over half that amount between 1925 and 1935 may also have had something to do with it.

14. La Rocque, *Disciplines d'Action*, Clermont-Ferrand, 1941, pp. 97–99.
15. La Rocque, *Service public*, pp. 160–62. See also Soucy, *The Second Wave*, pp. 153–54.
16. La Rocque cited by William Irvine in 'Fascism in France and the Strange Case of the Croix de Feu', pp. 292–93. See also *La Flamme*, 1 August, 1937, 10 February, 1938, 19 March, 1938, 20 May, 1938, 10 February, 1938.
17. The PSF was not a confessional party (it heralded its ecumenicalism), but most of its members, including La Rocque himself, were Catholic. However, under Vichy, La Rocque, like Hitler in Germany, was strongly opposed to Catholic Church leaders intervening in politics. La Rocque, *Disciplines d'Action*, p. 90.
18. Payne, *A History of Fascism*, pp. 9, 195.
19. Milza, *Fascisme français*, pp. 137–38.
20. 'La Rocque se réclamait du christianisme et déclarait son inspiration dans le catholicisme social, alors que, pour toute l'exploitation que Hitler et Mussolini faisaient de la religion, la contradiction de leur idéologie avec le christianisme apparaissait à quiconque prêtait attention à leurs propos.' Burrin, *Fascisme, nazisme, autoritarisme*, p. 259.
21. Payne, *A History of Fascism*, passim; S.J. Woolf, ed., *European Fascism*, New York, 1968, pp. 88–216, 280–336.
22. Payne, *A History of Fascism*, p. 345.
23. Alexander De Grand, *Fascist Italy and Nazi Germany: the 'Fascist Style of Rule'*, London and New York, 1995, p. 56.
24. S. Baranowski, *The Confessing Church, Conservative Elites, and the Nazi State*, Lewiston, Canada, 1986, pp. 48–49.
25. R. Rychlak, *Hitler, the War and the Pope*, Columbus, MS, 2000, p. 254.
26. J. Cornwell, *Hitler's Pope*, New York, 2000, p. 215.
27. D. Bergen, *The German Christian Movement in the Third Reich: Twisted Cross*, Chapel Hill and London, 1996, pp. 1, 2, 5–7, 8.
28. Cornwell, *Hitler's Pope*, pp. 121–24, 135–36, 147.
29. A. Costa Pinto, *Salazar's Dictatorship and European Fascism*, New York, 1995, p. 146.
30. Soucy, *The First Wave*, pp. 48, 49–50, 54–55, 83–85, 87, 101, 105–8, 113, 202–4, 230–31; Soucy, *The Second Wave*, pp. 39, 99–100, 130, 131, 136, 194–95.
31. Soucy, *Fascist Intellectual: Drieu La Rochelle*, Berkeley, Los Angeles and London, 1979, pp. 336, 338; Soucy, *The Second Wave*, pp. 296–97.
32. For the conservative (and dominant) wing of the Italian Fascist Party after 1924, see A. De Grand, *Italian Fascism: Its Origins and Development*, Lincoln, Nebraska and London, 2000, pp. 56, 140–46, 149.
33. Passmore, 'The Croix de Feu and Fascism', p.112.
34. See Soucy, *The Second Wave*, pp. 180–81.
35. Jackson, *The Popular Front in France*, p.46; Milza, *Fascisme français*, pp.135–36, 140–41; Berstein, 'La Ligue', pp. 101–3; Nobécourt, 'Le Pen a-t-il pris la suite de La Rocque?'; *Le Monde* 8–9 May, 1988; Nobécourt, *Colonel de La Rocque*, p. 347; Paxton, *French Peasant Fascism*, p. 158.
36. René Rémond has written that by providing French conservatives with a viable democratic alternative to fascism, the PSF served to 'immunize a sector of opinion against the fascist temptation'. Rémond, *Notre Siècle*, p. 216. See also Winock, *Nationalism, Anti-Semitism, and Fascism in France*, p. 190.
37. La Rocque cited in Soucy, *The Second Wave*, pp. 138–39.
38. Ibid., pp. 140, 141, 159; Le Flambeau, 25 May, 1935.
39. In July 1934, for example, 1,200 CF and JP activists in Paris staged a common gathering at the Arc de Triomphe. In 1935 in Lyon, Lille and Algiers, the CF held joint meetings with SF as well as JP members, and in October that year a CF meeting at Nantes was attended by both Action Française (AF) and SF members. Indeed, it was not uncommon for members of the AF, SF and JP to be members of the CF as well.

Kennedy writes: 'It is true that the Croix de Feu did not participate in actions such as throwing acid in Pierre Cot's face in May 1935. But it did not shy away from occasionally cooperating with the organizations that did, or from trying to attract their members'. When the anti-Semitic SF, with its blue shirts and fascist salutes, fell into financial difficulties in the spring of 1934, many of its members, including apparently the whole SF section in Montpellier, joined the CF. According to police reports, in several localities in France the CF was the primary beneficiary of the SF's collapse. Kennedy, 'Reconciling the Nation against Democracy', pp. 187–89, 255, 251–52. For more on the SF crossovers, see Archives Nationales, F7 13239, 17, 21, 26 July, 27 August and 18 October, 1934.

40.   Passmore, 'The Croix de Feu and Fascism', p. 111; *Le Flambeau*, 1 January and 12 October, 1935.

41.   *Le Fambeau*, 23 March, 1935.

42.   'La seule idée de briguer un mandat me donne des nausées : C'est une question de tempérament'. Archives Nationales, 451 AP 129, 2 January 1936. In 1941 La Rocque again expressed his 'aversion à l'égard des mandats électifs'. La Rocque, *Disciplines d'Action*, p. 15.

43.   'Mépriser le suffrage universel … ne résiste pas à l'examen. Ni Mussolini ni Hitler … ne sont tombé dans cette erreur. L'hitlérisme, en particulier, s'est hissé à la toute puissance par les élections. … L'hitlérisme est devenu une force politique prépondérante seulement le jour où, en [1930], il fait entrer 107 des siens au Reichstag.' Archives Nationales, Paris, 451 AP 91, document 162, Winter of 1935–36, pp. 3, 4–5.

44.   Griffin, *Fascism*, p .4.

45.   Kennedy, 'Reconciling the Nation against Democracy', pp. 280–82.

46.   Taittinger himself had been elected to the Chamber of Deputies in 1919 and was regularly reelected through 1935. In 1925, he called for the destruction of 'Parliament-King' and for a plebiscite to elect a leader who would be granted full powers. In 1926 he explained that although he regarded parliamentarianism as anachronistic and noxious he would use any weapon, including that of electoral politics, to defeat communism. 'If we vote,' he declared, 'it is not to serve this parliamentarianism but to make use of it.' This was the same rationale which Maurras gave for members of the AF who ran for the Chamber of Deputies in 1924 (AF candidates received 328,000 votes that year). In 1928, seventy-seven Deputies in the French parliament were either official members of the JP or financial donors. Soucy, *The First Wave*, pp. 25, 67. Paxton notes that Dorgères ran for a seat in the Chamber of Deputies in 1935 after spending years 'denouncing all parliamentary politics as a sink of iniquity.' Paxton, *French Peasant Fascism*, p. 64.

47.   Jackson, *The Popular Front in France*, p. 107.

48.   In 1937 the PDP questioned the 'depth of the [PSF's] commitment to democracy', and an FR spokesman accused the PSF of being 'fascistic'.

49.   'Si le mouvement croît spectaculairement après la dissolution des ligues, ce n'est pas, comme le veut l'école apologétique, parce que la masse des nouveaux adhérents s'enrôle dans un mouvement soudainement gagné aux vertus de la démocratie mais, au contraire, parce que de plus en plus nombreux sont alors ceux qui partagent le dégoût de l'ordre existant.' Sternhell, *Ni droite ni gauche* (3rd edition), Brussels, 2000, p. 92.

50.   Kennedy, 'Reconciling the Nation against Democracy', pp. 211–13.

51.   Cited in Soucy, *The First Wave*, p. 96.

52.   Kennedy, 'Reconciling the Nation against Democracy', pp. 186–87.

53.   Passmore, 'The Croix de Feu and Fascism', pp. 100–18.

54.   Kennedy, 'Reconciling the Nation against Democracy', pp. 270, 272.

55.   Ibid., pp. 216–18.

56. Ibid., pp. 218, 223, 286, 325, 331, 351–52.
57. Dobry, 'Février 1934', p. 511.
58. R.D. Zaretsky, 'Neither Left, nor Right, nor Straight ahead : Recent Books on Fascism in France', *The Journal of Modern History*, vol. 73, March 2001, p. 121.
59. Curiously, Zaretsky is aware of these stages in another part of his essay (ibid. p. 123), but ignores them on this issue.
60. Serge Berstein, for example, denies that La Rocque was a fascist partly on the grounds that La Rocque 'did not think at all of utilizing the force which he disposed of to overthrow the Republic and institute in France a strong regime'. Berstein, 'La Ligue', p. 100.
61. Archives Nationales, Paris, F7 12966, 20 February, 1937.
62. 'Nous aurions eu à supporter le double choc de foules grisées par la démagogie et de la force publique aux ordres gouvernementaux : la victoire des 'rouges' était certaine.' La Rocque, *Disciplines d'Action*, pp. 29–30.
63. Paxton, 'Five Stages of Fascism', *Journal of Modern History*, vol. 70, no. 1, March 1998, p. 17.
64. Archives Nationales, F7 13983, May 1936.
65. Soucy, *The First Wave*, pp. 57, 58, 179, 185, 186 and Soucy, *The Second Wave*, p. 68.
66. I. Kershaw, *Hitler 1889–1936: Hubris*, New York, 1998, pp. 349, 350.
67. 'Au-dessous d'énormes manchettes qui appellent à la guerre contre la trahison de l'intérieur, le ton se fait plus violent, le style plus démagogique, les attaques contre la gauche, Blum et le Front Populaire plus vulgaire'. Sternhell, *Ni droite ni gauche* (3rd edition), Brussels, 2000, p. 92.
68. Paul Creyssel, Parti Social Français, *A tous les patriotes quelles que soient leur origines, leur confessions, leur professions* (Paris, undated but situated in 1936), p. 51.
69. *Le Petit Journal*, 6 July and 7 July, 1937, 6 February, 1938; *Le Flambeau*, 9 July, 1939.
70. Burrin, *Fascisme, nazisme, autoritarisme*, p. 258. See also Milza, *Fascisme français*, p. 135.
71. See, for example, *Le Flambeau*, 11 April, 1936.
72. Colonel de La Rocque, *Service public*, Paris, 1935, pp. 263–64.
73. Kennedy, 'Reconciling the Nation Against Democracy', p. 227.
74. Cited in Laurent Bonnevay, *Les journées sanglantes de février 1934*, Paris, 1934, p. 144.
75. Milza, *Fascisme français*, p.135.
76. On 5 July 1936, PSF members clashed with police at the Place d'Étoile, and 105 people were injured. That same month Clermont-Ferrand's section of the PSF briefly occupied the prefecture of the Puy-de-Dôme, and in November PSF militants occupied factories in Troyes and Dijon to prevent workers from doing so. Kennedy, 'Reconciling the Nation against Democracy', p. 295.
77. Ibid., pp. 296–97.
78. In October 1936 in Beziers (Hérault), PSF activists assaulted Communist and Socialist demonstrators with phials of sulphurous gas. In November, police in Philippeville, Algeria reported that the PSF was more disrespectful of public order than their opponents and that they did not hesitate to cause disturbances. In the spring and summer of 1937, PSF members engaged in agricultural strike-breaking activities in the Aisne and the Seine-et-Marne. Robert Paxton recounts how in the Aisne in July 1937 the PSF brought in 200 'scabs' to help defeat a beetroot workers' strike. When these 'harvest volunteers' were prevented by the police from clashing with the strikers, the PSF claimed that the Popular Front government, by siding with the strikers, was promoting violence and that consequently farm owners had the right to restore order themselves. Paxton calls this argument a 'justification for agrarian vigilantism'. In October 1937, following a meeting in St Fons (Rhône), the local PSF ran into leftist counter-demonstrators, and some of its EVP (i.e. renamed dispos) opened fire on them with pistols. Kennedy, 'Reconciling the Nation against Democracy', pp. 295, 298, 305, and Paxton, *French Peasant Fascism*, p. 93.

79.   In February 1938, PSF militants in the Rhône disrupted a PPF meeting with stink bombs and flour bags, which led to a brawl with the PPF *service ordre* (security guards). In March, the PPF's Xavier Vallat was attacked by PSF militants while holding a meeting at Béthune, and in Algiers other PSF militants clashed physically on several occasions with their PPF counterparts. In Paris, some of Pierre Taittinger's JP meetings were also targeted by PSF militants. Kennedy, 'Reconciling the Nation against Democracy', pp. 333–34.

80.   Soucy, *The First Wave*, pp. 57–60, 61, 63, 111, 177, 185, 186, 199, 203, 206–9, 215; Soucy, *The Second Wave*, pp. 68–71.

81.   R. Soucy, 'French Press Reaction to Hitler's First Two Years in Power', *Contemporary European History*, vol. 7, Part I, March 1998, pp. 32–36.

82.   See Soucy, *The Second Wave*, pp. 126–27.

83.   Not only did the Blum government authorise police raids against PSF leaders after the Parc des Princes affair and launched an investigation into La Rocque's movement to see if it had reverted to its paramilitary practices, but following the 'Clichy massacre' of 17 March, 1937 (the PSF had attempted to hold a meeting in Clichy, a Popular Front stronghold , and the police killed five and wounded 300 leftists protesting the meeting), the Communist and Socialist press demanded that La Rocque be arrested for provocation. In neither case did the PSF's actions result in a ban, but the threat of being banned remained as long as the Popular Front was in power and doubtless would have increased had the PSF chosen to be more aggressive.

84.   B.Weisbrod, 'The Crisis of Bourgeois Society in Interwar Germany', in *Fascist Italy and Nazi Germany: Comparisons and Contrasts*, ed. R. Bessel, Cambridge, England, 1996, p. 35.

85.   Soucy, *The First Wave*, pp. 32, 39, 44–45, 48.

86.   Kennedy, 'Reconciling the Nation against Democracy', pp. 228, 307. As it turned out, Valois eventually violated his own position on the matter in November 1926 when, his patience having grown thin with Charles Maurras, who had launched a press campaign against the Faisceau, Valois sent ninety of his legionnaires to assault AF headquarters in Paris and 'shut up' Maurras. The royalists drove away the attackers with pistols, and the event led to a rash of resignations from the Faisceau. Soucy, *The First Wave*, pp. 183–84.

87.   Archives Nationales, Paris, 451 AP 81.

88.   *Manifeste de Croix de Feu* cited in Kennedy, 'Reconciling the Nation against Democracy', p. 284.

89.   *Le Flambeau*, 6, 13 June, 1936.

90.   Parti Social Français, *A tous les patriotes*, pp. 6,7.

91.   La Rocque, *Disciplines d'Action*, pp. 102, 109, 145–46.

92.   Ibid., p.102. Here are La Rocque's exact words in 1941: 'FAIRE DES EXAMPLES. Toute la question est, en période transitoire, d'appliquer des sanctions justifiées, impitoyables, visibles. Autorisera-t-on l'auteur de ce livre à puiser une preuve dans son passé militaire? J'ai tenu pendant deux ans, sur le 'front berbère,' un poste constamment harcelé par l'ennemi. ... C'était au début de la guerre 1914–1918. Or, je pus enfin rejoindre la bataille de France. Quelques semaines plus tard, mon premier successeur était assassiné, le deuxième, attiré dans un piège, était massacré avec la plus grande partie de mes chers goumiers. Voici quelle avait été ma méthode, generatrice de sécurité: moins indulgent que mes remplaçants, j'avais fait passer par les armes, selons les formes régulières, tout indigène convaincu de trahison ou d'intelligences avec l'adversaire ... Et le nombre de ces fusillés en deux ans n'avait pas atteint le dixième des soldats français massacrés par surprise dans les six mois qui suivirent mon départ. Les circonstances anormales où nous vivons [en 1941], pour le salut de la patrie et la protection de notre descendance, exigent des exemples implacables et publics, des disciplines unanimement observées.' See also pp. 56, 89, 101–2, 105, 110, 136.

93. T. Abse, 'Italian Workers and Italian Fascism', in Bessell, ed., *Fascist Italy and Nazi Germany*, p. 40.
94. Blatt writes: 'Arturo Bocchini, the chief of police, and Michelangelo Di Stefano, the head of OVRA, were reactionaries, anti-Communists, anti-Socialists, and anti-Liberals committed to keeping Mussolini in power. Unlike the heads of the KGB, Gestapo, and SS, they were not mass killers. If they could coerce, imprison, bribe, blackmail, or seduce opponents into conformity, they did it rather than murder them. They wanted control and would settle for control without killing in batches, if they could get it. The Italian Fascist regime did execute a small number of opponents. They killed a small number of the best leaders of the opposition: Matteotti, Amendola, Gobetti, Carlo and Nello Rosselli. Most activist opponents, though, were imprisoned or sent into confino (Carlo Levi was sent to Eboli where he produced his great book, *Christ Stopped at Eboli*).' Blatt warns, however, against 'normalizing' Italian Fascism – since it did, after all, establish a dictatorship and controlled the media, the judiciary, and labour. E-mails from Blatt to Soucy, 18 February and 17 May, 2001.
95. A.De Grand, *Italian Fascism: Its Origins and Development*, Lincoln, Nebraska and London, 2000, p. 148.
96. Colonel de La Rocque, *Disciplines d'Action*, p. 89. Jacques Nobécourt has disputed the 'inane' view that La Rocque's reference to 'continental collaboration' in 1941 meant continental collaboration with Nazi Germany, since in *Disciplines d'Action* the phrase itself is not followed in the text by 'with Nazi Germany'. For Nobécourt, La Rocque was referring to Europe as a whole after the war and not to collaboration with Germany during the war. Jacques Nobécourt, *Le Colonel de La Rocque*, p. 1120. Although it is true that La Rocque was indeed referring to an eventual 'rebirth' of France, he hardly rejected Nazi Germany as an acceptable partner in a new Europe. He did insist that France be treated as an equal partner and that such a collaboration have a 'spiritual' dimension, but otherwise he was quite open to collaboration with the Hitlerian regime and praised aspects of Nazi Germany that he admired. He wrote that, based on mutual respect, 'a "collaboration" between two great peoples like the French people and the German people' would be 'susceptible to reciprocal enrichments (p. 155)'. He added: 'Are not the results obtained by the national-socialist peasantry of a nature to inspire us, following our own paths to our traditions and our temperament?' (p. 156) The political and military context in which the words 'continental collaboration' were written also makes it difficult to believe that the postwar Europe La Rocque had in mind would not have entailed collaboration with Nazi Germany. *Disciplines d'Action* was published in 1941 when many observers thought that the Germans would win the war. In addition to his favourable remarks about Nazi Germany, La Rocque denounced Great Britain and De Gaulle and attacked political liberalism and democracy. These remarks were not a recipe for an antifascist postwar Europe. In *Disciplines d'Action*, La Rocque also blamed Jews, particularly the influx of foreign Jews into France in the late 1930s, for contributing to the 'mortal vices' of France. (pp. 91, 97–98).
97. Winock, *Nationalism, Anti-Semitism, and Fascism in France*, p. 193.
98. La Rocque, *Disciplines d'Action*, pp. 89, 104, 118, 134, 146, 156.
99. Rémond, *La Droite en France de 1815 à nos jours*, p. 12; Weber, *Varieties of Fascism*, pp. 41, 133–36, 137, 139–141; Milza, *Fascisme français*, pp. 136, 138, 141; Winock, *Nationalism, Anti-Semitism, and Fascism in France*, p. 189; Berstein, 'La Ligue', p. 103; Sternhell, *Ni droite ni gauche* (Paris, 1983 edition) pp. 21, 34; Griffin, *Fascism*, p. 4. Sternhell and Griffin have both distinguished between an 'authentic' or 'core' socially revolutionary fascism and 'whatever compromises it has had to make with existing elites and institutions to achieve and retain power in practice'. Griffin, *Fascism*, p. 9.
100. 'La Rocque ne remettent en cause ni l'ordre bourgeois ni les fondements économiques du système.' Milza, *Fascisme français*, p.136.

101. A. Lyttelton, 'The 'Crisis of Bourgeois Society' and the Origins of Fascism', in Bessel, ed., *Fascist Italy and Nazi Germany*, pp. 12–22; Abse, 'Italian Workers and Italian Fascism', and Paxton, 'Five Stages of Fascism', pp. 1–23. De Grand points out that even the Fascist programme of 1919 contained conservative elements that would later provide the basis for a further turn to the right. 'In fact, despite the leftist rhetoric, nationalism figured as the framework for all political action. The political target of the Fascist movement was not the capitalist or the landowner, rather it was the vaguely defined war profiteer and the Catholic, liberal, and socialist politicians who had opposed the war'. De Grand remarks: 'What fascism did has always seemed to me more important than what it said it wanted to do. … Thus, interpretations that highlight fascism's socialist and syndicalist origins in order to develop a theory of left-wing fascism or those that stress fascism's efforts to create a new type of Italian by means of mass mobilization and the sacralization of politics should not necessarily be dismissed but need to be treated cautiously and measured against economic, social, and political realities'. De Grand, *Italian Fascism*, pp. 141, 170.

102. De Grand, *Italian Fascism*, pp. ix, xv, 30.

103. Abse points out that the major anomalies were in Trieste, where fascists rallied ethnically Italian workers against local Slav workers, and in Porto Marghera, where a new industrial labour force was recruited from a peasantry with no traditions of agrarian class struggle. Outside of Trieste and Porto Marghera, however, 'there is no evidence of mass working-class membership in the Fascist party'. Between 1919 and 1922 workers fought fascists 'square by square, street by street, turning whole districts of cities like Livorno into "no go" areas for the Fascists and their allies in the security forces'. Abse notes that the '*tradizione souversiva*', the leftist subversive tradition among Italian workers, was never destroyed by Fascism. Many workers under Mussolini's regime found Fascist rhetoric about fascist socialism 'boring and laughable', and it was not uncommon for workers to parody Fascist songs and devise 'comic versions of Fascist slogans'. Abse, 'Italian Workers and Italian Fascism', pp. 42, 43, 54–55.

104. De Grand notes that Italian workers, 'unable to elect their own leaders and alienated by wage reductions, lost faith in the [Fascist] unions, which became a form of employment for lower-middle-class bureaucrats'. The result was a regime that 'satisfied the needs of the dominant interest groups … who had no interest in massive social experimentation. … Far from being a revolutionary system of government, Italian fascism succeeded best when it opted for compromise with the conservative order'. De Grand, *Italian Fascism*, pp. 71–120.

105. Joel Blatt, email, 18 February, 2001.

106. I. Kershaw, *Popular Opinion and Political Dissent in the Third Reich: Bavaria 1933–1945*, London, 1983; M. Kater, *The Nazi Party: A Social Profile of Its Members and Leaders, 1919–1945*, Cambridge, MA, 1983); Weisbrod, 'The Crisis of Bourgeois Society in Interwar Germany', p. 35; and T. Siegel, 'Whatever Was the Attitude of German Workers ?', in Bessel, *Fascist Italy and Nazi Germany*, pp. 61–77.

107. Kater, *The Nazi Party*, pp.139–68, 229–33; and Weisbrod, 'The Crisis of Bourgeois Society in Interwar Germany', pp. 24–34.

108. George L. Mosse, *The Crisis of German Ideology: Intellectual Origins of the Third Reich*, New York, 1964; F. Ringer, *The Decline of the German Manderins: The German Academic Community*, Cambridge, MA, 1969; and J. Weiss, *Ideology of Death: Why the Holocaust Happened in Germany*, Chicago, 1996.

109. Sternhell, *Ni droite ni gauche* (1983 edition); Z. Sternhell, M. Sznajder and M. Asheri, *Naissance de l'idéologie fasciste*, Paris, 1989; P. Burrin, *La Dérive fasciste : Doriot, Déat, Bergery 1933–1945*, Paris, 1986; Soucy, *The Second Wave*, pp. 53–58.

110. Paxton, 'Five Stages of Fascism', pp. 5, 14.

111. De Grand, *Italian Fascism*, pp. 30, 165.

112. Paxton, 'Five Stages of Fascism', pp. 17–18.
113. Kater, *The Nazi Party, 1919–1945*, pp. 20–22.
114. Cited in W.L. Shirer, *The Nightmare Years, 1930–1940* , New York, 1985, pp. 201–3.
115. Burrin, *Fascisme, nazisme, autoritarisme*, p. 253; Passmore, 'The Croix de Feu and Fascism: A Foreign Thesis Obstinately Maintained', pp.110–15; Griffin, *Fascism*, p. 9.
116. La Rocque, *Disciplines d'Action*, p. 128.
117. C. Hitchens, *Letters to a Young Contrarian* , Cambridge, MA, 2001, p. 77.
118. Left-wing populism has traditionally blamed upper-class individuals for many of its grievances and has supported labour unions, the right to strike and egalitarian values. By contrast, right-wing populism has traditionally railed against the evil influence of Marxists, liberals, Jews, Blacks or immigrants, and, rather than attacking upper-class material interests, has defended them by opposing labour unions and labour strikes and by channelling social anger towards racial or ethnic 'inferiors'. For a glaring example of right-wing populism in an American context, see the nature of the opposition to both labour unions and the civil rights movement described in D. McWhorter, *Carry Me Home: Birmingham, Alabama, The Climatic Battle of the Civil Rights Revolution* , New York, London, Toronto, Sydney and Singapore, 2001. For a discussion of a different brand of conservative populism in recent years, see T. Frank, *One Market Under God: Extreme Capitalism, Market Populism, and the End of Economic Democracy*, New York, London, Toronto, Sidney and Auckland, 2000.
119. Burrin, *La Dérive fasciste*, p.192; Burrin, *Fascisme, nazisme, autoritarisme*, p. 256.
120. Milza, *Fascisme français*, p. 138.
121. Griffin, *Fascism*, pp. 6, 9.
122. De Grand, *Italian Fascism*, p. 169.
123. De Grand defines intermediate elites as those who 'have a managerial function in society, transmit orders or ideas, enforce discipline or organize services'. These include journalists, teachers and professionals who justify the needs of the dominant interests in society, as well as mid-level personnel for political parties, labour unions, bureaucracies and business. The lower middle class is the 'seedbed' for these intermediate elites. De Grand, *Italian Fascism*, pp. 7–8.
124. J. Weiss, *Nazis and Fascists in Europe*, Chicago, 1969, p. 21.
125. Paxton, 'Review of Robert Soucy', p. 107.
126. Burrin, *Fascisme, nazisme, autoritarisme*, p. 263.
127. Paxton, 'Review of Robert Soucy', p. 108. Three years later, Paxton, without elaborating, added this qualification: 'Faced with aroused publics, authoritarians as well as fascists may attempt to create a Durkheimian "mechanical solidarity"'. He continued to emphasise, however, that fundamental differences between authoritarians and fascists keep them at odds, so that even when the borders between the two kinds of regimes are blurred 'neither gets its way'. Paxton, 'Five Stages of Fascism', p. 19, footnote 55. This was consistent with his 1997 assertion that fascisms that shared power with conservatives were 'incomplete'. Paxton, *French Peasant Fascism*, p. 158.
128. Kater, *The Nazi Party*, pp. 22, 64, 232–33, 236.
129. De Grand, *Italian Fascism*, pp. 139–46. De Grand objects to the idea that there was only one definition of fascism during the interwar period: 'there was no consensus about what fascism was, and people defined it as they went along'. Email from De Grand to Soucy, 14 January, 2002.
130. De Grand, *Italian Fascism*, pp. 20, 66–71, 111, 134–35.
131. For the first three, see ibid., pp. 36, 49. As for the fourth, on his road to power Mussolini went out of his way to curry favour with the army, and many former army officers held leadership positions within his movement. In 1922 two of Italy's most important military leaders, Marshals Armando Diaz and Pietro Badoglio, informed the King that the army favoured the Fascists. Ibid., pp. 46, 48–49, 76–77; and De Grand, *Fascist Italy and Nazi Germany*, pp. 56, 80.

132. M. Revelli (translated by Roger Griffin), 'Italy', in Detlef Mühlberger, ed., *The Social Bases of European Fascist Movements*, New York, 1987, p. 26.
133. Ibid., p. 7. For more on the dominating presence of elite conservatives within the PNF, see ibid. pp. 17–20, 23, 27 and 33.
134. Ibid., p. 33.
135. De Grand, *Italian Fascism*, pp. 145, 149.
136. Burrin, *Fascisme, nazisme, autoritarisme*, p. 248. However, Burrin also writes: 'For what brings the investigation to the French case, the anti-Semitism and racism of Nazism offers a point of comparison and reflection more appropriate than the Italian case.' Ibid., p. 249. Why this is 'more appropriate' is not clear.
137. Baranowski, *The Confessing Church, Conservative Elites and the Nazi State*, passim.
138. Baronowski writes: '[The timing of the attempted coup] suggests that the conspirator's rejection of National Socialism was neither absolute nor the simple product of idiosyncratic, a-contextual moral decisions. The erosion of the conservative–Nazi alliance forced some conservative elites to reject Nazi means but few Nazi ends. Outside of the Socialists, none of those most closely associated with the plans for the coup [names provided] opposed rearmament or revision of the Treaty of Versailles. ... Most in the resistance shared the view that Austria, Czechoslovakia, the Balkans and Poland should, at the very least, fall within the German sphere of influence. ... General Beck ... suppressed his reservations about the regime once convinced that the purge of the SA had restored the army to its rightful place. ... [Most everyone] in the resistance favored legal restrictions on the political rights of Jews. ... The *Generalität* provided the most vivid illustration of the bankruptcy of the conservative-Nazi alliance. ... Once the army lobbied intensively for rearmament and the expansion of troop strength, a bloated, socially heterogeneous officer corps, whose loyalty in a coup the generals could not seriously entertain, was the price. As [Ulrich von] Hassell observed in late 1939, no public sentiment existed to favor a coup, nor could the generals trust their officers 'from the rank of major down. ... Because the officer corps as a whole objected little to the regime's accelerated drive toward *Lebensraum*, or to the brutal colonialism which accompanied it, the generals could only follow nervously the Austrian corporal's lead.' Ibid., pp. 98–103.
139. Burrin, *Fascisme, nazisme, autortarisme*, p. 149; Paxton, 'Five Stages of Fascism', pp. 9–10.
140. Paxton, 'Five Stages of Fascism', pp. 4–6; Paxton, *French Peasant Fascism*, pp. 9, 97, 116, 159, 161.
141. One historian, Desmond Glynn, has suggested that the expression 'selective essentialism' is a bit like that of 'selective virginity' where 'ideological virtue' is concerned. The latter does not apply to Paxton's argument, however, since he repeatedly acknowledges episodes of conservative 'complicity' with fascism.
142. The answer seems clear in the case of Valois's Faisceau. In 1925–26, several thousand French conservatives joined his movement in reaction to the election of the Cartel des Gauches, and in 1926 many of these same conservatives departed his movement when the democratic conservative Raymond Poincaré defeated the Cartel and rendered authoritarian solutions unnecessary. Soucy, *The First Wave*, pp. 188–90. In 1936–38, French conservatives faced a much greater threat from the Popular Front, and those who went over to La Rocque, like those who had gone over to Valois, may be said to have changed their political 'essences' in the process, at least where their previous allegiance to democratic values were concerned. Did La Rocque change his 'essence' in reverse and become a genuine political democrat when he founded the PSF in 1936? To believe so, one would have to believe that his conversion was 'sincere' (as some scholars do), ignore his previous denunciations of 'electoralism', 'politicians', and

'moderates', disregard the political fears and hatreds of those who supported him, neglect the tactical (and undemocratic) reasons he gave in the winter of 1935/36 for opting for the electoral path to power, and discount the impact of the banning of the CF in June 1936 and that of the police raids against PSF headquarters in Paris and the homes of fifty of its leaders in October 1936.

143. Paxton, *French Peasant Fascism*, p. 158.
144. Ibid.
145. Paxton,'Book Review of Robert Soucy', p. 108.
146. Paxton, 'Five Stages of Fascism', p. 3.
147. Pinto, *Salazar's Dictatorship and European Fascism*, pp.189, 656, 659.
148. P. Preston, *Franco*, London and New York, 1994, pp. 440–41, 536.
149. Regarding (2), La Rocque, like most fascists, was highly critical of 'the search for petty comfort' and denounced 'bourgeoisisme' in this regard, without threatening bourgeois wealth or incomes. In 1941 he blamed 'twenty years of degeneracy' for France's military defeat. Regarding (3), La Rocque held up as an example of the 'new man' Jean Mermoz, a famous aviator of the era and a member of the CF. The CF's male youth organisation, the Volontaires Nationaux, and the CF and PSF in general honoured the 'virile' values which Mermoz represented. Regarding (6), the CF/PSF was not only the largest mass movement on the French Right between 1936 and 1939, but unlike one of its major rivals, the Fédération Républicaine, which relied on local notables and a minimum of demagoguery to get out the vote, La Rocque's movement, according to William Irvine, 'eschewed elite politics in favor of mass mobilization' and was 'at home with mass rallies.' Irvine, 'Fascism in France and the Strange Case of the Croix de Feu', p. 295. For some examples of the CF/PSF's mass mobilisation activities, see Soucy, *The Second Wave*, pp. 111–12, 113–14. None of these activities prevented La Rocque from receiving important financial support from members of France's traditional elites. Ibid.,123–28. Regarding (7), (8), and (9), see ibid., pp. 190–191, 104–14, 123–36, 140–52, 160–61, 176, 178, 196, 202–3 and Soucy, 'Functional Hating: French Fascist Demonology Between the Wars', pp.162–70.
150. For Valois, see Soucy, *The First Wave*, p.170. For La Rocque, see Soucy, *The Second Wave*, p.187.
151. Kershaw writes that without the presence of favourable political circumstances, beginning with the right-wing backlash to the 'Red Revolution' in Bavaria in 1918, Hitler 'would have found himself ... without an audience, his "talent" pointless and unrecognized, his tirades of hate without echo, the backing from those close to the avenues of power, on whom he depended, unforthcoming.' 'The origins of the leadership cult reflected mentalities and expectations prevalent in some sectors of German society at the time, more than they did the special qualities of Hitler. ... Without the changed conditions, the product of a lost war, revolution, and a pervasive sense of national humiliation, Hitler would have remained a nobody.' Kershaw, *Hitler 1889–1936*, pp. 131–32.
152. La Rocque cited in Winock, *Nationalism, Anti-Semitism, and Fascism in France*, p. 189.
153. Payne, *A History of Fascism 1914–1945*, pp. 7, 8, 10.
154. E. Weber, *Varieties of Fascism*, New York, 1964, pp.138–42.
155. Paxton, 'Five Stages of Fascism', pp. 4–5.
156. Griffin, *Fascism*, p. 8.
157. The PSF, it is true, did organise private charities for the underprivileged but at the same time opposed raising the taxes required for increased government aid to the needy while insisting that the new government benefits proposed by the Popular Front (which the PSF wished to reduce) be administered to only 'faithful' workers by their employers. For further discussion of fascist 'rationalism', see Soucy, 'Functional Hating: French Fascist Demonology Between the Wars', pp. 158–76.

158. See Vicky Caron, 'The Antisemitic Revival in France in the 1930s: The Socioeconomic Dimensions Reconsidered', *Journal of Modern History*, vol. 70, March 1998, pp. 137–38, 145, 167 and V. Caron, *Uneasy Asylum: France and the Jewish Refugee Crisis 1933–1942*, Stanford, 1999. There were also, of course, a number of irrational feelings and cultural stereotypes that abetted the revival of political anti-Semitism in France in 1935–36. However, these factors had existed in the previous three decades (when popular anti-Semitism had waned following the defeat of the anti-Dreyfusards) without having nearly as great an impact. That the revival of anti-Semitism in the mid-1930s coincided with the right-wing backlash to the rise of the Popular Front and with the selfish economic considerations mentioned above suggests that there was more involved than cultural 'constructions', however much cultural, economic and political anti-Semitism came to reinforce one another at this point in time. See Soucy, 'Functional Hating', pp. 159–61, 172–74, for more on this issue.

159. See R. Soucy, 'French Press Reaction to Hitler's First Two Years in Power', *Contemporary European History*, vol. 7, Part I, March 1998, pp. 21–38.

160. In April 1998, Maurice Papon, a former Vichy official charged with abetting the Holocaust, suggested at his trial that to find him guilty would be to besmirch 'France'. He told the jury: 'Be careful that France does not get hurt by this verdict outside our borders.' In December 1998, when Bruno Megret of the Front National challenged the leadership of Jean-Marie Le Pen, Le Pen accused him not only of 'a crime against the Front National' but also of 'a crime against France'. In February 2001, a supporter of Mirko Norac, a former Croatian major general suspected of having committed atrocities during the Bosnian war, said: 'We are all Mirko Norac. By prosecuting Norac, they want to prosecute the Croatian army and the Croatian people.' In February 2002, Slobodan Milosevic, the former president of Yugoslavia, defending himself before the Hague tribunal against sixty-six counts of genocide and other war crimes, claimed that the case against him was against the Serbian people: 'Our citizens stand accused, citizens who lent their massive support to me.' An official of the ruling Democratic Party in Serbia commented: 'Milosevic is on trial for what he has done personally. Rather than defending himself, he is trying to hide behind Serbia's citizens.' *United Press/Cleveland Plain Dealer*, 19 December, 1998, 2 April, 1998, 12 February, 2001, 15 February, 2000.

161. Hitler's party had only 107 of 608 seats in the Reichstag in 1930 when it became a major player in German politics, and in 1932, on the eve of its coming to power, it received only a third of the vote. Mussolini's party did even less well electorally before it came to power: in the Italian elections of May 1921, the Fascists won only 35 of 535 seats in parliament. According to Philippe Machefer, had the 1940 elections in France not been cancelled because of the war, the PSF might have won as many as 100 of 618 seats in the Chamber of Deputies. Machefer, 'Sur quelques aspects', p. 36.

162. Soucy, 'French Press Reactions to Hitler's First Two Years in Power', pp. 30–38. For additional reasons for the failure of fascism to come to power in France in the late 1930s, see Soucy, *The Second Wave*, pp. 315–19 and Paxton, *French Peasant Fascism*, pp. 161–64.

4

The Five Stages of Fascism*

Robert O. Paxton

A full ten years before the 'Sternhell controversy', Robert Paxton had already created a stir in France with the publication in 1972 of his *Vichy France: Old Guard and New Order, 1940–1944*. This went straight into French translation a year later as *La France de Vichy*, a significant choice of title, as Henry Rousso has pointed out, for hitherto 'Vichy' had denoted a government, a regime, a period – not France as a whole. Paxton's interpretation challenged several features of what by then had become the established view of things: that, far from playing a 'double game', Vichy had taken the initiative in seeking to persuade the occupier to accept a policy of collaboration right from the outset; that, far from there being 'two Vichys', the Révolution Nationale and the policy of collaboration were intimately linked; finally, that far from Vichy's domestic reforms being inconsequential, they reflected an ambitious attempt to transform state and society, and in some respects prefigured the economic modernisation process of the 1950s and 1960s. Paxton's detailed examination of Vichy's internal programme also revealed the extent to which the regime's anti-Jewish measures were devised and applied quite voluntarily, without specific pressure from the occupier, evidently an explosive issue and one which Paxton would pursue more extensively in his coauthored *Vichy France and the Jews* (1981).

As Henry Rousso records, Paxton's intervention drew some criticism from the Left (for exploding the notion that it was mainly the elites that had collaborated), from Gaullists (for suggesting that the Fifth Republic was building on a Vichy reform legacy), and from sections of the Resistance community (for neglecting 'les résistants de la première heure'); but generally the Left defended Paxton, and the most vitriolic reactions came from the Right, who accused him of failing to appreciate the difficulty of the circumstances in which people were forced to make choices in the wake of defeat and occupation. As for the response of French historians, Rousso's conclusion is that 'those who agreed with Paxton regretted (with good reason) that the job had not been done by a native specialist, while those who were hostile were rarely able to dispute Paxton's arguments by referring to other sources, because the French archives were largely closed'.

It was not, of course, Robert Paxton's principal concern in *Vichy France* to decide whether or not the regime could legitimately be described as 'fascist', though on this issue he adopted a view that would later become the orthodox one, and which he would still hold twenty-five years later: namely that 'the Vichy regime was closer to an authoritarian-clerical model than to a fascist one, at least until its last desperate days'. However, to suggest that the regime enjoyed not just elite connivance but also a considerable degree of mass support certainly raised the question of where that support had come from and how it had been prepared. Not surprisingly, therefore, Paxton would eventually turn his attention to the interwar period and to the activities of the various right-wing political movements that campaigned against parliamentary democracy in the 1930s. In choosing to study Henri Dorgères's Greenshirts, Professor Paxton was not only filling a major historiographical gap in the coverage of the interwar 'leagues', he was also offering a potentially fruitful angle of comparison with Italy and Germany: to quote, 'rural fascism is particularly important because both Mussolini and Hitler had their first success with farmers ... that being the case, no study of the successes and failures of fascism in France can afford to neglect the countryside' (see *French Peasant Fascism*, p.154)

Thus Paxton is not averse to using the term 'fascist' in the French context, and as we have seen, Zeev Sternhell is convinced that Paxton does eventually accept that the Greenshirts were a mass fascist movement. However, while Paxton acknowledges that Dorgères's rhetoric, programme and style bear all the hallmarks of fascism, he clearly feels uneasy with the label, and suggests that account must also be taken of the functions of fascism ('how it works' rather than 'what it says': *French Peasant Fascism* p.157) and of the circumstances which allow fascism to flourish. So Paxton's position is clearly more nuanced on this issue than that of our two previous contributors. His functionalist approach is arguably closer to Soucy, his willingness to take seriously the radical populist features of fascist discourse places him nearer to Sternhell, his reluctance to commit himself unequivocally sets him apart from both. On the issue of the Croix de Feu/PSF for example, he remains unconvinced by Soucy's arguments. But nonetheless, he undoubtedly rejects any notion that France was 'allergic to this particular political virus'. He goes on:

> There was no mysterious antibody to it in French political culture. Indeed no Western country was exempt during the periods of fascist glamor and success, and France was not exceptional in this point. On the contrary, France produced one of the most luxuriant growths in the Western world of fascist or near fascist intellectual expressions. *But* [editor's emphasis] there were concrete social, cultural and political obstacles in French rural society to Dorgèrism. (*French Peasant Fascism*, p.161)

In the wake of this definitive study of the Greenshirts, Professor Paxton turned his attention to concepts of generic fascism, and began to develop his comparative model of the developmental stages of fascism. His new book on this subject, *The Anatomy of Fascism* (available also in French, Italian and Spanish editions), appeared in spring 2004. An earlier version of the essay that follows was published in *Journal of Modern History*, vol. 70, 1998. It has been updated and revised to give the French case greater prominence.

Robert O. Paxton is Professor Emeritus of History at Columbia University.

At first sight, nothing seems easier to understand than fascism.[1] It presents itself to us in crude, primary images: a chauvinist demagogue haranguing an ecstatic crowd; disciplined ranks of marching youths; uniform-shirted militants beating up members of some demonised minority; obsessive preoccupation with community decline, humiliation or victimhood; and compensatory cults of unity, energy, and purity, pursued with redemptive violence.

Yet, great difficulties arise as soon as one sets out to define fascism.[2] Its boundaries are ambiguous in both space and time. Do we include Stalin? Do we reach outside Europe to charismatic dictators in developing countries like Nkrumah, with his single party and official ideology of Nkrumaism, or Saddam Hussein, gigantic statues of whose own forearms once raised crossed swords over a Baghdad avenue?[3] What about imperial Japan in the 1930s, or the nationalist syndicalism of Juan Perón in Argentina (1946–55)? How far back in time must we go? If we choose to trace a conservative pedigree, we may reach all the way back to Joseph de Maistre, whose dark vision of violence and conspiracy in human affairs and conviction that only authority could repress human destructive instincts offer a prophetic glimpse, according to Isaiah Berlin, of twentieth-century totalitarianisms of Left and Right.[4] If we prefer to trace a lineage within the Left, drawing upon the Enlightenment's own perception that individual liberty can undermine community, some have gone back as far as Rousseau.[5]

Even if we limit ourselves to our own century and its two most notorious cases, Nazi Germany and Fascist[6] Italy, they display profound differences. How can we lump together Mussolini and Hitler, the one surrounded by Jewish henchmen and a Jewish mistress,[7] the other an obsessed anti-Semite? How equate the militarised regimentation of Nazi Party rule with the laxity of Mussolinian Italy? Such eminent authorities as the late Renzo De Felice in Rome and Karl Dietrich Bracher of the University of Bonn have denied that German Nazism and Italian Fascism belong to the same category.[8] This article argues for their conceptual kinship, for reasons that we will develop as we proceed.[9]

Five major difficulties stand in the way of any effort to define fascism. First, a problem of timing. The fascist phenomenon was poorly understood at the beginning partly because it was so unexpected. Until the end of the nineteenth century, most political thinkers believed that widening the vote would inevitably benefit democracy and socialism. Friedrich Engels, noting the rapid rise of the socialist vote in Germany and France, was sure that time and numbers were on his side. Writing the preface for a new edition in 1895 of Karl Marx's *Class Struggles in France*, he declared that 'if it continues in this fashion, we will conquer the major part of the middle classes and the peasantry and will become the decisive power.'[10] It took two generations before the Left understood that fascism is, after all, an authentic mass popular enthusiasm and not merely a clever manipulation of populist emotions by the reactionary Right or by capitalism in trouble.[11]

A second difficulty in defining fascism is created by mimicry. In fascism's heyday, in the 1930s, many regimes that were not functionally fascist borrowed elements of fascist décor in order to lend themelves an aura of force, vitality and mass mobilisation. They were influenced by the 'magnetic field' of fascism, to employ Philippe Burrin's useful phrase.[12] But one can not identify a fascist regime by its plumage. The English writer George Orwell understood at once that fascism is not defined by its clothing. If, some day, an authentic fascism were to succeed in England, Orwell wrote as early as 1936, it would be more soberly clad than in Germany.[13] The exotic black shirts of Sir Oswald Mosley are one explanation for the failure of the principal fascist movement in England, the British Union of Fascists. What if they had worn bowler hats and carried well-furled umbrellas? The adolescent skinheads who flaunt the swastika today in parts of Europe seem so alien and marginal that they constitute a law and order problem rather than a recurrence of authentic mass-based fascism, astutely decked out in the patriotic emblems of their own country. Focusing upon external symbols, subject to superficial imitation, adds to confusion about what may legitimately be considered fascist.

This leads to the third problem with defining fascism, posed by the dauntingly wide disparity among individual cases in space and in time. They differ in space because each national variant of fascism draws its legitimacy, as we shall see, not from some universal scripture but from what it considers the most authentic elements of its own community identity. Religion, for example, would certainly play a much greater role in an authentic fascism in the United States than in the first European fascisms, which were pagan for contingent historical reasons.[14] They differ in time because of the transformations and accommodations demanded of those movements that seek power. A little circle of dissident nationalist syndicalists, such as those whom Zeev Sternhell studies, functions differently from a party in search of alliances and of complicities within the country's elites. Disparate in their symbols, décor, and even in their political tactics, fascist movements resemble each other mainly in their functions (a point to which we shall return).

A fourth and even more redoutable difficulty stems from the ambiguous relationship between doctrine and action in fascism. We shall have to spend much more time with this problem than with the others. As intellectuals, almost instinctively, we classify all the great political movements – all the 'isms' – by doctrine. It is a time-honoured convention to take for granted that fascism is an 'ism' like the others, and so treat it as essentially a body of thought.[15] By an analogy that has gone largely unexamined, much existing scholarship treats fascism as if it were of the same nature as the great political doctrines of the long nineteenth century like conservatism, liberalism and socialism. This article undertakes to challenge that convention and its accompanying implicit analogy.

The great 'isms' of nineteenth-century Europe – conservatism, liberalism, socialism – were associated with notable rule, characterised by deference to educated leaders, learned debates, and (even in some forms of socialism) limited popular participation. Fascism is a political practice appropriate to the mass politics of the twentieth century. It bears a different relationship to thought than the nineteenth-century 'isms'. Unlike them, fascism does not rest upon formal philosophical positions with claims to universal validity. There was no 'Fascist Manifesto', no founding fascist thinker. Although one can deduce from fascist language implicit Social Darwinist assumptions about human nature, the need for community and authority in human society, and the destiny of nations in history,[16] fascism does not base its claims to validity on their truth. Fascists despise thought and reason, abandon intellectual positions casually, and cast aside many intellectual fellow-travellers. They subordinate thought and reason not to faith, as did the traditional Right, but to the promptings of the blood and the historic destiny of the group. Their only moral yardstick is the prowess of the race, of the nation, of the community. They claim legitimacy by no universal standard except a Darwinian triumph of the strongest community.

Fascists deny any legitimacy to universal principles to such a point that they neglect even proselytism. Authentic fascism is not for export.[17] Particular national variants of fascism differ far more profoundly one from another in themes and symbols than do the national variants of the true 'isms'. The most conspicuous of these variations, one which leads some to deny the validity of the very concept of generic fascism, concerns the nature of the indispensable enemy: within Mediterranean fascisms, socialists and colonised peoples are more salient enemies than Jewry.[18] Drawing their slogans and their symbols from the patriotic repertory of one particular community, fascisms are radically unique in their speech and insignia. They fit badly into any system of universal intellectual principles. It is in their functions that they resemble each other.

Further, the words of fascist intellectuals – even if we accept for the moment that they constitute fundamental philosophical texts – correspond only distantly with what fascist movements do after they have power. Early fascist programmes are poor guides to later fascist policy. The sweeping social changes proposed by Mussolini's first Fascist programme of April 1919 (including the vote for women, the eight-hour day, heavy taxation of war profits, confiscation of Church lands, and workers' participation in industrial management) stand in flagrant conflict with the *macho* persona of the later *Duce* and his deals with conservatives. Similarly, the hostility of the Nazi Twenty-five Points of 1920 to all capitalism except that of artisan producers bears little relation to the sometimes strained though powerfully effective collaboration for rearmament between German business and the Nazi regime.[19]

Zeev Sternhell responds to this line of argument by asserting that every political movement deforms its ideology under the constraints of exercising power.[20] Fascism, however, (unlike Stalinism) never produces a casuistical literature devoted to demonstrating how the leader's actions correspond in some profound way to the basic scriptures. Being in accord with basic scriptures simply does not seem to matter to fascist leaders, who claim to incarnate the national destiny in their physical persons.

Feelings propel fascism more than thought. We might call them mobilising passions, since they functioned in fascist movements to recruit followers and in fascist regimes to 'weld' the fascist 'tribe' to its leader.[21] The following mobilising passions are present in fascisms, though they are often articulated only implicitly:

- the primacy of the group, towards which one has duties superior to every right, whether universal or individual;
- the belief that one's group is a victim, a sentiment which justifies any action against the group's enemies, inside as well as outside;
- dread of the group's decadence under the corrosive effect of individualistic and cosmopolitan liberalism;
- closer integration of the community within a brotherhood (*fascio*), whose unity and purity are forged by common conviction, if possible, or by exclusionary violence if necessary;
- an enhanced sense of identity and belonging, in which the grandeur of the group reinforces individual self-esteem;
- authority of natural leaders (always male) throughout society, culminating in a national chieftain who alone is capable of incarnating the group's destiny;
- the beauty of violence and of will, when they are devoted to the group's success in a Darwinian struggle.

Programmes are so easily sacrificed to expediency in fascist practice that, at one point, I was tempted to reduce the role of ideology in fascism to a simple functionalism: fascists propose anything that serves to attract a crowd, solidify a mass following, or reassure their elite accomplices. But that would be a gross oversimplification. Ideas count in fascism, but we must be precise about exactly when and how they count. They count more at some stages than at others. At the beginning, their promise of radical spiritual-cultural renewal and restored national community helped fascists recruit a broad and varied public, including some respectable intellectuals.[22] Early fascist ideas helped amplify the disrepute of the liberal values to which the broad middle classes had largely adhered up to the First World War. But it was only by distancing themselves from those elements of the early radical programmes threatening to conservatives that certain fascist movements were been able to gain and exercise power. What Roger Chartier had to say about cultural preparation as the 'cause' of the French Revolution is exactly right as well for the history of fascism: 'attributing "cultural origins" to the French Revolution does not by any means establish the Revolution's causes; rather it pinpoints certain of the conditions that made it possible because it was conceivable'.[23]

In power, what seems to count is less the faithful application of the party's initial ideology than the integrating function that espousing one official ideology performs, to the exclusion of any ideas deemed alien or divisive. Much later in the fascist cycle, at the climacteric moment, under the influence of war, parts of the original radical fascist programmes that do not threaten existing social or economic hierarchies (such as the Nazis' racial obsessions) may recover their ascendancy. We will return to these matters when we discuss the stages in detail. The contradictions that obscure every reading of fascist texts can be resolved, therefore, only by the study of the choices made by the fascists in their daily actions.

To illustrate this proposition, consider the two most ambiguous concepts in the fascist lexicon: revolution and modernity. Fascists like to call themselves revolutionaries, but one discovers best by their actions what they really want to change. Their revolution consists of hardening the character, and purifying and energising the community, rather than making the social structure or the economic system more just or free. Fascist militants proclaim themselves antibourgeois; what they hate in the bourgeoisie, however, is not exploitation but softness. Zeev Sternhell has put his finger precisely upon what distinguishes those revolutionaries who abandon early fascism, when it begins to reposition itself for power, from those who remain faithful to it through all its transformations: the first remain committed to a change in the socioeconomic order. The faithful, by contrast, preach a moral revolution in order to create 'the new fascist man'.[24] Fascist 'revolutionaries' believe in change in the sense used by Tancredi, scion of the decaying noble Sicilian family in Giuseppe di Lampedusa's great novel *The Leopard*: 'if we want things to stay as they are, things will have to change'.[25]

Similar confusions surround the fascist understanding of modernity. Hitler loved to arrive theatrically aboard a supercharged Mercedes, or by airplane. It is true that he nursed the archaic dream of installing German peasant colonies in the plains of eastern Europe, but this dream could be realised only by modern weaponry. Hitler execrated the Bauhaus style; the young Mussolini, on the contrary, was attracted to aesthetic modernism.[26] It has been traditional to try to resolve these conflicts by scrutinising fascist texts.[27] These conflicts can best be resolved, however, by examining fascist actions: all fascists seek technical and military power, while simultaneously trying to escape the destabilising social effects of the industrialisation such power requires. They combine technical modernity with a system of authority and discipline intended to suppress the disorderly social consequences of industrial expansion. The meanings that fascists give to the concepts of revolution and modernity, ambiguous in the texts, become comprehensible in their concrete applications.

The fifth and final difficulty with defining fascism is caused by overuse: the word 'fascist' has become the most banal of epithets. Everyone is someone's fascist. Consider the American radio commentator Rush Limbaugh's 'femi-nazis'. Several summers ago, I heard a young German call Western-sponsored birth control programmes in the Third World 'fascist', forgetting that the Nazis and the Italian

Fascists were, for once, agreed in encouraging large families – except, of course, among those considered either eugenically or racially inferior. Those were condemned to sterilisation, if not worse.[28] The term 'fascist' has been so loosely used that some have proposed giving it up altogether in scholarly research.[29]

Nevertheless, we can not give up in the face of these difficulties. A real phenomenon exists. Indeed fascism is the most original political novelty of the twentieth century, no less. It successfully gathered, against all expectation, in certain modern nations that seemed firmly planted on a path to gradually expanding democracy, a popular following around hard, violent, antiliberal and antisocialist nationalist dictatorships. Then it spread its 'politics in a new key'[30] through much of Europe, assembling all nationalists who hated the Left and found the Right inadequate. We must be able to examine this phenomenon as a system. It is not enough to treat each national case individually, as if each one constitutes a category in itself. If we can not examine fascism synthetically, we risk being unable to understand the twentieth century, or the present one. We must have a word, and for lack of a better one, we must employ the word that Mussolini borrowed from the vocabulary of the Italian Left in 1919,[31] before his movement had assumed its mature form. Obliged to use the word fascism, we ought to use it well.

Unfortunately, much scholarly work on fascism complicates things still further by two very widespread errors of approach. First, most authorities treat generic fascism in a static manner. With several remarkable exceptions – I think particularly of Pierre Milza and Philippe Burrin[32] – they look for a fixed essence: the famous 'fascist minimum'. Secondly, most works consider fascisms in isolation, without sustained reference to the political, social and cultural spaces in which they navigate. Together these two common errors of approach produce what we might call 'bestiaries' of fascism. Like medieval naturalists, they present a catalogue of portraits of one beast after another, each one portrayed against a bit of background scenery, and identified by its external signs.[33]

We can get beyond the 'bestiary' approach by adopting three quite simple historical strategies. One is to study fascism in motion, paying more attention to processes than to essences. Another is to study it contextually, spending at least as much time on the surrounding society and on fascism's allies and accomplices as on the fascist movements themselves.[34] The more actively a fascist movement participates in the political life of its country, the less one can understand it in isolation. It is ensnared in a web of reciprocal influences with allies or rivals in its country's civil society. Finally, we can put the disconcerting malleability of fascisms in time and in space to good use. That malleability is not necessarily an obstacle to understanding. It may even make understanding easier, by making comparison possible. Comparison is 'a way of thinking more than a method',[35] and it works better when we try to account for differences than when we try to amass vague resemblances. Comparison works revealingly with fascisms, since every Western society has contained at least some marginal example. Their different fates across time and space in neighbouring settings should help us to identify the principal factors in the varying success of specific cases, and even to isolate the constants.[36]

However, one must compare what is comparable. A regime where fascism exercises power is hardly comparable to a sect of dissident intellectuals. We must distinguish the different stages of fascism in time. It has long been standard to point to the difference between movements and regimes. I believe we can usefully distinguish more stages than that, if we look clearly at the very different sociopolitical processes involved in each stage. I identify five of them:[37] (1) the initial creation of fascist movements; (2) their rooting as parties in a political system; (3) the acquisition of power; (4) the exercise of power; and, finally, in the longer term, (5) radicalisation or entropy. Since different kinds of historical process are involved in each stage, moreover, we must deploy different scholarly strategies in the analysis of each.

Consider the first stage. First-stage fascism is the domain of the intellectual historian, for the process to be studied here is the emergence of new ways of looking at the world and diagnosing its ills. In the late nineteenth and early twentieth centuries, thinkers and publicists discredited reigning liberal and democratic values, not in the name of either existing alternative – conservative or socialist – but in the name of something new that promised to transcend and join them: a novel mixture of nationalism and syndicalism that had found little available space in a nineteenth-century political landscape compartmented into Left and Right (though retrospect may reveal a few maverick precedents). This first stage is the part of the fascist elephant that scholars have found most congenial as a subject; examining one limb, of course, may mislead us about the whole beast.

Comparison is of little help to us at this first stage, for all modern states have had protofascist militants and publicists in the early twentieth century. Fascism can appear wherever democracy is sufficiently implanted to have aroused disillusion. That suggests its spatial and temporal limits: no authentic fascism before the emergence of a massively enfranchised and politically active citizenry. In order to give birth to fascism, a society must have known political liberty – for better or for worse.

However, early fascisms were so ubiquitous that we can hardly attribute their origin to any one particular national intellectual history. George Mosse has pointed to anti-Enlightenment Germany;[38] Zeev Sternhell singles out France around 1900, followed by Italian disciples.[39] A body of thought that one can call protofascist appeared in the United States, too, at the end of the nineteenth century. Brooks Adams, scion of a great New England dynasty, descendant of two presidents of the United States, lamented, in *The Law of Civilization and Decay* (1895), the moral decline of the United States as a result of financial concentration.[40] Later on, in 1918, Adams believed he had found the remedy to American decline in an authoritarian regime directing a state socialism. After the First World War, the United States, too, entered the 'magnetic field' of European fascisms. 'Coloured shirt' movements sprang up, such as the 'Silver Shirts' or 'S.S.' of William Dudley Pelley.[41]

But it is further back in American history that one comes upon the earliest phenomenon that seems functionally related to fascism: the Ku Klux Klan. Just after the Civil War, some former Confederate officers, fearing the vote given to African-Americans by the Radical Reconstructionists in 1867, set up a militia to restore an overturned social order. The Klan constituted an alternative civic authority, parallel to the legal state, which, in its founders' eyes, no longer defended their community's legitimate interests. By the adoption of a uniform (white robe and hood), as well as by their techniques of intimidation and their conviction that violence was justified in the cause of their group's destiny,[42] the first version of the Klan in the defeated American South was a remarkable preview of the way fascist movements were to function in interwar Europe. It is arguable, at least, that fascism (understood functionally) was born in the late 1860s in the American South.

Since fascisms take their first steps in reaction to claimed failings of democracy, it is not surprising that they should appear first in the most precocious democracies, the United States and France. But we come now to a paradox: it is not necessarily in the countries that generated the first fascisms that fascist systems have had, historically, the best chance of succeeding.

The second stage – rooting, in which a fascist movement becomes a party capable of acting decisively on the political scene – happens relatively rarely. At this stage, comparison becomes rewarding: one can contrast successes with failures. Success depends on certain relatively precise conditions: the weakness of a liberal state, whose inadequacies seem to condemn the nation to disorder, decline or humiliation; and political deadlock, because the Right, the heir to power but unable to continue to wield it alone, refuses to accept a growing Left as a legitimate governing partner. Some fascist leaders, in their turn, are willing to reposition their movements in alliances with these frightened conservatives, a step that pays handsomely in political power, at the cost of disaffection among some of the early antibourgeois militants.

To illustrate the issues raised by the rooting stage, consider the growth of fascism among farmers. I studied a peasant movement in the west of France in the 1930s, whose leader, Henry Dorgères, linked himself openly with fascism, at least at the beginning, in 1934. I chose this subject not because his Greenshirts played a major role in interwar France, other than several conspicuous crowd actions exaggerated by the press, but because it was in the countryside that German Nazism and Italian Fascism first succeeded in becoming the representative of an important social and economic interest. The comparison between the success of rural fascism in Germany and Italy and its relative failure in France seems to me a fruitful one. It permits us to identify those aspects of the French Third Republic that made it a less propitious setting than Weimar Germany or the Italian liberal monarchy for the political rooting of the local variety of fascism.

All three of these countries experienced massive strikes of agricultural workers: east-Elbian Germany during the postwar crisis in 1919–23;[43] the Po Valley and Apulia in Italy in 1920–21;[44] and the big farms of northern France and the Paris Basin during the two summers of the Popular Front, in 1936 and 1937.[45] The German strikes were broken by vigilantes, armed and abetted by local army authorities, in cases where the regular authorities were too conciliatory to suit the landowners. The Italian ones were broken by Mussolini's famous blackshirted *squadristi*, whose vigilantism filled the void left by the apparent inability of the liberal Italian state to enforce order. It is precisely in this direct action against farmworkers' unions that second-stage fascism was born in Italy, and even launched on the path to power, to the dismay of the first Fascists, intellectual dissidents from national syndicalism. Many militants from the first stage resigned from second-stage Fascism at this point, complaining of being transformed into 'watchdogs' for the big planters.[46]

France had *squadristi*, too: Henry Dorgères's Greenshirts (*chemises vertes*), active during the great strikes of agricultural workers in the hot summers of 1936 and 1937. But the Greenshirts' role was limited to several symbolic actions in the big northern wheat and sugar beet farms of the north and northwest (Aisne, Somme, Seine-Maritime, Pas-de-Calais). It was the French *gendarmerie*, even with Léon Blum in power, who put down the agricultural strikes in France. The French landowners didn't need the *chemises vertes*. The authority of the state and the power of the conservative farmers' organisations left hardly any space in the French countryside for the rooting of a fascist parallel power. These differences in available space and allies seem to me much more influential than any differences or resemblances in vocabulary or programme among rural fascists in France, Germany and Italy.

That is to say, the most significant differences that comparison reveals to us concern the setting as much as the character of the fascist movements themselves. This seems to be a quite fundamental principle of good comparative method [see note 36 above]. The description of fascist movements in isolation does not explain much. It leads us straight back to the bestiary, or, even worse, to pruriency, as in Visconti's film *The Damned*, which invites us to leer at the decadent perversity of fascist personalities.[47] We learn much more if we focus our gaze on the circumstances that favour the fascists – polarisation within civil society and deadlocks within the political system – and on the fascists' accomplices and allies. It is in the surrounding conditions that one must seek the differences that count, for movements that sound rather similar in their rhetoric have arrived at very different results in different national settings.

Therefore the methods of intellectual history become much less helpful beyond the first stage in the fascist cycle. Every fascist movement which has rooted itself successfully as a major political contender, thereby approaching power, has betrayed its initial antibourgeois and anticapitalist programme. The processes to be examined in later stages include the breakdown of democratic regimes,[48] and the success of fascist movements in assembling broad catch-all parties that attract a mass following across the classes and hence seem attractive allies to conservatives looking for ways to perpetuate their shaken rule. At later stages successful fascist parties also position themselves as the most effective barriers, by persuasion or by force, to an advancing Left, and prove adept at the formation, maintenance and domination of political coalitions with conservatives. But these political successes come at the cost of the first ideological programmes. Demonstrating their contempt for doctrine, successfully rooted fascist parties do not annul or amend their early programmes. They simply ignore them, while acting in ways quite contrary to them. The conflicts of doctrine and practice set up by successful fascist movements on the road to power not only alienate many radical fascists of the first hour; they continue to confuse many historians, who assume that analysing programmes is a sufficient tool for classifying fascisms. The confusion has been compounded by the persistence of many early fascisms that failed to navigate the turn from the first to the second and third stages, and remained pure and radical, but marginal, as 'national syndicalisms'.

A thoughtful look at the first two stages in the original fascist cycle – the creation and emergence of such movements as plausible players on the political stage – shows how much improvisation was involved in the first steps of Mussolini and Hitler. Mussolini evidently believed in 1919 that his new *Fasci di combattimento* were destined to gather discontented veterans together with other discontented nationalists, from both Left and Right, in a vast movement for profound social change. We have noted how the first Fascist programme, drafted in spring 1919, mixed nationalist territorial claims with social reforms that are astonishingly radical in the light of Mussolini's later actions and *macho* persona. That early fascism was decisively defeated in the elections of 1919, for there was no space in Italian politics for a party that was both nationalist and Left. Mussolini would be totally forgotten today if some of his lieutenants in the provinces had not discovered different vocations – bashing Slovenes in Trieste in July 1920 and bashing socialist organisers of farm workers in the Po Valley in fall and winter 1920–21. Mussolini supported these new initiatives by the *ras*,[49] and his movement turned into something else, thereafter prospering mightily. Hitler's efforts to recruit urban and working-class voters faltered through 1928; he began assembling a mass electorate in 1929–30 when he turned his attention to recruiting rural populations afflicted by the collapse of farm prices.[50] The two apprentices learned how to be second-stage fascists by trial and error. Their adaptations to the available space undermine any effort to portray historical fascism as the consistent expression of one coherent ideology.

At the third stage, the arrival in power, comparison acquires greater bite. What characteristics distinguished Germany and Italy, where fascism took power, from countries like France and Britain, where fascist movements were highly visible but remained far from power? We need to recall that fascism has never so far taken power by a coup d'état, deploying the weight of its militants in the street. Fascist power by coup is hardly conceivable in a modern state. Fascism can not appeal to the street without risking a confrontation with future allies – the army and the police – without whom it will not be able to pursue its expansionist goals. Indeed fascist coup attempts have commonly led to military dictatorship, rather than to fascist power (as in Romania in December 1941). Resorting to direct mass action also risks conceding advantages to fascism's principal enemy, the Left, still powerful in the street and workplace in interwar Europe.[51] The only route to power available to fascists passes through cooperation with conservative elites. The most important variables, therefore, are the conservative elites' willingness to work with the fascists, along with a reciprocal flexibility on the fascist leaders' part, and the depth of the crisis which induces them to cooperate.

Neither Hitler nor Mussolini took the helm by force, even if they used force earlier to destabilise the liberal regime, and later to transform their governments into dictatorships.[52] They were invited to take office as head of government by a head of state in the legitimate exercise of his official functions, on the advice of his conservative counsellors, under quite precise circumstances: a deadlock of constitutional government (produced in part by the polarisation that the fascists abetted); conservative leaders who felt threatened by the loss of their capacity to keep the population under control, often at a moment of massive popular mobilisation; an advancing Left; conservative leaders who refused to work with that Left, and who felt unable to continue to govern against the Left without further reinforcement.

Comparison with the quite varied cases where fascism flourished but failed to take power can be instructive at this stage. France has provoked the most intense debate. On the one hand stand many French scholars who argue that the strength of republican tradition, with its values, institutions and habitual political practices, made France 'allergic' to fascism. According to this view, those French movements and intellectuals that were indubitably influenced by fascism between the wars amounted to little more than a 'homeopathic dose' of foreign influences, a 'coat of Roman whitewash' applied to a 'the old caesarist, authoritarian and plebiscitary legacy' left over from Bonapartism,[53] or 'little more than a veneer'.[54] The opposite point of view has been argued by other scholars for whom France was the 'real cradle of fascism'.[55] Indeed, Sternhell considers that it is by studying interwar France, where fascism 'impregnated' political culture in a pure form uncompromised by the exercise of power, that 'one can fathom its deeper significance'.[56]

While the 'allergy' hypothesis rightfully focuses our attention on settings, its unfortunate medical language makes it easy to deform into assumptions about inherent national character. Distinguishing stages helps sharpen the focus of this debate. The existence of first-stage fascism in interwar France seems beyond doubt.[57] It is equally evident that fascism never reached stage three in France. Although the demonstrations of 6 February 1934 succeeded in driving a legitimate government from office, that very success broke the movement's momentum and obliged its organisers to conclude that a forceful seizure of power in France was impracticable[58] – as it had been in Germany. Sternhell himself admits that 'on the continent of Europe, France was the only important country where liberal democracy successfully resisted the impact of fascism and Nazism'.[59]

Even the Vichy regime was not fascist at the outset, for it had neither a single party nor parallel institutions. Most extreme Right leaders remained in opposition in Paris, where German power and money permitted them to complete what Burrin calls their 'fascisation'.[60] Only as Vichy became transformed into a police state under the pressures of war, did parallel institutions appear – the *Milice* or supplementary police; the 'special sections' in the judiciary; the Police for Jewish Affairs – and figures close to fascism like Déat and Darnand obtain office.[61]

The difficult questions are posed by the second stage: did any fascist movements root themselves in French public life to the extent of becoming major players and establishing parallel structures? Asking the question in this way perhaps allows us to advance the argument beyond the labelling exercises and numbers-counting that have dominated the discussion up to now. The PPF, it might be argued, was sufficiently rooted in Doriot's fief of Saint-Denis that some of his original working-class clientele followed him from communism to fascism, making the PPF easily the most proletarian of the French far Right movements. Dorgères' s Défense paysanne – marginally fascist – came close to supplanting the state briefly in a few communes of the French west.

The key to the matter is the largest extreme-Right movement in interwar France, Colonel François de La Rocque's Parti Social Français, successor to his paramilitary league, the Croix de Feu, dissolved in 1936. If the PSF (with an estimated 800,000 members at its peak in 1938) was fascist, then fascism was a major force in interwar France. Most scholars have concluded that it was not.[62] A few, mostly foreign, have argued that both of La Rocque's movements were fascist.[63] Important differences, however, separated the Croix de Feu, with its paramilitary exercises and its talk of 'H hour' and its apparent readiness to supplant state authority, from the more cautious PSF. The paramilitary character and threatening demonstrations of the Croix de feu persuade the British historian Kevin Passmore that it was fascist; but he believes that the PSF settled gradually into constitutional conservatism.[64] It is impossible not to notice that the second came much closer to being rooted – here we need to examine its associational life as well as its electoral prospects and its effect on the political system as a whole – than the first.

Fascism faced additional obstacles in France beyond the undoubted strength of the republican tradition. One was the reluctance of French nationalists to emulate foreign examples. Nazi Germany seemed an alien world even to some French fascists (Brasillach, for example), and even French admirers of Mussolini criticised Italian Fascist statism. The French Right found the Belgian fascist Léon Degrelle a less threatening example, and it found most admirable the authoritarian (but nonfascist) regimes of Salazar and Franco. French fascism was also exceptional in operating within a nation without expansionist aims and with an overwhelming antipathy to another war. Indeed, it became pacifist as war against Hitler became more closely identified with Soviet foreign policy. When it became collaborationist under Nazi occupation, some have concluded that it was at best a derivative or secondary fascism.[65]

It is not sufficient to examine French fascist movements in isolation, of course. The space available is a crucial variable. Fascism did best wherever traditional conservatism lost credibility and the centre crumbled; the first began to happen in France but the second did not. The most interesting aspect of Passmore's work is his demonstration that La Rocque's star rose in proportion to the failures of

French conservatism to surmount its divisions and deal effectively with the problems of the day. By 1936, however, large parts of the centre had been drawn back into the republican fold by the Popular Front, and by 1938 the Daladier government had developed a broad centrist conservatism that came closer than anything heretofore to the British Tory example. The space available for the French extreme Right thereby became all the narrower.

To continue our survey of states that had conspicuous fascist movements between the wars but no fascist regime, Britain offered less space to fascism than France between the wars, despite the greater severity of its economic crisis. A centrist and solidly implanted Conservative Party succeeded in ruling consensually there from 1931 to 1945.[66] Authoritarian dictatorships often preempted fascist movements, as did Franco, or even destroyed them, as did Antonescu in Romania and Salazar in Portugal, after copying some of their techniques of popular mobilisation.[67]

The fourth stage – the exercise of power – is powerfully conditioned by the manner in which fascism arrives in power. The fascist leaders who have reached power, historically, have been condemned to govern in association with the conservative elites who had opened the gates to them. This sets up a four-way struggle for dominance among the leader, his party (whose militants clamour for jobs, perquisites, expansionist adventures, and the fulfilment of elements of the early radical programme), the regular state functionaries such as police commanders and magistrates, and the traditional elites – churches, the army, the professions,[68] and business leaders.[69] This four-way tension is what gives fascism its characteristic blend of febrile activism and shapelessness.[70]

The tensions within fascist rule also help us clarify the frontiers between authentic fascism and other forms of dictatorial rule. Fascist rule is unlike the exercise of power in either authoritarianism (which lacks a single party, or gives it little power)[71] or Stalinism (which lacked traditional elites).[72] Authoritarians would prefer to leave the population demobilised, while fascists promise to win the working class back for the Nation by their superior techniques of manufacturing enthusiasm.[73] Although authoritarian regimes may trample due process and individual liberties, they accept ill-defined though real limits to state power in favour of some private space for individuals and 'organic' intermediary bodies such as local notables, economic cartels, families and churches. Fascism claims to reduce the private sphere to nothing, though that is propaganda (quite successful, moreover, even with scholars).[74] Stalin's Communist Party governed a civil society radically simplified by the Bolshevik Revolution, while, under Hitler, the party, the bureaucracy and the traditional elites jostled for power. Even if Stalin's techniques of rule often resembled those of fascism, he did not have to concern himself with concentrations of inherited autonomous social and economic power.

The exercise of power involved the same elements in Mussolini's Italy[75] as in Nazi Germany. It is the balance between the party and traditional institutions that distinguishes one case from the other. In Italy, the traditional state wound up with primacy, largely because Mussolini feared his own most militant followers, the local *ras* and their *squadristi*. In Nazi Germany, the party came to dominate, especially after war began. This interplay between single parties and traditional elites helps us classify borderline regimes, especially if we bear in mind that the frontiers were fluid between authoritarian and fascist regimes, and might be crossed in either direction. Authoritarian regimes, especially those that managed to remain neutral, such as Spain and Portugal, steadily reinforced the predominance of the traditional state over their small fascist movements.

In the long run (the fifth stage), fascist 'dual power' can evolve in two directions: radicalisation or entropy. Mussolini's regime subsided towards routine authoritarianism after the establishment of the dictatorship in 1925–26, except during colonial campaigns. The Ethiopian War (1935–36) set off a 'rivoluzione culturale' and 'svolta totalitaria'[76] in which the Fascist regime tried to shape the fascist 'new man' by instituting 'fascist customs', 'fascist language' and racial legislation. Within the sphere of colonialist action, first in Libya and then in Ethiopia, the party's arbitrary rule and policies of racial discrimination were free to set the tone.[77] The radicalism of Italian Fascism's early days resurfaced in the phantom Republic of Salò that governed the north of Italy under German tutelage after September 1943.

Nazi Germany alone experienced full radicalisation. A victorious war of extermination in the East offered almost limitless freedom of action to the 'prerogative state' and its 'parallel institutions', released from the remaining constraints of the 'normative state', such as they were. In the 'no man's land' of what had been Poland and the western parts of the Soviet Union they put into application their ultimate fantasies of racial cleansing.[78] Extreme radicalisation remains latent in all fascisms, but the circumstances of war, and particularly of victorious wars of conquest, give it the fullest means of expression.[79]

Focus on processes and discrimination among stages – this article's principal methodological proposals – cast a clarifying light on many specialised themes in the study of fascism. Social composition, for example, changes with each stage. Any study that proposes a single, fixed social composition inherent in fascism is flawed.[80] It also becomes doubtful that we can identify a single unchanging fascist aesthetic that would apply to all the national cases.[81] The *macho* restoration of a threatened patriarchy comes close to being a universal fascist value, but Mussolini advocated female suffrage in his first programme, and Hitler did not mention gender issues in his Twenty-five Points.[82]

Having picked fascism apart, have we escaped from the nominalism of the 'bestiary' only to fall into another nominalism of processes and stages? Where is the 'fascism minimum' in all this? Has generic fascism evaporated in this analysis? Have we lost its 'essence' by exposing its complex tensions (political revolution versus social restoration, order versus aggressive expansionism, mass enthusiasm versus civic submission)?

It is by a functional definition of fascism that we can escape from these quandaries. Through all its stages, fascism promises to perform functions that neither conservatives, liberals, nor socialists can perform: to impose unity, energy and purity, by force if necessary, upon communities frightened by division, decline and foreign influence. It promises to undo the harm alleged to have been done by liberalism and democracy, and the even greater harm threatened by socialism, by employing levels of propaganda, community pressure, force and violence that traditional conservatives are unable to muster because they have no link to a mobilised mass following. It admits no legal or moral limits to what it will do to make its community prevail.

Defining fascism functionally, together with distinguishing clearly among successive stages, also helps us answer the burning question of this moment: can fascism still exist today, in spite of the humiliating defeat of Hitler and Mussolini, the declining availability of the war option in a nuclear age, the irreversible globalisation of the economy, and the triumph of individualistic consumerism? After ethnic cleansing in the Balkans, the rise of exclusionary nationalisms in post-communist Eastern Europe, the 'skinhead' phenomenon in Britain, Germany, Scandinavia and Italy, the participation of the former Movimento sociale italiano, rechristened Alleanza nazionale, in the Berlusconi governments of 1994[83] and 2000, and the participation of the Freiheitspartei in the Austrian government in 2000, it would be hard to answer no to that question.[84]

The most interesting cases today, however, are not those that imitate the exotic coloured-shirt movements of an earlier generation. New functional equivalents of fascism would probably work best, as George Orwell reminded us, clad in the mainstream patriotic dress of their own place and time. An authentically popular fascism in the United States would be pious and antiblack; in Western Europe, secular and anti-Semitic, or, more probably these days, anti-Islamic; in Russia and Eastern Europe, religious and slavophile. It is wiser to pay attention to the functions fulfilled by new movements of an analogous type, to the circumstances that could open a space to them, and to the potential conservative elite allies ready to try to coopt them, rather than look for echoes of the rhetoric, the programmes, or the aesthetic preferences of the protofascists of the last *fin de siècle*. We may legitimately conclude, for example, that the skinheads are functional equivalents of Hitler's SA and Mussolini's *squadristi* only if important elements of the conservative elite begin to cultivate them as weapons against some internal enemy, such as immigrants.

The right questions to ask of today's neo- or protofascisms are those appropriate for the second and third stages of the fascist cycle. Are they becoming rooted as parties that represent major interests and feelings and wield major influence on the political scene? Is the economic or constitutional system in a state of blockage apparently insoluble by existing authorities? Is a rapid political mobilisation threatening to escape the control of traditional elites, to the point where they would be tempted to look for tough helpers in order to stay in charge? It is by answering those kinds of question, grounded in a proper historical understanding of the processes at work in past fascisms, and not by checking the colour of the shirts, or seeking traces of the rhetoric of the national-syndicalist dissidents of the opening of the twentieth century, that we may be able to recognise our own day's functional equivalents of fascism.

Notes

1. This article has also been published in French translation in a book edited by Michel Dobry, *Le mythe de l'allergie française au fascisme*, Paris, 2003. An earlier version was delivered as the Marc Bloch Lecture of the Ecole des Hautes Etudes en Sciences Sociales, Paris, on 13 June 1994 in the Grand Amphithéâtre of the Sorbonne and was published in *Journal of Modern History*, no. 70, 1998.
2. Following a period of active study of generic fascism in the 1960s and early 1970s, scholarly activity shifted after about 1975 away from generic fascism to particular cases. See Tim Mason, 'Whatever Happened to Fascism?', in *Reevaluating the Third Reich*, ed. T. Childers and J. Caplan, New York, 1993, pp. 253–62. During the 1990s, scholars returned to the study of generic fascism. R. Griffin, *The Nature of Fascism*, London, 1993 and *International Fascism: Theories, Causes, and the New Consensus*, London, 1998; and R. Eatwell, *Fascism: A History*, London, 1996, define fascism as a doctrine. S.G. Payne, *A History of Fascism, 1914–1945*, Madison, 1995, provides an encyclopaedic empirical survey.
3. Samir el-Khalil, *The Monument*, Berkeley, 1991. The author evokes fascism only indirectly.
4. Sir I. Berlin, 'Joseph de Maistre and the Origins of Fascism', in *The Crooked Timber of Humanity*, New York, 1991.
5. J.L. Talmon, *The Origins of Totalitarian Democracy*, Boston, 1952. Talmon's student Zeev Sternhell is the preeminent scholar today of fascism's intellectual roots in a heresy of the Left, national syndicalism. See, among many works, Z. Sternhell, M. Sznajder and M. Asheri, *Naissance de l'idéologie fasciste*, Paris, 1989, dedicated to Talmon.
6. We capitalise Fascism when referring to the Italian party, and refer to generic fascism in the lower case.
7. The formidable Margherita Sarfatti, patron of the arts and Mussolini's official biographer, is the subject of P. Canistraro and B. Sullivan, *Mussolini's Other Woman*, New York, 1993. Mussolini's most notorious Jewish henchman was Aldo Finzi, implicated in the murder of the socialist leader Giacomo Matteotti in June 1924. About a third of adult Italian Jews were members of the Fascist Party in 1938. See A. Stille, *Benevolence and Betrayal: Five Italian Jewish Families Under Fascism*, New York, 1991, p. 22, and Susan Zuccotti, *The Italians and the Holocaust*, New York, 1987, p. 27.
8. R. De Felice, *Fascism: an Informal Introduction to its Theory and Practice: an Interview with Michael A. Ledeen*, New Brunswick, NJ., 1976, pp. 15, 55–56, 67, 94–96; K.-D. Bracher, *Zeitgeschichtlichen Kontroversen. Um Totalitarismus, Faschismus, Demokratie*, Munich, 1976, p. 20.
9. R. Bessel, ed., *Fascist Italy and Nazi Germany: Comparisons and Contrasts*, Cambridge, 1996, the papers of a conference in honour of Tim Mason, is the latest examination of the complex but fundamental conceptual unity of the two regimes.
10. Friedrich Engels, 1895 preface to Karl Marx, *Class Struggles in France, (1848–50)*, in R.C. Tucker, ed., *The Marx-Engels Reader*, 2nd edition, New York, 1978, p. 571.
11. After 1968, Western Marxists criticised Stalin's interpretation of fascism and found an alternate tradition in August Thalheimer and Antonio Gramsci. See, for example, N. Poulantzas, *Fascisme et dictature*, Paris, 1970 and A. Rabinbach, 'Toward a Marxist Theory of Fascism and National Socialism', *New German Critique*, no. 3, Fall 1974, pp. 127–53. Wolfgang Wippermann surveys German views in 'The Postwar German Left and Fascism', *Journal of Contemporary History*, vol. 11, no. 4, October 1976, pp. 185–219, and in *Faschismustheorien zum Stand der Gegenwart*, new edition, Darmstadt, 1989.
12. P. Burrin, 'La France dans le champ magnétique des fascismes', *Le Débat*, no. 32, November 1984.

13. G. Orwell, *The Road to Wigan Pier*, New York, 1961, p.176. See also *The Lion and the Unicorn* (1941), quoted in *The Collected Essays, Journalism, and Letters of George Orwell*, ed. S. Orwell and I. Angus, Vol. III: My Country Right or Left (1940–43), New York, 1968, p. 93.

14. Payne, *History*, pp. 490, 518, considers fascism as inherently anticlerical; religious fundamentalisms, he asserts, are more likely today to produce authoritarianism than neo-fascism. In practice, however, fascisms have historically been close to churches identified with the national cause, as in eastern Europe, as Payne himself shows.

15. Roger Griffin and Roger Eatwell [see note 2 above] assert vigorously that fascism is to be understood as a doctrine. The most ambitious effort is Griffin's; he overcomes the problems of variation and contradiction by paring the fascist minimum down to national regeneration. Even Stanley Payne's more narrative *History of Fascism* says 'reading fascist programs' is his methodological starting point (pp. 11, 472).

16. An excellent review of these assumptions within Nazism, with an extensive bibliography, is found in Michael Burleigh and Wolfgang Wippermann, *The Racial State: Germany 1933–1945*, Cambridge, 1991.

17. M.A. Ledeen, *Universal Fascism: the Theory and Practice of the Fascist International, 1928–1936*, New York, 1972, explores Mussolini's short-lived attempt to gather the other fascist movements around himself in an international organisation. Hitler manifested little interest in his foreign disciples, showing notable reluctance to entrust the governance of conquered territories to quislings like the original Quisling in Norway (out of power until 1942), Mussert in Holland and Degrelle in Belgium. A recent study is M. Conway, *Collaboration in Belgium: Léon Degrelle and the Rexist Movement*, New Haven, 1993.

18. E. Gentile, *The Sacralization of Politics in Fascist Italy*, Cambridge, MA, 1996, pp. 24–25 examines the ritual purificatory burning of captured socialist materials by the *squadristi*. For Italian Fascist racialism (more cultural than biological), directed first against Slovenes and then against Libyans and Ethiopians, see note 64 below.

19. Current authors still sometimes claim that the Nazis violated the aspirations of big business (Payne, *History of Fascism*, p. 190). In fact, most German business leaders, whose negative memories of Weimar and the Depression were still fresh, swallowed their reluctance about Nazi autarky and thrived handsomely from rearmament. P. Hayes, *Industry and Ideology: IG Farben in the Nazi Era*, Cambridge, 1987, finds an 'intersection, not an identity, of interests' (p. 120). Daimler-Benz found particular favour with the regime. See B.P. Bellon, *Mercedes in Peace and War*, New York 1990. The most important common interest, of course, was the emasculation of the labour movement. These issues are magisterially treated by Charles Maier, 'The Economics of Fascism and Nazism', in Maier, *In Search of Stability: Explorations in Historical Political Economy*, Cambridge, 1987.

20. Sternhell et al., *Naissance*, p. 311 argues that actions conflict with programmes no more with fascism than with other political currents.

21. I draw these terms from Marc Bloch's description in summer 1943 of the two political systems then engaged in a life-and-death struggle: 'the tribe that a collective passion welds to its leader is here – that is, in a republic – replaced by a community governed by laws.' Marc Bloch, 'Pourquoi je suis républicain,' (*Les Cahiers politiques*, organe du Comité général d'études de la Résistance, #2, juillet 1943), one of the 'écrits clandestins' published in *L'Etrange défaite* , Paris 1993, p.215. He evoked the same distinction in *L'Etrange défaite*, p.176: Hitlerism 'remplace la persuasion par la suggestion émotive.'

22. W.L. Adamson, 'Modernism and Fascism: the Politics of Culture in Italy, 1903–1922', *American Historical Review*, vol. 95, no. 2, April 1990, pp. 361, 363, holds that the principal effect of Mussolini's association with modernist intellectuals was the legitimation this lent early Fascism. 'The important issue ... is not the content of fascist ideology but the cultural sources of fascist rhetoric and of the secular-religious aura it sought to project.'

23. R. Chartier, *The Cultural Origins of the French Revolution*, trans. Lydia G. Cochrane, Durham, 1991, p. 2.

24. Sternhell *et al.*, *Naissance*, pp. 258–60, 334.

25. Giuseppe di Lampedusa, *The Leopard*, translated from the Italian by Archibald Colquhoun, New York, 1950, p. 40.

26. Barbara Miller Lane, *Architecture and Politics in Germany, 1918–1945*, New York, 1985; W.L. Adamson, *Avant-garde Florence: Between Modernism and Fascism*, New York, 1993.

27. J. Herf, *Reactionary Modernism*, Cambridge, 1984, tries, with great erudition, to extract the meaning of the 'modern' from within fascist texts.

28. G. Bock, *Zwangssterilisation im Nationalsozialismus: Studien zur Rassenpolitik und Frauenpolitik*, Opladen, 1986, has transformed our understanding of Nazi family policy by underlining the anti-natalist character of its programmes of obligatory sterilisation for foreigners, the incurably ill, Jews and Gypsies. These anti-natalist policies coexisted, however, with a natalist policy for 'the master race'. See A. Grossmann, 'Feminist Debates about Women and National Socialism', *Gender and History*, vol. III, no. 3, Autumn 1991, pp. 350–58.

29. Henry A. Turner, Jr., doubted that generic fascism is a valid or useful concept in 'Fascism and Modernization', in Turner, ed., *Reappraisals of Fascism*, New York, 1975, pp. 132–33. Gilbert Allardyce pushed scepticism furthest in 'What Fascism is Not: Thoughts on the Deflation of a Concept', *American Historical Review*, vol. 84, no. 2, April 1979.

30. The term is from Carl Schorske, *Fin-de-siècle Vienna*, New York, 1980, Chapter 3.

31. The term *fascio* was used by syndicalists in the 1890s, as in the *fasci siciliani*; it emphasises the solidarity of brothers in action. Pro-war syndicalists brought the word into the nationalist lexicon in 1914 by creating the *fascio rivoluzionario d'azione interventista*, which Mussolini soon joined. See P. Milza, *Mussolini*, Paris, 1999, p. 174. The term *fascismo* seems to have been Mussolini's own invention in 1919.

32. Pierre Milza (see note 37 below) presents a four-stage model of fascism; P. Burrin, *La Dérive fasciste*, Paris, 1986, traces elegantly the itineraries, pulled between constraints and choices, by which Jacques Doriot, Marcel Déat and Gaston Bergery shifted from the Left to fascism.

33. An extreme case of this genre, An. Joes, *Fascism in the Contemporary World: Ideology, Evolution, Resurgence*, Boulder, 1978, includes practically every dictatorship in the developing world.

34. An example of superior quality is A. Lyttleton, *The Seizure of Power: Fascism in Italy, 1919–1929*, 2nd edition. Princeton, 1987.

35. R. Grew, 'On the Current State of Comparative Studies', in *Marc Bloch Aujourd'hui. Histoire comparée et sciences sociales*, ed. H. Atsma and A. Burguière, Paris, 1990, p. 331.

36. Marc Bloch, a great exponent of comparison in history, distinguished two kinds: the juxtaposition of similar phenomena in different cultures, such as feudalism in the West and in Japan; and the parallel study of 'neighboring and adjacent societies' having known 'change in the same direction'. Bloch, 'Pour une histoire comparée des sociétés européennes', *Revue de Synthèse* (1928). This second type of historical comparison, confronting different outcomes for the same process in two neighbouring regions, is the sharper tool. One thinks of the two halves of the *département* of the Sarthe, one republican and the other counterrevolutionary, compared so fruitfully by Paul Bois, *Paysans de l'ouest*, Paris, 1971, and of Maurice Agulhon's comparison of the different reception of republicanism in the early nineteenth century in two sectors of the Var, one of them 'quasiment immobile' and the other 'touché par la fièvre industrielle du capitalisme adolescent', *La République au village*, Paris, 1979, p. 32.

37. Pierre Milza proposes four stages in *Fascisme français: passé et présent*, Paris, 1987, pp. 43–53, and *Les fascismes*, Paris, 1985, pp. 132–38: a 'premier fascisme', marginal movements of intellectuals from both Right and Left; second, the fascism of militant anti-Left activists on the road to power; third, exercising power; and fourth, under the pressures of war.

38.   G. Mosse, *The Crisis of German Ideology*, New York, 1964, and other works.
39.   Z. Sternhell, *La droite révolutionnaire, 1885–1914: les origines françaises du fascisme*, Paris, 1978; Sternhell *et al.*, *Naissance*. See also E. Nolte, *Der Faschismus in seiner Epoche: Die Action française, Der italienische Faschismus, Der Nationalsozialismus*, Munich, 1966. Charles Maurras and Léon Daudet claimed in 1923 that the Action française preceded and influenced its 'twin sister', Italian Fascism, though later they underlined their differences with Fascist 'statolatrie'. Joel Blatt, 'Relations and Rivals: The Response of the Action française to Italian Fascism, 1919–1926', *European Studies Review*, vol. II, no. 3, July 1981, pp. 269–70.
40.   B. Adams, *La loi de la civilisation et de la décadence*, translated from English by Auguste Dietrich, Paris, 1899.
41.   S.M. Lipset and E. Rabb, *The Politics of Unreason: Right-wing Extremism in America, 1790–1970*, 2nd edition, New York, 1978 is a servicable 'bestiary' of many extreme right movements in the United States. Pelley is treated most fully in L.P. Riboffo, *The Old Christian Right: the Protestant Far Right from the Great Depression to the Cold War*, Philadelphia, 1983. For a subtle discussion of the appropriateness of the fascist label for the U.S. extreme Right during the 1930s, see A. Brinkley, *Voices of Protest: Huey Long, Father Coughlin, and the Great Depression*, New York, 1982, pp. 269–83.
42.   D.M. Chalmers, *Hooded Americanism: the First Century of the Ku Klux Klan, 1865–1965*, 3rd edition, Durham, NC, 1987, chapter 1. Correspondences between fascism and the Klan in the 1920s are explored by N. Maclean, *Behind the Mask of Chivalry: The Making of the Second Klan*, New York and Oxford, 1994, pp. 179–88.
43.   F. Wunderlich, *German Farm Labor, 1810–1845*, Princeton, 1961, pp. 52, 105–8; Erich D. Kohler, 'Revolutionary Pomerania, 1919–1920: A Study in Majority Socialist Agricultural Policy and Civil-Military Relations', *Central European History*, vol. X, no. 3, September 1976, pp. 250–93; M. Schumacher, *Land und Politik: Eine Untersuchung über politische parteien und agrarische Interessen*, Düsseldorf, 1978, pp. 294–309.
44.   P. Corner, *Fascism in Ferrara*, Oxford, 1976; F.M. Snowden, *Violence and Great Estates in the South of Italy: Apulia, 1900–1922*, Cambridge, 1986; S. Colarizi, *Dopoguerra e fascismo in Puglia, 1919–1926*, Bari, 1971.
45.   R.O. Paxton, *Le temps des chemises vertes*, Paris, 1996.
46.   The disillusioned words of Barbato Gattelli, a Fascist from the movement's first days, quoted in Corner, *Ferrara*, p. 224.
47.   S. Friedländer, *Reflections of Nazism: An Essay on Kitsch and Death*, Bloomington, 1993, explores the nihilistic and erotic undercurrents within aesthetic evocations of Nazism after the 1970s.
48.   It is curious to note how little research has been directed to this crucial aspect of the fascist seizure of power. The main work dealing with this subject is J. Linz and A. Stepan, eds, *The Breakdown of Democratic Regimes in Europe*, Baltimore, 1978.
49.   Local fascist leaders were called *ras* after Ethiopian chieftains, for the Ethiopians' defeat of the Italian Army at Adowa in 1896 still rankled Italian nationalists.
50.   The Nazi rural organisers had to overcome rural suspicions based on Point 17 of the Twenty-five points that called for expropriation without compensation of land needed for national purposes, the abolition of ground rent, and the prohibition of speculation in land. T. Childers, *The Nazi Voter*, Chapel Hill, 1983, pp. 149–51, 215–21; J.E. Farquharson, 'The Agrarian Policy of National Socialist Germany', in R.G. Moeller, ed., *Peasants and Lords in Modern Germany: Recent Studies in Agricultural History*, Boston, 1986, p. 236. See more generally J.E. Farquharson, *The Plough and the Swastika*, Berkeley, 1976; A. Bramwell, *Blood and Soil: Richard Walther Darré and Hitler's 'Green Party'*, Abbotsbrook, 1985.
51.   Interwar fascists could remember how a general strike had frustrated the Kapp *Putsch* in Germany in 1920.

52. Lyttelton, *Seizure* is still best for this process in Italy. For Germany, K.-D. Bracher et al., *Die nationalsozialistische Machtergreifung*, 3 vols., Cologne and Opladen, 1962 is still basic.

53. R. Rémond, *Les Droites en France*, Paris, 1982, pp. 206–8, (Editor's translation)

54. S. Berstein, 'La France allergique au fascisme', *Vingtième siècle: revue d'histoire*, no. 2, April 1984, p. 94. (Editor's translation).

55. Sternhell et al., *Naissance*, p. 12. See also n. 38 above. (Editor's translation).

56. Z. Sternhell, *Ni droite ni gauche: l'idéologie fasciste en France*, Paris, 1983, p. 293. (Editor's translation).

57. No one denies the label of fascist to Valois's Faisceau, Bucard's Francisme, Renaud's Solidarité française, Doriot's Parti populaire français, and the last phases of Marcel Déat's Rassemblement national populaire. See the scrupulously delimited list in P. Burrin, 'Le Fascisme', in *Histoire des droites en France*, ed. J-F. Sirinelli, Vol. I: Politique, Paris 1992, pp. 636–644. Berstein, 'Allergique' wrote more generally of 'germes isolés' of fascism (pp. 89–91) and of a 'disponibilité au fascisme … présente dans une partie de l'opinion publique' (p. 92). Raoul Girardet, in 'Notes sur l'esprit d'un fascisme français, 1934–1939', *Revue française de science politique*, V:3, July-September 1955, p. 530, while agreeing with Rémond that France had few truly fascist movements, argued that French nationalism underwent an 'imprégnation fasciste' between the wars that created a 'une résonance, une tonalité nouvelle, tout à fait originale dans son histoire'.

58. M. Dobry, 'Février 1934 et la découverte de l'allergie de la société française à la "Révolution fasciste"', *Revue française de sociologie*, vol. XXX, 1989, pp. 528, 531.

59. 'Sur le continent européen la France constitue le seul pays important où la démocratie libérale ait résisté au choc du fascisme et du nazisme.' Sternhell, *Ni Droite ni gauche*, p. 293, (Editor's translation).

60. Burrin, 'Fascisme', pp. 641–42. Burrin's method of following 'itinéraires' into fascism is enlightening.

61. R.O. Paxton, *Le Régime de Vichy, 1940–1944*, new edition, Paris, 1997, pp. 93, 280–86, 309–10, 320; M. Cointet-Labrousse, *Vichy et le fascisme: les hommes, les structures, et les pouvoirs*, Brussels 1987, pp. 161, 197–208, 225ff. An interesting attempt to evaluate Vichy's propaganda efforts as a failed fascist experiment is D. Peschanski, 'Vichy au singulier, Vichy au pluriel. Une tentative avortée d'encadrement de la société (1941–1942)', *Annales: économies, sociétés, civilisations*, 43e année, no. 3, May-June 1988, pp. 639–62.

62. Burrin, 'Fascisme', Milza, *Fascisme français*; Berstein, 'Allergique'; Rémond, *Droites*. J. Nobécourt, *Le Colonel de La Rocque, 1885–1946, ou les pièges du nationalisme chrétien*, Paris, 1996, an exhaustive sympathetic biography, portrays La Rocque as a conservative victimised by false accusations and personal rivalries.

63. R. Soucy, *French Fascism: the First Wave, 1924–1933*, New Haven, 1986, and *French Fascism: the Second Wave, 1933–1939*, New Haven, 1995; William D. Irvine, 'Fascism in France and the Strange Case of the Croix de Feu', *Journal of Modern History*, vol. 63, June 1991, pp. 271–95.

64. K. Passmore, 'Boy Scoutism for Grown-ups? Paramilitarism in the Croix de Feu and the Parti Social Français', *French Historical Studies*, vol. 19, no. 2, Fall 1995, pp. 527–57; idem, *From Liberalism to Fascism: The Right in a French Province, 1928–1939*, Cambridge, 1997. The mere fact of competing in elections, of course, does not make a party nonfascist, as the energetic electoral campaigning of both the Nazis and Italian Fascists makes clear. Authentic fascisms were distinguished by their capacity to play on both electoral and extraparliamentary boards.

65. Burrin, *La Dérive fasciste*, p. 414; idem., 'Fascisme', pp. 643–44. Zeev Sternhell, usually scrupulously exact, is in flagrant error (see chapter 2 above pp. 40–41) when he argues that the interwar French Right was expansionist. Its overwhelming dread of war after about 1934 is manifest in every right-wing publication of the period. Its renewed

interest in Empire in the late 1930s, usually referred to as a 'repli impérial' (a term Sternhell carefully avoids), was a defensive turn inward that signified the abandonment of European ambitions. To confuse the French interwar image of the 'poilus', the tenacious peasant boys who had held the trenches in 1914–18 in a spirit of 'ils ne passeront pas', with the aggressive toughs of Mussolini's squadristi or Hitler's SA seems particularly misplaced.

66. The most comprehensive account is R. Thurlow, *Fascism in Britain, 1918–1985*, revised edition, Oxford, 1998. See also M. Cronin, *The Failure of British Fascism*, London, 1996.

67. S. Payne, *The Franco Regime, 1936–1975*, Madison, 1987; P. Preston, *Franco, a Biography*, New York, 1994; A. Costa Pinto, *Salazar's Dictatorship and European Fascism*, Boulder, 1995. One does not need to conclude, however, with Payne, *History*, pp. 250, 252, 312, 321, 326, 395, 492, that authoritarian military dictatorships have been the most effective barrier historically against fascist acquisitions of power.

68. Racial hygiene has recently proven a fruitful subject because it links Nazi practice to professional interests. See M.H. Kater, *Doctors under Hitler*, Chapel Hill, 1989; R.J. Lifton, *The Nazi Doctors: Medical Killing and the Psychology of Genocide*, New York, 1986. Burleigh and Wippermann, *The Racial State* (note 16 above), p. 353 n. 1, advocate, convincingly, a more anthropologically informed study of how fascist regimes interacted with various social groups.

69. Perspicacious contemporary observers saw this compound quality of fascist rule as a 'dual state', where the 'normative state' jostled for power with a 'prerogative state' formed by the party's parallel organisations. See E. Fraenkel, *The Dual State*, New York and Oxford, 1941, and F. Neumann, *Behemoth*, New York and Oxford, 1942. The compound nature of fascist rule has been conceptually refined since the 1970s by the 'polyocratic' interpretation. See M. Broszat, *Hitler's State*, London, 1981; Hans Mommsen in many works, including *From Weimar to Auschwitz*, Cambridge, 1991; and G. Hirschfeld and L. Kettenacker, ed., *Der Führerstaat: Mythos und Realität*, Stuttgart, 1981. For an analagous reading of Fascist Italy, see E. Gentile, 'Le rôle du parti dans le laboratoire totalitaire italien' and P. Burrin, 'Politique et société: les structures du pouvoir dans l'Italie fasciste et l'Allemagne nazie', both in *Annales: économies, sociétés, civilisations*, 43e année, no. 3, May-June 1988.

70. H. Arendt, *The Origins of Totalitarianism*, 2nd enlarged edition., New York, 1958, pp. 389–90, 395, 398, 402. She credits 'shapelessness' to Neumann, *Behemoth*.

71. Juan J. Linz has made the classic analysis of authoritarianism as a distinct form of rule, most recently in *Totalitarian and Authoritarian Regimes*, Boulder, 2000. Zeev Sternhell, in this volume and elsewhere, seconded by Soucy, prefers to classify everything to the right of centre in interwar France as fascist. This requires a definition of fascism so broad (rejection of the Enlightenment) that it could include the Pope and believers in divine-right monarchy. Political categories, of course, are only human contrivances that exist solely to help clarify our understanding of the political landscape. I believe that our understanding of the Right in the twentieth century is aided by a relatively circumscribed definition of fascism and a clear understanding of its borders with traditional conservatism and authoritarian dictatorship. To analyse them, one must not only amass similarities (as Sternhell does) but consider an entire balance-sheet of similarities and differences.

72. Arendt, *Origins*, included Stalin and excluded Mussolini, as did C. Friedrich and Z. Brzezinski, *Totalitarian Dictatorship and Autocracy*, New York, 1956. By the late 1960s, the totalitarianism concept had come to seem a Cold War artefact and remains in use today only in popular language. See Benjamin R. Barber, 'The Conceptual Foundations of Totalitarianism', in C.J. Friedrich et al., *Totalitarianism in Perspective: Three Views*, London, 1969.

73. The borders between the two kinds of regime are blurred here, for, in practice, neither gets its wish. Faced with aroused publics, authoritarians as well as fascists may attempt

to create a Durkheimian 'mechanical solidarity': see P. Brooker, *The Faces of Fraternalism: Nazi Germany, Fascist Italy, and Imperial Japan*, Oxford, 1991. Fascists may achieve no more than a 'superficial' and 'fragile' consent. V. De Grazia, *The Culture of Consent: Mass Organization of Leisure in Fascist Italy*, Cambridge, 1981, p. 20 and chapter 8, 'The Limits of Consent'.

74. Robert Ley, head of the Nazi Labour Service, said that the only private individual in the Nazi state is a person asleep. Arendt believed him. *Origins*, p. 339.

75. Although Fascist Italy has been less studied than Nazi Germany in 'polycratic' terms, E. Gentile, *La via italiana al totalitarismo: il partito e il stato nel regime fascista*, Rome, 1995, the most recent demonstration of the regime's far-reaching totalitarian aspirations, concedes that is was a 'realtà composita' (p. 136) marked by 'sorda lotta' among its factions (p. 180). Jens Petersen and Wolfgang Schieder give the issue more direct attention in several works, most recently in *Faschismus und Gesellschaft in Italien: Staat, Wirtschaft, Kultur*, Cologne, 1998. See also the articles of Gentile and Burrin cited in note 69.

76. The terms are Renzo De Felice's in *Mussolini: il Duce: lo stato totalitario, 1936–1940*, Turin, 1981, p. 100; for this and other controversial judgements by Mussolini's principal biographer, see B.W. Painter, 'Renzo De Felice and the Historiography of Italian Fascism', *American Historical Review*, vol. 95, no. 2, April 1990.

77. C. Segrè, *The Fourth Shore: the Italian Colonization of Libya*, Chicago, 1974; Angelo Del Boca, 'Le leggi razziali nell'impero di Mussolini' and Nicola Labanca, 'L'amministrazione coloniale fascista. Stato, politica e società', in *Il Regime Fascista: storia e storiografia*, ed. A. Del Boca, M. Legnani and M.G. Rossi, Rome/Bari, 1995.

78. In the debate about what drove radicalisation, the artificial dichotomy between 'intentionalists' and 'functionalists' has been resolved, most effectively by Christopher Browning, in favour of an interaction between the leader's intentions and competitive harshness among subordinates who counted on his approval. Browning's most recent analysis is *Nazi Policy: Jewish Workers, German Killers*, Cambridge, 2000.

79. Omer Bartov makes a somewhat different point about how the special conditions of the Russian campaign inured the Army as well as the SS to brutality. See *The Eastern Front, 1941–1945: German Troops and the Barbarization of Warfare*, New York, 1986, and *Hitler's Army: Soldiers, Nazis, and War in the Third Reich*, New York and Oxford, 1991.

80. Stein U. Larsen et al., eds, *Who were the Fascists? Social Roots of European Fascism*, Oslo, 1980, surmounts this problem better than most. More recent work avoids both class and Hannah Arendt's mass society, preferring to explore links with more particularly defined groups: professions (note 68 above), clubs, fraternities and other 'intermediary bodies'. See R. Koshar, 'From *Stammtisch* to Party: Nazi Joiners and the Contradictions of Grass Roots Fascism in Weimar Germany', *Journal of Modern History*, vol. 59, March 1987, pp. 1–24; and idem, *Social Life, Local Politics, and Nazism: Marburg, 1880–1935*, Chapel Hill, 1986.

81. Susan Sontag made an interesting effort to extract the elements of a fascist aesthetic from the work of Leni Riefenstahl: 'Fascinating Fascism' in Sontag, *Under the Sign of Saturn*, New York, 1980, but it may apply only to German culture.

82. Still basic in English is J. Stephenson, *Women in Nazi Society*, New York, 1975; Burleigh and Wippermann, *The Racial State* [note 16] have an up-to-date chapter on women in Nazi Germany and, more innovatively, one on men. Essential for Italy is V. De Grazia, *How Fascism Ruled Women: Italy, 1922–1945*, Berkeley, 1992.

83. Mirko Tremaglia, a veteran of Mussolini's last regime, the Republic of Salò, was elected chairman of the Foreign Affairs Committee of the Italian Parliament in 1994.

84. Stanley Payne, *History*, p. 496, along with all others who consider fascism a specific doctrine born of late nineteenth- century national syndicalism, is obliged to conclude that 'the same forms of fascism could not not be effectively revived' after 1945.

5

February 1934 and the Discovery of French Society's Allergy to the 'Fascist Revolution'

Michel Dobry

Unlike the other contributors to this volume, Michel Dobry is not a historian, but works rather in the field of political sociology. He is one of the promoters and intellectual leaders of the process of renewal this discipline has undergone in France over the last fifteen years. Before taking up his current post at the Sorbonne, Michel Dobry was the founder, and director from 1993 to 2003, of the Laboratoire d'Analyse des Systèmes Politiques (CNRS), and from 1994 to 1999 he was co-president of the European Science Foundation's international research network 'Social Transformations in Central and Eastern Europe'. His principal sphere of interest has been the problems associated with the analysis of political crisis, which is the subject of his book *Sociologie des crises politiques* (1986, Paris: also widely available in translation) and of several articles. His other works have focused above all on collective action and political competition in 'complex' contemporary societies. More recently he has written extensively on the politics of transition and democratisation: he edited *Democratic and Capitalist Transitions in Eastern Europe: Lessons for the Social Sciences* (Dordrecht, 2000) and a special issue of *Revue Française de Science Politique* on this topic, also in 2000.

The chapter that follows first appeared as an article in the French journal *Revue française de sociologie* in 1989, and indeed focuses on a particular political crisis, namely the events of 6 February 1934. The terms of reference are, however, much wider than that. It is a sustained critique of the standard historical interpretation of the politics of the French extreme Right between the wars, calling into question the methodological foundations of what Professor Dobry refers to here as the 'immunity thesis'. The importance of this landmark article has been acknowledged by every other contributor to this volume. For these reasons, we make no apologies for reproducing the original article here unamended in English translation.

The reader will observe that Professor Dobry is not interested in taking sides in the debate about whether or not French extreme Right formations were fascist, indeed he explicitly refuses to do so. This has not prevented some of the revisionists invoking Dobry's essay in support of their own case, omitting to point out that this was not his intention. He, on the other hand, has been careful not to level equal blame at the proponents of the immunity thesis and some of their detractors: in his view, the latter are much less mistaken than the former, because at least they have not underestimated the political importance of the radical Right in 1930s France. Michel Dobry has recently published an important edited volume of essays on this subject, prepared under his direction, *Le mythe de l'allergie française au fascisme* (Paris, 2003).

Michel Dobry is Professor of Political Science at the Université Paris I, Sorbonne.

Author's note
This article, first published in French fourteen years ago, does not require any modification or revision. My critique of the 'immunity thesis' remains equally pertinent today. Two or three brief observations will allow me to explain why.

Firstly, the arguments developed in this article have, in various ways and sometimes unintentionally, been confirmed, reinforced or developed by subsequent works. This is particularly evident in the analysis of certain key movements of the French authoritarian Right in the first half of the twentieth century, notably the Action française (see especially Bruno Goyet, *Charles Maurras*, Paris, 2000; Brian Jenkins, 'L'Action française à l'ère du fascisme: une perspective contextuelle', in Michel Dobry, ed., *Le mythe de l'allergie française au fascisme*, Paris, 2003) and La Rocque's Croix de Feu/Parti social français (see in particular Jacques Nobécourt, *Le Colonel de la Rocque, 1885–1946, ou les pièges du nationalisme chrétien*, Paris, 1996, a biography whose author claims to be an 'amateur' historian and who makes no attempt to hide his sympathy for La Rocque, but who nonetheless assembles a mass of material which contradicts the standard view of the PSF and its leader developed by proponents of the 'immunity thesis'; Kevin Passmore, *From Liberalism to Fascism: The Right in a French Province, 1928–1939*, Cambridge, 1997; Robert Soucy, *French Fascism. The Second Wave, 1933–1939*, New Haven and London, 1995; William D. Irvine, 'Fascism in France. The Strange Case of the Croix-de-feu', *Journal of Modern History*, 1991, pp 271–95; Didier Leschi, 'L'étrange cas La Rocque', in M. Dobry, ed., *Le mythe de l'allergie française au fascisme*; finally, as D. Leschi points out, Zeev Sternhell's recent revision of his views on La Rocque's movement clearly follows in the wake of the reflections developed in my article below; cf. Zeev Sternhell, preface to the 3rd edition, *Ni droite, ni gauche. L'idéologie fasciste en France*, Paris, 2000).

This does not mean that the authors cited above have all necessarily understood one of the key intentions of my article, far from it! I deliberately sought to demonstrate the futility of the classificatory approach adopted by the immunity thesis, but some of these authors are themselves ensnared in this same classificatory logic; thus, for example, Robert Soucy (in a work which frequently sheds interesting light on the French authoritarian Right between the wars) is mistaken when he interprets what I have to say about the PSF in my article as an invitation to classify the PSF under the heading of 'fascism' or 'authentic fascism' (R. Soucy, *The Second Wave*); as Brian Jenkins has indeed recognised, my intention was quite the opposite, namely to escape from the false embrace of *la logique classificatoire* (see B. Jenkins, 'Robert Soucy and the "Second Wave" of French Fascism', *Modern and Contemporary France*, 1996, no 2, pp. 193–208); for a more systematic treatment of this discussion, see Michel Dobry, 'La thèse immunitaire face aux fascismes. Pour une critique de la logique classificatoire', in M. Dobry, ed., *Le mythe de l'allergie française au fascisme*).

Finally it is also significant that in recent years the immunity thesis has been increasingly reluctant to manifest itself, except in disguised or euphemistic form; in response to circumstance, it has undergone numerous 'adjustments' and 'adaptations', thus becoming a *moving target* for would-be critics. However, these 'adaptations' are no more than 'tactical withdrawals' as far as its proponents are concerned, because at the same time they are quite determined to safeguard the essential core position of the thesis, namely the supposed exceptionalism of French society as regards fascism. One of these 'adaptations', tellingly enough, is purely *cosmetic*: since the publication of the article which follows, most partisans of the immunity thesis have noticeably avoided using the word 'allergie'.

The nature of a crisis is revealed just as much by the way in which it develops as by its origins: from this point of view, nothing proves more conclusively that [the crisis of February 1934] had no revolutionary impulse – fascism, at least at the outset, had a revolutionary side – than the outcome of that crisis. (René Rémond, *Les droites en France*, p. 210.[1])

This short extract from one of the 'classics' of contemporary 'political history' sums up the standard interpretation of the crisis of February 1934, a view still widely held today by French historians specialising in the period.

There are two reasons for beginning with this point. Firstly, the above quotation confirms that, in the analysis of crises and their attendant social phenomena, great importance has traditionally been attached to their 'outcomes', their 'results', their consequences. In this particular case the 'outcome' was the call to Gaston Doumergue, that hardened veteran of 'party politics', on the day after the 6 February events, inviting him to form a government. If Doumergue's cabinet did not actually stop the 'agitation' (demonstrations, counter-demonstrations and clashes continued well beyond 7 February), then at least it brought an end to the political crisis itself. After more than a month of street disturbances in the wake of the Stavisky scandal, the political regime of the Third Republic was able to struggle on for a few more years.

This habit of constructing historical interpretations on the basis of the 'outcomes' of crises is very common and goes far beyond the debate on the 'meaning' of 6 February. The aim of this article is to show that it is rather 'imprudent' (to use a euphemism) to claim with such conviction that the 'outcome' of a crisis 'reveals its nature'.[2] However, to return to the specific context of our opening quotation, Rémond believed that it was possible to make a further deduction from the 'outcome' of this particular crisis: namely that there was no significant fascist component in French political life in the 1930s. Indeed, the claim that the events of February 1934 had little immediate effect is one of the central arguments used by some (mainly French) historians to demonstrate that fascism was practically non existent in the country at that time, but for a few small ephemeral groups, and to prove that French society rejected fascism – a position we refer to here as the 'immunity thesis'.[3] It was partly on this basis that these same historians took issue with the very different perceptions of the period presented by various foreign authors, and especially by Zeev Sternhell,[4] whose work provoked a series of critical reactions. These responses have been very valuable for our own purposes here, because they have (albeit rather untidily) updated and systematised the immunity thesis. Furthermore, the violence of these reactions is a sure sign that this is rather a sore point, and not just on a methodological level.[5]

However, the aim of this article is not to take sides in *this* debate on Sternhell's ideas.[6] I will not be concerned with trying to locate the origins of fascism, nor indeed with attempting to *classify in any other way* the groups that, in 1930s France, were associated with the 'radical' Right or, if one prefers, the 'fascistoid' Right.[7] Nor will I seek to assimilate the latter with an 'authentic' fascism, pure and uncompromising, or similar in every detail to what could be seen in Italy or Germany at the time. The problems raised are in a manner of speaking 'disengaged' from the debate that we have just outlined; they are basically methodological, but nonetheless they probably have serious implications for our understanding of France between the wars.

What is at stake here is the intellectual stance of these advocates of the immunity thesis. And it is this stance – the interpretation of crisis situations in terms of their 'outcomes' – which leads to the discovery (or should I say the invention?) of the alleged 'allergy' of French society to fascism. It is this latter supposition that shapes the questions these historians then pose, that defines their field of enquiry and restricts their field of vision. It is this supposition that leads them quite simply to *miss what is truly specific about the object of their research*, to search for what is singular and particular where they are least likely to be found, whilst persistently refusing to see these things when they are staring them in the face. It also prevents them from perceiving clearly what is different, and also what is sometimes similar, between the political processes at work in interwar France, and the development paths of 'authentic' or 'complete' fascisms (and we shall see later how our historians tend to equate 'authentic' fascism with the 'complete' end-product of the fully-fledged fascist regime). In this sense, the notion of 'allergy' is a major obstacle to any comparative analysis of these processes and paths, and yet it is only by using this kind of analysis that the historian can establish a plausible relationship between 'results' or 'outcomes' (his starting point) and the 'causes' that he attributes to them.[8]

In other words, this article also suggests a way of overcoming this obstacle, by a device which, at first sight, may seem surprising to some historians and indeed to some sociologists. When the objects of our study are critical processes (whether 'crises', 'revolutions', 'riots' or indeed 'moves towards fascism') we should take the methodological decision to place the 'outcomes' or 'results' of these processes in parentheses, leaving them out of the picture for just a little while. This approach, I freely admit, is not the easiest, especially as the 'outcome', *once it has taken effect*, often has a considerable determining influence on the fate of peoples and societies. However, this would appear to be the only way of escaping from the illusion that the 'outcomes' reflect the critical processes that led to them.

Thinking from the 'outcome'

The proponents of the immunity thesis are not much given to methodological doubt and debate, and it seems unlikely that they are particularly aware of the intellectual logic which underpins their argument. Unrecognised, uncontrolled, this habit of reinterpreting historical processes according to their 'results' or 'outcomes' is nonetheless laden with consequences. A prime example of this is the way the events of February 1934 have been decoded, as the text quoted at the beginning of the article shows. There may be some individual or even seasonal variations of approach, but the overall picture is nonetheless remarkably clear.[9]

Unfortunately the use of the 'outcome' of 6 February to define the 'nature' of the crisis and of the processes that preceded it, without recourse to any other evidence, cannot be attributed simply to some stylistic vanity. It is quite clear that, in the immunity thesis, the formation of the Doumergue cabinet serves as a benchmark for measuring (which here means *eliminating*) the notion that prior to February 1934 there was an 'authentically fascist' element ('revolutionary ... at least at the outset' in Rémond's words) of any real political significance. Because the result, the 'outcome', was the survival of the Third Republic, the conclusion is that nothing in the events and mobilisations that produced it, nothing even in the articulation of these events and mobilisations, could bear meaningful comparison with the processes which had brought the fascists into power elsewhere. So the natural deduction is the *absence* of any genuine 'radicalism' in this 'radical Right', or, in other words, the respectable conservatism of all those who took part in the mobilisations.

Armed with this conviction, the historian (normally so attentive to the views, aspirations and feelings of the actors) will be indifferent to the fact that, for most people who mobilised and doubtless for many others besides, 6 February (precisely *because* the Third Republic survived!) was later regarded as a great 'missed opportunity' to do away with '*la gueuse*', the hated and reviled regime they contested with such passion. Instead the historian will ascribe to them motives and sentiments which fit better with the outcome – the return of a 'distinguished parliamentarian' – and will dismiss any awkward contrary testimony by filing it away under the convenient catch-all heading of 'myth'. Anything else (what participants actually said, sometimes loud and clear, at least in 1934–35) can be put down to 'pseudo-revolutionary language', words for words' sake, devoid of any 'serious' intent. After all, how can we tell the difference between 'pseudo-revolutionary' and 'authentic revolutionary', especially in the domain of language, except by referring to the fact that in the end the 'revolution' never happened? So evidently none of these individuals, movements and statements should be *taken seriously*. Are we still not convinced? In that case our historian will take great pains to establish that, in the run up to 6 February, *there was no real conspiracy* jointly engineered by the Jeunesses Patriotes, Action Française and the Croix-de-Feu (though the conspiracy theory is quite plausible). For, as everyone knows, conspiracy is an absolutely vital stage of the process in any 'serious' political crisis!

However, when we look at all the works subscribing to the immunity thesis, this regressive rereading of the processes that preceded the 'outcome' does not stop with the detail of the events themselves. The thesis has no trouble identifying diverse other 'causes' in the near or distant past that can all be deduced from this failure of the *ligues* in February 1934. Notably, among many others, the political weakness of their leaders or their lack of 'charisma', the inconsistency of their programmes, the absence of any coherent political strategy or structured ideology, their unrealistic ambitions, their marginal social bases, their fake belligerence and (the final stage in this rereading of history) the *specificity* of French society, i.e. its *political culture* (a notion sufficiently elastic to stretch around most arguments), and above all its 'allergy to fascism', the ultimate cause of the 'outcome' of the events of February 1934.

This, then, is the more explicit side of the immunity thesis, which seems at least to be clearly articulated. But this too proves to be an illusion! Closer examination reveals, to our astonishment, that the plausibility of the theory depends on an unavowed telescoping of events, a strange confusion or, at the very least, a surreptitious sleight of hand. From the question of the label of 'fascism' or 'authentic fascism' from which the organisations and militants of the radical Right have to be exonerated (this, apparently, is the major 'theoretical' preoccupation of our historians), we find ourselves constantly sliding away to consider another question, namely the alleged social or political 'marginality' of the radical Right, its marginal impact on the political contest. There is no doubt that by eliding these two issues, it has been possible to increase the demonstrative value of the immunity thesis – as if the plausibility of the answer to the first question depended on the answer given to the second.

However, this apparent methodological laxity has much deeper and more constraining roots; it is structurally linked to the intellectual logic that underpins the whole of the interpretation being discussed. This logic derives from an implicit (and dangerous) assumption or postulate: namely that for every 'outcome', for every consequential phenomenon, for every specific result – for example the 'outcome' of February 1934 – there must be a corresponding *specific historical path*. But then, the reader may anxiously ask, can we really do otherwise? After all, is such an assumption not absolutely indispensable to the work of any historian or sociologist? And, consequently, is it not the task *par excellence* of the historian to identify and describe this path by means of *regressive analysis* using the 'outcome' as the starting point? Indeed, should his work not be judged precisely by his ability to reveal what is singular about the historical path associated with a given type of result or outcome?

It will be easier to judge the significance of the above postulate if we remind ourselves of the multiplicity of 'outcomes' the historian may have before him. Bearing this in mind, the postulate corresponds to the following confident (but highly debatable) proposition: namely that for each type of 'outcome', effect or result (be they 'revolutions', 'fascisms', 'adjustments to democracy', 'moves towards authoritarianism') there must, necessarily, be specific types of historical path, which differ from those leading to other types of 'outcome'. Whence, as we will see, the bizarre view that the immunity thesis has of Italian and German fascisms, a view which is duplicated in the way it defines them. And this is particularly relevant given that the credibility of the immunity thesis depends largely on the contrast it draws between 'authentic fascism' and the political path of the French radical Right. It thus becomes a little clearer why the 'lack of seriousness' attributed to the latter also strangely concurs with the rejection of the label of 'fascism'.

Shameful historicism

Thus the regressive and selective identification of historical 'facts' has a dual dimension. First of all, on the face of it, selection on the basis of the result or 'outcome' seems to be giving proper attention to the deep historical context of the event or episode being examined. However, the selection of 'facts' is also being conducted in another way, one that is more often than not implicit or even unconscious. Namely the result, the starting point of the analysis, is itself used to identify all those historical cases that may legitimately be considered 'comparable' with one another. It singles out all those cases which display the features used to define the effect or 'outcome', the features which make this 'outcome' different from all other types of 'outcome'. And then, of course, in these same cases we will look for a similarity, or at least a proximity, of historical paths *preceding* the 'outcomes'.

The informed reader will by now have recognised that this pattern for decoding historical reality is very similar to what we used to call 'natural history', with Crane Brinton's 'natural history of revolutions' as the classic model.[10] It will be recalled that, by systematically comparing a number of 'great revolutions' (notably France 1789, England 1642 and Russia 1917), Brinton sought to show what they had in common and what was more specific in their trajectories. Thus we are introduced to the historical sequence of events organised into the famous 'stages', namely: the warning signs of the coming revolution (whose 'symptoms' range from accelerated economic growth to the transfer of the allegiance of the intellectuals); the 'fever' stage (the seizing of power by the 'moderates'); the 'crisis' stage (the coming to power of the radicals, in France the Terror); and finally the convalescent stage of a society returning to a tolerable normality (in France, Thermidor). In an admittedly cruder version, the intellectual logic of this 'natural history' approach can be detected in the perspectives of proponents of the immunity thesis, even though they neither intended it, nor were necessarily conscious of it: each type of result or 'outcome' must have its own specific 'natural history'.

It is perhaps becoming apparent that to interpret the processes in question – and critical processes in general – from the starting point of their results or 'outcomes' is not as harmless or neutral, in methodological terms, as common sense suggests or would have us believe. The historian's multifarious fascination with results goes hand-in-hand with an unacknowledged but nonetheless resilient historicism. Rare, of course, are those partisans of the immunity thesis who would openly admit what their approach is ultimately designed to prove: namely that, from the 'preconditions' of its emergence, from its very birth onwards, the process under consideration (the one that leads notably to the 'outcome' of February 1934) is almost genetically determined by an inner *nature' which is accomplished in this result* and which, at every turn, orients this process in the direction of the result and not in any other. But in reality, all their interpretation, selection and construction of the 'facts', their whole construction of the historical 'intrigue' tends towards this teleological view of the 'course of history'.[11]

In the light of this it is scarcely surprising that, when dealing with events like those of February 1934, our historians refuse to admit that one type of phenomenon may in certain circumstances become another (albeit one that closely resembles it). Not only on the abstract methodological level, but also in the substance of their work on the 1930s, they find it hard to accept that local nuances or minor changes can have 'great' effects, and can even upset 'major trends', long-term' evolutions or 'structural realities'. For them, if the leagues missed their chance to seize power, it was because they were not 'serious'! And if the 'outcome' of the crisis of February 1934 was the survival of the Third Republic, then that was because, when all is said and done, the 'nature' of the process which led to it meant that this was the only possible result. That is why this 'outcome' is so important to the immunity thesis.

The authentic and the complete

To illustrate what the above critique means in practice, let us now look at the way the promoters of the immunity thesis portray the German and Italian fascisms. The reader will be aware that these authors have criticised Sternhell, often in contradictory ways, for not having given any definition of what he understands by 'fascism', or for giving one that was too vague, or on the contrary, too narrow. Strangely, the counter-definitions they provide are themselves not always made fully explicit, far from it, in fact. The most developed definition (by Serge Berstein) attempts to define fascism 'in practice' and not, as Sternhell is accused of doing, as an 'ideology'.[12] The idea is an excellent one, but it should be looked at a little more closely. Four 'criteria' of fascism are proposed, which should allow us to cast a little light on a muddled reality. These criteria are: (1) Fascism is defined firstly by its link with the arrival of the masses on the political stage, and is associated with the problem of integrating these masses into political systems; in this sense, it becomes a 'phenomenon specific to a period' (the end of the nineteenth/beginning of the twentieth centuries) and in a specific geographical area. (2) The role of the Great War which, in a number of ways, not only encourages the awakening of a consciousness of the importance of political power, but also undermines the structures of societies, attaches new value to the 'principle of authority' within them (their efficiency in conducting the war), and gives rise to the 'reds under the bed' psychosis. (3) Fascism is also characterised by the contents of its programme, which reflects the coming together of 'third way' ideologies between liberalism and socialism, authoritarian and antidemocratic 'currents of influence'(?) derived from the war, the use of violence to establish a new order, and the 'regimentation of the masses behind a charismatic leader to create a military-type society'. (4) And finally, state totalitarianism based on the principle of the primacy of the ideology, and whose privileged instrument is the single party – which in turn supposes the destruction of all other organisations that could challenge its authority. However, adds the author, suddenly seized by quite justifiable doubts, this totalitarianism will already have been 'tendentially present in the ideology before arrival in power'.

What should we make of these four 'criteria'? Firstly, it should be apparent to everyone that the first two, however we understand them, are in no ways 'criteria' in that they do not distinguish what we call 'fascism' from other types of social phenomena. At best they are plausible *preconditions* for fascism – but not solely for fascism – and this suggests the definition is very much of the 'natural history' type. The fourth criterion only reveals itself, so to speak, after the *outcome* of the 'seizure of power' by the fascists, and this represents the end point of the developmental path. As for the third criterion, essentially it just describes a few ideological traits shared by the German and Italian fascist parties (but not only by them), their view of the world rather than their 'programmes', and moreover it telescopes these traits with what the fascists more or less did when they attained power. So the only real points of discrimination made by this definition of fascism concern the *result* of the process it attempts to define; it is all about the effective 'seizure of power' and the subsequent construction of a 'power system' or an original 'regime' by the fascists. It is *this* 'criterion', and none of the others, which enables the author to classify (in other words to demarcate) the movements of the radical Right in 1930s France in relation to fascism. However, the other criteria leave the historian free to conduct, at each stage, a *random search for any difference* between those paths that led to this type of result (fascism) and those which (as in 1930s France) led to different 'outcomes'.

We must try not to forget that, here at least, we are seeing a real attempt at definition. In most cases (and leaving aside the more ludicrous examples[13]) things tend to be covered a lot more hastily and summarily. Thus, for example, the following 'definition' which is typical of the debate, and which simply reiterates three common uses of the term 'fascism' (ruling out the third of course): 'fascism designates firstly (meaning no.1), the regime of Mussolini between 1922 and 1943. In this sense it is a term applied specifically to Italy in that period. By extension, it has become customary to group under the generic term fascism (meaning no. 2) all similar regimes that arose between the wars, and in this sense of the term Mussolini's Italy is not in any way an archetype ... rather it is Hitler's Nazi fascist regime (1933–1945) which serves as the model – though never replicated. Thirdly (meaning no. 3), in current political language, the word fascist has become a throwaway insult ...' (the italics are mine).[14]

When it comes to classifying or characterising the French radical Right between the wars, nearly all the works associated with the 'immunity thesis' assume, more or less implicitly, that the true character of fascism is revealed by those cases where it was 'successful', where it seized power and set up regimes. This always produces the same effect, the same approach to the interpretation of reality. The historian reconstructs the path prior to the result by using as his vantage point the specific nature of this result. He identifies, selects and interprets his 'facts', and makes them converge towards this same result. In this way, he will have no difficulty in recognising the 'marginality' and the 'lack of serious intent' that characterises this particular segment of the French political spectrum between the wars, and the chasm, the fundamental 'difference of nature', that separates it from the 'fascist model(s)'. This particular approach to history-making has left its mark on every component in the edifice of the immunity thesis.

On imprecision and the boundaries of ideologies

Let us reexamine one of the major themes of the immunity thesis (which is rooted in the most traditional 'history of ideas' approach), namely that the ideological formulations of the French radical Right between the wars were ambiguous, confused, tentative, in short 'vague'. For the sake of argument, we will accept the point, even though we have serious reservations and would prefer a more nuanced verdict: for example, the doctrinal systems elaborated by Action Française or even G. Valois's ephemeral Faisceau are not entirely lacking in coherence!

It is true that the French authoritarian movement largely failed to produce anything like the solid corpus of ideas on which Sternhell based his 'ideal-type' of fascist ideology. We should nonetheless avoid outrageous simplifications. Are we really so sure, for example, that the 'regressive', 'backward-looking' and 'antimodern' features that we like to think are peculiar to these ideologies are entirely absent from the Nazi *Weltansschauung*? That would be a little too hasty. Similarly, this supposed 'vagueness' does not seem to have prevented certain ideological elements – anti-parliamentarianism, hatred of democracy, the seductive appeal of authoritarian remedies in neighbouring states, 'anti-Marxism' etc. – from providing a solid foundation for these ideological formulations.

However, the real difficulty lies elsewhere, namely in the conclusions that the historian feels able to deduce from this 'vagueness'. Do we seriously believe that this was one of the decisive factors in the political 'failure' of the *leagues*, in the 'outcome' of February 1934? Do we really believe that this was what prevented the radical Right from gaining power? Winock himself (admittedly while discussing Sternhell's argument) cannot help pointing out that 'authentic' fascist ideologies were no less 'vague' than the ideologies of the French radical Right – as in the Italian case, *before* the seizure of power.[15]

But there is evidence that is even more damning and even more significant for the immunity thesis. Our historians refuse to see that this 'vagueness' does not affect just the 'content' of these ideological formulations, it affects the *boundaries* that define them. In the everyday use that they make of ideological resources, members of the *leagues* and their sympathisers dip indiscriminately into a sort of common pool – which includes the elements listed above – without troubling themselves about organisational loyalties, without paying too much attention to the boundaries that the *leagues* liked to draw around their individual identities. Thus for example, despite its monarchist banner, the doctrines of Action Française lend the whole of the radical Right very valuable resources in terms of intellectual *cachet*. Similarly, it would be at the very least naïve to attribute the fierce battle waged – both figuratively and literally – between Action Française and Valois's Faisceau to some imaginary, insurmountable divide between social conservatism and fascistoid radicalism. Valois's operations were clearly sanctioned by the leaders of the parent organisation (even though its profascist orientation was obvious to everyone) for as long as there were no signs of an attempt to create a *rival organisation*, one which threatened (as it later did with some initial success) to win over the Action Française's own clientele, *cadres* and financial backers.

As far as ideological formulations are concerned, the *boundaries were vague* even between the radical Right and conservative parliamentary Right; or to be more precise, they were of a *variable consistency*. As is shown by the periods 1924–26 or 1932–34, the boundaries could harden or soften according to the political conjuncture, and depending largely on how close the Left, even in its most moderate guise, was to taking power. Such manoeuvering lies behind the more programme-oriented shifts of organisations which were willing to cross over into the legitimate political arena; thus, for example, when the Jeunesses Patriotes, after their unsuccessful flirtation with respectability in 1928–32, decided in the autumn of 1933 to strike the 'revolutionary' chord,[16] there is no need to accuse them of any particular duplicity or 'two-facedness' for adapting their ideology in this way.

This perspective also sheds light on those hybrid ideological formulations that we associate with the so-called 'spirit of the thirties'. For the immunity thesis, the main task is to clear this phenomenon of any suspected kinship or proximity with fascistic views of the world. As a result it misses the opportunity to make sense of some of the fundamental features of the ideological 'climate' and debate of the time. If we accept that it is important to understand how representations of reality 'catch on' in society – irrespective of what historians may later say about the *viability* of such representations – then surely we have to acknowledge the significance of this constant *blurring of boundaries and collective identities*, which allowed the 'non-conformists of the thirties' to make such an original contribution. For it was through this multiplicity of transfers and exchanges with authoritarian or fascistoid ideologies that the latter became *socially plausible*, i.e. they became able to effectively 'represent' reality, and thus to shape it.[17] In other words, these meetings, transactions, and complicities of discourse around the theme of banishing 'old' divisions and 'old ideologies', of exploring 'new' ways (often the 'third way', because the political imagination of 'non-conformism' was very limited after all) were a vital resource for authoritarian ideology. They gave the seal of intellectual approval to its rather meagre, muddled and vague formulations, and thus helped it to win the support of large segments of French society, and to influence how 'reality' was interpreted, defined and perceived. They constituted one of the levers by which authoritarian ideologies became commonplace, acquired the 'density' or 'objectivity' of things that are taken for granted (for example, the widely felt 'inadequacy' of parliamentary institutions and political democracy in general).

The dilemma of the authoritarian nationalist

That leaves one last boundary to explore, this time an 'external' one. The propagators of the immunity thesis are keen to show how anxious the radical-Right movement was to distinguish itself ideologically from the Italian and German 'models', and they conclude from this that their 'natures' were radically different. In the world of pure essences, this may well be true. But in the context of 1930s France, this approach prevents us from understanding how Italian fascism and German Nazism were received in France. Not that anyone actually ventures to deny the admiration these foreign 'models' inspired – that would be absurd when it is made so explicit in the discourse of the radical Right, and often elsewhere, at least where the Italian version is concerned. But in practice our historians seem to ignore the fact that these representations, ideologies and world-views cannot be regarded as ideal self-contained entities wholly disconnected from the everyday tactics, stratagems, gambles, calculations, positions or perceptions of those who 'use' them. These historians require the radical Right not only to define itself with more clarity than the original – Italian – fascism, but also to undertake everything, immediately and openly. In a way they banish the whole notion of time, of that lengthy 'apprenticeship period' which allowed the leagues and many others – notably their opponents – to absorb the Italian and then the German experiments and to draw lessons from them; in other words, they banish the historicity of their perceptions and positionings.

This false perspective also leads our historians to misunderstand one of the central dilemmas of the radical Right as it develops its ideology, *the dilemma of the authoritarian nationalist*. Here are people who consider themselves nationalists, and thus germanophobes, but who also find themselves being seduced – too weak a term in many cases – by the authoritarian movements and authoritarian 'solutions' that have taken root precisely in neighbouring Germany: a country which, moreover, now contests everything these French nationalists thought they had won in 1918. This dilemma is the key to much of the imaginative ideological handiwork (*bricolages idéologiques*) that went on: it was designed precisely to resolve this dilemma. Thus we see the more or less systematic construction of a series of distinguishing disparities (*décalages de distinction*) which differentiate the subject from the ideological formulations of Italian fascism and, even more so, from those developed by the National Socialists in Germany. For this reason, too, we see a whole range of attempts to 'gallicize' these ideologies, including Valois's quite economical solution, which argued that the product was not an import at all, but was firmly rooted in French culture (and on this point perhaps Sternhell is simply following his lead).[18]

This is why it is misleading to talk of a 'magnetic field' of European fascisms, when seeking to explain how their ideological formulations were received in France. The metaphor is seductive but really rather feeble. It ignores all the work of reappropriation, reformulation and reinvention that the term 'importation' implies, the way these resources were redeployed for home consumption, how they were adapted to what we might call the 'rules of the game', the constraints, opportunities and political dynamics of France between the wars.[19]

The dilemma of the authoritarian nationalist is far from being the only or even the main mechanism by which such an attitude towards foreign fascisms emerges. Strategies for achieving ideological distinctiveness can also be more banal, though their consequences were no less important. Thus, however fascinated the Action Française and its leadership were by the Italian 'example' – and they were staunch defenders of it later in the decade – they nonetheless refused to abandon their own *pretensions*, and still claimed not only an original identity, but also indeed seniority and paternity. And this reflects not so much the Action Française's clientele or its conservatism, and all the attendant social prejudices, but the vanity of the intellectuals dominating the movement, and the image they had of themselves. And, since they needed to find ideological differences with foreign fascism, the ideologists were all too eager to take issue with Mussolini's 'statolatry', even his 'legalism'![20]

The autonomisation of the non-parliamentary Right

Far from there being firmly drawn, impregnable frontiers between backward-looking conservatism and hard-line (marginal) fascistoid radicalism, the 'ideological vagueness' of the leagues reveals a kind of 'force field' where everyone adopts a position in relation to the manoeuvres of everyone else; in other words, a system of *interdependence*, which conditions and sometimes limits the tactical choices and actions of each participant. One of the great weaknesses of the immunity thesis is its inability to recognise that, in the period before February 1934, a particular 'space' or 'zone' in French politics began to achieve a degree of autonomy. Here genuinely original 'political enterprises' entered into competition and conflict with one another, diversified, and took organisational shape. Their 'originality' consisted not only in their distinctive ideological posture, but also in the fact that they all concentrated their activity in the extraparliamentary arena. There is a very close correlation between the phased development of this zone and the occasions when the Left, albeit 'moderate', was in government. Thus in 1924–26, the veteran Action Française was challenged by the formation of new league-style organisations, such as the Jeunesses Patriotes or the Faisceau (by 1926, this political 'space' counted around 150,000 members). After the 1932 elections, new groups sprang up, varying greatly in size and importance but which nonetheless seemed to indicate a new generation.This is particularly evident in the development, at a quite remarkable rate, of the Croix de Feu, whose field of recruitment very quickly moved beyond the nucleus of war veterans on which it was initially based. In any case, we are certainly not dealing with an esoteric world of small irrelevant groups. On the eve of February 1934, these various organisations between them had over 300,000 direct members, and many more activists overall than the parties of the parliamentary Right. In the years that followed, this process took on quite spectacular numerical proportions. It involved nothing less than a political earthquake across the entire spectrum of the Right, and many of its dimensions still remain to be explored.

The concentration of the activity of these organisations in the extraparliamentary arena has implications for this analysis. Firstly, it shows that it is at the very least misguided to present the formation of paramilitary units, their parades, exercices, hierarchies, uniforms, in short their whole style of action, as so much surface froth; as superficial manifestations of phenomena which are allegedly much 'deeper' (and closer to the underlying 'nature' these organisations are supposed to have); as pale and inconsequential imitations of 'foreign experiments'. Similarly, it is naïve to assimilate this transformation, this *enlargement of the Right's repertoire of political activity*,[21] to the purely manipulative view that certain conservative politicians (not least Poincaré and Tardieu) and some business milieux seem to have had from the 1920s onwards: namely that these extraparliamentary political resources could be held 'in reserve' and used when the 'collectivist menace' became particularly threatening. It is no surprise that certain actors may have subscribed to this instrumental view of political action: it is common enough, especially though not exclusively among members of the political elite, and such illusions may indeed have some effect on their style of action. On the other hand, the historian who adopts this same view as an explanation for the 'weakness' of the radical Right and as a confirmation of the immunity thesis should perhaps remember that, in Italy and Germany, other politicians and businessmen also believed themselves able to 'control' their own native 'back-up forces'.

Indeed, this 'functionalist' vision of the radical Right founders above all on the fact that this particular political 'space' was characterised by *internal competition*. In the *key periods* for the radical Right (1924–26 and even more after 1932), the dynamics of the rivalry between the different groups tends to nullify any fantasies that conservatives might have had of keeping them in check and controlling them. Moreover, it would be wrong to assume that such competition is necessarily detrimental to collective action. If that was the case, no sense at all could be made of the way the events of February 1934 unfolded. The famous 'six février' owes a great deal to the almost daily violent demonstrations that preceded it for more than a month, initiated at first, it is true, by Action Française, but very quickly fuelled by the intense interorganisational rivalry which progresssively dragged the whole movement into the action, including the Croix de Feu.[22] This competitive process had a very typical side-effect: these mobilisations were used by the militants of the different leagues as a mutual testing ground, where each sought assurance of the others' resolution and assessed whether the movement was 'taking off'; the 'six février' did not exactly appear out of thin air.

The costs of extraparliamentarianism

It was in these key periods that contacts with certain sections of the parliamentary Right were made more openly and, indeed, acquired greater legitimacy. The 'disloyal'[23] opposition (the *leagues*) began to be seen as potentially 'cooptable' in the political arena, at the very moment that they were physically demonstrating their extraparliamentary vocation. Clearly, in such circumstances, the capacity to be active simultaneously in the extraparliamentary sphere and in the arena of legitimate politics was a considerable political asset. The ability to do precisely this was surely, in February 1934, one of the major tactical advantages enjoyed by the Jeunesses Patriotes, especially through the use they made of their seats on the Paris municipal council. Thus, to say that the ability to act in diverse political arenas is proof of the non radical 'nature' of the groups concerned is nonsense; and the error is compounded if it leads us deliberately to ignore, for example, that the Italian fascists, and to an even greater extent the German Nazi party, were very far from investing all their energy in the extraparliamentary domain.

On this point, permit us to digress for a moment on a matter related to the aftermath of February 1934. We know that the issue of how to label and classify Colonel de La Rocque's Parti Social Français (formed immediately after the government disbanded the group that had succeeded the Croix de Feu) is, together with the events of February 1934, central to the elaboration of the immunity thesis. In circumstances still marked by the electoral victory of the Popular Front and the subsequent strikes, the PSF had considerable success which transformed the competitive balance on the radical Right (with the PSF becoming the dominant force). Indeed, that success can be measured by a membership that probably exceeded 800,000 (that is, roughly the same as the size of the Nazi vote in 1928!). The electoralist line La Rocque seems to have opted for, and his stated intention of competing in elections, becomes, for our historians, the best possible 'proof' of the immense gulf that supposedly separated the new party from the radical Right. The enforced change from a paramilitary formation into a political party, if we are to believe them, eliminated in one fell swoop all the doubts they had had about the nature of the Croix de Feu in the previous period. Suddenly, we are just a short step away from saying that the PSF is a kind of scout movement for adults – and that step is soon taken![24]

Here we can clearly see how the methodological slant of the immunity thesis leads it to sketch out an image of fascism – Italian and German – which precludes any participation in electoral processes, any use of the electoral arenas and resources, and instead suggests that its activity is focused exclusively on street violence. And thus, because they have in their minds this entirely imaginary model of fascism, our historians fail to notice an absolutely vital aspect of the political processes prior to February 1934: namely the cost, in terms of political effectiveness, of the extravagant extraparliamentarianism of the radical Right (with the JP here being the exception), a feature that is doubtless not unrelated to its very competitive structure.[25] If there was any 'weakness' in French fascism, it was above all that the various movements had difficulty getting a foothold in the electoral process. In this respect, quite apart from the tactical choices made by the *leagues*, it may well be that an old-fashioned look at the operation of the electoral system might shed some explanatory light on the matter.

The radical Right's emphasis on extraparliamentary activity can also help to explain one strange result of 6 February 1934, namely the *leagues'* inability to rapidly 'exploit' their success. For it was indeed a success, *at the time*: The resignation of Daladier seemed to have totally wiped out the electoral victory of the Left in 1932. Despite the presence of the Radicals, Doumergue's cabinet, which included leaders of the parliamentary Right, notably Tardieu and Louis Marin – and, already, Pétain – marked a brutal rupture with the 'Radical Republic'. Too brutal perhaps, for both the fact and the scale of the breach had the initial effect of *stopping the mobilisation in its tracks*. And this had nothing to do with their programme, or even with the tactical know-how of the leagues' leaders. Mobilisations are not driven by the clarity of their programmatic objectives. Once Daladier had stepped down, the day after he had been invested by a comfortable parliamentary majority, there was quite simply no longer a *focal point* which would allow organisations to forget their rivalries and mobilise in concert. The leagues, who, on the morning of 7 February had experienced an insurrectional climate in Paris, very quickly realised this fact. The formation of the Doumergue government also had another effect. It channelled the calculations, anticipations and perceptions of all those involved in the crisis back into the official political arena; and more importantly back into the routine processes, the habitual reference points, the implicit and explicit rules of that official arena; in other words it put an end to a state of *political fluidity*,[26] and it was because of this that it appeared to be a 'solution' to the confrontations.[27]

These observations, however, should also lead us to consider other aspects. The decisive factor in the 'solution', Daladier's resignation, arose partly from the fact that certain 'strategic' state sectors (and not just their leaders) resisted governmental decisions – among them the army, the justice department and the police. This resistance took the form of inertia or prevarication, as well as a *definition of the probable outcome*, namely the likelihood of a rising tide of violence.

Political cultures, values and calculations

This brings us to one last, and spectacular, blind spot of the immunity thesis. Its proponents tend to submerge the real processes that contributed, both before and even after February 1934, to the survival of the Third Republic, under the umbrella heading of 'political culture', and it is this which ultimately is meant to explain the supposed allergy of French society to fascism. The concept of a 'political culture' is unfortunately one of the most uncertain notions to have sprung from contemporary political science. So the use of this idea by historians who, however learned they may be, are largely unaware of the problems associated with it, gives every reason for concern. To tell the truth, it is not always easy to grasp what exactly was this distinctive political culture, which had supposedly made French society – in its entirety ! – impermeable to fascist penetration. Subscribers to the immunity thesis lump together under this one label political organisations, partisan ideologies and the mind-sets attributed to diverse social groups, notably the middle classes. When we try to put a little order into these formulations, it becomes clear that the term 'political culture' is being used to refer to certain *values* expressed in people's convictions, modes of thought and habits, and that these are supposed to stem from two distinct factors: the longevity of the democratic regime in France and the existence of structures of mass membership, especially in the middle classes (organised, in particular, by the Parti Radical), structures which direct their members towards the values of democracy.

First of all, a preliminary remark about these membership structures. Curiously enough, although its proponents do not realise it, the immunity thesis is perfectly in line here with an observation made about 'authentic' fascisms. The latter were, to use Linz's expression, 'late-comers', movements characterised by their late arrival on the political scene, at a time when the political arena was already fully occupied and demarcated, and when their potential 'clients' had already been claimed.[28] This idea is clearly not absurd and, at first sight, it even seems to help the immunity thesis, by introducing for once a genuine *relational perspective* instead of the usual *classificatory* preoccupation with 'essences' or 'natures'. But it immediately comes up against a major problem, at least where the internal coherence of the theory is concerned, namely the success of at least some of these *late-comers* who managed to conquer the political space and gain social support *despite* their late entry onto the scene. And, as the reader has no doubt already concluded, it would not be unreasonable to place in this subcategory of successful late-comers a significant part of the interwar French radical Right.

But despite this (admittedly significant) qualification, we are still left feeling dissatisfied as soon as we test the strength of this key link in the immunity thesis. There are many reasons for this and they do not all have the same importance. First it assigns a quite unwarranted autonomy to a purely *political* culture – namely to the way people perceive political institutions or political activity – which is strictly speaking an imaginary construction. Equally questionable is the related idea whereby this 'political culture' is supposed to be internally coherent, or indeed the whole of French society culturally homogeneous. But these are trifling matters, of interest only to devotees of methodological debate, and there are other points that are much more disturbing and embarrassing for the immunity thesis.

It is easy to imagine how puzzled the reader will be to find that, in other works on closely related topics, these selfsame authors seem to contradict their thesis and give a quite different analysis of the 1930s. Over many pages, and in great detail, they describe the acute, multifaceted, omnipresent and persistent *crisis* in this same democratic political culture, in its values and its agencies, as manifested in the Parti Radical in particular.[29] The Radical Party and the 'republican synthesis' have lost their force. It is another quite different political culture, 'anti-parliamentarian and favouring the establishment of authoritarian government', that henceforth seems to be in the ascendancy. The problem is that, this time, our historians are doubtless correct. But where does that leave the immunity thesis? What should 'immunise' citizens against the temptations of authoritarianism apparently collapses as soon as these appear on the horizon. The proponents of the immunity thesis apparently forget all this once they become absorbed in defending their theory, gripped by the same relentless intellectual logic whose mechanisms we have been endeavouring to reveal.

If one of the key arguments in the immunity thesis thus seems to have disqualified itself, there is one consolation: it provides us with a real historical 'mystery' to solve. The interesting thing – once we stop trying to explain what did not happen by the fact that it could not have happened – is that the Third Republic showed genuine resilience, sometimes despite the values of those whose role it was to 'serve' it. In a way, our historians are not very wide of the mark when they attach importance to the longevity of France's democratic institutions, but what we need to understand is exactly *how* this longevity affects the question. To do this, we would need to revise dramatically the picture we have been given of what constitutes a 'political culture'. That does not just mean taking account of the observations made above (or of many others we could make). Nor does it just mean making clear our objections to the truly *mechanistic* nature of this view, which tends to treat acts and behaviours as mere 'applications', 'realisations' or 'executions' of a 'political culture' (as if it could only be used in one way). No, the real problem is that the longevity of the institutions does not solely, or principally, depend on the values that people have. The notion of a 'political culture' is only useful if we can stop thinking of it only, or even primarily, in terms of values which give coherence to the political representations of individuals or groups, or indeed to their actions.

If, between the wars, the strategic sectors of the state remained 'loyal', it was because in addition to their democratic values, which anyway they did not all share, we must also take account of their self-interested *calculations*. And this involves not just the everyday routines and mind-sets of bureaucratic life, but also notions of what was feasible and what was not, what was risky and what was not, what was possible and what was probable. Some of these notions, which took shape after the great political confrontations at the end of the nineteenth and beginning of the twentieth centuries, are of particular relevance here. Notably, there was the conviction that a coup d'état would not work; that in France it was impractical and would expose its authors to considerable risk. Such axioms were rarely questioned, except in times of considerable political fluidity, as for example for a brief period in the winter of 1934. Even if they had been more powerful, more united, better led, equipped with perfectly tailored programmes and ideologies, the leagues were probably incapable of simply manufacturing such situations at will. But, after the event, the radical Right was doubtless justified in regretting the 'missed opportunity' of February 1934.

As for the importance of (democratic) 'values', some time after February 1934 history offered counter-evidence in the shape of 1940. As Paxton and Sternhell both suggest in their different ways, this could truly be regarded as a 'test' case for the hypothesis. People will no doubt object that these were exceptional, dramatic circumstances, and totally confusing for all those involved. Well, most certainly they were … and what better conditions in which to judge what values are really worth?

(Translated from the French original by Brian Jenkins)

Notes

1. R. Rémond, *Les droites en France*, Paris, 1982 (modified re-edition of *La droite en France*, Paris 1954).
2. In this essay we will also avoid all reference to the 'origins' of crises, because unfortunately these confront the researcher with problems that are just as daunting as those posed by 'outcomes'. On the most complex of these difficulties, the etiological illusion, see M. Dobry, *Sociologie des crises politiques. La dynamique des mobilisations multisectorielles*, Paris, 1986.
3. Among the other components making up this interpretation we should particularly note those, no less strategically important, that serve to qualify both the nature (again!) of the Vichy regime, namely the theory of the 'two Vichys' which has since been seriously undermined by the translation into French of Robert Paxton's classic study (*La France de Vichy, 1940–1944*, Paris, 1973), and the 'nature' of the Parti Social

Français, which has been reduced in retrospect, and despite obvious difficulties in establishing the relationship, to being simply a pale precursor to De Gaulle's RPF.

4.   In particular, Z. Sternhell, *La droite révolutionnaire: les origines françaises du fascisme*, Paris, 1978; and especially his *Ni droite ni gauche: l'idéologie fasciste en France*, Paris, 1983. See also Z. Sternhell, M. Sznajder and M. Asheri, *Naissance de l'idéologie fasciste*, Paris, 1989.

5.   See, among others, S. Berstein, 'La France des années trente allergique au fascisme. A propos d'un livre de Zeev Sternhell', *Vingtième Siècle*, no. 2, April 1984; J. Julliard, 'Sur un fascisme imaginaire: à propos d'un livre de Zeev Sternhell', *Annales ESC*, 39e année, no. 4, July–August 1984; S. Sand, 'L'idéologie fasciste en France', *Esprit*, no. 8–9, August-September 1983; M. Winock, 'Fascisme à la française ou fascisme introuvable?', *Le Débat*, no. 25, May 1983. For an excellent – and unclouded – analysis of this debate and its stakes, see A. Costa-Pinto, 'Fascist Ideology Revisited: Zeev Sternhell and His Critics', *European History Quarterly*, vol. 4, no. 16, 1986.

6.   Some of the criticisms directed at Sternhell are not without pertinence. For example, in his attempt to prove the genesis in France of an indigenous fascist ideological tradition (and its persistance after the First World War), Sternhell's work (*Ni droite ni gauche*) has the weakness of adopting the methodological approach implicit in traditional 'history of ideas'; namely the tendency to identify origins, derivations, affiliations, continuities and breaks in ideological currents independently of the social arena in which ideas 'operate'. By doing this, ironically he reproduces some of the same methodological errors as the historical theory which he is really attacking – and which, it must be acknowledged, *has not survived the assault*. We are referring to the claim that for a long period, over a century, 'right-wing opinion' was structured (and, according to the argument, still is!) around three coherent and clearly distinct ideological traditions, 'legitimism', 'Orleanism' and 'Bonapartism' (Rémond, *Les droites en France*).

7.   Without abandoning the classificatory aims of the immunity thesis, Philippe Burrin, *La dérive fasciste: Doriot, Déat, Bergery, 1933–1945*, Paris, 1986, uses the expression 'fascistoid nebula' to designate the relationships linking the 'minuscule circle of jack-booted, black-shirted groups' to much broader elements of French political life in the 1930s.

8.   Critics may well argue that the research approach we have described here may not be the only reason for the errors and deficiencies of the immunity thesis. They may suggest that other factors, having little to do with 'methodology', may have played a part (including, notably, the period when this historical interpretation was first propounded, namely the beginning of the 1950s at the time of the amnesty laws, 'voluntary amnesia' and 'reconciliation'). I would simply note that this type of objection *in no way* relieves us of the obligation to examine as rigorously as possible, and for their own sake, the research approach, its intellectual logic, and, of course, its empirical relevance.

9.   It is impossible here to draw up a complete list of the works based on this interpretation; as regards the points made in this essay, they almost always say the same thing. In addition to the works mentioned in notes 1 and 5, there is another book and another article by Berstein (S. Berstein, *Le six février*, Paris, 1975; idem, 'L'affrontement simulé des années 30', *Vingtième Siècle*, no.5, January–March 1985). Pierre Milza's book on the question of fascism in France (P. Milza, *Fascisme français. Passé et présent*, Paris, 1987) has the unusual feature of distancing itself in a number of discreet and often pertinent ways from the imagery of the immunity thesis, but without challenging its overall validity.

10.   C. Brinton, *The Anatomy of Revolution*, New York, 1965 (first published 1938). The fourth case examined by Brinton, the 'American revolution', is sufficiently atypical for its classification to be problematic in 'natural history' terms.

11. P. Veyne, *Comment on écrit l'histoire. Essai d'épistémologie*, Paris 1971.

12. Berstein, 'La France des années trente allergique au fascisme'.

13. For example: 'In our opinion, there are two ways of approaching fascist thought … . The first is that of the historian, and it involves critical engagement with thinkers who consider themselves to be fascist or who have supported fascist movements and regimes, by examining their theories in the light of the historical situations on which their thinking is based … . The second approach, that of the *"politologue"* – and I would hardly place myself in that category – involves constructing a set of detailed criteria, a sort of grid or pattern serving to identify an ideology, and then applying this grid to the various currents of thought at a given period in history, in order to distinguish those that present the traits of the ideology in question' (S. Sand, 'L'idéologie fasciste en France' p. 150). Curiously, this type of accusation (and also the lack of understanding it reveals about the use of 'ideal-types' in the social sciences) seems to be aimed solely at the works of Sternhell, and does not go on to question, for example, the significance of R. Rémond's sketchy attempt to recycle his three ideological traditions of the French Right (see note 6 above) as 'ideal-types', thereby hoping no doubt to breathe fresh life into his work (*Les droites en France*, p. 39).

14. Julliard, 'Sur un fascisme imaginaire'.

15. Winock, 'Fascisme à la française ou fascisme introuvable?'

16. On this point, see in particular the pertinent analyses of R. Soucy, *French Fascism: The First Wave, 1924–1933*, New Haven 1986. (esp. pp. 215–16).

17. For a good introduction to these points, see P. Berger and T. Luckmann, *The Social Construction of Reality*, London, 1971.

18. See, in particular, Sternhell, *Ni droite ni gauche* and Y. Guchet, *Georges Valois: L'Action française, le Faisceau, la République synicale*, Paris, 1975.

19. Burrin, *La dérive fasciste*. Despite his stated intention of not 'reducing fascism in France to the distinction between home-grown and imported fascism', Burrin fails to recognise the importance of all the work the radical Right put into the construction of a distinctive 'identity' for itself, even if he appears to have some intuition of this. Thus he still remains imprisoned in the view that 'repeated refusals to recognize foreign fascisms as role models' indicate an 'immunity to fascism'.

20. J. Blatt, 'Relatives and rivals: the Response of the Action Française to Italian Fascism, 1919–1926', *European Studies Review*, vol. 2, no. 3, July 1981; see also E. Weber, *L'Action Française*, Paris, 1964, with useful additional material from J. Linz, on 'protofascist' movements (J. Linz, 'Political space and Fascism as latecomer', in *Who were the Fascists? Social Roots of European Fascism*, ed. S.U. Larsen et al., Bergen, 1980, p. 173ff.).

21. On the repertoires of collective action, see, especially, C. Tilly, *From Mobilization to Revolution*, Reading, MA, 1978.

22. The choice by the different organisations of widely dispersed assembly points is both an effect and a faithful reflection of this competition. So too was La Rocque's curious tactic of an orderly and disciplined show of strength. Having been forced – rather late – to take to the streets, he thereby tried to show, not unsuccessfully, that his group was different from the others.

23. On the distincion between 'loyal' and 'disloyal' opposition, see J. Linz, *Crisis, Breakdown and Reequilibration*, Baltimore and London, 1978.

24. Rémond, *Les droites en France*, p. 213.

25. The competitive balance within this particular segment of political space was decisively changed in 1936 with the aforementioned emergence of one dominant pole, the PSF. This is a critical point when we are trying to appreciate both the tactics used by Colonel La Rocque to affirm group distinctiveness – see, in particular, the incident of the 'Front de la Liberté' (P. Machefer, 'L'union des droites, le PSF et le Front de la Liberté, 1936–1937', *Revue d'histoire moderne et contemporaine*, vol. 17,

January–March 1970) – and the fierce struggles that opposed the PSF to practically all the other groups of the radical Right. The inability to understand the virulence and far-reaching effects of this rivalry and, especially, of the changed competitive environment, explains why so many have failed to make sense of the anti-PSF coalition that crystallised at this time (notably during the Pozzo di Borgo/La Rocque trial, hastily decoded as being an effect of the 'moderation' of La Rocque). It is, then, hardly surprising that this broad alliance, ranging from Doriot's PPF and the Action Française to large segments of the parliamentary Right, is perceived by subscribers to the immunity thesis as an 'unnatural' coalition.

26.   On the contexts of political fluidity, characterised notably by the collapse of effective markers and routine instruments for evaluating and defining situations, for estimating the ' value' of political resources and, more generally, for political calculation, see Dobry, *Sociologie des crises politiques*.

27.   In addition to Daladier's resignation, this 'solution' included, among other things, the broad similarity perceived between the situation in 1926 and that in 1934. This enabled Doumergue – whose very active role as President of the Republic in 1926 was widely recognised – to appear as an excellent focal point for a number of heterogeneous protagonists all looking for an 'outcome' to the crisis.

28.   J. Linz , 'Some Notes Towards a Comparative Study of Fascism in Sociological Historical Perspective', in *Fascism: A Reader's Guide*, ed. W. Laqueur, Harmondsworth, 1979; idem. 'Political Space'). On the subject of Italian fascism, however, Leonardo Morlino observes that this was, in a sense, an *early-comer*: it represents the first experiment in this type of 'response' to mobilisations 'from below' and it also emerged in a political space that was far from being definitively demarcated.

29.   For example, Berstein, 'L'affrontement simulé', and, above all, idem, *Histoire du parti radical*, vol. 2: *Crise du radicalisme*, Paris, 1982.

6

The Construction of Crisis in Interwar France[1]

Kevin Passmore

Over the last ten years or so, Kevin Passmore has established himself as one of the leading academic authorities on La Rocque's Croix de Feu/Parti Social Français. His articles have explored the problematic definition of the movement, the nature and purpose of its paramilitarism, and perhaps most significantly, the political and socioeconomic context in which it emerged. His monograph *From Liberalism to Fascism: The Right in a French Province, 1928–1939* uses an archive-based microstudy of the Right in Lyons during the 1930s to throw light on developments at national level, namely the unfolding political crisis of French conservatism. As a product of this process, La Rocque's movement is characterised by Passmore as belonging to a category which he defines as the 'authoritarian-populist Right', of which fascism is a subset. What makes fascism distinctive, he argues, is its use of paramilitarism as a means of mass mobilisation, its deployment of what Roger Griffin has called 'palingenetic' ultra-nationalism based on a myth of historical rebirth, and its mercurial combination of radical and conservative impulses. On this basis, Passmore concludes that the Croix de Feu may indeed be described as fascist, although (unlike Sternhell and Soucy above) he believes that once the movement became the PSF it moved towards constitutional conservatism, and thus ceased to be fascist (whilst remaining 'authoritarian-populist').

While Passmore regards the term 'fascism' as useful for explanatory purposes, he is not primarily concerned with the definitional issues that have so preoccupied the previous generation of historians. The main theoretical underpinning of his work is his insistence on the complexity and diversity of social power in early twentieth-century France (capitalism, catholicism, gender, profession), the competitive nature of social-elite relationships and strategies, the impact on right-wing politics not only of dominant but also of subordinate social groups, and the consequent fragmentation and ill-discipline of this sector of the political community. This perspective challenges not only the Marxist tendency to see the Right in terms of (increasingly unified) dominant class interests, but also Rémond's over-simplified view of three distinct and coherent ideological traditions or *mentalités*, and Stanley Hoffman's notion of a broad social consensus between bourgeoisie and small producers underpinning the so-called 'stalemate society'. Instead, Passmore emphasises the social diversity and the internal divisions (both material and ideological) of the French Right's clientele, the range of social alliances and mobilisational strategies available to political formations, the importance of the details of historical context and political conjuncture as explanatory tools.

In Passmore's view, some participants in the fascism debate have exaggerated the 'conservatism' of the Croix de Feu/PSF and others have exaggerated its desire for revolution; in his view both reactionary and revolutionary sides of fascism are important – fascism sees itself as a kind of popular insurrection in the name of order. The importance of the relationship between right-wing politics and subordinate social groups, and the changing evocation of the 'people' in right-wing discourse, is a central theme of the book he is currently preparing on the French Right during the Third Republic. In the chapter below, however, he returns to the issue of the 'stalemate society' thesis, the notion of a social compromise which held back the forces of modernisation, and which has often been used in support of the argument that interwar France was unpropitious terrain for the development of fascism. He suggests that the stalemate society thesis can be seen as an historiographical legitimation of the current French political system, and that rather than being a 'scientific' diagnosis of objective problems in French society, it is actually an academic systematisation of prejudices and assumptions that were current on the Right in the Third Republic. He argues that there was actually no consensus on the nature of French social and political institutions; that there were powerful forces favouring authoritarianism of various sorts, including fascism; that the French Right had traditionally defined itself in terms of both nationalism and admiration of foreign systems, and so it is impossible to see fascism as a foreign import.

Kevin Passmore is Lecturer in History at Cardiff University.

How many regimes have evolved thus – at first rendering services, only to do more harm than good afterwards? The absolute monarchy was like that. We are in the same bad situation. Neither in the management of finances, the direction of the public mind, nor in the conduct of foreign affairs, is the elective regime, in its present form, sufficient to its task, and it could be carried off in a single day of panic. Profound corrections are needed to save it. (A. Tardieu, *L'Heure de la décision,* p.36[2])

Everyone knew and everyone knows that the Third Republic was in crisis in the 1930s, that the symptoms were parliamentary instability, financial and economic mismanagement, and impotence in foreign affairs, and that the failure of the regime was not merely contingent: the Republic was out of tune with history. Equally axiomatic was that the solution was authority. Tardieu again: 'They proclaim this truth on the left. They proclaim it on the right. They whisper it in the centre. No body without a head; no collectivity without a leader. Who then is a leader in France?'[3] The appeal to authority was evident in demands for 'reform of the state', fascination with foreign dictatorships, routine recourse to special powers to issue laws, and calls for the banning either of the leagues or of the Communist Party (PCF). Historians have largely agreed with contemporaries. Parliamentary instability was self-evidently a problem rooted in the laws of history: the Third Republic had not 'modernised'. Its problems were resolved only by the presidential Fifth Republic.

Even if it is agreed that there was a social crisis in the 1930s, it was not inevitable that contemporaries should have considered that this necessitated remodelling of the political system. Was it necessarily so that the repeated overthrow of cabinets harmed the national interest (whatever that was)? Some have argued that cabinet instability masked considerable continuity in the tenure of particular ministries.[4] Whatever the case, whilst instability might have disrupted government action, it might also have permitted more flexible policy formulation. Even if we could agree on what constitutes political effectiveness, there would be no scientific formula for achieving it. It might be more appropriate for historians to focus on *perceptions* of the regime. Undoubtedly people in 1930s France believed there was a crisis, and since they did, there was a crisis. But what did they think constituted a successful political system and why did they believe that the Third Republic could not resolve contemporary problems? My answers do not pretend to completeness. I shall focus less upon the traditional Catholic integrist and monarchist enemies of the Republic – whose contribution to the fall of the regime was nevertheless essential[5] – and follow a recent historiographical trend in primarily discussing the republican origins of authoritarianism.[6]

In particular I shall examine the influence upon historians of the 'stalemate society' thesis – the contention that stability in the Third Republic was produced by a social compromise between 'traditional' and 'modern' classes, ideas and political systems. This pact with tradition is said to have delayed modernisation and produced objective dysfunctions in the system, rendering the Republic unable to cope with the Depression and the rise of Hitler. Only an elite of politicians, businessmen, trade unionists, administrators, journalists and intellectuals understood the true causes of the problems of the Republic. Their exceptional enlightenment enabled them to stand above the petty concerns of their contemporaries.

The stalemate society thesis remains central to the explanation of recent French history in spite of the discredit in the wider historiographical community of the functionalist sociology and modernisation metanarrative on which it is based. The teleological assumptions inherent in the concept of modernisation, as well as the conviction that a properly functioning society depends on a 'common culture' have both been challenged. Actually, the Third Republic always rested on a narrow political base and had always been contested, even in its so-called stable period. The problem is therefore to explain why the events of the 1930s should have been perceived as a regime-threatening crisis. The failure of the Third Republic resulted from a complex set of contingencies, which are explicable in terms of the meanings given to events by contemporaries, and in many respects the diagnoses of contemporaries matched the assumptions of the stalemate society thesis.

The stalemate society thesis has resisted attack partly because it provides legitimacy for the Fifth Republic. Paradoxically, it supports criticisms of the Fifth Republic too. Indeed, the stalemate society thesis was always as much a political intervention in French history as a scientific diagnosis of real difficulties. It might even be said that the stalemate society thesis was a major *cause* of the instability of republican politics in the 1930s. This is not to say that the crisis of the 1930s was invented, but that contemporaries made sense of their circumstances within the framework of a set of expectations and fears. Examination of these conceptions might explain why a seemingly minor financial scandal could have been seen as the visible manifestation of a crisis of historic proportions.

The stalemate society thesis

The term 'stalemate society' is not used by all the historians discussed in this essay. I want to argue, nevertheless, that many historians of modern French history share certain assumptions, and it is therefore convenient to use the term. The stalemate society thesis has heterogeneous origins, traceable to nineteenth-century myths of progress, political and economic liberalism and academic sociology, anthropology and history. More particularly, the stalemate society thesis represents a blend of Alexis de Tocqueville's critique of the weakness of associations in French democracy with the sociology of the American Talcott Parsons. The latter was derived in turn from a very particular reading of the sociology of Max Weber and Émile Durkheim.

In view of the international origins of the stalemate society thesis it is appropriate to begin with Stanley Hoffmann, an Austrian Jew who fled from Nazism first to France and then to America, where he imbibed functionalist social science. He is one of those persons described by cultural transfer theorists as transnational 'mediators'.[7] As such he reminds us that the stalemate society thesis, although purporting to be a story of national exception, actually contains much that might be considered 'foreign'. Negative views of German history and idealised selections from British and American history are essential to the view of French history presented in the stalemate society thesis, and indeed by those who claimed in the 1930s that institutional reform was a national necessity.

For Hoffmann the Third Republic was underpinned by a compromise between 'modern' forces represented by the bourgeoisie, and 'traditional' forces represented by 'independents' (small business and the peasantry).[8] Recruited from the naturally cautious peasantry, and impressed by the resistance of the aristocracy to the great Revolution, the French bourgeoisie was bathed in premodern values. Its economic activity was designed to preserve family stability rather than to maximise production. The bourgeoisie desired limited economic expansion and social mobility, but only so long as they did not endanger this family-based order.

The political system likewise was seen by Hoffmann as a mixture of traditional and modern. It was neither authoritarian and hierarchical nor democratic and egalitarian. At the centre was a parliamentary government strong enough to defend the stalemate society against those excluded from it (workers and aristocrats) but not so effective that its interventions could throw the stalemate society out of kilter. Parliament was the preserve not of parties organised around clear programmes, but of 'notables' – men who owed their position to family, money and land, and so were in tune with the values of the stalemate society. Individuals expected these notables to defend their interests for them, rather than look after their own affairs in voluntary associations (such as trade unions and business organisations). Strong interest groups, like strong parties, might have endangered the stalemate society. France was thus an individualist society, yet one in which individuals refused to take responsibility for themselves through participation in voluntary associations. These personal failings could be traced back to the days of absolute monarchy, which seemed to offer the choice only between total resistance and total subservience to authority. French people kowtowed to authority, but, in the right circumstances, would rebel against it.

The problems of French society derived from incomplete modernisation. Normally, progress should be driven by an enterprising liberal-democratic bourgeoisie, the actions of which would be fruitful because in tune with progress. France's failure to modernise (like the failure of Germany, Italy, Spain and Japan to do likewise) is found in the 'abnormal' attraction of the bourgeoisie to traditional values. Hence the view that French politicians were 'cut off' from the real needs of French society – they did not recognise the direction of history.

Hoffmann's emphasis upon the aberrant traditionalism of the bourgeoisie is reinforced by the functionalism of the Parsonian model. Functionalism assumes that society naturally tends towards harmony, and judges social and political phenomena according to their contribution towards the reproduction of the existing social system. Shared core beliefs, in turn, ensure that each individual and group fulfils their allotted role. In the Third Republic the blend of traditional and modern beliefs described by Hoffmann provided society's value system. But these core beliefs were not in tune with the age – semi-traditional beliefs were dominant in a period in which modern values 'ought' to have predominated. Hence the historiographical clichés such as 'Third Republican politicians responded to twentieth-century problems with nineteenth-century solutions' or 'the problem of the Radical Party was its preoccupation with anachronistic religious problems at a time when economic issues were more pressing'.

Hoffmann regards the 'underlying' social compromise of the stalemate society as more significant than party politics. In the Third Republic, he writes, 'political life came close to the model of a pure game of parliamentary politics'.[9] Only the feeble remnants of the aristocracy and the more powerful working-class parties contested the system, and even the latter were increasingly sucked into it. The only meaningful political conflict was between conceptions of how to manage the status quo. Those whom Hoffmann calls liberals – one supposes the Radicals – wanted further democratisation of the constitution. Of more direct concern in the present context is that others, for example 'Bonapartists' such as the Croix de Feu, wanted a more authoritarian constitution. The extreme Right was not clearly differentiated from the parliamentary Right in terms of its 'fundamental' purpose.

It follows, for Hoffmann, that change could not come from within the system, and that the causes of the breakdown of the Republic in the 1930s were external. The dynamism of Nazism, Stalinism, the New Deal and Swedish Social Democracy, Hoffmann argues, exposed France's economic lethargy and the loss of its status as a beacon of progress in the world at large. Militarily, France dug in behind the Maginot line, yet this defensive reflex did not shield the country from domestic turmoil. Since economics had hitherto been a matter for consensus, no party was equipped to deal with the challenges of the Depression. The government's initial response – wage and price deflation – was designed to freeze the stalemate society at a low level. But deflation provoked colossal resentment. Some disillusioned voters turned to the Popular Front. They were disappointed, however, for its leaders, reflecting the Socialists' increasingly unadventurous posture, proved unable to break out of the stalemate society. Meanwhile, those who believed that only authority could preserve the stalemate society turned to the Croix de Feu/PSF. Hoffmann emphasises its attraction for conservatives like Xavier Vallat, Philippe Henriot and Georges Scapini, who accepted the Republic only so long as it guaranteed conservative bastions such as the banks, industry and administration [sic]. Even on its deathbed, the regime perpetuated the old way of doing things.

The crisis did, however, provoke a minority of dissidents to rethink the Republic. They included left-wingers (principally Marcel Déat, Jacques Doriot and Gaston Bergery), moderate Republicans (such as André Tardieu), fascists, hitherto apolitical intellectuals, engineers from the École Polytechnique, students, trade unionists and veterans' organisations. These dissidents agreed on the need for a stronger state, a less individualist society, reform of capitalism (either through state planning or privately initiated cooperation between large firms) and a 'moral reformation'. These dissidents stood apart from the usual social and political circuits, and it is from their ranks that change eventually came during and after the Occupation. In their independence, exceptional foresight and insight into the movement of history, they anticipated modern academic proponents of the stalemate society thesis. In the short term the dissidents achieved little, for they were politically divided, and ultimately captured by the system. The dissidents were especially compromised by alliance with 'the group of disgruntled conservatives [allied to the dissidents], trembling sheep with wolves' voices, like La Rocque', who attacked the political arrangements of the Third Republic, but not the underlying social compromise.[10]

Michel Winock's analysis of the recurrent crises of the French political system since 1870 shares many features of the stalemate society thesis.[11] Like Hoffmann, he argues that the experience of living under absolute monarchy, coupled with the extensiveness of peasant proprietorship, had inculcated in the French a combination of anarchic distrust of, and abject worship of, authority. The French were unsuited to association, so a genuine democracy could not develop. Deprived of the associative life-blood of democracy, parliament was cut off from the people and was incapable of dealing with the inevitable difficulties of 'modern' life. In 1934 (as in 1889, 1899 and 1958) the inadequacy of parliament caused widespread demands for reform. In 1936 the regime was saved by an alliance of bourgeoisie and socialists. As in Hoffmann's interpretation the latter abandoned their revolutionary rhetoric and chose republican defence. As usual voters chose the least adventurous option and the status quo was preserved.

Winock differs in identifying the leagues primarily with Catholic nationalist opposition to the Republic rather than with Bonapartism. The instability of French history, he argues, resulted from struggle between the absolutist principles of monarchy and Church and their nemesis, the Revolution. Moderate reformism could not develop in such conditions. Winock argues, nevertheless, that the wartime *Union sacrée* and in 1926 the Papal condemnation of Action Française, integrated many Catholics into the Republic and made possible the joining together of Catholics with conservative republicans in an anti-Marxist coalition. One of the alleged preconditions of a successful democracy – a united parliamentary Right – came into being. The Left, in contrast, remained locked into the absolutes of the past. It was able to win elections, but because the Communists and Socialists had not cast off the inflexible Revolutionary ideal, the Left could not form a stable governing coalition – hence the cycle of left-wing electoral victory, paralysis in government, right-wing reaction, and reversal of majorities.

For Winock, the Croix de Feu represented the coming together of two responses to this 'blockage' in the system. Parliamentary instability outraged a good many ordinary republicans, who wanted simply to render the regime more effective. Yet this 'justifiable' discontent provided the professional opponents of the Republic – a small number of Catholic nationalists – with an audience. Whereas for Hoffmann the Croix de Feu/PSF was a part of the stalemate society, Winock saw it as led by Catholic intransigents, and followed by ordinary citizens vaguely desirous of government in tune with 'modernity'.

It would be wearisome to list all the historians who have argued similarly. Suffice it to note that René Rémond's contention that the Croix de Feu/PSF were Bonapartist rests on the view that Bonapartism had discarded its radical Jacobin wing in the late nineteenth century, and had become a movement of conservative notables.[12] For Pierre Milza, the Croix de Feu/PSF was dominated by Catholic paternalists who rejected the innovative technocratic and corporative schemes of members such as Pierre Pucheu and Bertrand de Maudhuy, out of fear of upsetting their bourgeois clientele.[13] For both these historians the values of the conservative stalemate society, coupled with the deep roots of democracy, preserved France from fascism, yet left it vulnerable to traditionalist authoritarianism in the form of Vichy.

It is perhaps more interesting to examine Christophe Charle's recent critique of what he calls the 'comforting' view of French history. In his comparison of Britain, France and Germany, Charle accepts many of the so-called 'Anglo-Saxon' criticisms of the stalemate society thesis, and highlights the profundity of the crisis of the 1930s.[14] Yet his break with the Hoffmann interpretation is more apparent than real, for its proponents had always emphasised the collapse of the stalemate society in the 1930s and invoked this as a cause of the turn to Vichy. Charle's chapter on the interwar years is revealingly entitled 'La république enlisée'. Recent research is assimilated into the familiar framework. Peasant life is marked by routine and dependence on the state; the workers are excluded from mainstream society, and organisationally weak. 'Failure' of immigrants to assimilate into the common culture is a sign of harmful social disunity.

Charle's debt to the stalemate society thesis is evident above all in his stress upon the 'Malthusianism' of French society. Studies of social mobility are used to demonstrate the Malthusian closure of the professional and administrative bourgeoisie, its obsession with corporatist self-defence, and frustration of all attempts at educational reform. Charle takes up the argument of interwar pronatalists that Malthusian attitudes towards the family, coupled with war deaths, increased the weight of the older generations and reduced the level of initiative in French society. French generals were considerably older than their German counterparts, and this explains the defensiveness of French military planning.[15]

Charle declines to join 'theological' disputes on the definition of the Croix de Feu, but one would guess that the movement would represent one more manifestation of this conservative, Malthusian, tendency. What is clear is that innovation 'ought' to have come from the elites. Various schemes for a 'third way' and constitutional reform were produced in the early 1930s, but the elites were too divided to bring them to fruition, and soon the coalition of innovators was sucked back into the divisions of French society, as they were in Hoffmann's account.

Like Hoffmann, Charle assumes that a properly functioning society requires consensus (of the right sort), but updates functionalist sociology's stress on the collective consciousness with the concept of *habitus* – a notion also susceptible to a determinist reading. Charle's method is to detail the 'construction of a national habitus' on the basis of social dynamics supposedly particular to each of the three countries under consideration. He particularly emphasises the failure of French elites to unite. And because intermediary associations were weak, there was no way to spread a sense of national purpose to society at large. The consequent lack of consensus proved fatal in wartime.

Charle's major contribution is to make explicit the international comparison implicit in the stalemate society thesis. At each step of his argument French society is contrasted negatively with British, unconsciously echoing a longstanding theme of the conservative republican critiques of the system.[16] The British elites are socially and politically more unified, younger, more closely connected to the population at large, more dynamic and possessed above all of a 'will' which shames the Malthusian, habit-bound French. The French war premier, Paul Reynaud (born 1878), is compared unfavourably with Winston Churchill (born 1874), confirming Julian Jackson's remark that the myth of Britain's wartime spirit survives only in France. Whereas historians such as Milza and Rémond assume proximity between Britain and France because of their shared history of democracy, Charle sees France as a sort of middle term between Germany and Britain. France was marked by similar social problems to those which caused the collapse of Weimar, yet was preserved from the Nazi extremism by an education system able to inculcate democratic values. The comforting belief that France was preserved from fascism by the republican tradition enters through the back door.

There is no greater testimony to the influence of the stalemate society thesis than the fact that even historians who contested the once orthodox view that France was allergic to fascism have borrowed heavily from it. It is rarely noticed that Zeev Sternhell's explanation for the precocious appearance of fascism in France depends upon it. Like Hoffmann, he depicts France as a country of slow industrialisation, in which the values of the Revolution were strongly entrenched. Since socialism had largely been absorbed into the system, the regime was strong enough to resist any attack upon itself. For Sternhell fascism derived from the convergence of extremists of left and right against the immobile centre, and 'the history of fascism was in many respects the history of a will to modernisation'. The very stability of the Republican consensus provoked a radical, modernising, critique in the form of fascism, but guaranteed that fascism could not become a mass movement – just as modernising intellectuals were outside the system in Hoffmann's thesis. It follows that for Sternhell the Croix de Feu, as a mass organisation, represented a conservative safeguard for the stalemate society, rather than a fascist opposition.[17] Interestingly, Sternhell has recently modified his argument. He now holds that the Croix de Feu shared the 'third way' ideology that characterised fascism as he defined it. The stalemate society thesis, however, remains intact. The Croix de Feu just joins the ranks of the system's opponents.[18]

Marxist historical writing on France also shows some interesting parallels with the stalemate society thesis -- both, after all, see capitalism as historically necessary, and both require auxiliary hypotheses to explain history's perverse refusal to tread its allotted path. One could cite Albert Soboul's view that the development of industrial capitalism in France was retarded by the need for the French bourgeoisie to ally with the peasantry in order to overcome the resistance of the aristocracy.[19] In his study of conservative politics in the early Third Republic, Herman Lebovics explicitly acknowledges a debt to Hoffmann. He adds only that the alliance of bourgeoisie, landowners and peasants in the stalemate society was part of a conscious conservative strategy.[20]

The overlap between Marxist and non-Marxist understandings of the nature of Third Republican history is plain in the work of Gérard Noiriel. He set out as a *Marxisant* labour historian interested in ethnic cleavages in the working class, but has recently used a variety of the stalemate society thesis to underpin a critique of the racist structures of Third Republican political culture.

Like Charle, Noiriel places international comparison at the heart of his method. His *Origines républicaines de Vichy* begins by restating Norbert Elias's account of the triumph of Nazism in Germany (a thesis later perfected by *Sonderweg* historians).[21] Thanks to the failure of bourgeois revolution in Germany, it is said, aristocratic traditionalism, antimodernism and obsession with decadence spread through German society. Nazism represented an exacerbation of the antimodern mentality of the Germans. In France too, premodern values survived in the Third Republican present. Noiriel's argument is familiar: the combination of monarchical centralism under Louis XIV, coupled with the strength of peasant proprietorship, permanently inscribed an amalgam of individualism and respect for authority upon the French 'habitus'.

The originality of Noiriel's argument lies in his integration of ethnic cleavages into the stalemate society thesis. In the classic manner he argues that before 1914 the Republicans achieved a compromise between the industrial bourgeoisie and small producers. Protectionism was an important element of this alliance since it defended small property against foreign competition. But by retaining the peasantry on the land, protectionism potentially created a labour shortage in industry. In any case, peasants' individualism made them reluctant to abandon their properties, and when they did leave the land they preferred state employment to factory work. The employers' solution was to import foreign workers, whilst subjecting them to discrimination, regulation and harassment in order to appease French workers' hostility to cheap competition. Foreign workers, and even newly naturalised immigrants, were barred from state employment, thereby permitting French citizens privileged access to these jobs. The Republic also endeavoured to integrate workers into the Republic through the enactment of social legislation, the benefits of which were restricted to citizens. Meanwhile labour organisations were weakened by the use of a reserve pool of cheap labour. Thus the Republican compromise was underpinned by discrimination against immigrants. Noiriel sums up his argument thus:

> The Third Republic was able to profit from these three years of prosperity to realise a political project founded upon the maintenance of a balance between the different sectors of the economy and upon an ideal of social mobility. This republican compromise allowed the attenuation of the violence of the changes that resulted from industrialisation. This is one reason why fascist movements never gained a social base as strong as they acquired in Italy and Germany. But at the same time the republican compromise permitted social groups belonging to sectors condemned by the development of capitalism (petty agricultural and artisanal property) to conserve the bulk of their strength, thereby providing traditionalist parties with a considerable social base.[22]

As in all other versions of the stalemate society thesis, the French were too democratic to be attracted to fascism, but insufficiently democratic, too individualistic and too reliant upon the state to make a liberal democracy work.

For Noiriel, Malthusianism in the face of perceived *déclassement* helped prepare the way for Vichy. Industrial rationalisation during the 1930s forced French workers to take unskilled jobs, while the democratisation of secondary education created fear of overcrowding of the professions. The incompatible demands of increasingly corporatist interests undermined parliamentary government, which became distanced from the nation. Unelected 'experts' (Charle calls them occult experts) displaced parliamentary government. Faced by social unrest and the discredit of parliament, the bourgeoisie abandoned the regime and turned to Vichy. Noiriel parts company, however, with those who see Vichy as an exclusively traditionalist regime. Vichy remained faithful to the republican project of integrating the people into the nation. It sought to restore the republican compromise by authoritarian rather than democratic means. It used traditionalist residues in the French national psyche to legitimate an authoritarian version of the republican project.

Critique

The long survival of the stalemate society thesis owes something to its usefulness as a means of legitimating the Fifth Republic. To illustrate this point, let us glance at Jean-Pierre Rioux's history of the Fourth Republic.[23] Following Hoffmann, and many others, Rioux argues that the Resistance produced a general aspiration for a break with the practices of the Third Republic. However, the Resistance failed to found a lasting political movement, and the parties reasserted themselves within a constitution resembling that of the old Republic. The parties – remember Hoffmann's description of the parliamentary game – were cut off from French society, perverted the popular will for change expressed in elections, and were incapable of governing a 'modern' society. The parties were united only by anticommunism, and so part of the working class was excluded from the nation. The Algerian crisis brought these problems to a head. Politicians, as ever, were responsive more to military and economic lobbies than to the people (recall the 'occult experts' who determined policy in the Third Republic). Unlike de Gaulle, they did not recognise the public's desire for peace, prosperity and effective government (read 'modernity'). De Gaulle established a regime in which a strong executive was directly responsive to the electorate, and like all 'great men' his actions were effective because in tune with progress. Under de Gaulle the parties, dominated by local interests, were sidelined in favour of strong associations reflecting the 'real' needs of the people. The Fifth Republic solved the problems of French history.[24]

One cannot dismiss a historical interpretation just because of its political implications. For one thing, Noiriel uses the categories of the stalemate society thesis to criticise republican political culture. For another, historians must write the history they are interested in, and all history begins in bias. This does not absolve us from treating interpretations on their merits. Nevertheless, historians on both sides of the debate about fascism in France should be aware that the stalemate society thesis represents an academic synthesis of criticisms of the republican system current in the interwar years in the mainstream and the Leagues as well as the 'dissidents'.[25] Hoffmann had after all lived in France in the 1930s, and many of his criticisms of the regime recur in every other edition of every other right-wing newspaper in the 1930s – the image of parliamentary representatives 'playing a rather Byzantine game of pure politics in the house without windows' (i.e. the Chamber of Deputies); the conviction that notable-politicians milked the state for the benefit of local interests; Radical committees' distortion of the democratic process.[26] Hoffmann's solutions to the problem of the Republic, moreover, matched those advanced by more liberal reformers at the time – a stronger and more interventionist state; use of referenda; negotiation of social policy between freely organised interest groups.[27] His specific contribution was to underpin these recipes with the 'scientific' theory of necessary modernisation, but even this had been implicit at the time in warnings of the dire consequences of attempting to swim against the tide of 'progress'.

The problem with the stalemate society thesis is not so much that it is political, but that its partisans do not distinguish between 'how/why' and 'ought' questions. Why and how something happened is a matter on which historians can claim special expertise. What *should* have happened is a question of moral and political choice, on which historians are no better qualified to pronounce than anyone else. Yet the stalemate society thesis assumes that what is regarded as politically desirable – liberal democracy and the market economy – is historically necessary, and that deviations from the expected norm are both dysfunctional and morally reprehensible. French history is judged (in all senses of the word) against the expected outcome of modernisation, and people, institutions and events are graded according to whether they retard or stimulate modernisation – de Gaulle was great because he recognised the direction of history.

Since no-one really knows the direction of history, value judgements take the place of genuine explanation. Thus Winock's argument rests on the scientific *validity* of criticisms of parliament in the 1930s and he lauds the constitutional reforms proposed by conservatives such as André Tardieu. His logic is that since antiparliamentarianism was the response to a 'real' malfunction in the system, fixing the problem was a neutral (and necessary) technical matter. Although vulnerable to exploitation by a fringe of intransigent Catholic nationalists, the great majority of those who attacked parliamentarianism were merely concerned citizens and not fascists.[28]

Furthermore, as a diagnosis of ills and prescription of remedies, the stalemate society thesis relies on some dubious assumptions. We may start with 'modernisation'. Hoffmann posits a law – modernisation – and then attempts to explain away deviations from it. It is only possible to do so by recourse to sweeping generalisations, such as 'the French are unable to take responsibility for their own lives', or 'the French are more concerned with stability than innovation'. Law-based explanations are invoked at all levels of explanation. Charle explains social discontent in the 1930s as a product of the law of disappointed rising expectations.[29] Michel Winock's *Fièvre hexagonale* is organised in the classic positivist manner: observation of a series of crises permits the establishment of laws governing 'fevers' (note the medical term) in French society which can then be used to explain each crisis and suggest prognoses and remedies.

Societies have certainly changed and will continue to do so. But no law guarantees this. Rising production is only an 'explained trend' and as such it relies on conditions – such as rising food supply and the availability of raw materials – which might not last.[30] We cannot assume that people will recognise change, or that change creates some kind of existential crisis with which contemporaries must 'come to terms', to use the psychobabble term. We cannot foresee the ways in which societies will change, or in which change will be conceived; we cannot predict the relationship between the 'dimensions' of change. There is no necessary reason, for example, why industrial capitalism should develop in tandem with liberal democracy. Some seek to render the concept of modernisation more flexible by suggesting that some parts of society progress faster than others. Indeed, the problem of the Third Republic, according to the stalemate society thesis. was precisely that mentalities remained traditional in a modernising economic and international environment. Even if we accept that society can be separated into parts moving at different speeds, the teleological assumptions of modernisation remain untouched. Mentalities *should* evolve in tandem with the demands of the age. Because they did not in early twentieth-century France, the political system was dysfunctional.

In any given society there are competing, and often conflicting, projects to define the future shape of society. One could perhaps refer to these as visions of modernity. Furthermore, many of the projects around in the 1930s anticipated the stalemate society thesis, and they must be taken seriously as political interventions. Indeed, many people were so convinced that France had problems akin to those later systematised by Hoffmann that they were prepared to join a mass paramilitary organisation in order to realise their desired solutions. The Third Republic did not fall into crisis because its leaders were ignorant of the old mole of history burrowing away beneath their feet, but because many people, rightly or wrongly, believed that the Republic did not, could not, and perhaps should not, work.

Put another way, we must focus on both the objective structures of the Republic, and on perceptions of them. We must examine the complex genesis of ideas about society in France and the way people used and manipulated them. Constitutional prescriptions and wider understandings of the modern were not exactly 'invented', but they were constructed from diverse materials. These included not just 'pure' economic, social and political ideas, but beliefs about ethnicity, gender, religion, science and so on, which at first sight have nothing to do with politics.

The diversity of understandings of change in French society points to another problem with the stalemate society thesis: the idea that societies must possess cohesive beliefs, a common culture, or dominant ideology, which allows people to contribute to the good of society as a whole.[31] All such contentions, whether derived from a Durkheimian notion of common culture, a Marxist concept of social control, or even from a certain reading of the Foucauldian power–knowledge axis,[32] rely on the dubious contention that ruling ideas are somehow 'internalised' by the masses (often through propaganda, repetition and ritual). Dominant groups certainly attempt to propagate ideologies designed to legitimate the status quo. But the masses are often sceptical of the claims made by their betters. They perceive them in the light of their own views of the world; they adapt dominant ideologies to their own purposes, and they sometimes use dominant ideas to expose what they see as the hypocrisy of the ruling class. Anyway, the ruling class rarely presents a single ideology to the masses. Division of, and contest over, the meaning of ideas is the normal state of society. Revolution is nevertheless infrequent because of what Abercrombie, Hill and Turner refer to as the 'dull compulsion of economic necessity'. Structural change, if it is seen as possible at all, is regarded as costlier than the potential benefits. Most regimes are able to provide *some* reward for their members, and they may resort to compulsion.

If conflict is regarded as intrinsic to any society then the stalemate society thesis's stability–crisis–collapse chronology must be questioned. The early history of the Third Republic is beyond the scope of this chapter. But it is worth remembering that contemporaries did not perceive it as a golden age. No sooner had the republicans consolidated their victory over the monarchists than they were faced by Boulangism. A decade later the Dreyfus Affair ripped apart a nascent conservative coalition and precipitated years of bitter religious conflict at all levels of French society. The 1900s were also marked by unification of the socialist movement on a revolutionary programme and syndicalist-inspired strikes. In the years immediately preceding the war fear of revolution and foreign invasion coalesced in the controversy over the three-year military service law. Discourses of social and moral degeneration and decay were very common.

The difference in the 1930s was that a powerful threat to the parliamentary republic emerged in the form of a mass movement of the extreme right, while under Doumergue in 1934 and especially Daladier in 1938–40 the regime became increasingly authoritarian. Why was this? There is no standard by which the 'seriousness' of a crisis can be measured, given that it depends on so many variables, including people's perceptions. The relationship between the gravity of a crisis and the emergence of movements of the extreme Right is complex anyway – as the absence of a significant fascist movement in Depression America and the high vote for Jörg Haider in prosperous contemporary Austria both confirm. It is insufficient for historians who wish to explain the emergence of authoritarianism in interwar France merely to list problems such as unemployment, the rapid overthrow of cabinets, and the rise of the Left. None of these alone or in combination will inevitably produce an authoritarian response. We must interrogate the concepts through which particular groups understood the political system and the expectations they had of it.

To do this it is necessary to understand the importance of religion and secularism to contemporaries, for the conflict between them influenced the way in which social problems were perceived (conversely competing social conceptions influenced ways in which religion and secularism were understood). The stalemate society thesis necessarily relegates religious differences to secondary status in order to sustain the argument that the Republic was underpinned by a social compromise between bourgeoisie and petty bourgeoisie. The Dreyfus Affair and subsequent religious conflicts are ignored by Hoffmann, just as they are in Lebovics's Marxist interpretation of the period. The stalemate society thesis assumes that militant Catholicism and anticlericalism would disappear with modernisation – just as Republicans believed that organised religion would be cast off by men (not women) and societies as they 'grew up'. Therefore the revival of religious conflict in the mid-1920s is interpreted as a sign of the preoccupation of the regime with 'archaic' conflicts at a time when 'modern' economic concerns were objectively more pressing. We shall see, however, that whilst the nature of religious conflict changed, it remained folded into other issues.

A further problem with the stalemate society thesis is its assumption that the nation-state is the fundamental unit of historical analysis. Nations are conceived of as vessels containing autonomous economic and social processes, and this is the condition of the possibility of national comparison. This nation-centred approach also permits René Rémond to relegate features of the leagues he regards as borrowed from abroad to secondary status. Fascism can thus be depicted as alien to France.

Privileging of the nation-state found a receptive audience partly because it connected with certain trends in the Annales school. Both the stalemate society thesis and the dominant school in French historiography were indebted to Durkheim's preoccupation with collective beliefs, and both focused upon the deep mental and social structures allegedly underlying French history. *Annaliste* concern with the 'past in the present' matched Hoffmann's conviction that residues of tradition were responsible for the problems of the Third Republic. Marc Bloch himself had argued that historic patterns of landholding, reinforced by the Revolution, explained the self-sufficiency, individualism and backwardness of the French peasant compared to the American farmer.[33] Most importantly, the 1960s and 1970s 'third generation' of Annales historians devoted much attention to national memories.[34] Some Annalist historians came to view the nation as a social and psychological unity, determined by deep structures that had evolved over centuries. Even Braudel, who had begun his career with a study of the 'Mediterranean World', was in 1991 'fired with enthusiasm for "the weightiness of our origins"', and he wanted to write a history of 'France's past as a whole' since the Roman conquest.[35] Annaliste geographic determinism chimed with a French nationalist tradition which emphasised the roots of the national psyche in the soil, and which was as evident in the novels of the antirepublican Maurice Barrès as it was in the academic geography of the republican Roger Vidal de la Blache. The stalemate society thesis's recourse to the contention that a French national character (or 'habitus' in contemporary usage) was formed in the seventeenth century by the experience of absolute monarchy and peasant proprietorship is not innocent. Noiriel rightly criticises Annales historians for treating France as if it were a person with a collective memory accessible using psychological techniques, and suggests that this approach is based on a misreading of the social psychology of Maurice Halbwachs. Yet his own argument that national memories were specific to social classes is scarcely less reductive, and he repeats the old arguments about the impact of peasant mentality upon twentieth-century French political culture.[36]

This approach had not always been followed by the founders of the Annales. Marc Bloch and Lucien Febvre's goal was precisely to question the primacy of the national framework, and thereby to undermine the dominant position of diplomatic history in interwar historiography. Bloch denied that social structures could be enclosed within national boundaries or the reigns of kings; he studied feudalism as a transnational phenomenon. The nation is indeed only one of several power networks within which individuals and social groups are situated. A citizen of France was part of a global complex of economic exchange, and might have been a member of a Church that looked to Rome. He or she might also be aligned with a pan-national concept of civilisation against the barbarians within and without. The political activist had access to a pool of pan-European ideas and models of political organisation.[37] As cultural-transfer theorists argue, thinkers selectively appropriate, use and modify indigenous and international ideas. Even national identity – what is seen as 'one's own' – is bound up with what is conceived of as 'other', as not part of the nation. It is absurd, therefore, to speak of unitary national characters or even of the apparently more respectable idea of the national habitus.[38]

The implication of these considerations for our particular subject is that the emergence of right-wing authoritarianism in interwar France cannot be seen as the product of French developments alone. Authoritarianism was a response to wider problems, and quite naturally drew from a pool of ideas and institutional precedents beyond French borders. Developing Zeev Sternhell's argument, we might say that 'French' ideas were selectively appropriated by Italians and Germans, and reappropriated by French citizens. This approach also problematises the 'inter-national' comparison inherent in the stalemate society thesis. If national paths cannot so easily be separated, then it is difficult to posit a normal historical development, and the authoritarian turn in the 1930s was not simply 'French'.

Finally, it follows from the above remarks that we can measure neither the Croix de Feu/PSF nor any other manifestation of authoritarianism in the period, against an ahistorical standard of modernity. Rather we should regard authoritarianism as the product of a global crisis, and we should see projects for constitutional reform as contributions to complex debates about how to organise French society. Neither should we expect either the Right or extreme Right to have espoused consistent or unanimous views of the issues they perceived. Their ideas about polity, economy and society were diverse, and cannot easily be summed up by concepts such as conservative, traditional or modern.

The political elite

We are still some way from a convincing alternative picture of the history of the Third Republic. However, cultural and prosopographic methods have begun to revise our view of the Republic's governing class, and its conceptions of society and politics. In this section I shall draw together some of the insights of this research. I shall contend that reforming discourses, which anticipated the stalemate society thesis, came as much from within as from without the system. It is hard to distinguish modernisers from traditionalists or conservatives from progressives. Rather there was a complex struggle between liberals and interventionists, Catholics and secularists, within which competing groups deployed the same vocabulary of 'competence', 'expertise' and 'experience', and endeavoured to depict their opponents as relics of the past. Although there were significant changes in the nature of the ruling elite in this period, they are too subtle to be reduced, say, to an opposition between 'experts' and 'politicians', or 'traditionalists' and 'modernisers'. It follows that reform programmes were not simply a response to malfunctions in the Republic, and so neither was the stalemate society thesis. They all originated within the Third Republic from a *mélange* of languages which cannot be entirely separated, including moderate republican and monarchist distrust of democracy, specific conceptions of progress, assumptions about the relationship between national power, population and social cohesion and a selective borrowing from and rejection of foreign models. The stalemate society thesis represents one of several variants of the Republican elite's reformist programme, and it cannot be understood separately from its origins.

Competence

The stalemate society thesis, in its various versions, advances three propositions concerning the Republican elite:

1. It was more an agglomeration of the local interests represented by 'notables' than a genuinely national government representing the interests of the nation.
2. It was increasingly divided.
3. Its only common feature was its antimodernity.

Nothing illustrates the stereotypicality of this view of the Republic better than the success of Gabriel Chevallier's satirical novel, *Clochemerle*, published in 1934. The latest in a long line of parodies of political life, it tells the story of a 'querelle de clocher' in a Beaujolais village. A dispute about the building of a public lavatory in a passageway adjacent to the Church escalates into a national political crisis, and causes the failure of a major international conference. Amongst the characters is the deputy Alexandre Bourdillat, who left Clochemerle to work as a waiter in a Parisian café, married the owner's daughter, and set up on his own. Since his café was used as a headquarters by various political parties, Bourdillat made enough friends to become a deputy. Once in the chamber, he agitated for a ministerial portfolio on the grounds that his serving of aperitifs had rendered greater services to the party than those 'grand messieurs with their great speeches'. Bourdillat was eventually suggested to Clemenceau as an 'honnête moyenne' and the Prime Minister included him in his government because 'plus j'aurai d'imbéciles autour de moi, plus il y aura de chances qu'on me f… la paix!'[39]

The fascinating researches of Gilles Le Béguec demonstrate that this picture of a republic of over-promoted provincial nobodies like the fictional Bourdillat – the 'république des sous vétérinaires' in contemporary parlance – is wrong. Neither was the Republic a regime of local notables reliant upon 'traditional' authority, family or heredity.[40] The governing instances of the Republic recruited largely from the petty bourgeoisie and especially the bourgeoisie, but within that limit the system was highly selective – no less so than the Fifth Republic, although the criteria for advancement differed. In the Third Republic the route to power lay in medical and especially legal faculties, the Paris Bar and the École libre des sciences politiques. Those stars of the Bar who were selected as *secrétaires de stage*, and who had complemented legal training with attendance at the École libre, were virtually guaranteed political preferment – especially if they understood the conventions of parliamentary oratory. Louis Marin, leader of the Fédération républicaine and minister in several Union nationale cabinets, was typical. He had been part of the Progressist Bar at the turn of the century, taught at the École libre, and became a deputy in 1905. In parliament he soon secured a reputation as an effective speaker. This is not to say that local roots did not matter. Marin believed that reelection required direct experience of his constituents' concerns. His status as the son of a local notable, and the successful conduct of delicate negotiations with rival conservative parties were also preconditions of his success.[41]

Already before 1914 this elite crossed political boundaries, providing the leadership of the Radical Party, the secularist Centre Right and the more moderate wing of the Catholic Right. It was also well represented in para-political bodies, from natalist associations and social policy institutes like the Musée social to employers' organisations.[42] In the interwar years this Paris-based elite gained much ground at the expense of provincially trained lawyers, and indeed provincials in general.[43]

It is no more accurate to sum up the Republican elite's outlook as 'antimodern' than it is to see it as 'local'. The elite's intellectual training was distinctive and deserves close attention. To start with, elite culture was generalist and eclectic. It rejected the specialised academic knowledge of new university disciplines, such as the scientific history (in different forms) of a Seignebos or later a Bloch.[44] This generalism was seen as essential to the education of the well-rounded man, and on this ground the elite defended classicism too. In the 1930s engineering schools insisted on generalist education as a means of defending their profession against competition from autodidacts.[45]

Generalism was closely linked to the notion of 'competence'. It would be tempting to see deployment of this term as evidence of an impulse to technocracy and modernity in the elite, and it does indeed call into question simplistic categorisations. But we must understand the contemporary meanings of competence. The elite defended generalism on the grounds that coupled with 'experience' of life it provided the 'competence' necessary for government. In 1923 the deputy Georges Noblemaire wrote that elites were formed by 'contact with the real', and that regular involvement in a profession gave one the right to speak of things that deputies only experienced from a distance.[46] This is why Marin argued in 1937 that a deputy did not know everything ('n'a pas la science infuse'). He must learn by experience and direct contact with his electors.[47] This idea can be traced back to the 1870s at least, and was part of a critique of Radicalism advanced by moderate republicans (especially the followers of Thiers in the Centre Left) and by monarchists of various shades. These diverse groups agreed that the Radicals overemphasised abstract knowledge and paper qualifications. Radicals were said to have entered parliament only because they had failed as doctors and lawyers, and so they were cut off from the world. Moderate Republicans and monarchists depicted themselves as men who had succeeded in other spheres of life, and so could bring their experience to government. This desire to involve the 'interests' in policy formulation reappeared in various guises throughout the life of the Republic, from the Duc de Broglie's advocacy of a Senate designed to represent the 'interests' to the vogue for corporatism in the 1930s.[48]

Needless to say, competence was in the eye of the beholder. It could express the opposition of displaced monarchist elites to a new knowledge-based ruling class. Yet it was also espoused also by moderate republican elites and some Radicals, who were at the heart of government. In the hands of André de Fels, 'competence' designated the small elite of fifty politicians, habituated to the workings of the administration, who carried out most of the legislative work in the parliamentary commissions, and saved France in the Great War – 'a veritable elite of tested competence', 'strangers to superficial agitation and corridor intrigues', they 'deliberated', 'in the calm intimacy of the inner circle'.[49]

After the rapprochement of Ralliés and moderate republicans in the 1890s, the competence discourse became central to moderate republicanism. Charles de Benoist – an Orleanist turned moderate republican, and another professor at the École libre – produced various schemes for a professional franchise.[50] In the 1900s he argued that a regional list system of proportional representation would encourage men of talent to enter parliament, for the nomination of candidates would no longer be in the hands of blinkered local committees.[51]

'Competence', as the term was deployed in the antiparliamentarian discourse of the 1930s, owed much to its fusion with theories of rationalised management during the Great War. In a parliamentary debate on 7 February 1916, Benoist claimed that the principle of republican administration was that 'since no matter who is suited to no matter what, one can, no matter what, put anyone anywhere'.[52] He took advantage of the military crisis to echo the old demand of the Right that those with specialist knowledge derived from general experience should be brought into government. In fact, the government had already called on 'experts' from outside the usual parliamentary and administrative circles – demonstrating again the malleability of competence. In 1914 the War Ministry gave the Polytechnique-trained businessman, Louis Loucheur, the task of organising artillery production. Loucheur regarded the Conseil des ministres as too large for its purpose and as 'a milieu where imprecision was the rule'. He praised Minister of Commerce Clementel for speaking the 'precise language of the businessman'. Loucheur wanted to apply the lessons of industrial organisation to political decision making, and this was the thinking behind demands for simplification of parliamentary procedure that began to be voiced in those years. Loucheur also cultivated the idea of the politician-expert, allegedly refusing to give even Clemenceau his opinion on issues upon which he was not 'qualified' to speak.[53]

Finally, competence entailed financial caution. Attacks on left-wing fiscal irresponsibility were an old theme of the Right. In the 1885 election it had been the main justification for the Right's opposition to Republican education reforms. Since the theme was electorally productive the 1885 election acquired mythical status and finance became a constant of conservative propaganda. A discourse of the natural probity of the peasant was counterpoised to the allegedly wasteful deputy. Fiscal worries were reinforced by the difficulties resulting from the Great War and by socialist calls for a tax on capital. In 1926 Maurice Bokanowski argued that the citizens of France were like shareholders in the 'great firm' of France. As such they had the right to be suspicious of 'board members' who asked them for more money, yet who failed to develop a proper plan of action. A coherent policy could be developed only if party politics were suspended. Bokanowski's implicit ideal was the 'competent' businessman-politician, defined in opposition to the left-wing Cartel politician. The Cartel he typically regarded as an alliance of Radical committees, which exploited the state on behalf of local interests, with socialist ideologues, who supposedly valued abstract knowledge more than the practical knowledge of men of the world.[54] Likewise, those charged with organising the international exhibition of 1937 saw it as an opportunity to advertise 'the French firm'.[55]

The notion of competence cannot be associated either with the defence of a 'traditional' ruling class or with technocracy in an abstract sense. It was, nevertheless, related in its republican version to a scientist ideology. In the 1870s this science was associated with figures such as Ernest Renan and Hippolyte Taine, both of whom were monarchists who rallied to the Republic. Taine, of course, had succeeded Auguste Comte as the champion of positivism. His approach to history, based on the triptych of race, milieu and moment, contained a large dose of what would now be dismissed as pseudo-science, but which was then entirely respectable. In the 1890s this scientism was updated by a mélange of Social Darwinism and neo-Lamarckianism, scientific conceptions of racial hierarchy, anthropology, and social psychology. Specialist academics in the new disciplines of sociology and history were somewhat suspicious of this eclecticism, and they became more so in the interwar years – the Sorbonne historian François Aulard, for example, attacked Taine's history of the French Revolution. This science nevertheless provided the core of the curriculum in the École libre, which Taine had helped to found, and in the generalist Medical and Law Faculties. These institutions trained the republican elite throughout our period. Pierre Favre argues that 'from the Great War to the 1930s French political science produced no more innovative work', and the École libre was now the 'école du pouvoir'.[56] The conservative Louis Marin may again be taken as emblematic. In the 1930s he defended conservative gentlemanly anthropology quite successfully against the new anthropology of the left-wing Marcel Mauss.[57]

Generalists were marked by their readiness to intervene directly in the formulation of government policy. In contrast, specialist historians and sociologists were aware of the political implications of their work, but saw distance from day-to-day politics as a guarantee of professional neutrality.[58] This was why professional historians like Bloch preferred to study the medieval period. Specialists intervened significantly in politics only after 1934, when fascism appeared to threaten the very principle of free intellectual inquiry. Generalists had no such qualms about political engagement. The founding principle of the École libre was that science could be applied to contemporary problems. Some generalists, such as Gustave le Bon, were said to have compensated for lack of recognition amongst professional academics by seeking salon success. Le Bon, moreover, was able to write leading articles for a moderate republican weekly, *L'Opinion*, in which he pronounced on contemporary issues. Experts justified intervention in the lives of others by defining as scientific questions those which others might have seen as moral, such as the right to regulate family size.

It is often argued that, beginning with the Great War and culminating with the Laval and Daladier governments, experts increasingly displaced politicians. This is true in the sense that parliament lost ground to unelected policy makers, and the Daladier government issued a mass of legislation by decree. But the notion of a category of experts separate from the usual political personnel needs to be reconsidered. 'Experts' shared a similar intellectual formation, attended the same salons and joined the same think-tanks as politicians. Many 'experts' actually had political mandates. The businessman Louis Loucheur became a deputy; the natalists Georges Pernot and Louis Duval-Arnould did so too. The rise of expertise did not see the arrival in power of a new group, so much as a partial political shift within the ruling elite. Above all, there was a greater openness to the moderate wing of Catholicism (evident in the role of figures like Pernot, Boverat and others in formulating family legislation), and there was a weakening of liberalism. It is also possible that Polytechnicians such as Alfred Sauvy returned to the centres of political power, from which they had been somewhat estranged since 1924, but more research needs to be done on this question. Thirdly, a host of business and other special interests found it easier to secure specific legislation under Laval and Daladier – note, for example the role of the Chamber of Commerce of Lyons in obtaining a decree permitting the formation of a compulsory *entente* in the silk industry. This was something like the government of the competent. There was, as we shall see, no more unity of views amongst those formulating policy under Daladier than there had been under any previous administration. The example of the silk *entente* shows the futility of any attempt to understand policy making in terms of a struggle of modernisers against traditionalists. But all policy makers shared certain preoccupations.

This elite espoused a neo-mercantilist conception of political economy which took from Social Darwinism the notion that a nation's fitness to compete with rivals was determined by the quantity and quality of its population, which had to be large enough to provide sufficient soldiers, producers and consumers.[59] Countries which did not increase their populations would be militarily defeated and colonised by others. In 1922 Comte André de Fels, a leading figure in the democratic Centre Right, argued that French geography provided its inhabitants with a position from which to lead the world, but also rendered it vulnerable to open and covert invasion by enterprising and adventurous races which sought to use French soil as a point of departure for world domination. French strength depended upon clear policy and a strong birth rate.[60]

These conceptions were not specific to France, but they were given an original twist by amalgamation with Lamarckian biological science, according to which progress depended upon 'balance' of active and passive elements.[61] According to this view it was possible to contain the international struggle through economic cooperation. Likewise, industry and agriculture, towns and countryside, male and female virtues must be balanced. Noblemaire, using the determinist, racial and Lamarckian assumptions of the generalist intellectual, suggested that the French mentality was one of 'moderation', the result of a fusion of virile northern tenacity with southern, implicitly female, enthusiasm.[62]

It was equally necessary to balance the mass and the elite. The former was regarded equivocally. The people were potentially a reservoir of common sense, but also alternated between passivity and feminine passions – just as in the stalemate society thesis the French people swung between blind opposition and subservience. Again as in the stalemate society thesis, progress depended on the ability of the elite to guide the masses. In 1932 Marin argued that the leadership of an elite was particularly necessary given that in 'this age of universal suffrage, all those things which bitter experience has shown to be so fatal both for peoples and individuals -- base demagogy, brutality and facile illusion – threaten to overwhelm us'.[63] Fédération républicaine activists, serving a France tempered over centuries, would save the nation. Joseph Barthelémy, a typical moderate republican at that time, believed that modernity had 'de-brained' the masses and produced hatred of anyone who rose above the common herd.[64]

The nation was at the core of the republican elite's world-view. French republicans rejected the biological definition of citizenship advanced by Germans. But they espoused a cultural and historical definition that was potentially highly exclusionary. French identity was said to be the product of a long history, in which the political work of the monarchy and Revolution, coupled with contact with the land, were particularly important. Renan argued in his famous definition of the nation that over the centuries the French acquired a 'common psychology' and this idea was reinforced by concepts of social psychology at the turn of the century.[65]

Belief in national indivisibility was important in two ways. First, the idea of a French national psyche, formed by contact with the land, individual property and the central state, is as crucial to the stalemate society thesis as it was to Third Republican thinkers. Gérard Noiriel shows that André Siegfried was a crucial mediating figure between early twentieth-century conceptions of the nation and modern political science and history.[66] Secondly, the belief in a unitary French nation underpinned the belief that party competition undermined national unity. *Pace* Winock, the idea that a healthy democracy depended upon '*alternance*' in power of Right and Left was quite alien to French conservatives in the interwar years.[67] The Fédération républicaine hysterically denounced left-wing governments: the Radicals were said to be in the thrall of the Socialists, and the Socialists in the thrall of the Communists. Communism and socialism, the former supported by immigrants and autonomists in Alsace, were both foreign ideologies bent upon the destruction of the French nation. Ideas of this sort were not confined to the Catholic Right. As might be expected of a party dominated by the republican elite, the Alliance démocratique advocated government by independent men of the upper class and regarded parties ambivalently. Donald Wileman has shown that the Alliance regarded left-wing governments as illegitimate. The Alliance was less hostile to the Radicals than was the Fédération, but it aimed to detach the Radicals from the Socialists in order to exclude the Left from power permanently. An unimpeachable liberal like Joseph Barthelémy, a follower of Flandin, hoped that electoral reform would put an end to party rule and return the honest men to government.[68] Antisocialism combined with nationalism defined the limits of the elites' commitment to democracy. Thirdly, belief that the nation ought to cohere entailed suspicion of immigrants and made xenophobia attractive as a means to unite France in the troubled 1930s.

Elite nationalism was nevertheless compatible with admiration of foreign systems of government. Advocates of constitutional reform routinely referred to the American and especially English practices. Indeed, their knowledge of foreign constitutions helped distinguish the elites from the masses. In terms of Lamarckian thinking the masses were creatures of their environments, while the elites were able to escape determination because of their unusual endowment with reason.[69] Likewise historiographical critics of the stalemate society, from Bloch to Charle, tend to emphasise their knowledge of non-French history and implicitly to contrast themselves with the narrowness of their colleagues.

Faith in French 'grandeur' and uniqueness, paradoxically, entailed membership of a group of similarly superior nations which France ought in key respects to resemble. For much of the history of the Third Republic, France was seen as part of a community of constitutional nations. During the Great War she had fought as part of a community of 'ancient nations' against the tyrannical and uncivilised Austrian and German Empires (a view easier to sustain after the fall of Tsarism). Even then, anti-Germanism was tempered by admiration, for since the 1870 disaster many had been convinced that Germany was better placed to cope with the modern world because she was governed by 'les compétences'.[70]

In the interwar years the notion of civilisation was redefined by colonial rebellion, the rise of Japan, and fear of 'Asiatic' communism, to include, with qualifications, Fascist Italy and sometimes, with many more qualifications, Nazi Germany. Although most commentators insisted that France was not suited to dictatorship, many granted that Fascism and Nazism were necessary defences against communism in Italy and Germany. Since Robert Paxton's *Old Guard, New Order*, historians have rightly emphasised the roots of the Vichy regime in a French potential for authoritarian and exclusionary nationalism. Nevertheless, French conservatives had long been selectively open to wider influences. Neither imitation of fascist paramilitarism nor collaboration with Germany – so long as France preserved its specificity in the wider struggle against communism – was unprecedented. Moderates like Flandin, Laval and Barthelémy all advocated reconciliation with Germany in the 1920s, and did not revise their views in 1933 or 1940. In the 1930s politicians from La Rocque to Tardieu meditated the lessons of the dictatorships. After 1935 conservatives increasingly believed that war against Hitler would benefit only Stalin. Policies as diverse as the Popular Front's leisure programme and Daladier's Family Code were elaborated in imitation of and competition with the dictatorships.[71]

Policy making

Four major policy areas concerned the republican elite. Each area was connected with the conceptions of national power described above. The first was pronatalism. It is well known that pre-1914 fears of population decline had been exacerbated by the loss of a generation of potential fathers in the Great War. The War also provoked alarm that women had taken over male jobs, and perhaps put careers before marriage and childbirth. The Bloc national tightened up restrictions on abortion and contraception; Fascist and Nazi pronatalism reinforced fears for the future of the French 'race' and provided a widely cited model for imitation; in 1939 a range of natalist measures were introduced in the Family Code. This preoccupation with the birthrate and traditional family *could* be seen as supporting the stalemate society thesis. Yet pronatalist projects could just as well be seen as modernising attempts to overcome the 'Malthusianism' of the stalemate society. Indeed, Charle sees Malthusianism, with its effects on the birth rate, production and the level of imagination and enterprise, as one of the objective problems of French society.

As Mary-Louise Roberts has demonstrated, fears about depopulation and the break-up of the family were not a straightforward reflection of real changes in demography or the sexual division of labour.[72] In a culture where it was conventional to use gendered metaphors to signify social relationships, perceived changes in the roles of women were used to give meaning to other social problems. To give just one example, Georges Noblemaire argued that the failure of the Bloc national government of 1919–24 was due to the domination of parliament by men who resembled the 'garçonne', or 'any other bitch (garce)', rather than 'honest women'.[73] Politicians of Left and Right assumed that reestablishment of normality following the war depended upon restoration of 'normal' gender relations. This is not to deny demographic realities. But it is not inevitable that sluggish population growth should have been regarded as a 'problem', or that it should have led to demands for the return of women to the home. Labour shortages could have been overcome through technological innovation and by immigration.

Indeed immigration was the second major area of interest of the experts. As Noiriel argues, given that it was politically difficult to detach the peasantry from their land, and that the birthrate was unlikely to rise in the short term, French business had little choice but import foreign labour in the 1920s. Business also saw immigration as a means to discipline French workers.[74] Republicans generally believed in assimilation, for according to Lamarckian principles it was possible for acquired characteristics to be handed down the generations. Immigration could therefore help solve the population problem. The citizenship law of 1927 was relatively liberal in its provision for foreigners to acquire French nationality. But as Noiriel has demonstrated, assimilationism was combined with some distinctly illiberal attitudes. There was debate about the amount of time it required and about which groups could most easily be absorbed. The Left held that the children of immigrants were assimilated by the inculcation of French history in state education. But the Left was somewhat suspicious of adult immigrants who had not attended French schools, and were happy to exclude them from public employment and to subject them to petty regulation. At the other extreme, the heirs of Barrès felt that centuries of contact with French soil were necessary for the creation of a citizen, and they wondered whether some groups, particularly Jews and non-Europeans, could ever be assimilated. All, however, agreed that policy towards immigrants was not a social question, as contemporary social policy assumes, but one of nation and ethnicity. Experts on race were called upon to determine French policy towards immigration.[75] In spite of a rejection of crude racism, hostility towards foreigners provided a potential meeting point with popular xenophobia.

The third area of concern for the 'experts' was social and economic organisation. Many senior business figures, as well as those who ran employers' organisations, shared the 'scientific' assumptions of the governing elite and pronatalist experts, and assumed that military strength, international competitiveness, industrial production and demography were linked. Already before 1914 such figures advocated, as an alternative to left-wing plans for nationalisation, employer-run cartels, which would cooperate with the state in a programme of 'economic rearmament'.[76] During the Great War the entry of businessmen such as Loucheur into the government strengthened this tendency. In 1923 Loucheur argued that current economic problems were not just due to the war, but resulted from a more fundamental disorder. The solutions were coordination of state and business action in a system of ententes, rationalisation of production in order to reconquer foreign markets and improvement of the purchasing power of the colonies.[77] It was also hoped that rationalisation, coupled with the use of semi-skilled immigrant labour, would undermine trade unionism. Ideas of this order were shared by a host of businessmen in the 1920s, of whom the best known were Auguste Detoeuf of Alsthom and Ernest Mercier of the Compagnie générale d'électricité. In 1926 they set up Redressement français to promote 'neo-capitalism'. Mercier was influential in the Tardieu governments of 1929–30.[78]

'Progressive' businessmen are often conceived of as maverick and/or unusually enlightened critics of the stalemate society. In fact there is no clear division between modernisers and traditionalists or insiders and outsiders, at least in the ranks of big business. Jean Peyerimhoff, head of the coal mining employers' association, André Lambert-Ribot, head of the Comité de Forges, and René Duchemin, president of the Confédération générale de la production française, have all been seen variously as the epitome of routine and as innovators.[79] Whatever the case, they were all part of the circuits of power in the Third Republic.

Furthermore, 'modernisers' shared the broader assumptions of the Republican elite. Use of the term 'Malthusian' to designate both economic conservatism and refusal to have children suggests that the 'traditional' French businessman might have been as mythical as the 'modern woman', and that ideas about business organisation were not just 'technocratic' responses to purely economic problems. As Jackie Clarke argues, business-intellectuals synthesised wider concerns, and advanced a historically constructed conception of modernity. She shows that the Polytechnique-educated engineer, Jean Coutrot, combined humanist and rationalist notions in a manner designed to avoid the excessive rationalisation associated in the public mind with Fordist America.[80] Likewise, Roland Ziegel explained to X-Crise in 1935 that decentralisation of production would raise productivity, wean workers away from communism, increase the birthrate and reverse the morally dangerous tendency towards urbanisation. In this plan one sees the typical preoccupation with balance, the connection between birthrate and national power, and the belief that national identity resided in the land.[81] Neocapitalists were prominent in the natalist movement: Paul Lefebvre-Dibon, president of Air liquide, along with Mercier, sat on the board of the Alliance nationale pour l'accroissement de la population française. Redressement français did not envisage the elimination of peasants and small producers but their 'modernisation', and held that medium firms were the real enemies of small business, not big capital.[82] Although less critical of traditional/modern categories, Shanny Peer shows how the promoters of the Regional Centre at the 1937 World Exhibition promoted a 'modern regionalism' designed to avoid the perceived dangers of American-style productivism.[83]

The fourth area of interest was constitutional reform, in pursuit of which a huge number of projects were produced in this period. Let us take that of Redressement français, published in 1927, as exemplary, for it emanates from a group often seen as having protested vainly against the immobility of the stalemate society.[84] The fact that Redressement's proposal was produced by a committee chaired by Raphaël Alibert, supporter of the neo-royalist Action française and future counsellor of Pétain, should warn us against understanding these proposals in terms of modern-traditional dichotomies.[85] Nevertheless, the project begins with the language of the stalemate society thesis: reform is necessary because a constitution already 'archaic' in 1914 had been completely vitiated by the Great War.[86] France now required an assembly able to legislate competently and rapidly. To this end 'technicians' (i.e. experts from business and elsewhere), should be involved in parliamentary committees. Parliament would be forbidden to amend projects agreed in committee; its right to interpellate governments would be restricted, and the state would be strengthened in unspecified ways. Redressement's proposals represented one more project for reduction of the alleged gap between government and the country – that is, to place government in the hands of the 'competent'. Equally predictable was the justification of a single-round electoral system as a means to prevent parties from perverting the democratic process. Redressement's proposals were intended not just to improve legislative and economic efficiency, but to raise the birthrate. Redressement proposed the enfranchisement of women, coupled with extra votes according to the number of children in the family, as a means to ensure that the voice of the family – the true social unit – was heard in the legislative process. This, it was felt, would meet the demands of feminists without harming the family.

In many ways Redressement's critique anticipates that of the stalemate society thesis: the inappropriateness of current institutions to the modern age, the gap between parliament and the people, and the selfishness of the parties are all present. Redressement's project also reveals the roots of the stalemate society thesis in a scientific world-view that is largely rejected by contemporary scholars, in the culture of competence, and in immediate issues such as the perceived danger of feminism and communism. Furthermore, Redressement's assumptions were shared in the Republican elite as a whole. It was not a critique from without.

A divided elite

The Republic was governed by a class whose power depended upon a distinctive combination of material resources and cultural capital. This class shared ideas about national identity, economic organisation, relations between men and women and political representation. Its political centre of gravity rested in the

Centre Right, but extended into both the Radical Party and SFIO and the Catholic Fédération républicaine. Yet there were fundamental disagreements about the meanings of key concepts, and projects for constitutional reform were deployed as much in pursuit of factional struggles within the elite as in response to perceived problems in the system. The stereotypes of the expert-politician and its other, the provincial under-vet, were so well rooted in elite culture that they were useful weapons in these quarrels. Even Socialist and Radical reformers used the concept of competence to depict the capitalist elites as backward-looking remnants of feudalism (a notion appropriated by the Croix de Feu).

Confining our attention to the Right, the first area of conflict concerned liberalism. The conservative, neo-mercantilist, natalist world-view described above was compatible with both increased state intervention (even fascism) and with political and economic liberalism.[87] Thus the ultraliberal Auguste Isaac agreed that the birthrate was a question of life or death for France, but felt that financial encouragement of births was pointless. Only moral reformation of the elites, the presentation of a more positive image of the *mère de famille*, and the suppression of anti-family propaganda, could be effective.[88] Liberal opposition to interventionist natalist measures explains the apparent paradox that in spite of near unanimous belief in the dangers of depopulation, little legislation was introduced before the implementation of the Code de la famille by decree in 1939.

Liberal opposition also delayed or scuppered schemes for social reform, whether they were proposed by the Left, centre-right partisans of economic organisation, or Social Catholics. This had happened before the Great War,[89] and afterwards liberals ensured that efforts to make some of the institutions of the war economy permanent foundered.[90] Likewise, the moderately reformist and interventionist governments of André Tardieu and Pierre Laval in 1929–32 were undermined by opposition from liberals in the Fédération républicaine. The Fédération attacked social insurance legislation and excessive government spending as interference in the market.[91] In the 1930s, liberal financial orthodoxy helped ensure that devaluation would not be adopted as a means of combating the Depression.[92]

Next, whilst all – including so-called modernisers – agreed that social stability required equilibrium between large and small production, the nature of this balance was contested. Alliance with 'les petits' could mean the promotion of shareholding, and therefore of big business, or it could mean defence of the family farm. Protection of the latter could mean retreat into a subsistence economy, or 'modernisation' through cooperation and consolidation of landholdings. Whilst many Radicals lauded the small shopkeeper, right-wing and business groups almost universally blamed shopkeepers for profiteering on foodstuffs, raising wages and depriving peasants of their rightful income. In the 1930s the Right tried to set consumers against shopkeepers. Bakers were attacked for defrauding consumers through debasement of the quality of bread – an ironic comment on a current advertising campaign for bread made to 1930s standards, and another reminder of the constructed nature of historical categories used to understand the world.[93]

The complexity of relations between and among industrial and rural producers was especially evident in the Lyonnais silk industry. In the 1920s legislative attempts to protect artisans exacerbated tensions in the industry. The exemption of artisans from labour legislation, especially the eight-hour law, coupled with the electrification (modernisation, some might say) of the countryside, made rural weaving extremely profitable. Some silk manufacturers saw this as a positive development, permitting the industry to respond to rapid changes in demand. They spoke of the 'social interest' of home weaving and of the iniquity of regulation of individual producers.[94] Others thought differently. Jean Vautheret praised family workshops, but evoked the 'rabbit hutches' masquerading as workshops at Chauffailes in Saône-et-Loire. At a time when home workshops were diverted from their true vocation, Vautheret said, industry suffered from ever greater regulation and could not compete.[95] In this example attempts to protect 'small producers' – to create something like a stalemate society – provoked much hostility between businessmen and helped push a few into opposition to the regime.[96] Even without taking into account the different ways in which anticlerical and Catholic businessmen conceptualised economic issues, it is possible to see that the relationship between large and small producers was conceived in many ways.

Our third source of division is that between republican and Catholic elites. Some sections of the elite possessed economic power and cultural capital, but were partially excluded from political power because of their Catholicism. Catholics, whether of professional, academic or business backgrounds, were still in the interwar years barred from certain areas of state employment, including the Prefectoral Corps, the Council of State (with a few exceptions) and the Education Ministry. Catholics rarely became government ministers.[97] The Catholic political party, the Fédération républicaine, was often called upon to support right-wing governments in parliament, but its members rarely entered the cabinet. Marin, a practising, but far from fanatical, Catholic, served briefly in Union nationale cabinets, but only in secondary posts.[98]

Catholic resentment at this bar may be traced back to monarchist opposition to the Third Republic in the 1870s, and it was one of reasons for the demand for government by the competent. It is important, however, to bear in mind divisions amongst Catholics, for some Catholics were closer to the republican elite than others, and some were more open to the scientific world-view we have been describing. In the interwar years, thanks to the disappearance of the explicitly Catholic party, the Action libérale populaire, Catholic conservatives who accepted the Republic had little choice but to back the liberal-conservative Fédération républicaine, which became the unofficial voice of the Church in parliament. One of the effects was that a small group of practising Catholics, who had long sought to reconcile religion with the scientist and secular ethos of the Republic, became prominent in the leadership of political Catholicism. These Catholics could trace their origins back to the Centre gauche of the early republic, and in our period Louis Marin was the best known. While such figures never occupied first-rank ministerial office, they had some hope of minor posts, and they were prominent in the think-tanks which were so influential in policy making in this period. Ferdinand Boverat, the son of a Parisian banker, was a Catholic natalist activist, and was significant in the shift to the right of the Alliance nationale pour l'accroissement de la population française, of which he became president in 1938. Boverat's right-wing sympathies did not prevent him from serving on the Daladier government's Haut comité de la population in 1939, in which he helped elaborate the Code de la famille.[99]

Doubtless the growing political importance of figures such as Marin and Boverat was partly responsible for the rapprochement between the Catholic and lay Rights in the interwar years, a process facilitated by the condemnation of Action française in 1926. But these developments mask the persistence of the religious–secular cleavage *among* Catholics. The dissolution of Action française caused some monarchists to join burgeoning Catholic organisations or to join the Fédération républicaine – Xavier Vallat is a good example. Representatives of the ALP, such as Joseph Denais, also remained influential in the Fédération. The conflict between secularism and religion now ran through the Fédération républicaine. Louis Marin was too Catholic for the Republican establishment, to which he possessed so many ties. But he had to reckon too with a strand among Catholics, represented by Christian Democrats and Catholic nationalists, which sought to abolish the distinction between religious and secular politics.[100] In 1937 Marin complained lengthily to the Nuncio that the Church's refusal to allow him to attend a meeting of a Catholic agricultural association was undermining his electoral position in a constituency where the religious struggle remained bitter.[101]

Since the Ralliement conservatives had periodically expressed the need to unite Catholics and secularist conservatives in a single conservative party. Tardieu lamented that

> These parties [of the Right and Centre] have even less unity than their counterparts on the Left. For they are divided more or less equally between followers of the Catholic tradition and supporters of the French Revolution. This division in the ranks is the cause of their problems.[102]

Appeals for unity were generally based on the claim that religious struggles were 'anachronistic', and that in the modern age economics and social issues were more important. In the interwar years it was commonly claimed that the Great War had reconciled Catholics and Republicans but that conservatives were too concerned with the past to recognise this. Likewise, Marc Audigier, writing in 1995, describes the Alliance démocratique's desire to build a centrist coalition with the Radicals, as 'outdated' and argues that a more 'realistic' policy would have been to accept the 'reality' that France was divided into two blocs.[103]

The problem was that there was no agreement on the terms of the reconciliation. Had the republicans accepted the 'legitimate rights' of the Church in a 'Catholic France'? Had the Church accepted that religion was a private matter in a secular society? Moreover, the separation of religion and economics into separate 'factors' – as essential to contemporary thinking as to the stalemate society thesis – was difficult to maintain in practice. The elites failed to unite around economic issues because religious and secularist ideas influenced the very manner in which 'the economic' was defined.[104]

It is doubtful whether a successful political system (whatever that means) requires a united conservative party. But many conservatives believed that it did, and they attributed this failure to recognise the needs of a modern society to the average deputy's atavistic preoccupation with religious disputes and local matters. The desire to unite conservatives in circumstances where failure to do so was seen as a matter of life or death for the nation was a significant cause of the crisis of the 1930s.

The clerical/anticlerical conflict was entangled with a fourth area of contest – the nature and purpose of constitutional reform. Both wings of the Right invoked the need for competent and experienced men to govern and used similar language to attack parliament. But there were important differences. Broadly speaking, the formerly monarchist and Catholic Right demanded strengthening of the executive. Some spoke of a stronger presidency, others of granting the right of dissolution to the Prime Minister. Some, influenced by Bonapartism, wanted to combine a strong executive with the use of referenda. The continuity of the authority principle once represented by the monarch would be provided by a stronger executive. The monarchist inheritance was evident too in the belief that reform of the state would allow the competent to govern – those practical men who had been excluded from power by the parliamentary Republic of talentless lawyers and doctors. It is true that the establishment of the Republic had led to significant alterations in the conditions of access to political power, and that the installation of the Radical Republic in the 1900s had led to a degree of democratisation of access to the elite. Nevertheless, the Right's picture was a mixture of fact and myth, for we have seen that the republican elite too defined itself in terms of competence. The Catholic Right deployed class and cultural stereotypes in a complex struggle between factions of the Right.

Many centre-right politicians also deployed the language of competence, attacked parliamentary abuses, and adopted plans for constitutional reform which apparently differed only in detail from those of the Catholic Right. Moreover, André Tardieu of the Centre Right became the champion of a highly authoritarian programme for constitutional reform, and by 1940 Flandin, Barthelémy, Romier and other centrists were ready to endorse frankly authoritarian government.[105] In the early 1930s, however, the Centre Right's schemes were less antiparliamentarian than those of the Catholic Right. The Centre Right traditionally placed enormous faith in the value of parliamentary debate. At least until the mid-1930s their ideal was a parliamentary government, in which disinterested and experienced men (the competent) legislated in the public good through careful deliberation. Faith in parliament was strengthened by the belief – not entirely justified – that parliamentary government had won the Great War. But there was also concern to profit from the lessons of conflict – hence the aforementioned interest in improving parliamentary efficiency and rationalising its business. The great movement for constitutional reform of 1919, although it included many left-wing and conservative elements, largely thought in these terms, and did not espouse the more authoritarian antiparliamentarianism of the Catholic Right.[106]

Subsequently, there was a degree of convergence between the two currents – so much so that the movement for constitutional reform often seemed irresistible. Yet at the crucial moment the partisans of reform were unable to agree, for many on the Right, even the Catholic Right, refused to accept limitations on parliamentary sovereignty. Louis Marin, in the name of the rights of parliament, helped ensure the failure of a modest reform of parliamentary procedure in December 1919.[107] In 1933 Poincaré rejected Tardieu's plan and wanted to restrict action to parliamentary procedures.

These divisions within the elite take us some way towards understanding why the regime was perceived to be in crisis in the 1930s. Large sections of the parliamentary elite, together with the Right and not a few of the Radical and Socialist Left, felt that national unity was a precondition of national power, and had long felt that the governing class was inadequate to its task. Criticism of the Republic, both among insiders and outsiders, was as old as the Republic, and so the Right *expected* crisis.[108] The litany of demands was familiar. The administration must be rationalised and useless effort eliminated. Talkers must give way to doers. The state must cooperate effectively with business, whilst avoiding the dangers of socialist interventionism. The unity, quantity and quality of the population must be preserved. Without such measures, France would be unable to deal with the unavoidable demands of 'progress' and compete successfully in a potentially lethal struggle between nations. The stakes were high.

It is possible to detect a cycle of expectation and disappointment and a shift towards the extreme Right on the part of some of those most interested in structural reform – not least Tardieu. The elections of 1919, to use Gilles Le Beguec's expression, had seen a 'veritable mobilisation of competence'. Many graduates of the École libre were elected to parliament, and even a number of students of the École polytechnique, who normally shunned politics, became deputies. The businessman Auguste Isaac briefly became Minister of Commerce.[109] Yet the Bloc national's legislative record was seen as meagre, and many of those elected in 1919 did not stand in 1924, often complaining that they had been outmanoeuvred by politically astute parliamentary hacks. Some turned to extraparliamentary pressure groups, like Redressement français, and some of these placed their hopes in André Tardieu's government of 1929–30, only to be disappointed again. Others were attracted to antiparliamentary leagues. The pronatalist activists Fernand Boverat, Joseph Haury and Louis Duval-Arnould, studied by Cheryl Koos, were among their number. Mercier joined the Croix de Feu in the 1930s. It was not inevitable that disillusioned partisans of reform should have been attracted to right-wing extremism. Many were not, and some of those who were, like Duval-Arnould and Boverat, were also involved in the formulation of the Daladier government's policies. Nevertheless, this administration had broken with the parliamentary practice once idealised by the republican elite.

The elites and the masses

The stalemate society thesis makes a number of assumptions concerning mass politics:

1. The masses shared a common culture which mixed traditional and modern values, and combined family stability with individual social promotion. Only the workers were partially excluded.
2. The masses did not join associations, and were unwilling to take responsibility for their own lives.
3. They were more concerned with local than national politics (hence the continued domination of politics by notables).
4. The masses alternated between dismal submission to authority and anarchic rebellion.
5. The masses were not the primary source of opposition to the stalemate society. In some versions the mass support of the leagues desired defence of the status quo. At most the masses expressed through the leagues a vague 'common sense' desire for reform.

It is a cliché that 1934 witnessed the beginning of an unprecedented social and political mobilisation in France. On the Right, veterans' organisations like the Union nationale des combattants (UNC)[110] and the Ligue des contribuables[111] were both involved in the 6 February riots, and were at the forefront of the movement for constitutional reform. Henri Dorgères's quasi-fascist Défense paysanne was strong in many rural areas.[112] Hundreds of thousands of largely bourgeois men and women joined the Croix de Feu/PSF, along with many other discontented conservatives.[113] On the Left, semi-skilled workers without a history of trade union or political activism, many of them immigrants, joined the CGT and voted for the Communist Party, and the latter also increased its appeal to women.[114] Intellectuals felt compelled to issue manifestos favouring one side or the other. The authorities were threatened with potential or actual strikes by taxpayers, Parisian market gardeners and above all industrial workers. Veterans' organisations presented the government with an ultimatum in 1934. Much of this activism occurred outside the normal political channels, and to some extent the political battles of the period were fought out in the streets. This was unsurprising, for not only were Catholics and communists more or less debarred from governing coalitions, but the suffrage excluded the majority of adults. Women – more numerous than men in the adult population – did not have the vote. Neither did millions of immigrant workers.[115]

On the face of it, this mass activism could be seen as evidence of an objective crisis in the regime, especially as parliamentary government rested on a far from universal suffrage. Yet those excluded from decision making did not necessarily want to be included. Even though many people felt that constitutional methods of expressing their views were not working, we still have to explain why people believed that this was the case.

At this point we meet a problem. In the present state of research it is difficult to say very much about popular attitudes to the political system, especially about those of a right-wing disposition. Regrettably, moreover, the reaction against social history has led to neglect of the labour movement and peasantry as objects of study. Recent cultural history, important as it is, is largely concerned with the ways in which government policy and social and political theorists conceptualised, moulded, or attempted to mould, workers, peasants and women. German *Alltagsgeschichte*, which has done so much to illuminate workers' ambiguous relationship to Nazism, has no equivalent in French history.[116] Neither have historians of the interwar period emulated Alain Corbin's brilliant examination, using anthropological methods, of peasant Bonapartism in the 1860s and 1870s.[117] In the absence of studies of this type it is difficult to say with certainty how far the masses were integrated into a common culture, what expectations they had of the parliamentary republic, or why, if at all, they perceived it to be in crisis in the 1930s. The following remarks therefore concern activists as much as popular opinion proper.

The contention that French people were reluctant to join associations is dubious. True, political parties did not possess enormous memberships by European standards. Neither were trade unions numerically powerful – although this might have had as much to do with employer hostility as to worker apathy. Other kinds of associations did prosper, however. To start with there was an enormous number of women's groups – the Ligue patriotique des françaises alone had over one million members.[118] The Ligue patriotique was part of a vibrant network of Catholic organisations of both genders centred upon the parish, ranging from specialist Catholic Action groups to 'groupes d'hommes' devoted to boules and belotte. The Church was also involved in a network of economic associations, including farmers' groups and trade unions. Veterans' groups – chiefly the pro-Catholic UNC and the secularist Union fédérale – played a crucial role in rural and urban associative life in this period.[119]

The mobilisation of the 1930s was less an example of a swing from apathy to rebellion than a politicisation of existing networks. Both women's and veterans' groups had a history of moderate antiparliamentarianism. Conservative women's groups, drawing upon conventional stereotypes, contrasted the idealised family with the amoral male world of business and politics. Women's groups invested themselves with the task of moralising men through a kind of propaganda of example in the private sphere – broadly defined to include welfare.[120] Likewise veterans' groups contrasted the idealised moral-patriotic community of the front with the selfishness of politicians, and throughout the interwar years they expressed the hope that the *esprit ancien combattant* would cleanse parliamentary and social life. Some women's groups, as well as the UNC, were also influenced by

Catholic Action, which expanded from the late 1920s. Catholic Action too aimed to moralise social life through personal purity and example.[121]

None of these organisations intervened effectively in the political process. Catholic and women's organisations did not attempt to do so. Among the veterans' associations the UNC alone sought a political role, but its highly politicised leaders failed to convince the bulk of followers, especially outside Paris, of the wisdom of playing politics. Veterans' organisations were too diverse to be mobilised on a precise platform. Nevertheless, while we cannot say how deeply rooted antiparliamentarianism was in the population at large, we can see that it was a factor in the rich associative culture of the late Third Republic. It is no accident that the Croix de Feu should have recruited members from Catholic Action, veterans' associations and women's groups. Neither is it surprising that veterans in parliament should have used their status as old soldiers to depict themselves as outside the normal circuits of the system – even though most were actually experienced politicians.[122]

All of the aforementioned organisations participated in discussions about the shape of French society. The question of how to adapt American methods of mass production to French conditions was as likely to be discussed in local Catholic trade union newspapers as it was in the austere pages of Redressement Français's review. Discussions about corporatism in Lyons show how wide were debates about industrial, trade union and political organisations in that city. The contention that reform programmes were elaborated by an elite standing outside the stalemate society must be qualified, and the degree of separation between elite and mass politics can be exaggerated too. Whereas the stalemate society thesis assumes that reform programmes were elaborated by a group uniquely able to take an objective view of society, we have seen that diagnoses of the ills of the regime relied heavily upon gendered, religious and ethnic assumptions which were as deeply ingrained in the elites as the masses. Much of Third Republican political science was little more than systematised prejudice, and its legacy has not entirely disappeared.

The persistence of the religious question provides further evidence of the inseparability of elite and mass politics. Some versions of the stalemate society thesis argue that religious issues had been superseded by modern financial and economic questions. There is, however, plenty of evidence that religious disputes continued to divide. One might expect this in 'backward' Brittany, or Catholic Alsace. It is perhaps more surprising that in largely urban Rhône department the Fédération républicaine attributed its poor showing in rural areas in the general election of 1936 to the unwillingness of the peasantry and rural petty bourgeoisie to vote for the 'priest's candidate'.[123] In the industrial suburb of Neuilly gangs of Catholic and Communist children fought in the school playgrounds, the former with crosses on their rings, the latter with hammers and sickles.[124] There is no need to give more examples. The point is that religion continued to be a major element in social groups' self-definition.

Just as religious allegiance influenced access to governmental power, so it was a factor in the job market. This was particularly true in certain sections of state employment, especially education, in which anticlerical trade unions fought against the linked dangers of feminisation and Catholicisation. Denunciation of discrimination against Catholics in state employment was a major preoccupation of the Fédération républicaine, and was a source of solidarity between Catholics of all classes. The campaign against discrimination reinforced the conviction – which had some basis in fact – that the state did not treat all citizens equally, and that employment prospects did not depend on merit. Critiques of parliament in the name of competence therefore had some resonance in the Catholic population at large.[125] Interestingly, the same might be true of lay conservatives. As conservatives the Alliance démocratique too disliked the excessive influence of the anticlerical Syndicat national des instituteurs in the teaching profession, for it was seen as a bastion of Marxism. The Centre Right might have liked to purge teaching of left-wingers, but it did not do so because it feared that this would alienate secularist feeling.[126]

Furthermore, the religious quarrel had been rendered even more essential to popular politics by the development of state and private white-collar employment, and by the creation of a host of Catholic and *laïque* lobbies in education, agriculture and business. Conservative politicians could not afford to ignore these, and so attempts to unite conservatives were constantly disrupted.

The question of immigrant labour provided another linkage between elite and mass politics. State regulation of immigration was shaped partly by the knowledge that French workers, artisans, shopkeepers and their unions resented foreign competition. Moreover, the elites themselves, especially lawyers, doctors and students, had long demanded protection against foreign competition. Although during the 1930s expulsions and unemployment reduced the number of immigrants in France, hostility to immigrants remained high, not least because of the arrival of numerous political refugees. Meanwhile international tension spread fear of spies. Since intellectuals habitually thought in terms of racial and national characters, they were more than ready to deploy racial stereotyping in defence of their own corporative privileges.[127] The elites' fear of religious and class division in the social body meant that xenophobia was an attractive electoral tactic.

6 February 1934

It is hard to identify the precise moment when the Right became convinced that the problems of French society were so serious that they required fundamental reform of the regime, and perhaps even a change of regime. Examination of the press following the Left's electoral victories in 1924 and 1932 reveals a level of fear and hysteria which makes sense only if we understand the way in which the Right perceived the political process. It is illuminating, nevertheless, to conclude with consideration of the Right's views of the riots of 6 February 1934. This *journée* precipitated the long period of Franco-French conflict, which arguably came to a (temporary) end only with the centrist victory in the elections of 1951. Moreover, 6 February was perceived by many right-wingers as a turning point in the history of the regime. The Left had definitively demonstrated its inability to govern within a decadent system, and it seemed possible that a new order might rise from the 'cesspit' of contemporary France.

Some expectations are inevitably confirmed by events. If deputies are believed to be fundamentally corrupt, and if all deputies are held to be the same, then sooner or later evidence of corruption will appear. The failings of an individual will be but one manifestation of the failings of the category. The Stavisky scandal confirmed what a great many French people already knew – that deputies were out to line their own pockets at the expense of the state. This belief had been a staple of literature and the press, and was ingrained within women's and old soldiers' associations, and was not absent from left-wing discourses either (the idea that parliament was controlled by 'les gros' or by capitalists). The Stavisky scandal was especially suited to confirm right-wing expectations. Unlike the *Gazette du franc* and Oustric scandals, this affair involved left-wing politicians. In the figure of Stavisky it was possible to bring together all of the fears of the Right at a time when public opinion was concerned by financial crisis, socialist influence in government, the arrival of refugees from Germany and Nazi agitation in Austria. Of course, a leading role in ensuring public attention for the scandal was played by *Action française*. But it is noticeable that by the end of January even the moderate republican *Le Temps* and the Alliance démocratique were ready to endorse the use of violence to overthrow the Cartel government.

First, the scandal was evidence of a moral crisis. Much use was made of the term 'cesspit'. According to *Le Journal des Débats*, owned by François de Wendel, and close to Louis Marin's wing of the Fédération républicaine, the regime had caught a fever from living so long in the cesspit, and there were some infections from which the regime could not recover.[128] According to this logic, the scandal was not a problem of individual culpability, but an objective politico-medical problem requiring scientific-surgical intervention.

More precisely, Stavisky signified the government's crimes against financial good sense. The scandal revealed that the origins of the budget deficit lay in the willingness of deputies to pillage the state for the benefit of their clients. The possibilities for corruption were multiplied by the interference of the state in private matters – it was no accident that Stavisky had exploited the funds of local government and the state. In a society where individual initiative was no longer allowed, Stavisky was able to make use of the whole edifice of state regulation.[129] The moderate *Le Temps* added that agitation on the part of civil service trade unions, coupled with political interference in promotions, had corrupted the administration.[130]

Stavisky also represented the internationalism, or 'cosmopolitanism' of the Left. Moderate conservative newspapers did not, at least in those I have sampled, mention the fact that Stavisky was a Ukrainian Jew, and neither did the more conservative *Journal des Débats*. Explicit anti-Semitism remained largely confined to Action française. Nevertheless, in a context where artisans, shopkeepers, businessmen and the liberal professions were appealing for protection from immigrant competition, Stavisky symbolised the dishonest foreign merchant. Refugees from Germany were said by citizens and officials alike to be taking advantage of crisis in Germany to set up businesses in France. It is not surprising that the small business association, the Ligue des contribuables, should have participated in the 6 February riots.[131] Belief in the international dimensions of the scandal were explicit in references to Staviskites' mixture of 'profits and anti-French propaganda' and implicit in the oft repeated claim that the 'French' were ready to rise up against the 'thieves', and that the time had come for conflict between the Staviskite Cartel and the nation. According to *Les Débats* the scandal exposed the submission of parliamentarians to internationalism and their feebleness when confronted with German infiltration (in Austria).[132] Stavisky, then, evoked deep-seated fears about the international situation and the possibility that France might be absorbed by its more strongly governed, more fertile and productive, neighbours.

Condemnation of internationalism was closely related to identification of the Left with occult power. According to *Les Débats* the scandal was inexplicable without some 'great secret' at its base. The affair revealed the manipulation of the parliamentary system by committees and Masonic lodges (another manifestation of internationalism). Identification of 'Staviskites' with the Left as a whole effectively denied legitimacy to the government.[133] Furthermore, the departure from Daladier's administration of the centrists Fabry and Piétri, confirmed (if confirmation were needed) that the Radicals were dependent on the Socialists. The revolutionary intentions of the Socialists were in turn proved by the sacking of Jean Chiappe, the right-wing Prefect of Police.

From there it was a short step to endorsing 'defensive' violence (isn't it always?) against a government said to be bent on revolution. A month previously *Les Débats* had compared the current atmosphere of moral corruption with that prevailing in the Directory prior to Napoleon Bonaparte's coup, and could not believe that now, as then, the 'honest and hardworking' country would not demand the application of the scalpel. The first demonstrations outside the Chamber on 12 January were interpreted as a sign of the 'awakening of the people'.[134] On the morning of 6 February *Les Débats* declared that 'public opinion' would not accept a government dominated by Blum. The editorialist asked what would become of us given the state of our finances, the undermining of the army by internationalism, and the sacking of Chiappe?[135]

It is predictable that a Catholic nationalist like Jean Guiraud should also have spoken of the 'right of insurrection' against a tyrannical government.[136] But the historically moderate republican *Journal des Débats* too echoed the refrain that the government had used troops against peaceful veterans and expressed gratitude to those who had fought so disinterestedly.[137] Even more surprisingly, *Le Temps*, the bastion of conservative republicanism, was caught up in the populist mood. At first the newspaper had refused to identify a few criminals with the regime as a whole, and had accepted the Chautemps administration's word that it desired action against corruption. But *Le Temps* admitted there was a moral crisis, and argued that a 'party' had covered up the wrongdoings of a few guilty men. On 3 February, *Le Temps* gave Tardieu's *Heure de la décision* a positive review, and admitted that only public opinion, enlightened by the Stavisky Affair, could reform the regime. On the day of the riots, the newspaper evoked the divorce between parliament and the people, socialist tutelage of the government, and failure in the economic and international domains. The claim that Chiappe had been sacrificed to Marxist revolution effectively gave the red light to the leagues on the Place de la Concorde. On 9 February, *Le Temps*'s editorialist blamed the riots on the ministry, rather than the demonstrators, and saw statist confusion of the political and economic as the root cause of the crisis of the regime.[138] The views of the Alliance démocratique's journal were nearly identical. It spoke of the extent of corruption in the 'république staviskienne', the role of socialist revolutionaries in the Daladier regime, and attributed Daladier's fall to the fact that it was not possible to govern for ever in defiance of public opinion – represented by 'unarmed veterans'.[139]

Finally, there was common ground in diagnosis of the origins of the crisis. It is not usually noted that most factions of the Right deployed the concept of competence to make sense of the scandal and to propose solutions. According to the *Journal des Débats*, the professionalisation of politics was at the origin of the deputy's search for financial reward. As professionals, deputies saw it as their job to interfere in matters that did not concern them, including judicial activities. Politics had become a matter of party and clientele, in which Masonic orders were more important than ideas. In the good old days, parliamentarians took time out of their professional activities to devote themselves to public affairs, so they served the country rather than themselves.[140] The Right called for a government of 'character, independence and service'.[141] Doumergue was on the same wavelength. The deep cause of the crisis was lack of self-discipline. We are, he wrote shortly after the riots, too shut up in our 'specialisms'. Technicians were necessary in the modern world, and the head of the government must heed their advice. But the final decision, Doumergue said, must be taken by the head of government alone, on the basis of his 'culture and human and historical experience'. Classical education, which had formed so many great minds, must be restored.[142] Likewise, Flandin attributed the crisis to the fact that the regime paid for services rather than recognising 'virtue'.[143] On 7 February an *Alliance démocratique* editorialist claimed that Daladier fell because he had offered the country a government of unknowns, rather than one of 'worthy and respected men in whom the country could have confidence'.

A relatively minor financial scandal became a state crisis because it appeared to confirm that the governing class of the Republic was inadequate to its tasks. Since dislike of deputies was deeply rooted in the population at large, attacks on selfish deputies were always likely to resonate widely. The elites systematised this prejudice against deputies, together with their own resentments, into an objective critique of the parliamentary republic. A regime of notables, exploiting the state for the benefit of clients, local interests, committees and international socialism, was simply unable to deal with the concrete difficulties faced by the modern state. The parliamentary regime could provide neither economic and financial stability nor effective defence against resurgent Germany (which in turn depended on strong leadership, political unity, and a high birth rate). As André Maurois told the Cercle d'études of the Alliance démocratique on 18 January 1934, 'social transformations, which result from technical change, call forth political change'.[144]

The subsequent breakdown of the 'truce' represented by the Doumergue government does not directly concern us here. Suffice it to say that within a general belief in the necessity of authority, there was plenty of room for disagreement and for different political solutions. For Catholic nationalists the origin of the crisis of the regime lay in the decline of religious values, and the solution was the restoration of religious teaching in state schools.[145] Only under Vichy did Catholic intransigents play a significant political role. Intransigents, did, however, have a certain influence in the Fédération républicaine, which agreed on the need for a more authoritarian constitution, coupled with a thorough purge of vaguely defined 'Staviskites' and the repression of illegal trade unions, especially in state employment. While *Le Temps* called for 'pacification', the *Journal des Débats* declared that that was not enough. The people wanted something new.[146] Philippe Henriot, a link between Catholic integrists and the Fédération, rejected the idea that reform could come from within parliament – the heart of France, he said, was not in the Palais Bourbon.[147] This programme was tied up with resentment at discrimination against Catholics in employment, and was implicitly connected to the 'competence' discourse. For the Catholic Right the 'competent' were excluded from power even at the lower levels of state employment, in a regime that depended on patronage.

Lay conservatives shared ambient ideas about the gap between parliament and the people, the iniquities of parties, the revolutionary intentions of left-wing governments, and they had rarely condemned the notion that a government could fall as a result of riot. But with the exception of Tardieu, Franklin-Bouillon and a few others, lay conservatives believed that a government of 'worthy' men could be installed by reforming the procedures of parliament. The Loire federation of the Alliance argued that the only way to avoid popular rebellion was through revolution within the constitution. Public opinion would be expressed through proportional representation, which would put an end to 'immoral' electoral combinations, and allow the 'honest and laborious' people to express themselves. 'Honest people' would enter parliament and realise the long-expected economies, reform demagogic laws (i.e. 'statist' social insurance) and enact constitutional reform.[148] The Doumergue government's proposal to give the right of dissolution to the Prime Minister was unacceptable to many on the Centre Right, for it was seen as weakening the sovereignty of parliament.[149]

This opposition ensured the failure of constitutional reform and helped ensure Doumergue's fall. Tardieu later wrote that the withdrawal of Doumergue had convinced him that parliament could not reform itself.[150] Doumergue, moreover, had failed to resolve the economic crisis. His programme of spending cuts was as incoherent as that of the Radicals had been. The government failed to keep order on the streets, as the antifascist mobilisation, sealed by the formation of the Front commun in July, confronted the Right with violent opposition on the streets. The cycle of expectation and disappointment recurred, and this time many disillusioned conservatives turned to the Croix de Feu.[151]

The Croix de Feu is outside the scope of this article, but it is worth noting briefly where it stood in relation to the ideas we have been considering in this essay. The league played an equivocal role on 6 February, apparently spurning an opportunity to invade the Chamber of Deputies. This hesitation has sometimes been interpreted as evidence that the movement was essentially legalistic. This is not the place to enter into this debate. Suffice it to say that the Croix de Feu's justification for the 6 February riots scarcely differed from that of the mainstream Right. The rioters were protesting against a 'terroristic' government which had delivered France to the Mafia, decapitated the Parisian police, and opened the way to Revolution.[152] So if the Croix de Feu's analysis was unoriginal it was because the Right generally had largely abandoned legality as it had hitherto been understood. Indeed, it might be said that the parliamentary Right had legitimated paramilitary activism on the streets.

Unlike the lay Centre Right La Rocque had no faith in the ability of parliament to resolve its own problems, and unlike Tardieu he was unwilling to confine his action to the transformation of elite opinion.[153] For La Rocque the Doumergue government was a temporary palliative, and he more or less promised to act again, this time decisively, when the moment was right. For the moment his movement would respond to aggression with 'ironic silence', and hold itself ready for the 'last phase': the reestablishment of order.[154] This rhetoric more closely matched that of the right wing of the Fédération républicaine, which was more willing than the Alliance to endorse extra-constitutional action. Yet relations between the Croix de Feu and the Fédération were marked by suspicion, not least because many of those who joined the league did so out of disgust at the party. To cite just one example, André Aubeuf, Fédération mayor of Saint-Jean de Vence (Alpes Maritimes), led a whole section of three hundred men out of the party because Marin's record in government had allegedly been so ineffective. There had been no reforms and no activity appropriate to the gravity of the times – 'rien qu'une politique de bonnes femmes'. Significantly, Aubeuf promised that the people would soon sweep away career politicians.[155]

The Croix de Feu's appeal lay precisely in its claim that it would bring to power a team of 'new men' – highly qualified, courageous and full of dignity. La Rocque claimed that the Croix de Feu had not invaded the Chamber on 6 February because that would merely have permitted the replacement of one team of politicians by another. Union nationale government could work only if it was preceded by a 'prior civic reconciliation'.[156] The Croix de Feu was not very specific about the nature of this new ruling class, except in saying that it would be drawn from the 'génération du feu' allied to the best of the young generation. Closer examination reveals a considerable debt to the ideal of rule by men of experience – the competent. Typically, La Rocque held that parliamentarian leaders were too absorbed in the chase for honours, electoral mandates and sinecures to resolve the problems facing France. His own expert status as an ex-officer legitimated frequent writings upon military affairs,[157] and seemingly qualified him to see the 'problems of the age' in a way that career politicians could not. The Croix de Feu's debt to the culture of competence was nowhere more evident than in the rejection of theoretical constructs. France needed not sterile debate, a *Flambeau* journalist wrote, but practical solutions, applied by honest and disinterested people living in the real world.[158] Georges Lamirand, future Vichy youth minister, argued that it was insufficient for the engineer to master science and mathematics. Drawing upon Social Catholicism, he claimed that the engineer must have a 'vocation', be a leader, and reconcile capital and labour.[159] The Croix de Feu's ideas about economic and social organisation were typical of professional and academic circles in the Third Republic. One writer, an engineer, defended machines and technology as the means for man to liberate himself from animal tasks and move towards his destiny.[160] Typically, however, La Rocque criticised those who sang the 'hymn of production', and the Croix de Feu – like all so-called modernisers – stressed the need for balance and humanity in the economy.[161]

This does not mean that the Croix de Feu was simply a reedition of the old Right. The Croix de Feu differed in that it possessed a mass paramilitary movement, which promised to bring the competent (as the league defined them) to power through the implicit threat of force. This movement expected not only to crush the Left (defensively, of course) but to purge the existing ruling class on the grounds that it was more concerned with private gain than national issues. Competence served, once again, as a weapon in complex struggles within the Right, and cannot be seen simply as a response to objective dysfunctions in the system. Only careful studies of particular groups can uncover the meaning of these struggles for participants.

More generally, however, we can say that in the mid-1930s, the idea of competence enjoyed a new lease of life because of its deployment in the Italian Fascist regime, which also claimed to represent the supplanting of a corrupt and anachronistic ruling class by a new generation of the 'competent'. Many admirers of this project were to be found in France. In Lyons, for example, we could cite Johannès Dupraz, a leading figure in the regional employers' movement, who wrote for the PSF press. Dupraz published his laudatory *Regards sur le fascisme* on his return from a visit to Italy in 1935. Marcel Canat de Chizy, an engineer trained at the École centrale, and a leading figure in the Croix de Feu and PSF at Lyons, was well versed in all of the literature of economic and political reform and was a keen student of social legislation in Germany and Italy.[162]

Conclusion

To say that the Croix de Feu's critique of the Third Republic was a variant of well-worn themes does not mean that the parliamentary Right in the 1930s or the stalemate society thesis were sub-fascist. Many of the central criticisms of the regime were contested. Also, the ideas that generated the stalemate society thesis could be harnessed to very different political projects. The point of this essay has been to demonstrate that the stalemate society thesis represented one of a number of reform programmes which rested on common foundations. These foundations were empirically erroneous (the belief that the Republic was ruled by provincial notables), essentialist (the belief that the French character was formed by the experience of peasant proprietorship and subservience to a centralising state), teleological (the belief that the Republic failed because its institutions were inappropriate to the modern phase of historical development), functionalist (the belief that society depended on a common culture), and unfalsifiable (the belief that there was a 'gap' between society and parliament).

It might be objected that there is a major discontinuity between 1930s and postwar reform programmes, especially those of the Fifth Republic, in that the latter opted unequivocally for a democratic, industrial and urban society. In fact, however critical of routine reformers have been, politicians have rarely envisaged abandonment of the rural sector to the rigours of the market. Rather, the binary categories are still taken as self-evident, while debates upon the *meaning* of the relationship between urban and rural society have persisted. In the late 1940s, for example, policy makers embraced plans for mechanisation of agricultural production and consolidation of holdings that had been advocated in many quarters in the Third Republic. Now the emphasis has shifted back to small-scale quality production as part of an alternative conception of globalisation (an earlier age spoke of modernisation). The notion that a unitary French identity is rooted in contact with the soil and assimilation into national culture through the village persists too, as Nicolas Philibert's film *Être et Avoir* (2002) testifies.

This reminds us that neither the ideas synthesised in the stalemate society thesis nor the many reform programmes on offer were clearly differentiated from the ambient prejudices of the late Third Republican ruling class, and these prejudices were not clearly separate from the ethnic and religious prejudices of the masses. Moreover, reform programmes were constructed from ideas which were not intrinsically related to the actual functioning of the regime – Darwinist and Lamarckian notions of science and organic balance, conventional conceptions of gender and class, religion and ethnicity, and the culture of generalism and competence. Finally, I have suggested that the emphasis on national uniqueness masks the extent to which the stalemate society thesis depended, despite assertions to the contrary, upon borrowings from foreign regimes. Imitation of fascist 'style' by the French Leagues cannot be dismissed as 'superficial' and collaboration with Germany was not unprecedented.

The stalemate society thesis is nevertheless historically important, for in one way or another most politicians, business leaders, civil servants, natalists and other experts subscribed to its tenets, and the stereotypes on which it depended were routinely deployed in political conflict. Reformers did not fail because they were voices crying in the wilderness, but because of fundamental disagreement over the meaning of key elements of reform. Who were the competent? Were they Catholic or laïque, liberal or interventionist, parliamentarian or extraparliamentarian, male or female? Given that reformers believed that the very survival of the nation depended on the achievement of national unity, raising the birthrate and reconciliation of the elites with the people, failure caused many to turn to radical solutions. By the time of the 6 February riots hardly any conservatives were prepared to condemn the overthrow of a corrupt majority through action on the streets. In turn the failure of Doumergue permitted the Croix de Feu to use a populist version of the stalemate society thesis against established conservatives.

Notes

1. I would like to thank Garthine Walker and Jackie Clarke for their perceptive and helpful comments on an earlier draft of this article, and Brian Jenkins for his patience and equally helpful suggestions.
2. A.Tardieu, *L'Heure de la décision*, Paris, 1934, p. 36.
3. Ibid., pp. 233–34.
4. R. Warwick, *The French Popular Front: A Legislative Analysis*, Chicago and London, 1977; G. Martinez, 'Joseph Barthelémy et la crise de la démocratie libérale', *Vingtième siècle*, no. 59, 1998, pp. 28–47.
5. The evolution of the Catholic Right is discussed in my forthcoming, *The Right in the French Third Republic*.
6. See especially G. Noiriel, *Les origines républicaines de Vichy*, Paris, 1999. Although I have disagreed at certain points with this brilliant interpretive essay, I must acknowledge my debt to it.
7. M. Espagne and M. Werner, *Transferts. Les relations interculturelles dans l'éspace Franco-Allemande*, Paris, 1988.
8. S. Hoffmann, 'The French Political Community', in *In Search of France*, ed. S. Hoffmann, C. Kindleburger, L. Wylie, J.R. Pitts, J.-B. Duroselle and F. Goguel, New York, 1963, pp. 1–117.
9. Hoffmann, 'The French Political Community', pp. 15–16.
10. Ibid., p. 33.
11. M. Winock, *La Fièvre hexagonale. Les grandes crises politiques, 1871–1968*, Paris, 1986, pp. 375–412.
12. R. Rémond, *Les Droites en France*, Paris, 1982.
13. P. Milza, *Fascisme français, passé et présent*, Paris, 1987, pp. 134–41.
14. C. Charle, *La crise des sociétés impériales. Allemagne, France, Grande-Bretagne (1900–1940)*, Paris, 2001, pp. 358–414.
15. In fact, the defensive Maginot line was designed to preserve the freedom of manoeuvre of the best French troops in the northeast. A. Tardieu, *Sur la pente*, Paris, 1935, p. 92; J. Jackson, *The Fall of France*, Oxford, 2003.
16. E. Demolins, *A quoi tient la supériorité des Anglo-Saxons?* Paris, 1903.

17. Z. Sternhell, *Ni droite, ni gauche: L'idéologie fasciste en France*, Paris, 1983, pp. 20, 41.
18. See Sternhell, chapter 2 above.
19. A. Soboul's view in 'Survivances "féodales" dans la société rurale française au XIXe siècle', *Annales ESC*, 1968, pp. 965–72.
20. H. Lebovics, *The Alliance of Iron and Wheat in the Third French Republic 1860–1914: Origins of the New Conservatism*, London and Baton Rouge, 1988, pp. 7, 8, 204–5.
21. G. Noiriel, *Les origines républicaines de Vichy*, Paris, 1999, pp. 45–98.
22. Ibid., pp. 77–78.
23. J.-P. Rioux, *La France de la Quatrième république*, 2 vols, Paris, 1980 and 1983.
24. For the classic statement of the view that Gaullism solved the problems of French history see J. Charlot, *Le phénomène gaulliste*, Paris, 1970.
25. J. Clarke, 'Engineering a New Order in the 1930s: The Case of Jean Coutrot', *French Historical Studies*, vol. 24, no. 1, 2001, pp. 63–86 points out that the first postwar academic accounts of modernisation were written by 1930s advocates of modernisation such as Alfred Sauvy. See also H. Chapman, 'Modernity and National Identity in Postwar France', *French Historical Studies*, vol. 22, no. 2, 1999, pp. 291–314, who makes the same point about recent studies of postwar modernisation in France.
26. Hoffmann, 'The French Political Community', pp. 15–16.
27. Only in advocating a creative alternation in power of Left and Right did Hoffmann really differ from interwar modernisers. The latter were extremely suspicious of left-wing government.
28. Winock, *La fièvre hexagonale*, pp. 204–6, 235–38: '[La journée du six février] a mis à nu la crise du parti radical et, au-delà, l'usure de la "synthèse républicain".' See also François Monnet, *Refaire la république: André Tardieu, une dérive réactionnaire, 1876–1945*, Paris, 1993, pp. 178–79, 190, 196–97. Monnet too insists on the correctness of Tardieu's diagnosis of the Republic's ills. The regime was already 'obsolete' before 1914, but problems had temporarily been masked by victory in the Great War.
29. Charle, *La crise des sociétés impériales*, p. 399.
30. K. Popper, *The Poverty of Historicism*, London, 1989 (first published 1957), pp. 105–19.
31. N. Abercrombie, S. Hill and B.S. Turner, *The Dominant Ideology Thesis*, London, 1980.
32. Foucault's view can, of course, be formulated in more than one way.
33. M. Bloch, *Les caractères originaux de l'histoire rurale française*, Paris, 1931, pp. 230–49.
34. M. Middel, 'The Annales', in *Writing History: Theory and Practice*, ed. S. Berger, H. Feldner and K. Passmore, London, 2003; Julian Jackson, 'Historians and the Nation in France', in *Writing National Histories*, ed. S. Berger, M. Donovan and K, Passmore, London, 1999, pp. 239–51.
35. F. Braudel, *L'Identité de la France*, 3 vols, Paris, 1989–92, I, p. 18.
36. Noiriel, *Origines républicaines de Vichy*, pp. 33–38.
37. M. Mann, *The Sources of Social Power*, Volume I: *A History of Power from the beginning to A.D. 1760*, Cambridge, 1987, pp. 14–17.
38. Espagne and Werner, *Transferts*; Berger, 'Comparative History', in *Writing History*.
39. G. Chevallier, *Clochemerle*, Paris, 1989, pp. 111–12.
40. G. Le Béguec, 'L'Entrée au Palais-Bourbon: les filières privilégiées d'accès à la fonction parlementaire 1919–1939', unpublished thesis (doctorat d'état), Université Paris X Nanterre, 1989.
41. Ibid., pp. 75–78; Archives nationales [AN] 317 AP 119, Fonds Louis Marin, Marin to Valeri, 19 February 1937; J. Vavasseur-Desperriers, 'Associations politiques et groupes parlementaires: Groupe progressiste et Fédération républicaine (1905–1914)', in *Les modérés dans la vie politique française (1870–1965)*, ed. F. Roth, Nancy, 2000, pp. 123–38.

42. P. Nord, 'Social Defence and Conservative Regeneration: the National Revival, 1900–14', in *Nationhood and Nationalism in France: From Boulangism to the Great War*, ed. R. Tombs, London, 1991, pp. 211–28.

43. Le Béguec, 'L'Entrée au Palais-Bourbon', pp. 86–88, 95–98.

44. See the attacks on the 'nouvelle Sorbonne' in the moderate republican *L'Opinion*, 23 July, 13 August 1910.

45. A. Grelon, ed., *Les ingénieurs de la crise: Titre et profession entre les deux guerres*, Paris, 1986.

46. G. Noblemaire, *Carnet de route au pays des parlementaires*, Paris, 1923, pp. 14–15, 19–20.

47. 317 AP 119, Marin to Valeri, 19 February, 1937.

48. K. Passmore, *The French Right in the Third Republic*, forthcoming, chapter 1.

49. Comte André de Fels, *Essai de politique expérimentale*, Paris, 1922, pp. 142–48.

50. C. Benoist, *L'Organisation du suffrage universel*, 3 vols, Paris, 1895–99.

51. Le Béguec, 'L'Entrée au Palais-Bourbon', pp. 232–41.

52. Quoted in G. Bonnefous, *Histoire politique de la troisième république*, Vol II, *La grande guerre*, Paris, 1957, pp. 120–21.

53. L. Loucheur, *Carnets secrets 1908–1932*, Brussels and Paris, 1962, pp. 29–36; R. Péret, *L'Alliance démocratique*, 28 March 1915; R.F. Kuisel, *Capitalism and the State in Modern France*, Cambridge, 1981, pp. 31–50.

54. M. Bokanowski, *Pas de salut financier sans la confiance … pas de confiance sans l'union*, Paris, 1926, pp. 16–17.

55. S. Peer, *France on Display: Peasants, Provincials, and Folklore in the 1937 Paris World's Fair*, Albany NY, 1998, pp. 23–49.

56. P. Favre, *Naissances de la science politique en France (1870–1914)*, Paris, 1989, pp. 307–15.

57. H. Lebovics, *True France: The Wars over Cultural Identity 1900–1945*, Ithaca and London, 1992, pp. 32–36.

58. Noiriel, *Origines républicaines de Vichy*, pp. 261–62.

59. G. Clemenceau was especially impressed by Darwinism and this underlay his belief that pronatalist measures were a necessary accompaniment to the Versailles Treaty.

60. For a clear statement of this view see de Fels, *Essai de politique expérimentale*, pp. 17–20; C. Koos, 'Engendering Reaction: the Politics of Pronatalism and the Family in France, 1919–1944', unpublished Ph.D. thesis, University of Southern California, 1996, pp. 43–45.

61. R. Nye, *Masculinity and Male Codes of Honor in Nineteenth-Century France*, Oxford, 1993, pp. 74–88.

62. Noblemaire, *Carnet de route*, pp. 9–11.

63. '[Dans] notre époque de suffrage universel, la basse démagogie, la brutalité, l'illusion facile, tout ce que l'expérience implacable de la vie montre mortel pour les peuples comme pour les individus, déborde sauvagement.'

64. *La Nation*, 21 May 1932; Martinez, 'Joseph Barthélémy', pp. 36–37.

65. Noiriel, *Origines républicaines de Vichy*, pp. 234–37.

66. Ibid., pp. 254–61.

67. The Left was hardly less doubtful of the legitimacy of right-wing governments.

68. D.G. Wileman, 'L'Alliance républicaine démocratique: the Dead Centre of French Politics, 1901–1947', unpublished Ph.D. dissertation, York University Toronto, 1988, pp. 248–51; Martinez, 'Joseph Barthélémy', pp. 32–34.

69. Passmore, *The Right in the Third Republic*, chapter 3.

70. See for example the Bonapartist Fernand Engerand, in *L'Echo de Paris*, 19 July 1917; De Fels, *Essai de politique expérimentale*, pp. 23–25.

71. Peer, *France on Display*, pp. 31–32.

72. M.-L. Roberts, *Civilization Without Sexes. Reconstructing Gender in Postwar France, 1917–1927*, Chicago, 1994.

73. Noblemaire, *Carnet de route*, pp. 18–19.
74. H. Bertrand, *Soierie lyonnaise. Chardonne et soie ordinaire. Évolutions récentes; situation actuelle*, Lyon, 1930.
75. Noiriel, *Origines républicaines de Vichy*, pp. 129–49, 222–72.
76. Nord, 'Social Defence and Conservative Regeneration', pp. 211–15.
77. Loucheur, *Carnets secrets*, pp. 158–61.
78. F. Monnet, *Refaire la république: André Tardieu, une dérive réactionnaire, 1876–1945*, Paris, 1993, pp. 103–74.
79. For opposing views on these figures see Martin Fine, 'Towards Corporatism: The Movement for Capital-Labour Collaboration in France, 1914–1936', Ph.D. dissertation, University of Wisconsin, 1971, pp. 146–47 and Ingo Kolboom , *La revanche des patrons. Le patronat français face au Front populaire*, Paris, 1987, pp. 76–98.
80. Clarke, 'Engineering a New Order' and 'Imagined Productive Communities: Industrial Rationalisation and Cultural Crisis in 1930s France', *Modern and Contemporary France*, vol. 8, no. 3, 2000, 345–57.
81. Clarke, 'Imagined Productive Communities'.
82. R.F. Kuisel, *Ernest Mercier. French Technocrat*, Berkeley, 1967, pp. 53–54.
83. Peer, *France on Display*. See also M. Beale, *The Modernist Enterprise: French Elites and the Threat of Modernity, 1900–1940*, Stanford, 1997. Much of this is anticipated in L. Boltanski, *Les Cadres: la formation d'un groupe sociale*, Paris, 1982, which is heavily influenced by Pierre Bourdieu's cultural approach.
84. Kuisel, *Capitalism and the State*, pp. 88–92.
85. 'Organisation politique et administrative. La Réforme parlementaire, *Cahiers du Redressement français*, 25, Paris, SAPE, 1927.
86. Note that French scholars often use 'archaïsme' to refer to the concept of 'tradition'.
87. N. Carre de Malberg, 'Les limites du "libéralisme économique" chez les inspecteurs des finances sous la IIIe République', *Bulletin du centre d'histoire de la France contemporaine*, 1985, vol. 6, pp. 37–67, shows that these supposed guardians of economic orthodoxy were divided on the precise limits of state intervention.
88. A. Isaac, *La Plus grande famille*, Paris, 1917.
89. J.F. Stone, *The Search for Social Peace: Reform Legislation in France 1890–1914*, Albany, 1985.
90. N. Rousselier, *Le Parlement de l'éloquence. La souveraineté, de la délibération au lendemain de la Grande Guerre*, Paris, 1997, pp. 72–76, 106–9.
91. K. Passmore, *From Liberalism to Fascism: the Right in a French Province*, Cambridge, 1997, pp. 140–57.
92. J. Jackson, *The Politics of Depression in France*, Cambridge, 1985; K. Mouré, 'French Reluctance to Devalue, 1933–6', *French Historical Studies*, vol. 15, 1987, pp. 479–505.
93. A few decades earlier Henri Flamans, *L'Alliance démocratique*, 14 December, 1913, declared that modern industrial bread was a 'danger national' which had 'contribué à, affaiblir notre race'.
94. Archives Justin Godart (AJG), Carton 1, Fructus to Godart, 30 September, 1935 and Rapport Isaac, 13 October, 1935.
95. AJG Carton 1, Vautheret to Godart, 5 November, 1934.
96. K. Passmore, 'Business, Corporatism and the Crisis of the French Third Republic: the Example of the Silk Industry in Lyon', *Historical Journal*, vol. 38, no. 4, 1995, pp. 959–87.
97. M. Larkin, *Religion, Politics and Preferment in France since 1890: la Belle Époque and its Legacy*, Cambridge, 1995, pp.147–73.
98. K. Passmore, 'Catholicism and Nationalism: The Fédération républicaine, 1927–1939', in *Catholicism, Society and Politics in Twentieth-Century France*, ed. K. Chadwick, Liverpool, 2000, 47–72; W.D. Irvine, *French Conservatism in Crisis: the Republican Federation of France*, Baton Rouge and London, 1979.

99. Koos, 'Engendering Reaction', pp. 21–45, 195–200.
100. For a Catholic conservative attack on those who mixed 'discreet Catholicism' and 'revolutionary principles' see Georges Vinacé, *La Croix*, 27 January 1934.
101. Passmore, 'Catholicism and Nationalism', pp. 47–72; AN 317 AP 119, Marin to Valeri, 19 February 1937.
102. 'Ces partis [de la droite et du centre], ont encore moins d'unité que les groupes de gauche. Car ils se composent, a peu près par moitié, de tenants de la tradition catholique, et de tenants de la Révolution française. Cette division à la base a causé leur malheurs.' Tardieu, *Sur la pente*, p. xxxvi.
103. F. Audigier, 'L'anachronisme de l'Alliance démocratique (1933–37)', *Vingtième siècle*, no. 47, 1995, pp. 147–57.
104. This is one of the major contentions of my *From Liberalism to Fascism*. For the uncertainties of the Fédération républicaine see Passmore, 'Catholicism and Nationalism', pp. 60–63.
105. Martinez, 'Joseph Barthelémy'.
106. Monnet, *Refaire la république*, pp. 185–88; Roussellier, *Le Parlement de l'éloquence*, pp. 9–22; Passmore, *The French Right in the Third Republic*, chapter 3; Le Béguec, 'L'Entrée au Palais-Bourbon', pp. 279– 402.
107. Rousselier, *Le Parlement de l'éloquence*, pp. 55–56.
108. Monnet, *Refaire la république*, p. 195.
109. Le Béguec, 'L'Entrée au Palais-Bourbon', pp. 393–402.
110. A. Prost, *Les anciens combattants et la société française*, 1914–1939, 3 vols, Paris, 1977.
111. W.A. Hoisington Jr, *Taxpayer Revolt in France and the National Taxpayers' Federation, 1928–1939*, Stanford, 1973.
112. R.O. Paxton, *French Peasant Fascism: Henry Dorgères's Greenshirts and the Crisis of French Agriculture, 1929–1939*, Oxford, 1997.
113. K. Passmore, '"Planting the tricolor in the citadels of communism": Women's Social Service in the Croix de Feu and Parti social français', *Journal of Modern History*, vol. 71, no. 4, 1999, pp. 814–51.
114. S.B. Whitney, 'Embracing the Status Quo: French Communists, Young Women and the Popular Front', *Journal of Social History*, vol. 30, no. 1, 1996, pp. 29–53.
115. S. Reynolds, *France Between the Wars: Gender and Politics*, London, 1996, pp. 25–26.
116. See for example P. Fritzsche, 'Where Did All the Nazis go? Reflections on Resistance and Collaboration', *Tel Aviver Jahrbuch für Deutsche Geschichte*, vol. 23, 1994, pp. 91–214. See also the fascinating J. Lawrence, *Speaking For the People: Party, Language and Popular Politics in England, 1867–1914*, New York, 1998.
117. A. Corbin, *The Village of the Cannibals: Rage and Murder in France, 1870*, trans. Arthur Goldhammer, Cambridge, MA., 1992.
118. F. Blum, C. Chambelland and M. Dreyfus, 'Mouvements de femmes 1919–1940', *Vie sociale*, vol. 11/12, 1984, pp. 507–653; O. Sarti, *The Ligue patriotique des françaises: A Feminine Response to the Secularization of French Society*, New York, 1992.
119. Prost, *Les Anciens combattants*.
120. Sarti, *The Ligue patriotique des française*.
121. B. Smith, *Ladies of the Leisure Class: the Bourgeoisie of Northern France in the Nineteenth Century*, Princeton, 1981; Prost, *Les anciens combattants*; Le Béguec, 'L'Entrée au Palais-Bourbon', pp. 332–66.
122. Passmore, 'Planting the Tricolor'; Passmore, *Liberalism to Fascism*, p. 223.
123. *L'Union républicaine*, 21 June 1936
124. L.L. Downs, *Childhood in the Promised Land: Working-class Movements and the Colonies de vacances in France, 1880–1960*, Durham and London, 2002, p. 243.
125. Passmore, 'Catholicism and Nationalism', pp. 56, 59.
126. Wileman, 'L'Alliance républicaine démocratique', pp. 184–85.

127. R. Schor, *L'Opinion française et les étrangers 1919–1939*, Paris, 1985, pp. 549 ff.
128. *Journal des Débats*, 6 January, 1934.
129. Ibid.
130. *Le Temps*, 13 January 1934.
131. R. Schor, *L'Opinion française et les étrangers*, Paris, 1985, pp. 597–612; R. Schor, *Histoire de l'immigration en France*, Paris, 1996, pp. 130–31; Mary Dewhurst Lewis, 'The Company of Strangers: Immigration and Citizenship in Interwar Lyon and Marseille', unpublished Ph.D. dissertation, New York University, 2000, pp. 265–67.
132. *Journal des Débats*, 11, 23, 31 January, 1934. Jean Guiraud in *La Croix*, 30 January 1934.
133. *Journal des Débats*, 23, 31 January, 1934.
134. Ibid., 5, 13 January, 1934.
135. Ibid., 6 February, 1934.
136. *La Croix*, 9 February, 1934.
137. *Journal des Débats*, 9 February, 1934.
138. *Le Temps*, 6, 9 February, 1934.
139. *L'Alliance démocratique*, 10 January, 7 February, 1934.
140. *Journal des Débats*, 23 January, 1934.
141. Ibid., 29 January, 1934.
142. Cited in *Journal des Débats*, 9 February, 1934.
143. *L'Alliance démocratique*, 10 January, 1934
144. Ibid., 18 January, 1934.
145. *La Croix*, 19 January and 12 February, 1934.
146. *Journal des Débats*, 10 February, 1934.
147. P. Henriot, *L'envers du décor du Palais Bourbon*, Paris, 1934.
148. *L'Alliance démocratique*, 18 January, 1934.
149. N. Rousselier, 'André Tardieu et la crise du constitutionalisme libéral (1933–1934)', *Vingtième siècle*, no. 21, 1989, pp. 57–70; Monnet, *Refaire la république*, pp. 188–89; Martinez, 'Joseph Barthélémy, pp. 32–34.
150. *Gringoire*, 10 March, 1936.
151. Passmore, *From Liberalism to Fascism*, pp. 198–99.
152. *Le Flambeau*, 1 March, 1934.
153. For Tardieu's view of the leagues see *Gringoire*, 25 December 1936.
154. *Le Flambeau*, 1 March, 1934.
155. AN 317 AP 72 Fonds Marin, Aubeuf to Guiter, 14 June 1935, and Guiter to Marin, 17 and 20 June, 5 July, 1935.
156. *Le Flambeau*, 1 March, 1934; AN 451 AP 81 Fonds La Rocque, Special Instruction of 5 February, 1934.
157. *Le Flambeau*, 1 January, 1934.
158. Ibid., 1 June, 1934.
159. Ibid., 1 December, 1933.
160. Ibid., I January, 1934.
161. Ibid., 1 May, 1934; Passmore, *From Liberalism to Fascism*; see also a discussion which perhaps depends too heavily on a desire to categorise as traditional and modern: S. Kalman. 'Vers un ordre nouveau: The Concepts of Nation and State in the Doctrines of the Faisceau and Croix de Feu/Parti Social Français', unpublished Ph.D thesis, McMaster University, 2001.
162. Passmore, *From Liberalism to Fascism*, pp. 272–73.

7

Conclusion: Beyond the 'Fascism Debate'

Brian Jenkins

In a landmark article written in 1988, the American John Sweets – reviewing the historiography of fascism, collaboration and resistance in France – called on his fellow historians to 'hold that pendulum'.[1] In his view, revisionist writers had gone too far in their efforts to correct the errors of mainstream ('immunity thesis') historians, producing a version of the past that was similarly exaggerated and one-sided. It was time to stop the process of overcompensation and overreaction, to take stock and attempt to reach a more balanced judgement. Having assessed the work of Sternhell and Soucy before turning to recent books by Pierre Milza and Philippe Burrin, Sweets concluded that 'the best work of the revisionists' was indeed being absorbed into mainstream French historiography. There was a greater willingness to accept that fascism had distinctively French intellectual origins, and while René Rémond himself refused to revise his original view that fascism only affected a small minority in France, Pierre Milza was ready to concede that 'it was neither absolutely marginal nor of foreign manufacture'.[2]

If this was a 'concession' it hardly seemed substantial enough to justify Professor Sweets's optimism, and indeed seven years later a fresh intervention by Milza offered little evidence that mainstream historiography had shifted its ground any further.[3] In his essay on *Fascisme français* in Sirinelli's historical dictionary (1995), Milza even insists that the core arguments developed by René Rémond remain 'globally valid'.[4] The lively debate provoked by Sternhell's work has, in Milza's view, exposed the flaws in two 'equally exaggerated' (*symétriquement caricaturales*) positions.[5] One of these – the tendency to underestimate the impact of a specifically French form of fascism – has by implication long since been corrected. On the other side, however, the error persists, with Sternhell continuing to apply the term fascism to 'all expressions of hostility to bourgeois parliamentary democracy'.[6] In other words, the ball is firmly back in the revisionists' court.

So what modifications have been made to the classical orthodoxy? Certainly Sternhell's work on the intellectual origins of fascist ideology in France during the Belle Epoque is now routinely acknowledged in most of the literature, and some of the criticisms levelled against it cannot be attributed to the 'immunity thesis' as such. For example, Jacques Julliard and Michel Winock have warned against a 'history of ideas' approach which neglects social and political context.[7] Similarly, Pierre Milza spoke for many when he argued, in an earlier piece (1990), that the pre-history of fascism was 'transnational' and 'European' rather than 'especially French, as Zeev Sternhell suggests'.[8] However, in his 1995 essay Milza shifts onto more familiar ground when he complains that Sternhell neglects the *German, Austrian* and *Italian* roots of fascist ideology.[9] He thus seems to imply that we should look for the ideological antecedents of fascism above all in those countries where fascist regimes were eventually to be established. This in turn suggests that fascism is the product of peculiar *national* histories and cultures rather than something more generic (albeit with national variations) derived from similar historical processes and circumstances in similar countries. The impression is reinforced when Milza goes on to claim that in France the most 'fascist' formations were modelled on the Italian example, while those that were 'deeply rooted in national history were not *stricto sensu* fascist'[10]. Are such notions of national path-dependence, and therefore of French exceptionalism, the hidden structures of the 'immunity thesis'? And is this in turn largely driven by a deep reluctance to accept the possibility that France produced its own indigenous brand of fascism?

This underlying notion that fascism was an alien import has proved hard to shift. As Michel Dobry has pointed out, the core proposition that France was 'allergic' to fascism has retained its credibility by incorporating certain 'fall-back positions', namely that French movements that looked or claimed to be fascist were usually not homegrown, and were anyway of marginal political importance. Thus, in the interwar period, the term has most readily been applied to small formations that openly emulated the Italian or German example, like Valois's Faisceau or, in cruder form, Bucard's Françisme and (more hesitantly) to François Coty's Solidarité Française.[11] Increasingly, Doriot's much larger Parti Populaire Français has been recognised as a more authentically 'indigenous' version, though very frequently this concession is hedged about with qualifications ('fascisant' rather than fascist, the nearest French approximation, etc). There is certainly never any question of including the intellectually influential Action Française, and the numerically more significant organisations – Jeunesses Patriotes and above all the Croix de Feu/PSF – within the definition. Milza's 1995 'state of the art' summary thus concludes with the judgement that, except during the first two years of Doriot's movement, French fascism was 'marginal'[12] (not 'absolutely marginal' maybe, but marginal nonetheless).

There are signs of a rather more substantial shift of position in Philippe Burrin's important 1992 essay,[13] where he recognises the need for some refinement of Rémond's classic typology of *les trois droites*. Thus he suggests that the post-Boulangist nationalist Right, though derived from the Bonapartist tradition, could usefully be divided into two subsets: national-caesarism and national-populism.[14] This may be seen as a response to the argument of Sternhell and others that there is a decisive historical break in the last quarter of the nineteenth century with the advent of mass politics, industrial society and populist nationalism, and that thereafter the concept of Bonapartism loses its explanatory power. While Burrin does not explicitly reject Rémond's notion of a continuous Bonapartist tradition, his subdivision of the category is nonetheless a significant innovation. It is open to question how useful or valid is the distinction he makes between leaders who are conventional authority figures, like Taittinger or La Rocque (national-caesarists), and sons of the people or *déclassé* adventurers, like Dorgères and Coty (national-populists). But the overall effect of the innovation is, of course, to build an outer ring of conceptual defences around the immunity thesis. National-populism (a term first deployed by Pierre-André Taguieff[15] in a different context) is defined in such a way as to incorporate many of the features commonly associated with fascism, its boundaries with fascism are seen as 'permeable', and yet it remains qualitatively distinct from fascism.[16]

When it comes to identifying exactly what makes authentic fascist movements so different from the main formations of the French extreme Right, there are almost as many answers as there are authorities on the subject. The defenders of the so-called 'immunity thesis' are far from being a monolithic group. One of the more consistent themes, as we have seen, is that the French movements were too 'conservative' to qualify – that is, insufficiently plebeian in their recruitment, too closely associated with traditional social elites, insufficiently antibourgeois in their rhetoric and in their programmatic commitments. This is linked to another line of argument, namely the supposed modernising thrust of authentic fascism as against the defensive traditionalism of the French extreme Right. A second major theme is the totalitarian character of fascism, allegedly already visible in the movement before the seizure of power, and reflected in the attempt of a single party to mobilise, unite and organise the entire community around an ultranationalist project of violent renewal – on this issue there are subsidiary points about the supposed 'legalism' of the Croix de Feu/PSF and the defensive (or even symbolic) nature of its paramilitarism, but the main argument seems to be that as no single party achieved hegemony in France, none of them can have entertained 'totalitarian' ambitions.

The revisionist response to these arguments has in some cases involved presenting a rather different definition of fascism from the one shared by most proponents of the immunity thesis. It has also often challenged the empirical and methodological foundations of mainstream interpretations of the French extreme Right. But given that the whole debate hinges crucially on cross-national comparisons, revisionists have been equally concerned to correct what they see as misrepresentations of the German or Italian cases. For example, the traditionalist features of Nazi ideology and the absence of real totalitarian control in Mussolini's Italy are not given prominence in the 'immunity thesis' for obvious reasons. And as Michel Dobry has pointed out,[17] the tendency to measure French extreme Right movements against fully-fledged fascist regimes infringes one of the most elementary principles of the comparative method.

This issue of comparison is of course crucial to a theme we have already touched on, namely national path-dependency and French exceptionalism. French historians like Serge Berstein and Michel Winock, and the Swiss scholar Philippe Burrin, tend to agree that two crucial sets of historical developments paved the way for fascism: first, a series of interdependent changes at the end of the nineteenth century that mark the advent of 'modernity', namely the emergence of the modern nation-state, urbanised industrial society, mass politics and modern political ideologies; second, the First World War, the Russian Revolution and all the consequences that flowed from these two decisive events. A third factor is also regarded as vital, namely the configuration of severe economic and social problems which were endemic between the wars and which above all reached crisis point in the world economic Depression of the 1930s. Admittedly, as Dobry points out in his critique of Serge Berstein above,[18] these are 'pre-conditions' of fascism rather than genuine criteria for identifying it, but it is nonetheless revealing to consider how these developments in European history have been applied to the French case.

Evidently, for René Rémond himself, the decisive watershed was the French Revolution and the precocious ideal of popular sovereignty. His *trois droites* defined themselves in relation to this event, and have enjoyed an unbroken continuity ever since. As we have seen, many of Rémond's successors, and notably Philippe Burrin, have acknowledged that the transformation of European societies between 1870 and 1914 was equally momentous, that France was caught up in this dramatic process of continental change, and indeed was deeply involved in shaping the political and ideological responses to it. Zeev Sternhell can claim considerable credit for having shifted the French historiographical consensus that far. However, even Philippe Burrin cannot bring himself to see the late nineteenth century as a point of *rupture* and thus break with the Rémondian model. The continuity of the Bonapartist tradition, though shaken, remains intact – and with it the notion that the French Right is best understood in terms of an exceptional and distinctive national past rather than in relation to wider transnational developments.

Michel Winock remarked, in his critique of Sternhell, that fascism was derived not from books but from the Great War and its revolutionary aftermath.[19] Many would agree that it is virtually impossible to imagine the rise of Italian fascism and German Nazism outside this context. The 'immunity thesis' therefore needs to demonstrate that the French experience was somehow qualitatively different from that of her neighbours across the Alps and the Rhine, and this is problematic. Studies of the period constantly emphasise the deep economic, social, demographic and psychological dislocations wrought by the war; the heightened class tensions produced by the Russian Revolution; the destabilisation of the political system; the rise of paramilitarism, antiparliamentarism, racism and xenophobia. How the scale and intensity of any of these phenomena compare with analogous developments elsewhere is a matter of judgement. The single most important distinction that has been drawn is of course the fact that France (unlike Germany) was victorious in 1918, that (unlike Italy) she achieved most of her objectives at the Versailles Peace Conference, and therefore did not harbour those feelings of national humiliation and resentment which Mussolini and Hitler were able to exploit. Aggressive territorial expansionism has thus been promoted by several 'immunity thesis' historians to the status of one of fascism's core defining characteristics.

The impact of the economic depression is, of course, the key historical backdrop to the victory of Nazism and to the rise of parallel movements in many European countries. In this context France's experience was indeed distinctive – the visible effects were less spectacular, though the downturn was protracted and debilitating – and this is certainly often cited as a further factor insulating the country against fascism. More balanced studies have revealed that the social effects were more severe than the official statistics suggest, and certainly the political consequences in the mid-1930s were dramatic enough. But in fact, immunity thesis historians do not make this issue a central element in their case. Berstein, for example, reminds us that both the U.S.A. and Britain experienced high levels of unemployment, and yet remained virtually untouched by the 'contagion' of fascism. This leads him to endorse René Rémond's original analysis, and to conclude that 'the countries that escaped fascism are the old democracies where this form of regime is long established and deeply entrenched in political culture, while the nations that did experience fascism are ones where democracy was merely a recently constructed façade'.[20]

The discussion in the preceding paragraphs reveals a curious methodological feature of the 'immunity thesis'. Under the pretence of asking the question 'Was there a significant French fascism?' it is often asking a quite different question, namely 'What are the historical explanations for the absence of a significant French fascism?', or even, dare we suggest, 'Why was it historically impossible for fascism to make significant headway in France?'. The original question is thus entirely prejudged, and these 'explanations' (France was an old democracy, was victorious in the Great War, did not suffer so badly in the Depression, was less fearful of social revolution) are then presented as if they were 'evidence' (rather like using a character reference as 'proof' that someone did not commit a murder). Of course, other ancillary arguments are also deployed, usually based on typological distinctions, but here again we encounter the same chicken-and-egg problem. Is it the particular (objective) definition of fascism which just happens to exonerate France, or is it the prior assumption that France is historically exceptional and therefore exempt which leads fascism to be defined in this way?

The methodological loopholes in all this are revealed rather well by the issue of France's so-called 'democratic political culture', which might almost be described as the 'bedrock' of the immunity thesis. Supposedly it was these deeply entrenched democratic instincts and traditions which more than anything else rendered

France impermeable to fascism between the wars. And yet, in the terminology used by scholars like Berstein and Burrin to describe French extreme Right formations in this period, we find constant reference to their antiparliamentarism and antiliberalism, to their impatience with democracy and civil liberties, to their contempt for the *pays légal* and the 'political class'. Indeed, Pierre Milza, while insisting that such movements were not really fascist, says that 'this does not mean that they were any less dangerous for the institutions of the Republic'.[21] So on the one hand, hostility to democracy was rife in interwar France, and on the other hand, France's democratic political culture explains why fascism supposedly made so little headway. In the face of such contradictions, proponents of the 'immunity thesis' can always shift the argument onto other terrain, citing the deep-seated conservatism of France's 'stalemate society', and indeed of the prevailing ideologies of the French Right, as additional barriers to the 'modernising' thrust of fascism. For at least some of the 'revisionists', however, the only way out of this methodological maze is to return to the starting point, and question the principles that underpin the entire thesis.

Common ground

As we have seen, the contributors to this volume approach the subject with different perspectives, different concerns, different aspirations, and they reach different conclusions. They do not all define fascism in the same way, and they have different views about the extent of its impact in interwar France. Indeed, not all of them are even convinced that it is particularly useful to measure French extreme-Right movements against some generic concept of fascism. However, they would all reject the notion that French society had somehow been rendered 'immune' (allergic, impermeable) to fascism by an historical *Sonderweg* and a peculiarly resistant political culture.

This latter point requires a little elaboration, because it may not be immediately obvious that our contributors do indeed share much common ground. For example, as regards the designation of this or that formation of the French extreme Right as 'fascist', Robert Paxton uses the term more sparingly than Sternhell or Soucy, and is particularly wary of applying it to La Rocque's movement. For Paxton, there is a useful distinction to be made between fascism and conservative authoritarianism, and he also believes that there were specific political conditions in 1930s France which help explain why fascist movements were less successful there than they had been, for example, in the closing years of the Weimar Republic. Indeed, in his view one of these conditions was the existence of a robust republican tradition, of which the antifascist Popular Front movement was a concrete expression. However, we would argue that Paxton's position is far removed from the view that France's exceptional history had somehow left the country culturally and politically inoculated against the affliction of fascism. Paxton rejects the notion of the 'antibody' as explicitly as any of the other contributors.

This leads to significant *methodological* differences between the two camps. As Michel Dobry has pointed out, while Milza and Burrin in particular have refined the original Rémond version of the 'immunity thesis', these are 'tactical withdrawals' which leave the essence intact: namely 'the supposed exceptionalism of French society in the face of fascism'.[22] This leads to an approach which seeks out the continuities of national ideological and political tradition, which uses comparison largely to underline national specificities, and which (as Paxton says above) too easily degenerates into assumptions and assertions about national character.[23] Our authors in contrast bring a rather different methodological perspective to bear – one which places much greater emphasis on the importance of historical *context*, and which uses comparison as much to underline transnational *similarities* and *parallels* as to identify national distinctions.

Thus, whatever their disagreements with Sternhell on the details of his analysis and on the conclusions he draws, our other contributors would nonetheless accept that French thinkers pre-1914 contributed significantly to the stock of ideas on which European fascist movements subsequently drew. Similarly, while Passmore examines the political crisis of the 1930s much more minutely than his fellow authors, there is a shared recognition that the Third Republic between the wars encountered significantly similar problems to those that are commonly cited to explain the success of Italian fascism and German Nazism. In short, the contributors to this volume recognise that France was implicated in developmental processes that transcended national frontiers, and that in such a context the rather parochial distinction between indigenous (rooted, authentic) ideologies and imported (alien, imitative) ones is artificial and misleading. As Michel Dobry's chapter indicates, we should be wary of taking the '*décalages de distinction*' at face value, and of failing to recognise the deeper common impulses driving similar movements in different countries.[24]

However, even if we screen out the 'immunity thesis' and the assumptions on which it rests, we are left with a range of important issues on which our authors implicitly or explicitly disagree. Our coverage of these in this brief concluding essay cannot be comprehensive, let alone exhaustive, and indeed that would not be our intention even if space allowed. We would prefer to end on a rather more contentious note, by suggesting that some of the more obvious areas of disagreement between our authors have already been sufficiently explored, and that further debate is unlikely to yield anything new, let alone resolve outstanding differences. Instead we will try to focus on fields of enquiry where further work needs to be done and where argument promises to be more productive.

Defining fascism

The most obvious bone of contention between proponents of the so-called 'immunity thesis' and those we have referred to as 'revisionists' has been over the *definition* of fascism. In general terms it may be said that the former have developed a rather detailed and precise delineation of the chief political and ideological features of fascism, and on this basis have concluded that most of the potential French contenders fail to fit the bill. They also argue that revisionists like Nolte, Sternhell, Irvine and Soucy, whatever their individual differences, all commit the error of defining fascism too loosely, too broadly, too vaguely, and it is this lack of precision which allows them to apply the term 'fascist' so freely in the French context.

We will not rehearse that debate any further, but it is worth dwelling for a moment on the divergences among contributors to this volume, and especially on those between Sternhell and Soucy, whose definitions of fascism are radically dissimilar even if their conclusions increasingly converge. The most obvious difference is that Sternhell has consistently emphasised the synthetic nature of fascist ideology, which in his view draws sustenance as much from dissident left-wing thought as from right-wing integral nationalism, whereas Soucy insists that fascism is a predominantly right-wing movement, distinguishable from conservatism more by its means than by its ends. These apparently irreconcilable positions are partly derived from very different spheres of interest and different methodologies. Sternhell has hitherto focused above all on the world of ideas and intellectual *minorités agissantes*, on the long gestation of ideologies and how they impregnate social and political values over time. Soucy, on the other hand, is engaged in the categorisation of specific political movements on what purports to be an empirical basis, and in his view the occasional leftist flourishes in fascist discourse are submerged in what is overall a profoundly right-wing ideology.

In certain respects Sternhell's approach curiously resembles that of his 'immunity thesis' critics. Like him, many of them also draw heavily on the history of ideas, and emphasise the *radicalism* of fascist ideology (though without insisting as much on its specifically left-wing origins). Arguably there is a further methodological parallel. Michel Dobry's critique of the immunity thesis starts with the claim that it is teleological, that it judges historical processes in terms of their outcomes. Thus the ultimate survival of the Third Republic is used retrospectively to prove that fascism was always a marginal force in France. Has not Sternhell simply chosen a different 'outcome' (Vichy) to prove the opposite case? It would certainly be wrong to suggest that Sternhell's argument is teleological in the same way: the sequence of his work on France confirms that he is not reconstructing history from the vantage point of Vichy. But when he portrays Vichy as the culmination of an antidemocratic authoritarian French intellectual tradition dating from Boulangism, is he not making the implicit assumption that (to quote Dobry) 'for every "outcome" ... there must be a corresponding *specific historical path*'?[25] Is he not presenting historical processes in too linear, too reductionist a fashion?[26]

Whatever doubts may have been raised about the methodology,[27] it has to be acknowledged that Sternhell's work has weakened the credibility of two key propositions of the immunity thesis – first, the supposed hegemony of France's democratic political culture, and, second, the alleged continuity of France's right-wing traditions (*les trois droites*). His evocation of the political and ideological novelty of France's turn-of-the-century has been a decisive historiographical contribution.

Robert Soucy's contribution has also been important, though very different. His sceptical empiricism is designed to remind us that in the 'real world' fine ideological distinctions are of little account, and tend to crumble once a rigorous comparative approach is brought to bear. He has certainly helped to highlight the concrete parallels between French formations and their German or Italian counterparts, and the fluidity of political boundaries on the Right. His no-nonsense attitude to the anticapitalist or antibourgeois features of fascist discourse, which he tends to dismiss as rhetorical window-dressing, will be seen by some as entirely justified given the record of fascist movements in power. Others, however, will feel that this perspective underestimates the capacity of fascism to exercise mass appeal, and fails adequately to examine the complex mechanisms of that process.[28]

Of course, as Soucy has written elsewhere, those who set out to define fascism often bring their own political baggage with them.[29] Conservatives will tend to emphasise its left-wing roots, socialists will be more likely to see it in terms of capitalist class interests, liberals will identify its totalitarian features, and so on. However, even when different interpretations have this political edge, they may all offer insights on which a more synthetic position can draw. Thus, while I share Soucy's scepticism about the left-wing credentials and working-class appeal of the Italian Fascist and German Nazi parties, the fact remains that these were mass movements which mobilised support well beyond the constituencies normally associated with traditional conservatism. Whatever their (conservative) objective function in terms of capitalist class relations, these parties were able to win over many (white-collar employees, self-employed artisans, shopkeepers, small farmers, and indeed some industrial workers) whose values and interests were far from identical with those of the social and economic elites. How this was achieved is a legitimate field of enquiry, and it is in this context that the notion of *populism* has recently gained wider currency, as an umbrella term characterising the various methods used by the Right (traditionally identified with elites) to attract mass support.[30]

The different ways in which La Rocque's Croix de Feu has been classified by historians may serve to clarify the point made above. For proponents of the immunity thesis, and indeed for Zeev Sternhell until recently, the Croix de Feu is too *conservative*, too much identified with traditional values and established elites, to qualify as fascist, because fascism has this radical *populist* dimension. Soucy's riposte is to say that this populism (in as far as it is identified as left-wing) has been greatly overplayed, that in fact the Fascist and Nazi parties were violent, authoritarian, but essentially *conservative* in terms of programme and support, just like the Croix de Feu and all the other French extreme right-wing formations, which can therefore also be labelled fascist. Kevin Passmore, on the other hand, sees fascism as an ultranationalist paramilitary variant of what he calls *authoritarian populism*, and in his view the Croix de Feu was indeed fascist. When it became the PSF the movement ceased to be fascist but it nonetheless remained authoritarian populist.[31]

Thus Passmore and Soucy agree that the CF was fascist, but for rather different reasons. They also converge in refuting the immunity thesis argument that the Croix de Feu (and indeed most other French *ligues*) were radically different from their Italian and German counterparts. Zeev Sternhell's view of fascist ideology is clearly more compatible with that of Passmore than with that of Soucy, but despite his claims about the influence of fascist ideas in French society, he was once very sceptical about the existence of a fascist mass movement in interwar France. Like his immunity thesis opponents, he regarded the Croix de Feu/PSF as too conservative to qualify, and paid little attention to it in earlier editions of *Ni droite ni gauche*.[32] As we have seen, his new stance involves the classification of both La Rocque's and Dorgères's movements as fascist, and certainly this reflects greater acknowledgement of the *populist* dimensions of the CF's discourse and appeal.[33] In this respect, he appears to follow Passmore. However, Sternhell's change of position also raises rather different issues about the relationship between fascist ideology and fascist movements, and about how to conceptualise the materialisation of fascism as a political force, which will be dealt with in the next section.

Fascism as essence versus fascism as process

The extreme polarisation around the use of the term 'fascism' in the French context has sometimes generated more heat than light. Sternhell and Soucy have both been key protagonists in this sometimes acrimonious dispute with French historians, and not surprisingly their perspectives on the subject are still largely defined by the parameters of that debate. It is understandable, therefore, if they sometimes misread the intentions of other scholars working in the field, who may be approaching the subject from a different angle. Thus Michel Dobry was surprised to see his arguments enlisted in support of Soucy's case that the PSF was fascist,[34] and Robert Paxton might well feel the same about Sternhell's interpretation of his work on Dorgères's Greenshirts.[35]

Of course, Soucy and Sternhell have every right to interpret the work of others and harness it to their cause, but in the process they may neglect or ignore features that deserve closer consideration, as we shall see. Paxton's essay in the present collection is a case in point. His notion of the 'five stages of fascism' seeks to move away from the treatment of fascism as a static and fixed essence, isolated from 'the political, social and cultural spaces in which (... fascist movements) navigate',[36] and focuses instead on *processes*. Thus fascism comes in different national guises, changes shape as it moves through the phases of ideology-movement-regime, interacts with other movements, adapts to shifting conjuncture.

Robert Soucy at first seems to approve of this approach, recognising that fascists are often 'opportunistic in reacting to changing circumstances',[37] and agreeing with Paxton's functionalist perspective whereby fascists are better judged by what they *do* than by what they *say*. But Soucy then complains that Paxton does not apply the same methodological principles when dealing with conservatives. If these flirt with fascism, they nonetheless remain in *essence* conservatives; allies or accomplices of fascism, but not fascists as such. Soucy welcomes Paxton's notion of a continuum between conservative authoritarianism and fascism, but wants to know at what point on this continuum a conservative becomes a fascist. He also clearly has difficulty with Paxton's notion that on this scale, no regime was 100 per cent fascist. These are interesting exchanges, for while both authors insist on the fluidity of boundaries between conservative authoritarianism and fascism, Paxton therefore accepts the notion of hybridity. For Soucy, however, this is a disguised form of essentialism (something can only be '80 per cent fascist' if measured against some absolute), and in his view fascism differs from conservative authoritarianism only *in degree* rather than *in kind*.

As we have seen, Zeev Sternhell finds Paxton's notion of hybridity and of 'incomplete fascism' equally unacceptable, but here the disagreement is even more fundamental. In developing his model of fascism as process rather than fixed essence, Paxton claims that it is not comparable to the other great political 'isms' (conservatism, liberalism, socialism), in the sense that it is not based as they are on 'formal philosophical positions with claims to universal validity'.[38] Fascist movements and leaders do not feel the need to justify their actions in line with these basic values, they are driven by 'feelings more than thought', and once in power they are not guided by initial ideological principles, rather the ideology is developed ad hoc or even post hoc to perform an 'integrative function'. This is a bold methodological move on Paxton's part, which certainly merits further discussion in the French context, but its implications for the Sternhell perspective are clearly dramatic.

As has often been pointed out, Sternhell's definition of fascist ideology is highly specific. From its initial pre-1914 version through to the interwar variants, it was forged from a synthesis of diverse currents of left revisionism with right-wing integral nationalism, and in this pure form was to be found on the political margins amongst relatively small groups of intellectuals. However, Sternhell's thesis has always been that this core ideology (like the tip of an iceberg) reflected a much wider diffusion of antidemocratic and antiliberal attitudes in French society at large, which eventually provided sufficient support and acquiescence to sustain Vichy's Révolution nationale. Until now, however, this scenario has not included the added dimension of genuine fascist mass movements active in France in the 1930s, and this major change of stance seems surprising at first. Earlier editions of *Ni droite ni gauche* studiously avoided the 'usual suspects' like Action Française, the leagues, Doriot, Brasillach, to focus on the more rarefied dissident circles of the *non-conformistes des années trente*,[39] and figures like Dorgères and La Rocque were largely passed over. Their sudden incorporation is grist to the mill of those 'immunity thesis' critics who have always argued that Sternhell, after giving a rather narrow definition of fascism's core ideology, then proceeds to find evidence of its political and intellectual influence in every dissident corner of French society between the wars.[40]

Sternhell's response, of course, is that fascism, like every other political movement, tends to compromise and deform its ideology in the pursuit and exercise of power. This does not mean that ideology should somehow be separated from behaviour, 'the myth from the application'. To continue the quote, '(just like communism, socialism, liberalism), fascism was at the same time a concept, an intellectual construction, and an historical reality whether expressed as a movement or a regime'.[41] In contrast, Paxton contends that fascism is a different kind of political phenomenon from liberalism or socialism, that it cannot be treated as a conceptual *unity* in this way, that it must be seen more as a process passing through distinctive phases, or indeed as a 'political practice appropriate to the mass politics of the twentieth century' which 'bears a different relationship to thought than the nineteenth-century "isms"'.[42]

Now it might be argued that although there is a considerable methodological gulf between them, both Sternhell and Paxton are trying in their different ways to come to terms with the shifting nature of fascism. Sternhell believes that ideology remains the defining and driving force for movement and regime, although intervention in the political arena inevitably involves adaptation and compromise. However, his insistence on the unicity of fascism is problematic in the French case because of the difficulty of establishing lines of historical and intellectual continuity between the birth and dissemination of 'fascist' ideology, the emergence of 'fascist' mass movements, and the establishment of a 'fascist' regime in the shape of Vichy.

Paxton, on the other hand, believes that very different sociopolitical processes are involved in each 'stage' of the development of fascism, and that a single mode of analysis is therefore not appropriate. Thus, for example, his understanding of the 'ideas' phase when fascist movements are first created is broadly in line with Sternhell's own study of pre-1914 protofascist ideology (antiliberal, antidemocratic national-syndicalism) but when he moves to 'stage two' (the 'rooting' of fascist movements) his emphasis shifts to the political setting in which these formations operated, the degree to which circumstances were favourable or allies available, the methods they used in pursuit of power.

Paxton's periodisation at first appears to offer a more flexible and discerning approach, but it nonetheless runs into problems of its own. For example, while he is sceptical about the prior existence of a coherent fascist ideology, and the degree to which ideas and programmatic commitments really influence fascist movements, he recognises that fascism is guided by what he describes as 'mobilising passions'. His list might be summed up as (to borrow Roger Griffin's phrase) 'palingenetic' ultranationalism , and some would argue that this does indeed correspond to an 'ideology', even though it cannot be identified with a clear philosophical position and a coherent body of texts. It is 'synthetic' and, in Paxton's view, it is driven above all by the 'irrational'. Thus the notion of the 'Other' is treated as part of the machinery for the forging of communal identity, not as the sublimation of very real fears and antagonisms which may have their origins in the 'rational' world of class interests. Paxton suggests, for example, that the targeting of socialists is more typical of Mediterranaean fascisms, and in terms of explicit *naming* that is no doubt true. But (as Paxton would certainly acknowledge) the hatred of 'Jewish' Marxism and socialist internationalism was equally endemic in German Nazism, and its appeal was thus to interests as well as to passions.

So Paxton does have a view of what fascism 'represents', and his treatment of 'stage two' of the process is therefore not entirely 'functional' (as he acknowledges). Yes, he does insist that fascist movements are easier to recognise by what they *do* rather than what they *say*, and in his comparison of rural fascist movements he pins this down: their key characteristic is that they supplant state authority and set up parallel power structures. But this still leaves the question of what they are doing this *for*. Not the pure pursuit of power, that would be too functionalist an answer, he agrees. So is it for the irrational mobilising passion of national regeneration? In the actual examples he draws from rural fascism in Italy, Germany and France, the armed bands which took the law into their own hands in local areas were engaged in strike-breaking; they were taking up cudgels on behalf of the big landowners because the public authorities were not dealing with the situation appropriately, they were setting-up 'parallel structures' to defend a particular set of socioeconomic interests. Can this engagement in class politics really just be dismissed as typical fascist opportunism? It is easy to understand at this point why Robert Soucy has doubts about the coherence of Paxton's approach.

There is a final methodological point. Paxton's model works well enough for the successful fascisms of Italy and Germany where single mass parties acceded to power and regimes evolved to their conclusion. With the benefit of this hindsight, it is easy to see the use of paramilitary force to subvert and replace the normal public authorities as in some way foreshadowing and paving the way for the eventual 'totalitarian' structures of the fascist state, and therefore as a defining feature of fascist movements. However, this approach proves to be somewhat unhelpful in the French context, where fascism never got beyond Paxton's 'stage two'. Clearly, French extreme-right formations did not 'supplant' the state or create 'parallel structures' to the same extent. Does this indicate that fascist movements were simply 'less successful' in France, or does it tell us that the French movements were less fascist than their Italian and German counterparts? The two issues are never effectively separated in Paxton's commentary, and this leaves the lingering suspicion that his argument is in fact teleological: that it falls into the trap of seeing successful fascism as the only real fascism, and thus (to borrow Dobry's phrase) of measuring processes by their outcomes.[43]

On methodology

This issue of teleology is of course one of the main preoccupations of Michel Dobry's article above. One of his key criticisms of the 'immunity thesis' is that it analyses historical processes in the light of 'outcomes'; to be more specific, that it constructs an historical narrative designed to explain why the French Republic 'survived', and in the process therefore treats French fascism as 'marginal' because ultimately 'unsuccessful'. Curiously enough, as we have seen, a similar (though not identical) objection could be levelled at Zeev Sternhell, who arguably presents Vichy's Révolution nationale primarily as the 'outcome' of the fifty-year process of France's unfolding antidemocratic counterculture.

There is a danger of teleology in Paxton's model as well. In his analysis of 'stage two', he seems to be suggesting that it is only if and when state authority begins to crumble that authoritarian movements will get the chance to set up parallel power structures and reveal themselves as genuinely 'fascist'. From this perspective, circumstance is the main motor and success the only gauge of fascism, while intention (whether driven by ideology, class interest, mobilising passion) is of little account. This is misleading, because in reality Paxton's position is far from deterministic and leaves more room for human agency. Indeed, he is much closer than either Sternhell or Soucy to Michel Dobry's *perspective relationnelle*, with its emphasis on the importance of process and conjuncture, political setting and space, the interaction with allies in a competitive environment.[44] But his insistence on 'establishing parallel structures' as a defining feature of fascist movements runs him into an impasse when dealing with French extreme-Right formations.

Kevin Passmore is also keen to differentiate fascist from other authoritarian-populist movements, and he too sees their *practice* as distinctive. For him, however, while fascists typically use paramilitarism as an instrument for imposing 'an historically conditioned worldview' (palingenetic ultranationalism)[45], this mobilising function does not necessarily involve supplanting the state and setting up 'parallel structures'. Under this definition, fascist movements may not need to directly confront or replace state authority, but may nonetheless use their extraparliamentary presence to reinforce their bargaining power in the mainstream political arena, and may find ways of subverting the constitutional framework from within. Passmore's extensive work on the nature of Croix-de-Feu paramilitarism, and of La Rocque's supposed 'republicanism' and 'legalism', is revealing in this respect.[46]

Passmore's work has also involved an ambitious sociological and ideological investigation of the relationship between the Right and the extreme Right in France, and in the process he has constructed a sophisticated conceptual armoury in which, as we have seen, fascism is identified as a subset of authoritarian populism. Michel Dobry, on the other hand, offers the methodologically more daring prospect of breaking entirely with what he calls the *logique classificatoire*. Not only does he place himself outside the debate on the nature of fascism, where it originated, and how significant a force it was in France between the wars, he also avoids discussion of how to 'classify in any other way' the groups associated with the French radical Right.

Although this argument was initially developed in the context of Dobry's critique of the immunity thesis, it clearly has implications for all those engaged in this field of study. The construction of detailed political and ideological typologies, the drawing of boundaries around fixed essences, is seen as a distorting lens. It fails to convey the fluidity and dynamism of political processes, the interactive environment in which political movements operate, the instrumental nature of ideology. Fifteen years after Dobry's landmark article, it might now also be argued that the preoccupation with proving or disproving the 'fascist' character of French political movements has ceased to be particularly productive. While in the past the cut and thrust of this debate may have helped refine the tools of analysis and extend the scope of research on both sides, in the future it risks becoming little more than the constant reformulation of entrenched positions. Maybe it is time for specialists in this area to move on, to address new questions, to pose the problem in different terms.

On first impression, Michel Dobry's methodological blueprint may look impossibly utopian. How can history be written without reference to outcomes and without recourse to classification? In practical terms, however, the objectives are more limited. It is merely being suggested that, for example, we should not analyse French extreme-Right movements through the filter of what we know happened later; that we should not *prejudge* their importance or their intentions by attaching weight to the fact that in the end they did not come to power. We should, as Dobry says, put the outcomes 'in parentheses'. Similarly, to refuse to measure such movements against some generic concept of 'fascism' is not to throw away all means of viable comparative analysis, far from it. Indeed, the constantly changing and deeply contested definitions of 'fascism' have become an increasing source of confusion, and have ceased to be the sort of stable conceptual reference point that eases communication between scholars. What remains as a stable and valid point of comparison is the actual political movements and regimes on which this abstraction was originally based, namely Italian Fascism and German Nazism in their many different facets, not to mention the many other comparable cases on which scholars have consistently drawn, such as Franco's Spain and Salazar's Portugal. And in this whole field of investigation, there are many concepts that are more specific and precise in their focus, and which therefore enjoy greater clarity and accuracy than the term 'fascism'.[47]

Much of the work that underpins the contributions to this volume would have equal value if it was set outside the framework of this increasingly stale debate, and some of the essays are in their different ways seeking to break out of the straitjacket. In this respect it is significant that the selection ends with the chapter by Kevin Passmore, who belongs to a new generation of historians in the field, who may be said to have 'cut his teeth' on the fascism debate, but who has chosen now to direct his attention elsewhere. His study of the 'stalemate society thesis', his attempt to reintroduce a more sophisticated sociological dimension to the analysis of the period, his focus on the problematic relationship of the political Right with the people, his evaluation of authoritarian tendencies in social and political elites including those identified with mainstream Republican opinion: all of these initiatives promise to shed greater light on the political crisis that affected

France in the 1930s (the analysis of which has not always been enhanced by preoccupation with the question of fascism).[48]

Passmore argues that the Croix de Feu/PSF was part of a wider current of authoritarianism in the 1930s, and that it owed much to traditional conservatism, though ultimately it was the product of a cycle of disappointment and radicalisation. So he sees the movement as simultaneously conservative and radical, and thus compatible with his own definition of fascism, in which conservatism and radicalism are inseparably linked. Arguably this successfully 'triangulates' the rival positions of Sternhell and Soucy (the former having more problems with the 'conservative' dimensions of fascism, the latter with its supposed 'radicalism'), though both would no doubt dispute the precise nature of the synthesis as outlined by Passmore. Similarly, Passmore's argument that the Croix de Feu was rooted as much in republicanism as in traditions associated with enemies of the regime raises difficult questions about the definition of *République/républicain*, and the drawing of boundaries around this political concept. Indeed, in Dobry's terms, despite Passmore's determination to move beyond the fascism debate, he has not truly escaped the *logique classificatoire*.[49]

As Michel Dobry has recently argued, the revisionists may have got caught up in the *logique classificatoire*, but they did not get things as badly wrong as their 'immunity thesis' opponents. They were at least able to recognise 'the real scale and impact on French society, especially in the 1930s, of the powerful authoritarian or antidemocratic currents which, unevenly and in different forms, affected most European countries'.[50] Passmore's attempt to redirect attention to the historical analysis of France's political crisis of the 1930s, and to do so without getting bogged down in the conceptual morass of the fascism debate, should therefore be welcomed and there is no doubt it points the way forward. Such an enterprise would be greatly enriched if it could also harness the range of skills, knowledge and experience that our other contributors have deployed in the present volume: Sternhell's understanding of *longue durée* cultural and ideological processes; Soucy's dogged and sceptical empiricism; Paxton's sensitivity to political process, setting, space and context; Dobry's telling methodological insights, and finally that genuinely comparative perspective which all our authors have brought to bear on France's role in a wider European drama.

Notes

1. J. Sweets, 'Hold that Pendulum! Redefining Fascism, Collaboration and Resistance in France', *French Historical Studies*, vol. XV, no. 4, Fall 1988, pp. 731–58.
2. P. Milza, *Les Fascismes*, Paris, 1985, p. 303 (quoted in Sweets, 'Hold that pendulum', p. 733).
3. P. Milza, 'Fascisme français', in *Dictionnaire historique de la vie politique* française *au XXe siècle*, ed., J.-F. Sirinelli, Paris, 1995, pp. 356–62.
4. Ibid., p. 356.
5. Ibid., p. 356.

6. '… toutes les manifestations d'hostilité à la démocratie bourgeoise et parlementaire'. Ibid., p. 357.
7. J. Julliard, 'Sur un fascisme imaginaire: à propos d'un livre de Zeev Sternhell', *Annales ESC*, no. 4, July-August 1984, pp. 849–59; M. Winock, 'Fascisme à la française ou fascisme introuvable', *Le Débat*, no. 25, May 1983, pp. 34–44.
8. P. Milza, 'Fascisme et Nazisme: qui a couvé l'oeuf du serpent?', in H. Shamir, ed., *France and Germany in an Age of Crisis 1900–1960*, Leiden, 1990, p. 270.
9. Milza, 'Fascisme français', p.357.
10. 'Celles qui peuvent être rattachées à une tradition fortement enracinée dans l'histoire nationale ne sont pas, *stricto sensu*, des organisations "fascistes"'. Ibid., p. 358.
11. For a discussion of the divided views on Solidarité Française, see K.-J. Müller, 'Fascism in France? Some Comments on Extremism in France Between the Wars', in Shamir, *France and Germany*, pp. 289–93.
12. Milza, 'Fascisme français', p. 359.
13. P. Burrin, 'Le fascisme', in *Histoire des droites en France*, Vol. 1. *Politique.*, ed. J.-F. Sirinelli, Paris, 1992, pp. 603–52.
14. Ibid., pp. 631–32.
15. P.-A. Taguieff, 'La rhétorique du national-populisme', *Cahiers Bernard Lazare*, vol. 109, June-July 1984; 'La doctrine du national-populisme', *Etudes*, vol. 364, January 1986. See also A. Collovald, 'Le "national-populisme" ou le fascisme disparu: Les historiens du "Temps Présent" et la question du déloyalisme politique contemporain', in M. Dobry, ed., *Le mythe de l'allergie française au fascisme*, Paris, 2003, pp. 279–321.
16. Burrin, 'Le fascisme', pp. 631–32. See also the definition of populism developed by Kevin Passmore, *From Liberalism to Fascism: the Right in a French Province, 1928–1939*, Cambridge, 1997, pp. 13–18, and his 'The Croix de Feu. Bonapartism, National-populism or Fascism?', *French History*, vol. 9, 1995, pp. 93–123.
17. M. Dobry, chapter 5 above, pp. 136–38.
18. Ibid., pp. 137–38.
19. Winock, 'Fascisme à la française', pp. 43–44.
20. 'Les pays qui ont échappé au fascisme sont les vieilles démocraties où cette forme de régime est implantée de longue date et profondément enracinée dans la culture politique, alors que les nations qui ont connu le fascisme sont celles où la démocratie n'était qu'une façade récemment édifiée'. S. Berstein, 'La France des années trente allergique au fascisme: à propos d'un livre de Zeev Sternhell', *Vingtième siècle*, no. 2, April 1984, p. 93.
21. '… ce qui ne veut pas dire qu'elles furent moins dangereuses pour les institutions de la République'. Milza, 'Fascisme français', p. 358.
22. M. Dobry, chapter 5 above, p. 131.
23. See Paxton, chapter 4 above, p. 117.
24. M. Dobry, chapter 5 above, p. 141.
25. M. Dobry, chapter 5 above, pp. 134–35.
26. Serge Berstein's main criticism is that Sternhell's understanding of what constitutes fascism extends across the whole ideological range of 'third-way' attempts to break the political mould in the 1930s ('on aboutit ainsi à considérer comme "fasciste" toute la génération des non-conformistes des années trente', Berstein, 'La France des années trente allergique au fascisme', p.85.). Michel Winock makes a similar point, but sees this error as derived from Sternhell's preoccupation with the history of ideas, his insufficient attention to events and context, his attempt to impose intellectual coherence on what is an historically complex phenomenon. In Winock's view, Sternhell's approach therefore ends up being teleological: for example, the ideas developed by the Belgian socialist Henri de Man in 1927, or by the French socialist Marcel Déat in 1930, are seen as somehow leading logically and inexorably to the fascist positions both will adopt under the Nazi occupation. (Winock, 'Fascisme à la française', p. 40.)

27. In an email to the editor, Zeev Sternhell takes issue with the charge of teleology, pointing out that historians always know the end of the story, and that to examine the intellectual roots of Vichy (or indeed of the American Declaration of Independence or the French Revolution) is not to imply that there were *no other causes* for these events. (Sternhell, email to Brian Jenkins, 21 August, 2003.)

28. See B. Jenkins, 'Debates and Controversies: Robert Soucy and the "Second Wave" of French Fascism', *Modern and Contemporary France*, NS4, no. 2, 1996, pp. 193–208.

29. R. Soucy, 'Fascism', *Encyclopaedia Britannica Online*, http://search.eb.com/eb/article?eu=127635, 2002, p. 4.

30. See for example K. Passmore, *The French Right in the Third Republic* (forthcoming). For a critique of the term 'populism' (and more especially 'national-populism'), see Collovald, 'Le "national-populisme" ou le fascisme disparu'.

31. In an email to the editor, Robert Soucy denies the suggestion (made by Passmore and others) that he underestimates the 'populist' dimensions of the Croix de Feu/PSF's appeal. Instead he insists on the importance of distinguishing left-wing from right-wing populism, both in terms of ideology and in terms of the social constituencies they address. In his view, it is the tendency to assume that fascist 'populism' must somehow have 'leftist' connotations which is misplaced. (Soucy, email to Brian Jenkins, 22 July, 2003). See also Soucy, chapter 3 above, note 118.

32. Sternhell, *Ni droite ni gauche*, Paris, 1983 and 1987.

33. It seems worth noting here that in making out the case that the movements led by La Rocque and Dorgères were both fascist, Sternhell often refers to their anti-Semitism. This might seem curious, given that anti-Semitism is associated above all with Nazism (which Sternhell explicitly excludes from his definition of fascism). See Sternhell, chapter 2 above, p. 46.

34. See Dobry, chapter 5, pp. 130–31, and Soucy, chapter 3 above, p. 67.

35. See Sternhell, chapter 2, pp. 52–53, and R. Paxton, *French Peasant Fascism: Henri Dorgères's Greenshirts and the Crises of French Agriculture, 1929–1939*, Oxford, 1997.

36. See Paxton, chapter 4 above, p. 112.

37. See Soucy, chapter 3 above, p. 87.

38. See Paxton, chapter 4 above, p. 109.

39. J.-L. Loubet del Bayle, *Les non-conformistes des années 30*, Paris, 1969.

40. See in particular Berstein, 'La France des années trente allergique au fascisme', p. 85.

41. See Sternhell, chapter 2 above, p. 54.

42. See Paxton, chapter 4 above, p. 109.

43. In a recent essay, Michel Dobry offers a rather different critique of Paxton's methodology. He notes that each of Paxton's 'stages' is implicitly a precondition for the next, whereas in reality rather different developmental trajectories are possible. But, more importantly, if each 'stage' involves different processes and settings, what is it that makes each stage distinctively 'fascist'? Dobry concludes that the answer lies in Paxton's 'functionalist' approach, but he notes that 'stage one' (ideological origins) does not have an obvious functional rationale, while later stages depend heavily on the (much contested) 'instrumentalist' perspective of conservative elites co-opting mass movements. See M. Dobry, 'La thèse immunitaire face aux fascismes', in Dobry, ed., *Le mythe de l'allergie française au fascisme*,. pp. 58–62.

44. Dobry acknowledges that Paxton's approach breaks with the *logique classificatoire*, locating movements in their political space and historical context. Ibid. p. 59.

45. Passmore, *From Liberalism to Fascism*, p. 211.

46. See Passmore, *From Liberalism to Fascism*; also 'Boy Scoutism for Grown-ups? Paramilitarism in the Croix de Feu and the Parti social français', *French Historical Studies*, no. 19, Autumn 1995, 527–57.

47. Michel Dobry has recently made some firm methodological proposals for the future development of research in this area. He suggests, for example, that the analysis

'instead of starting with some definition of fascism (or fascism*s*), should *delineate the object of study in some other way*, thus leaving it open for the historian or political scientist to find, at the end of their research, something different which falls outside the parameters of the original definition; even allowing them, perhaps, to detect *other* historical enigmas and intrigues which need to be unravelled.' Dobry, 'La thèse immunitaire face aux fascismes', p. 66, (editor's translation).

48.   See note 47 above; also Passmore, 'The French Third Republic: Stalemate Society or Cradle of Fascism?', *French History*, vol. 7, 1993, pp. 417–49; 'Business, Corporatism and the Crisis of the Third French Republic. The Example of the Silk Industry in Lyon', *Historical Journal*, vol. 38, 1995, pp. 959–87; 'The Croix de Feu. Bonapartism, National-populism or Fascism?', *French History*, vol. 9, 1995, pp. 93–123; 'Class, Gender and Populism: the Parti populaire français in Lyon', in N. Atkin and F. Tallet, eds, *The French Right, 1789–1997*, London, 1998; 'The Croix de Feu and Fascism: a Foreign Thesis Obstinately Maintained', in E. Arnold, ed., *The Development of the Radical Right in France. From Boulanger to Le Pen*, London, 2000; *The Right in the Third Republic* (forthcoming).

49.   Thus, in Didier Leschi's view, when Passmore argues that the PSF was more moderate than its Croix de Feu predecessor, his case is very similar to that made out by Rémond or Milza. It is La Rocque's decision to engage the movement in elections that is equated with a 'republican' commitment: 'c'est la volonté de participer aux échéances électorales qui, en quelque sorte, a déradicalisé le colonel de La Rocque. L'imprégnation républicaine aurait, contrairement à l'expérience italienne ou allemande, amené à une adhésion au régime'. D. Leschi, 'L'étrange cas La Rocque', in Dobry, ed., *Le mythe de l'allergie française au fascisme*, p. 159.

50.   '… l'ampleur et la portée considérables, dans les faits, qu'ont eues dans la société française, en particulier dans les années 30, les formidables poussées autoritaires ou antidémocratiques qui, inégalement et sous de formes variables, ont affecté alors l'essentiel des pays européens'. Dobry, 'La thèse immunitaire face aux fascismes', p. 58.

Select Bibliography

Arendt, H. *The Origins of Totalitarianism.* New York, 1951.

Aron, R. *Les Étapes de la pensée sociologique.* Paris, 1967.

Assouline, P. *Gaston Gallimard: un demi – siècle d'édition française.* Paris, 1984.

Azéma, J.-P. 'Le régime de Vichy' in J.-P. Azéma and F. Bédarida, eds, *La France des années noires. T.1: De la défaite à Vichy.* Paris, 1993.

Badinter, R. *Un antisémitisme ordinaire. Vichy et les avocats juifs (1940–1944).* Paris, 1997.

Balent, M.'La Réception des thèses de Zeev Sternhell par les historiens français', unpublished Masters dissertation, Université Pierre Mendès France, Grenoble, 1997.

Baranowski, S. *The Confessing Church, Conservative Elites, and the Nazi State.* Lewiston, New York/Queenston, Toronto, 1986.

Baruch, M.O. *Servir l'État français. L'Administration en France de 1940 à 1944,* Preface by J.-P. Azéma. Paris, 1997.

Bergen, D. *The German Christian Movement in the Third Reich: Twisted Cross.* Chapel Hill and London, 1996.

Berger, P.L. and Luckmann, T. *The Social Construction of Reality.* London, 1971.

Bergès, M. *Vichy contre Mounier. Les non-conformistes face aux années quarante.* Paris, 1997.

Bernardi, A. and De Guarracino, S. *Il fascismo. Dizionario di storia, personaggi, cultura, economia, fonti e dibattito storiografico.* Milan, 1998.

Berstein, S. *Le 6 février 1934.* Paris, 1975.

————. *Histoire du Parti radical,* vol. 2 'Crise du radicalisme'. Paris, 1982.

————. 'La France des années trente allergique au fascisme. À propos d'un livre de Zeev Sternhell', *Vingtième Siècle. Revue d'Histoire,* no. 2, April 1984.

————. 'L'affrontement simulé des années 1930', *Vingtième Siècle,* no. 5, January–March 1985.

————. 'La Ligue', in J.-F. Sirinelli, ed., *Histoire des droites en France.* Paris, 1992.

————. 'Le fascisme français a-t-il existé?', *L'Histoire,* no. 219, March 1998.

Berstein, S.and Milza, P. *Dictionnaire historique des fascismes et du nazisme.* Brussels, 1992.

Bessel, R., ed. *Fascist Italy and Nazi Germany: Comparisons and Contrasts.* Cambridge and New York, 1996.

Birnbaum, P. 'La France aux Français', in *Histoire des haines nationalistes.* Paris, 1993.

————. 'Sur un lapsus présidentiel', *Le Monde,* 21 October 1994.

————. *La France imaginée. Déclin des rêves unitaires.* Paris, 1998.

Blatt, J. 'Relatives and Rivals: The Response of the Action française to Italian Fascism, 1919–1926', *European Studies Review,* vol. 2, no. 3, July 1981, pp. 269–70.

Blinkhorn, M. (ed.). *Fascists and Conservatives.* London, 1990.

Boltanski, L. *Les Cadres: la formation d'un groupe sociale.* Paris, 1982.

Brinton, C. *The Anatomy of Revolution.* New York, 1965 (1st edition 1938).

Burrin, P. 'La France dans le champ magnétique du fascisme', *Le Débat*, no. 32, November 1984.

————. *La Dérive fasciste: Doriot, Déat, Bergery 1933–1945*. Paris, 1986.

————. 'Le Fascisme', in J.-F. Sirinelli, ed., *Histoire des droites en France*,Vol.I: Politique. Paris, 1992, pp. 603–52.

————. *La France à l'heure allemande 1940–1944*. Paris, 1995.

————. *Fascisme, nazisme, autoritarisme*. Paris, 2000.

Charle, C. La *crise des sociétés impériales. Allemagne, France, Grande-Bretagne (1900–1940)*. Paris, 2001.

Chavardès, M. *Une campagne de presse: la droite française et le 6 février 1934*. Paris, 1970.

Clarke, J. 'Engineering a New Order in the 1930s: The Case of Jean Coutrot', *French Historical Studies*, vol. 24, no. 1, 2001, pp. 63–86.

Cointet-Labrousse, M. *Vichy et le fascisme: les hommes, les structures, et les pouvoirs*. Brussels, 1987.

Collovald, A. 'Le "national-populisme" ou le fascisme disparu. Les historiens du "Temps Présent" et la question du déloyalisme politique contemporain', in M. Dobry, ed., *Le mythe de l'allergie française au fascisme*. Paris, 2003.

Comte, B. *Une Utopie combattante. L'École des cadres d'Uriage 1940–1942*. Paris, 1991.

Conan E. and Rousso, H. *Vichy: un passé qui ne passe pas*. Paris, 1994.

Cornwell, J. *Hitler's Pope*. New York, London, Victoria, Toronto, Auckland, 2000.

Costa-Pinto, A. 'Fascist Ideology Revisited: Zeev Sternhell and his Critics', *European History Quarterly*, vol. 4, no. 16, 1986.

————. *Salazar's Dictatorship and European Fascism*. New York, 1995.

De Grand, A. *Fascist Italy and Nazi Germany: the 'Fascist Style of Rule'*. London and New York, 1995.

————. *Italian Fascism: Its Origins and Development*. Lincoln and London, 1982.

Dobry, M. *Sociologie des crises politiques. La dynamique des mobilisations multisectorielles*. Paris, 1986.

————. 'Février 1934 et la découverte de l'allergie de la société française à la "Révolution fasciste"', *Revue française de sociologie*, vol. 30, no. 3/4, July–December 1989.

————. 'La thèse immunitaire face aux fascismes. Pour une critique de la logique classificatoire', in M. Dobry, ed., *Le mythe de l'allergie française au fascisme*. Paris, 2003.

Dobry, M., ed. *Le mythe de l'allergie française au fascisme*. Paris, 2003.

Douglas, A. *From Fascism to Libertarian Communism: Georges Valois against the French Republic*. Berkeley and Los Angeles, 1992.

Duclert, V. 'Histoire, historiographie et historiens de l'Affaire Dreyfus (1894–1997)', in M. Leymarie, ed., *La Posterité de l'Affaire Dreyfus*. Lille, 1998.

Eatwell, R. *Fascism: A History*. London, 1996.

————. 'On Defining the "Fascist Minimum": the Centrality of Ideology', *Journal of Political Ideologies*, vol. 1, no. 3, October 1996.

Espagne, M. and Werner, M. *Transferts. Les relations interculturelles dans l'éspace franco-allemande*. Paris 1988.

Favre, P. *Naissances de la science politique en France (1870–1914)*. Paris, 1989.

Felice, R. de. *Mussolini il fascista. I. La conquista del potere 1921–1925*. Turin, 1966.

Fleury, A. *'La Croix* devant la marée brune', *Vingtième Siècle. Revue d'Histoire*, no. 9, January-March 1986.

Foureau, C. 'La Revue universelle (1920–1940)', Ph.D. dissertation prepared at the University of Princeton under the supervision of Thomas Pavel, May 1999.

Friedrich, C., ed. *Totalitarianism*, proceedings of a conference held at the American Academy of Arts and Sciences in March 1953, Cambridge, MA, 1954.

Friedrich, C. and Brzezinski, Z. *Totalitarian Dictatorship and Autocracy*, Cambridge, MA, 1956.

Gaulle, Ch., de. *Mémoires de guerre: l'Appel 1940–1942*. Paris, 1954.

Germinario, F. 'Fascisme et idéologie fasciste. Problèmes historiographiques et méthodologiques dans le modèle de Zeev Sternhell', *Revue française des idées politiques*, vol. 1, no. 1, 1995.

Goguel, F. 'En mémoire d'André Siegfried', *Revue Française de Science Politique*, vol. 9, no. 2, June 1959.

Goodfellow, S.H. *Between the Swastika and the Cross of Lorraine: Fascisms in Interwar Alsace*. De Kalb, 1999.

Goyet, B. *Charles Maurras*. Paris, 2000.

————. *Henri d'Orléans, Comte de Paris (1908–1999). Le prince impossible*. Paris, 2001.

————. 'La "Marche sur Rome" : version originale sous-titrée. La réception du fascisme en France dans les années 20', in M. Dobry, ed., *Le mythe de l'allergie française au fascisme*, Paris, 2003.

Griffin, R. *The Nature of Fascism*. London, 1991.

————. *Fascism*. Oxford and New York, 1995.

Grynberg, A. *Les camps de la haine: les Internés juifs des camps français 1939–1944*. Paris, 1999.

Guchet, Y. 'Georges Valois ou l'illusion fasciste', *Revue française de science politique*, vol. 15, 1965, pp. 1111–44.

————. *Georges Valois, l'Action française, la République syndicale*. Paris, 1975.

Hébey, P. *La Nouvelle Revue française des années sombres, 1940–1941: des intellectuels à la dérive*. Paris, 1992.

Hellman, J. 'Bernanos, Drumont, and the Rise of French Fascism', *Review of Politics*, vol. 52, Summer 1992, pp. 441–59.

————. *The Knight-Monks of Vichy France: Uriage 1940–1945*. Montreal, 1993.

————. 'Wounding Memories: Mitterrand, Moulin, Touvier and the divine Half-Lie of Resistance', *French Historical Studies*, vol. 19, no. 2, Autumn 1995.

Hoffmann, S. 'Paradoxes of the French Political Community', in S. Hoffmann, S. (et al.) eds, *In Search of France: Renovation and Economic Management in the Twentieth Century*. New York, 1963. (Published in France as *A la recherche de la France*, Paris 1963.)

Irvine W.D. 'Fascism in France and the Strange Case of the Croix de Feu', *The Journal of Modern History*, vol. 63, no. 2, 1991.

Jackson, J. *The Politics of Depression in France*. Cambridge, 1985.

————. *The Popular Front in France : Defending Democracy, 1934–38*. Cambridge, New York, New Rochelle, Melbourne, Sydney, 1987.

————. *France: The Dark Years, 1940–1944*. Oxford, 2001.

————. *The Fall of France: the Nazi Invasion of 1940*. Oxford, 2003.

Jenkins, B. 'The Paris Riots of February 6th 1934: the Crisis of the Third French Republic', unpublished Ph.D. dissertation, University of London, 1979.

————. 'Robert Soucy and the "Second Wave" of French Fascism', *Modern and Contemporary France*, vol. 4, no. 2, 1996, pp. 193–208.

————. 'L'Action française à l'ère du fascisme: une perspective contextuelle', in M. Dobry, ed., *Le mythe de l'allergie française au fascisme*. Paris, 2003.

Julliard, J. 'Sur un fascisme imaginaire: à propos d'un livre de Zeev Sternhell', *Annales ESC*, 39e année, no. 4, July-August 1984, pp. 849–59.

Kalman, S. 'Vers un ordre nouveau: The Concepts of Nation and State in the Doctrines of the Faisceau and Croix de Feu/Parti Social Français', unpublished Ph.D. dissertation, McMaster University, 2001.

Kater, M. *The Nazi Party A Social Profile of Members and Leaders, 1919–1945*. Cambridge, MA, 1983.

Kennedy, S.M. 'Reconciling the Nation Against Democracy', Ph.D. dissertation, York University, Ontario, 1998.

Kershaw, I. *Popular Opinion and Political Dissent in the Third Reich: Bavaria 1933–1945.* Oxford, 1983.

——————. *Hitler, 1889–1936.* New York and London, 1998.

Kogan, N. 'Fascism as a Political System', in S.J. Woolf, ed., *The Nature of Fascism.* New York, 1969.

Koos, C. 'Engendering reaction: the Politics of Pronatalism and the Family in France, 1919–1944', unpublished Ph.D. dissertation, University of Southern California, 1996.

Kuisel, R. *Ernest Mercier. French Technocrat.* Berkeley CA, 1967.

Laborie, P. *L'Opinion française sous Vichy.* Paris, 1990.

Larkin, M. *Religion, Politics and Preferment in France since 1890: la Belle Époque and Its Legacy.* Cambridge, 1995.

La Rocque, Colonel de. *Service public.* Paris, 1934.

——————. 'Bab Allah', *Le Flambeau,* no. 36, August, 1932.

——————. 'Gloses', *Le Flambeau,* no. 67, 1 February, 1935.

——————. 'Dérèglement', *Le Flambeau,* no. 69, 1 August, 1936.

——————. 'Répères', *Le Flambeau,* no. 71, 22 August, 1936.

——————. 'Fait nouveau', *Le Flambeau,* 3ème série, no. 89, 9 January, 1937.

——————. 'Réalisme', Le Flambeau, no. 34, 5 December, 1936.

——————. *Disciplines d'Action.* Clermont – Ferrand, 1941.

Laughlin, M. 'Gustave Hervé's Transition from Socialism to National Socialism: Another Example of French Fascism?', *Journal of Contemporary History,* vol. 36, no. 1, January 2001, pp. 5–39.

Le Béguec, G. 'L'Entrée au Palais-Bourbon: les filières privilégiées d'accès à la fonction parlementaire 1919–1939', unpublished *Thèse pour le doctorat d'état,* Paris X Nanterre, 1989.

Lebovics, H. *The Alliance of Iron and Wheat in the Third French Republic 1860–1914: Origins of the New Conservatism.* London and Baton Rouge, 1988.

Le Clère, M. *Le 6 février.* Paris, 1967.

Leschi, D. 'L'étrange cas La Rocque', in M. Dobry (ed.), *Le mythe de l'allergie française au fascisme.* Paris, 2003.

Levey, J. 'Georges Valois and the Faisceau', *French Historical Studies,* vol. 8, 1973, pp. 279–304.

Linz, J. 'An Authoritarian Regime: Spain', in E. Allardt and S. Rokkan, eds, *Mass Politics: Studies in Political Sociology.* New York and London, 1970.

——————. 'Totalitarian and Authoritarian Regimes', in F. Greenstein and N. Polsby, eds, *Handbook of Political Science,* vol. 3, Macropolitical Theory. Reading, MA, 1975. (Reprinted and updated in Linz, *Totalitarian and Authoritarian Regimes.* Boulder, 2000.)

——————. *Crisis, Breakdown and Reequilibration.* Baltimore, London, 1978.

——————. 'Some Notes Towards a Comparative Understanding of Fascism in Sociological Historical Perspective', in W. Laqueur, ed., *Fascism. A Reader's Guide.* Harmondsworth, 1979.

——————. 'Political Space and Fascism as a Latecomer', in S. Larsen et al., eds, *Who were the Fascists. Social Roots of European Fascism.* Bergen, 1980.

Loubet del Bayle, J.-L. *Les non-conformistes des années 30.* Paris, 1969.

Lyttelton, A. *The Seizure of Power: Fascism in Italy, 1919–1929.* 2nd edition, London, 1987.

Machefer, P. 'Sur quelques aspects de l'activité du Colonel de La Rocque et du "Progrès Social Français" pendant la seconde guerre mondiale', *Revue d'Histoire de la deuxième guerre mondiale,* vol. 58, 1963.

——————. 'L'Union des droites:le PSF et le Front de la Liberté, 1936–37', *Revue d'histoire moderne et contemporaine,* vol. 17, 1970.

——————. 'Le Parti social français en 1936–37', *L'Information historique,* March–April 1972.

——————. *Ligues et fascismes en France, 1919–1939.* Paris, 1974.

Maier, C. *Recasting Bourgeois Europe*. Princeton, 1975.

Marrus, M. and Paxton, R.O. *Vichy France and the Jews*. New York, 1981.

Masgaj, P. *Action Française and Revolutionary Syndicalism*. Chapel Hill, 1979.

Meier, H. *The Lesson of Carl Schmitt. Four Chapters on the Distinction between Political Theology and Political Philosophy*. Chicago, 1998.

Michaud, E. *Un art de l'éternité. L'image et le temps du national socialisme*. Paris, 1996.

Milza, P. *Les Fascismes*. Paris, 1985.

————. *Le Fascisme italien et la presse française*. Brussels, 1987.

————. *Fascisme français. Passé et présent*. Paris, 1987.

————. 'Fascisme et Nazisme: qui a couvé l'oeuf du serpent?', in H. Shamir, ed., *France and Germany in an Age of Crisis 1900–1960*. Leiden, 1990.

————. 'L'Ultra-Droite dans les années trente', in M. Winock, ed., *Histoire de l'extrème droite en France*. Paris, 1993, pp. 157–89.

————. 'Fascisme français', in J.-F. Sirinelli, ed., *Dictionnaire historique de la vie politique française au XXe siècle*. Paris, 1995.

Monnet, F. *Refaire la république: André Tardieu, une dérive réactionnaire, 1876–1945*. Paris 1993.

Mosse, G. *The Crisis of German Ideology: Intellectual Origins of the Third Reich*. New York, 1964.

Müller, K.-J. 'French Fascism and Modernization', *Journal of Contemporary History*, vol. 11, 1976, pp. 75–107.

————. 'Die französische Rechte und der Faschismus in Frankreich 1924–1932', in Industrielle Gesellschaft und politisches System. Bonn, 1978, pp. 413–30. [Mainly on Jeunesses patriotes].

————. 'Fascism in France? Some Comments on Extremism in France between the Wars' in H. Shamir, ed., *France and Germany in an Age of Crisis 1900–1960*. Leiden, 1990.

Nguyen, V. *Aux origines de l'Action française: Intelligence et politique à l'aube du XXe Siècle*. Paris, 1991.

Nobécourt, J. 'Le Pen a-t-il pris la suite du colonel de La Rocque ?' *Le Monde*, 8–9 May, 1988.

————. *Le colonel de La Rocque 1885–1946, ou les pièges du nationalisme chrétien*. Paris, 1996.

Noiriel, G. *Les origines républicaines de Vichy*. Paris, 1999.

Nolte, E. *Der Faschismus in seiner Epoche: Die Action française, Der italienische Faschismus, Der Nationalsozialismus*. Munich, 1966 (Translated as *Three Faces of Fascism: Action française, Italian Fascism, National Socialism*, New York, 1966.)

Novick, P. *L'épuration française 1944–1949*. Paris, 1985.

Nye, R. *Masculinity and Male Codes of Honor in Nineteenth-Century France*. Oxford, 1993.

Ory, P. 'Le Dorgérisme: Institution et discours d'une colère paysanne (1929–1939)', *Revue d'histoire moderne et contemporaine*, vol. 22, April–June 1975.

Passmore, K. 'The French Third Republic: Stalemate Society or Cradle of Fascism?', *French History*, vol. 7, no. 4, 1993, pp. 417–49.

————. 'The Croix de Feu. Bonapartism, National-populism or Fascism?', *French History*, vol. 9, 1995, pp. 93–123.

————. 'Business, Corporatism and the Crisis of the Third French Republic. The Example of the Silk Industry in Lyon', *Historical Journal*, vol. 38, 1995, pp. 959–87.

————. 'Boy Scoutism for Grown-Ups ? Paramilitarism in the Croix de Feu and the Parti Social Français', *French Historical Studies*, vol. 19, Fall 1996.

————. *From Liberalism to Fascism. The Right in a French Province, 1928–1939*. Cambridge, 1997.

————. 'Class, Gender and Populism: the Parti populaire français in Lyon' in N. Atkin and F. Tallet, eds, *The Right in France: 1789–1997*, London, 1998.

————. 'The Croix de Feu and Fascism: a Foreign Thesis Obstinately Maintained', in E.J. Arnold, ed., *The Development of the Radical Right in France: From Boulanger to Le Pen*. London and New York, 2000.

————. 'Catholicism and Nationalism: The Fédération républicaine, 1927–1939', in K. Chadwick, *Catholicism, Society and Politics in Twentieth-Century France*. Liverpool, 2000, pp. 47–72.

Paxton, R.O. *La France de Vichy, 1940–1944*, new edition. Paris, 1997. (U.S. edition, *Vichy France: Old Guard and New Order, 1940–1944*, rev. edition, New York, 2001.)

————. *French Peasant Fascism: Henri Dorgères's Greenshirts and the Crises of French Agriculture, 1929–1939*. Oxford, 1997. (Also published in French as *Le temps des chemises vertes. Révolte paysanne et fascisme rural 1929–1939*, Paris, 1996.)

————. 'Five Stages of Fascism', *Journal of Modern History*, vol. 70, no. 1, March 1998.

Payne, S.G. *A History of Fascism 1914–1945*. Madison, 1995.

Péan, P. *Une jeunesse française. François Mitterrand, 1934–1947*. Paris, 1994.

Peer, S. *France on Display: Peasants, Provincials, and Folklore in the 1937 Paris World's Fair*. Albany NY, 1998.

Pellissier, P. *6 février 1934*. Paris, 2000.

Peschanski, D. 'Vichy au singulier, Vichy au pluriel. Une tentative avortée d'encadrement de la société (1941–1942)', *Annales: économies, sociétés, civilisations*, 43e année, no. 3 (May–June 1988), pp. 639–62.

Plumyène, J. and Lasierra, R. *Les fascismes français, 1923–63*. Paris, 1963.

Poznanski, R. *Être juif en France pendant la Seconde Guerre mondiale*. Paris, 1994.

Preston, P. *Franco: a Biography*. New York, 1994.

Rémond, R. 'Ya-t-il un fascisme français', *Terre humaine*, 2e année, no. 19–20, July–August, 1952.

————. *La Droite en France de la première Restauration à la Ve République*. 2nd edition. Paris, 1963 and *Les Droites en France*, 1982 edition.

————. *Notre Siècle, 1918–1988*. Paris, 1988.

————. 'Complexité de Vichy', *Le Monde*, 5 October, 1994.

Reveilli, Marco. 'Italy', in D. Mühlberger, *The Social Bases of European Fascist Movements*. London, New York, Sydney, 1987.

Ringer, F. *The Decline of the German Mandarins: the German Academic Community 1890–1933*. Cambridge, MA, 1969.

Romano, S. 'Sternhell lu d'Italie', *Vingtième siècle. Revue d'histoire*, no. 6, April–June 1985.

Rousselier, N. *Le Parlement de l'éloquence. La souveraineté, de la délibération au lendemain de la Grande Guerre*. Paris, 1997.

Rousso, H. *Le Syndrome de Vichy de 1944 à nos jours*. 2nd edition. Paris, 1990.

Sand, S. 'L'idéologie fasciste en France', *Esprit*, no. 8–9, August–September, 1983.

Schmitt, C. *La Notion de politique*. Preface by Julien Freund. Paris, 1972.

Schor, R. *L'Opinion française et les étrangers 1919–1939*. Paris, 1985.

Siegfried, A. *America Comes of Age. A French Analysis*. New York, 1927.

————. *Vue Générale de la Méditerranée*. Paris, 1943.

————. *L'me des peuples*. Paris, 1950.

————. *De la IIIe à la IVe République*. Paris, 1956.

————. *Tableau politique de la France de l'Ouest*. Presentation by Pierre Milza. Paris, 1995.

Singer, C. *Vichy, l'Université et les Juifs. Les silences et la mémoire*. Paris, 1992.

Sirinelli, J.-F. 'Les Intellectuels', in R. Rémond, ed., *Pour une histoire politique*. Paris, 1988.

Sirinelli, J.-F. ed., 'Introduction générale', in *Histoire des droites en France*. Vol. I, *Politique*. Paris, 1992.

Slama, A.-G. 'Vichy était-il fasciste?', *Vingtième Siècle. Revue d'Histoire*, special issue, July–September 1986.

Soucy, R 'The Nature of Fascism in France', in W. Laqueur and G.L. Mosse, *International Fascism*. New York, 1966.

Soucy, R. *Fascist Intellectual: Drieu La Rochelle*. Berkeley, Los Angeles, London, 1979.

————. *French Fascism : The First Wave, 1924–1933*. New Haven, 1986. (Also published in French translation as *Le fascisme français 1924–1939*. Paris, 1989.)

————. 'French Fascism and the Croix de Feu: A Dissenting Interpretation', *Journal of Contemporary History*, vol. 26, 1991.

————. *French Fascism: the Second Wave, 1933–1939*. New Haven and London, 1995.

————. 'French Press Reactions to Hitler's First Two Years in Power', *Contemporary European History*, vol. 7, part I, March 1998.

————. 'Functional Hating: French Fascist Demonology Between the Wars', *Contemporary French Civilization*, vol. 23, no. 2, Summer/Fall 1999.

————. 'Fascism', *Encyclopaedia Britannica Online*, http://search.eb.com/eb/article?eu=127635, 2002.

Soury, J. *Campagne nationaliste 1894–1901*. Paris, 1902.

Sternhell, Z. 'Fascist Ideology', in W. Laqueur, ed., *Fascism. A Reader's Guide: Analyses, Interpretations, Bibliography*. Berkeley, 1976.

————. 'Anatomie d'un mouvement fasciste en France: le Faisceau de Georges Valois', *Revue française de science politique*, vol. 26, 1976, pp. 5–40.

————. 'Strands of French Fascism', in S.U. Larsen et al., eds, *Who were the Fascists? Social Roots of European Fascism*. Oslo. 1980, pp. 479–500.

————. 'Sur le fascisme et sa variante française', *Le Débat*, no. 32 (November 1984), pp. 28–51.

————. 'The Political Culture of Nationalism', in R. Tombs, ed., *Nationalism in France from Boulangism to the Great War 1889–1914*. London and New York, 1991.

————. *Maurice Barrès et le nationalisme français*. Paris, 1972 (new French edition, Brussels, 2000).

————. *La Droite révolutionnaire: les origines françaises du fascisme*. Paris, 1978 (new French edition, Brussels, 2000).

————. *Ni Droite ni gauche: l'idéologie fasciste en France*. Paris, 1983 (new French edition, Brussels, 2000), translated as *Neither Right nor Left: Fascist Ideology in France*, Berkeley and Los Angeles, 1986.

Sternhell, Z., Sznajder, M. and Asheri, M. *Naissance de l'idéologie fasciste*. Paris, 1989 (new French edition, Paris, 2000).

Sweets, J. 'Hold that Pendulum! Redefining Fascism, Collaboration and Resistance in France', *French Historical Studies*, vol. 15, no. 4, Fall 1988, pp. 731–58.

Taguieff, P.-A. 'La rhétorique du national-populisme', *Cahiers Bernard Lazare*, vol. 109, June–July 1984.

————. 'La doctrine du national-populisme', *Etudes*, vol. 364, January 1986.

Talmon, J. *The Origins of Totalitarian Democracy*. London, 1952.

Tannenbaum, E. *Action Francaise: Diehard Reactionaries in 20th century France*. New York, 1962.

Tilly, C. *From Mobilization to Revolution*. Reading, MA, 1978.

Veyne, P. *Comment on écrit l'histoire. Essai d'épistémologie*. Paris, 1971.

Weber, E. *Action Française: Royalism and Reaction in 20th Century France*. Stanford, CA, 1962.

————. *Varieties of Fascism*. New York, 1964.

————. *The Hollow Years: France in the 1930s*. New York and London, 1994.

Weiss, J. *The Fascist Tradition*. New York, 1967.

————. *Ideology of Death: Why the Holocaust Happened in Germany*. Chicago, 1996.

Winock, M. 'Fascisme à la française ou fascisme introuvable?', *Le Débat*, no. 25, May 1983.

————. *Nationalisme, antisémitisme, et fascisme en France*. Paris, 1982 (translated as *Nationalism, Anti-Semitism, and Fascism in France*, Stanford, CA, 1998).

————. *La Fièvre hexagonale. Les grandes crises politiques 1871–1968*. Paris 1986.

————. *Histoire de l'extrême droite en France*. Paris, 1993.

Wohl, R. 'French Fascism Both Right and Left: Reflections on the Sternhell Controversy', *Journal of Modern History*, vol. 63, March 1991.
Woolf, S.J. ed. *European Fascism*. New York, 1968.
Zuccotti, S. *The Italians and the Holocaust*. Lincoln, 1987.

Index